TOWARDS SUSTAINABLE DEVELOPMENT, 2ND EDITION

Towards Sustainable Development, 2nd Edition

Essays on System Analysis of National Policy

KHALID SAEED
Social Science and Policy Studies Department
Worcester Polytechnic Institute

Ashgate

Aldershot • Brookfield USA • Singapore • Sydney

First published 1991, 2nd edition 1998

This edition published by
Ashgate Publishing Limited
Gower House
Croft Road
Aldershot
Hants GU11 3HR
England

Ashgate Publishing Company
Old Post Road
Brookfield
Vermont 05036
USA

British Library Cataloguing in Publication Data
Saeed, Khalid
  Towards sustainable development : essays on system analysis
  of national policy. - 2nd ed.
  1.Sustainable development 2.Sustainable development -
  Government policy
  I.Title
  338.9

Library of Congress Catalog Card Number: 97-076944

ISBN 1 85972 598 8

Typeset by Sripatchara Manakul

Printed in Great Britain by The Ipswich Book Company, Suffolk.

Contents

ix

Figures

xiv

xvii

Tables

Citation

Jay Wright Forrester Award 1995

The 1995 Jay Wright Forrester Award is presented to Khalid Saeed for his book, Towards Sustainable Development: Essays on System Analysis of National Policy. The book, published in 1991, presents a series of models of social and economic development, especially in the so-called 'less developed' countries. The book includes models of political instability in developing countries and the linkages between economic and political evolution. It includes models of income distribution, showing how income inequality and poverty can become institutionalized in a society, even as it enjoys aggregate economic growth. It includes theoretical and methodological papers advocating a dynamic systems perspective, and case studies showing how it is done.

The work is notable in several respects. First, the papers describe the evolution of developing nations from a systems point of view. These are not only models of economic development, political development, or natural resource policy, but integrated models in which the artificial boundaries imposed by traditional disciplinary distinctions are erased. Second, these are fully dynamic, disequilibrium, behavioral models, in which the actors in the system - the politicians, entrepreneurs, workers, farmers and political insurgents - behave not according to the narrow prescriptions of economic rationality but in richer, and more realistic, ways that better reflect field study and empirical knowledge. The models include the stocks and flows, broad boundaries, multiple nonlinear feedback processes, and other elements of dynamic complexity that often lead to counterproductive developmental policies and political and economic instability, and that often confound traditional analysis. The models are well described and documented and the results are replicable. In short, this is exemplary system dynamics.

Finally, much of the work in system dynamics has been focused on business organizations in highly developed economies. Khalid's work is focused sharply on what many believe to be a more important domain where the challenges are greater: the developing nations, where three-quarters of the world's people live and where, many believe, the future of the world system lies. Khalid is well qualified to address these issues. In addition to his skill as a model builder, he has observed these dynamics first hand. A native of Pakistan, Khalid is Professor at the Asian Institute of Technology in Thailand, where he works with a cross-disciplinary group of faculty members and students on these issues and catalyzes the growth of system dynamics throughout Asia.[1] It is a pleasure to present the 1995 Jay Wright Forrester Award to Khalid Saeed.

John D. Sterman
Chair, Jay Wright Forrester Award Committee

---

[1] The author worked at the Asian Institute of Technology from 1980 to 1997.

Preface to 2nd edition

This book is the second edition of a volume published in 1991 by Progressive Publishers, Lahore, Pakistan in a limited quantity. The first edition collected 10 published essays and 3 working papers written over an extended period of time by me together with my colleagues and students on generic issues concerning sustainable development and country case studies addressing developmental agenda. Sustainability subsumed a broad definition in these essays including also the social, political and organizational considerations besides the questions of physical resources and environment. The first edition unfortunately has not been easily available internationally, although it was recognized as an important attempt to apply system dynamics to the design of public policy for sustainable development and used as a reader in several courses on system dynamics and economic development while the models presented in the book were further built upon by many students and researchers working on economic development agendas. The first edition earned the Jay Wright Forrester Award in 1995, but it was already out of print by then.

The second edition includes the essays of the first edition as well as additional writings on sustainable development that I and my students formulated over the six years following the publication of the first edition. 2 of the working papers included in the first edition were revised and published in learned journals. The published versions now appear in this second edition. Furthermore, 4 new papers, all collected from published sources have been included. The Conclusion has been reformulated and now highlights the learning process entailed in modeling instead of presenting a summary of the essays of the book. The main insights gained from the extended research described in the book are now recounted in the

Introduction representing the text of the lecture the author delivered upon the receipt of the Jay Wright Forrester Award. The citation of the award precedes this preface.

The text of the book is divided into three parts. Part I comprises the first seven chapters that deal with modeling generic issues concerning sustainable development. They constitute the conceptual foundation for dealing with questions of sustainable development.

Chapter one deals with the role of the political organization in creating a sustainable civil society. It attempts to identify the organizational parameters of a political system that should enable a government to maintain its commitment to public welfare. Government action being essential to any public policy initiative, it is important to create a functional government role that should support welfare.

Chapter two deals with production and disbursement of income in a fixed economy framework to understand the variety of historical experiences and to identify entry points for sustaining economic growth while also maintaining an equitable distribution of income and wealth. Government intervention into the system is conceived in terms of fiscal and organizational measures that can be implemented in the existing institutional framework. Chapter three revisits past experience in development planning and attempts to understand the successes and the failures of the efforts to alleviate poverty and hunger using the model of chapter two, but relaxing its fixed economy assumption.

Chapter four reviews the technological and environmental perspectives on resource use and attempts to develop a framework for implementation of fiscal and institutional measures to attain a sustainable resource base. Chapter five applies the framework of chapter four to operationalize the normative recommendations made in respect of our resource base and environment by the famous Club of Rome study on limits to growth. It illustrates the difference between the normative and the operational policies and demonstrates how this difference can be bridged.

Chapter six revisits the role of technological development in shaping development policy. A modified version of the model of chapter two is employed to develop alternative technology policy levers to achieve growth with equity. Chapter seven attempts to define the parameters of an effective organization conducive to achieving innovation that should fuel technological development.

The second part comprising chapters eight, nine and ten, extends the concepts developed in the first part to the controversies on poverty and hunger, technological development, and entrepreneurship, which are based rather on parochial positions than on a shared common model. These chapters are conceptual extensions of the first part. They demonstrate how modeling and experimentation of the first part can be extended to address more general agenda of sustainable development.

The third part of the volume relates six case studies covering a variety of local issues in selected developing countries. Chapter eleven deals with agricultural development policy in Pakistan; chapter twelve examines the impact of the rural credit system on Thailand's agricultural economy; chapter thirteen deals with the pitfalls of oil dependent growth in Indonesia; chapter fourteen examines options for coping with the Philippines' debt problem; chapter fifteen addresses the problem of food self-sufficiency in Vietnam; chapter sixteen examines water resources management in Saudi Arabia. Although dealing with situation-specific issues, these case studies provide insights that can be generalized to some extent provided specific conditions of each case are kept in view.

The Conclusion summarizes the learning process underlying the modeling framework used and outlines the procedure to maximize the learning yield of the heuristical framework of system dynamics.

Each chapter of this volume was written as a self-contained essay and can be read independently of the other essays, yet all have a common thread in that they attempt to understand specific aspects of sustainability using an experimental process based on system dynamics.

Acknowledgments are due to *Behavioral Science, Higher Education Policy, Simulation, Socio-Economic Planning Sciences, System Dynamics Review* and *World Development* for their kind permission to reprint articles earlier published in those learned journals and to Sripatchara Manakul for typesetting the manuscript on computer and Pam Riley for making the final editing changes. Last but not least I am indebted to Amanda Richardson who very diligently edited the final manuscript to make sure that it is free of language errors and formatting inconsistencies. I am, of course, responsible for any errors still remaining.

Khalid Saeed
Social Science and Policy Studies Department
Worcester Polytechnic Institute
Worcester, MA 01609

Part I: Conceptual Foundations

Introduction
Sustainable development, old conundrums, new discords[*]

Khalid Saeed

Abstract

This paper represents the text of the obligatory talk given by the author on receipt of the 1995 Jay Wright Forrester Award for his book titled "Towards Sustainable Development, Essays on System Analysis of National Policy". The paper documents methodological and problem related insights created over the course of an extended research effort that yielded the essays of the book. The methodological principles elaborated include the use of a diverse data base for model development, the partitioning of a complex problem into tractable parts and the process of building confidence in a model. The problem-related insights cover the concept of economic value, its diverse manifestations and their implications for sustainable development. An attempt is made to extend the concepts learnt to the global economic system and research agendas are outlined for addressing the problems of global sustenance.

Introduction

In 1975, the system dynamics Ph.D. program at MIT admitted the largest group of students. System dynamics at that time was still considered a new area whose counter-intuitive insights had invoked many controversies with

[*] Reprinted from System Dynamics Review, 12(1), Khalid Saeed, Sustainable Development, old conundrums, new discords, pp.59-80, 1996, with kind permission from John Wiley and Sons, Ltd., Baffins Lane, Chichester, West Sussex PO19 1UD, UK.

the other disciplines. The Ph.D. students entering system dynamic first of all had to view these controversies as a challenge rather than a disadvantage. Secondly, they had to be willing to make concerted efforts to bridge the differences between system dynamics and other disciplines if they were to avoid isolation in their future careers. The members of the 1975 MIT Ph.D. entering class met those expectations by positioning themselves in special niches and bridging system dynamics with the other bodies of knowledge. To say the least, their collective endeavor was an ample success. This group consisted of four people, John Morecroft, Barry Richmond, Peter Senge and Khalid Saeed. All four have been honored for their contribution by our peers in system dynamics with the award of Jay Forrester Prize. I am the last of the four to receive this honor. Let me take this opportunity to say that I receive it with great pride both for myself and for the entering MIT system dynamics Ph.D. class of 1975.

Jay Forrester's name signifies innovation and progress in high technology, both in engineering and in social sciences. It is also notable that this year, the award bearing Jay Forrester's name recognizes a person who grew up in a small rural town in a low income country, far away from progress in high technology, and whose work also addresses the problems of the poor and the technologically backward. My first classroom had the blue sky as its roof, and my work has dealt with the problems of sustainability, welfare and governance for the low income countries. My coming to the classrooms of a most sophisticated institution of higher learning, MIT, to study an advanced methodology for application to addressing the problems of the poor might appear to be a study in contrasts, but this is not the subject of my talk today. I wish instead to talk about the old conundrums associated with sustainable development and what I have learnt from researching them with system dynamics. It is pertinent to say, however, that both the experience of having grown up in a low income country and the learning of system dynamics were important elements in the attainment that brings me to this gathering, since system dynamics made it possible for me to make productive use of my experience as a citizen of a low income country.

Another important factor that contributed to the quality of the insights gained was my anchoring myself into a selected problem area for an extended period of time. Tarek Abdel-Hamid, who received this award together with Stuart Madnick last year (1994) for their book *Software Project Dynamics* [Abdel-Hamid and Madnick 1991], referred to this process as the colonization of another field. Such colonization efforts by our colleagues have greatly helped in bridging the gap between system dynamics and other disciplines besides also enriching the colonized fields.

The work

The work for *Towards Sustainable Development* [Saeed 1991], the book cited by the award began some seventeen years ago when I prepared the first draft of my Ph.D. research proposal. This draft was seen quite appropriately as too ambitious by my advisory committee, which was chaired by Edward Roberts, and I was asked to carve out a tractable slice of the problem to work on for my thesis if I did not wish to spend some fifteen years on my Ph.D. Following this advice, I defined the boundary of my Ph.D. work around issues of sustainability of the economic relations, which also became the conceptual staring point for the remaining work reported in the book.

The current edition of *Towards Sustainable Development* collects thirteen papers written over a period of twelve years which deal with the various aspects of sustainability of the developing country socio-economic systems. Six of these papers are country-specific case studies; the first of which is based on my Ph.D. work while four others resulted from research done together with my students at AIT. Please allow me to acknowledge their contribution by calling their names. They are Jayprakashan Ambali from India, Tasrif Arif from Indonesia, Nguyen Luang Bach from Vietnam and Phares Parayno from Philippines. The sixth case study came from the work Tony Picardi and I did together at the Development Analysis Associates during my graduate student years. Twelve of the thirteen papers have been published in six learned journals, *Behavioral Science, Simulation, Socio-Economic Planning Sciences, System Dynamics Review, Technological Forecasting and Social Change* and *World Development*. The thirteenth paper, on entrepreneurship development, is based on a report prepared on a request from the UN Fund for Science and Technology for Development for a meeting held in Beijing in May 1990.

I must add that an extended dialogue with a spirited economist, my young colleague and friend, Mike Radzicki, over the years following the publication of *Towards Sustainable Development* opened for me a window to the Institutionalist and the Post Keynesian streams of economics to view my work in their context. What I saw through this window encouraged me to integrate my writings dealing with the basic concepts on sustainability into a second book *Development Planning and Policy Design*, published last year (1994) by Avebury [Saeed 1994]. I wish also to acknowledge the assistance of another young colleague, Kip Cooper, who provided critical support in the early stages of development of a user-friendly software that accompanies above book [Saeed 1994a].

5

Learning from researching old conundrums

In my own assessment, the most significant skill I have acquired over the course of my work on the old conundrums of development planning included in *Towards Sustainable Development* is to integrate a diverse information base containing quantitative data, experiential information and theoretical concepts into a unified theory. This is easier said than done, since the process seeking this integration is complex yet informal and has many pitfall in it. Indeed, as shown in a classical illustration by Jay Forrester [1980] reproduced in Figure 1, system dynamics requires integration of a whole spectrum of information in which experiential data represents the largest chunk.

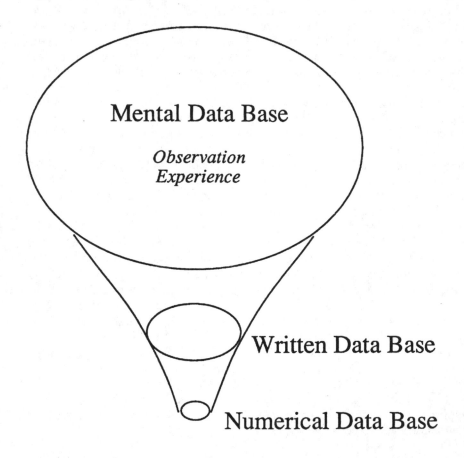

Figure 1   **Information base for system dynamics modeling**
Source: Forrester 1980

6

The various categories of data contained in the information base will often have inconsistencies resolving which is not only a challenge, it also creates a substantial learning opportunity. An episode would best illustrate this process. While trying to collect evidence on the incidence of agricultural feudalism in South Asia, which served as an empirical reference for my work, it appeared that the literature on economic development did not record any explicit starting point for feudalism, rather, it was seen to have existed since the medieval times. However, when I simulated the model of economic relations I had developed with the rules of land tenure pertinent for medieval India, the land tenure pattern the model generated was that of an egalitarian agricultural economy. This frustrated me and I spent considerable time and effort trying to find errors in the logic of my model, but without success. I finally turned to economic history, which corroborated my model rather than the vague records of agricultural feudalism in the economic development literature. According to the pertinent writings on economic history, medieval India enjoyed quite an egalitarian agricultural society where labor was internalized by the families tilling land, formal land ownership was absent, and the concessions for tilling were made according to the quantity of labor a family could internalize [Mukhia 1981]. Feudalism appeared in the agricultural economy of India when land ownership was formalized during the British colonial period and land began to be treated as a commodity rather than a common property resource, which was also corroborated by my simulation experiments with the model.

In retrospect, I tend not to dismiss above course as a routine. If the model were based only on a selected data category, the opportunity to resolve inconsistencies in a diverse information base would not arise. Needless to add that Forrester's experience of finding long wave in the empirical data after his model had exhibited it most certainly contributed to my search for a pattern consistent with the behavior of my model in which I seemed to have developed some confidence. However, the requirement to integrate a diverse information base into an experimental apparatus - the model - created the need to resolve inconsistencies in data, which is an important skill to be learnt in pursuing system dynamics.

The need to carve a slice out of a complex problem for my Ph.D. research helped me also to develop significant insights into the process of partitioning a complex problem without severing its important symbiotic relationships. This allowed me to divide my original research agenda into several parts, which could be dealt with independently of one another without seriously undermining the integrity of the whole. Thus, I was able to create a series of manageable research projects that I had the satisfaction of completing, some of them with the help of my students, while still continuing to work on a complex agenda over an extended period of time. A paper titled, *Slicing a Complex Problem for System Dynamics Modeling*, which appeared some time ago in *System Dynamics Review*, represents an

7

effort to document this experience [Saeed 1992].

Since models cannot be made overly complex if they are to remain understandable, complex problems must be sliced into smaller parts in a way that the parts meet the requirements of the intended policy design. This calls for separating the *multiple modes* contained in a complex historical pattern in a rather special way.

The term *multiple modes* is not new to system dynamics, although it is used a bit loosely. Not all classes of behavior implied by *multiple modes* may be relevant to creating a model for an effective policy design. In fact, many intuitively sensible schemes of partitioning a system may create models that do not incorporate policy space for investigating the possibilities of change. The *multiple modes* relevant to a problem may refer to the simultaneously existing components of a complex pattern of behavior that is exhibited by a system over a given period; they may represent patterns experienced over different periods of time in a system of relationships; or even patterns experienced in similar organizations that are separated by geographic space. The conceptual space in which *multiple modes* can be found is, therefore, three dimensional as shown in Figure 2.

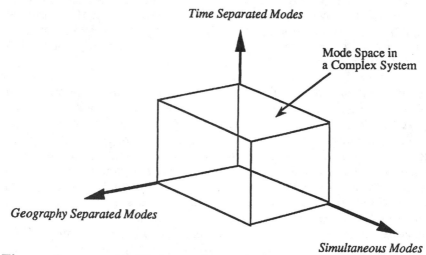

Figure 2　　　**Multiple mode space**
Source: Saeed 1992

When multiple modes contained in a complex historical series are the focus of a modeling effort, the complex modal space will be sliced as shown in Figure 3. The simultaneous modes constituting the complex historical pattern will be subsumed in a selected partition while the variety of patterns in the temporal and geographic dimensions is ignored. Such a problem slicing process will create situational theories and forecasting

8

models that may explain a unique and complex pattern, and also extrapolate it into the future, but without shedding any light on the possibility to change it.

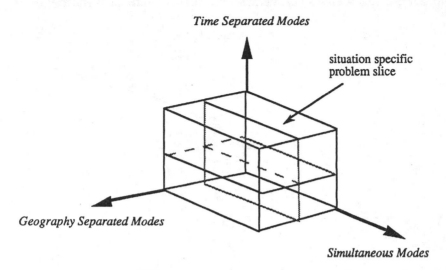

Figure 3   **Problem slices for developing forecasting models and situational theories**

On the other hand, when a model is intended for exploring policy options for system change, the complex modal space must be sliced as shown in Figure 4. The partition selected for modeling will subsume multiple modes that are separated by time and geography since only then its underlying structure would contain the mechanisms of modal change. It may not necessarily incorporate multiple modes that exist simultaneously in system behavior since interaction between the mechanisms creating these may not provide any additional policy space, although this may enhance a model's ability to track history accurately. When policy exploration rather than tracking history is the primary purpose of modeling effort, simultaneously existing multiple modes and their underlying structure can be separated and addressed in different models for limiting complexity contained in a single model.

Representing a complex system as a number of submodels that produce behavior different from what appears in the historical data will require defining reference mode differently from historical behavior. For example, each of the two complex time histories shown in Figure 5 contains a trend simultaneously existing with a cyclical tendency. To be able to address the two issues concerning the cycles and the trends, this problem may be represented by two models: One subsuming the multiple modes existing in the two trends, the other subsuming the cyclical mode existing in both of them. The two models so created will keep together the symbiotic processes underlying the potential multiple patterns thus providing the policy space to attempt a design for change. Also, the two components of the design so created can be pursued quite independently.

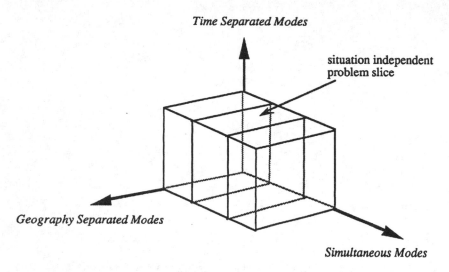

Figure 4   Problem slices for exploring policy design

Above partitioning process was instrumental in creating the models reported in *Towards Sustainable Development*. The variety of development patterns experienced in the low income countries over time and geography is quite staggering. These have sometimes led to controversial theories of economic development. The partitioning procedure I adopted allowed me to view such patterns as multiple modes of system behavior for creating unified theories or models for the various problems concerning sustainable development. Models so created not only allowed to identify specific conditions leading to each pattern, they also contained the policy space for exploring the mechanisms of change from one pattern to the other.

For example, the model investigating sustainable political organizational forms views a large variety of unstable political change patterns as its reference mode. The model investigating sustainable economic relations subsumes a large variety of economic growth and income distribution patterns implicit in the various economic development theories and the variety of experience in the low income countries. The model of resource system subsumes both technologist and environmentalist perspectives on resource depletion patterns. On the other hand, these models do not track precisely any specific time histories.

The case study models used had to be more specific since they ruled out subsuming variety along the dimensions we can find conflicting multiple modes. However, keeping focus on issues and emphasizing the qualitative characteristics of the reference mode, rather than the historical time series it is based on, allowed creating models that could serve as experimental instruments for understanding specific circumstances of each case rather than merely becoming vehicles for forecasting.

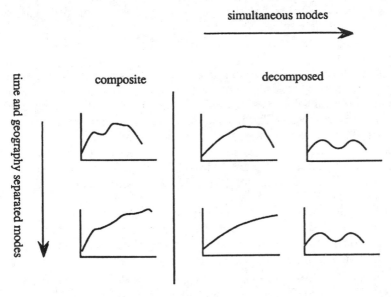

Figure 5   **Decomposing multiple modes for slicing a complex problem**
Source: Saeed 1992

An interesting aspect of the work also was that a unified basis for the multiple theoretical expositions existing in the literature was invariably discovered over the course of the modeling effort when an attempt was made to define a reference mode as a set of patterns separated by time and geography.

The economic growth model I developed could endogenously create a whole spectrum of growth patterns — medieval, classical, neo-classical, revisionist, dualist — that the various growth theories viewed as given. A perennial debate in economics concerns the theory of value, how the real prices of commodities are affected by the costs of the factors used in their production, which has been seen differently by the different theorists. However, as pointed out by Saraffa, a circularity exists between commodity prices and factor costs. While commodity prices will depend on factor costs, these costs cannot be independent of the claims to income their

11

suppliers are able to make, which depends on the commodity prices they are able to charge [Saraffa 1960]. Since these claims may be different from true factor contributions to the production process, it is not surprising that a variety of value patterns will be experienced, depending on the bargaining power enjoyed by the various cross-sections of the households providing inputs to the production process.

Thus, the bargaining position of the various cross-sections of the households and the degree of polarization in their control of production resources will really determine who can file a larger claim to the value created in production, the suppliers of capital or the suppliers of labor. The real problem, therefore, is to model the process of bargaining and how ownership of productive assets might become polarized, which came to fore only after I had spent considerable time examining the variety of growth theories as well as the variety of growth and income distribution patterns actually experienced. The model so created allows exploration of policies that could change the degree of polarization in the ownership of capital and change also the wage share in the value of production. It explains the dynamic relationship between the prices of commodities and production factors and outlines operational means which would influence this relationship.

The political dynamics model, likewise subsumes the variety of correlations between variables representing government power and the state of the economy observed by the various researchers, who have made conflicting statements about a government form appropriate for the developing countries. These researchers were often guided by patterns tied to specific situations bounded by spatial and temporal parameters. Only when an effort was made to subsume a collection of these situations into a model could a unified theory of political behavior be constructed. This model allowed also to search for a sustainable organizational form that should return continued support for welfare agenda.

The resource policy model on one hand contains a simplified archetype of the World3 model, whereas on the other, it elaborates the resource sector so it can subsume both technologist and environmentalist positions on resource use. The model cannot only create resource use patterns posited by the two sides, it is also able to deal with aspects of resource substitution and technological development which could not be addressed with the policy space of World3. In one of the papers presented at this conference, Surya Acharya and I have attempted to combine the structure of the resource sector in my resource policy model with World3 whose resource sector is based exclusively on the environmentalist position on resource use. This has made it possible to outline an operational framework to implement the main recommendations of the World3 study - namely reducing the strain on the resource base and limiting population. With the added policy space, these recommendations could be translated into fiscal and institutional measures that might be executed at the regional and national levels rather than being left to the world leadership at large [Acharya and Saeed 1995].

The case studies included in *Towards Sustainable Development* deal with a variety of issues concerning sustainable development, ranging from foreign debt to water supply. A common element in these studies is the focus on issues rather then on any concrete system. The models created exist for the problems they address. The abstract systems they represent are based on an extension of the concept of man-machine interaction in a broad sense; the interacting entities they deal with are the social institutions, the economy and the natural resource system. The insights provided by the case study models may not be transferred directly to the other cases, but they help to understand the special circumstances of each case, which opens a way to addressing other cases, and also to creating unified theories subsuming the multiple patterns the various cases exhibit.

In almost all instances, the modeling process led to two types of instruments for changing dysfunctional patterns — those creating fundamental forces of change and those facilitating change. These categories seemed to be analogous in their function to Herzberg's motivators and hygiene [Herzberg 1966], which was another important principle learnt over the course of the research. For example, to influence income distribution, the fundamental instrument of change was to tax the various forms of unearned income. The related facilitators included the well-known technological and financial development policies and community assistance programs which have been the main fare of the past development effort. To contain political instability, the fundamental measure was to guarantee civil rights that help the government to take notice of an impending dissonance and reform itself. The facilitators included productivity improvement efforts and giving priority to welfare remit of the government over is concerns for control. To sustain resources and environment, the fundamental measure was a schedule of severance taxes that should adjust the resource basket so their consumption and regeneration can be matched, while conservation and recycling were the facilitators.

Experimentation with my models repeatedly established that a mere implementation of the facilitating factors may not cause any change in the system behavior. This is also borne out by the experience of a number of the developing countries where policies posited by my experimentation as facilitators have often been ineffective in meeting their intended objectives. The facilitators may, however, speed up the process of change, if a primary source of change embodied in a fundamental policy is in place.

Let me hasten to add that the fundamental and the facilitating categories of policies may not hold in an absolute sense and may change with the model boundary, as should be expected from our knowledge of boundary sensitivity [Forrester and Senge 1980]. The question, however, is not only whether a policy sensitive boundary should be extended but also whether a

13

selected boundary is relevant to the problem at hand.

One issue dealt with indirectly in *Towards Sustainable Development* is the role of technological growth. Theodore Schultz was probably the first scholar of economic sciences to point out that the potential of human agents has been under-rated in the design of economic development policies for the poor [Schultz 1979]. Indeed, the studies on the sources of economic growth conducted in the western countries have established that growth from technological change, which arises largely from learning by human agents, is more significant than from the growth of capital and labor. Yet, development planning efforts in the low income countries have mainly sought capital formation and the transfer of equipment-embodied technology and production methods from the developed countries rather than nurturing indigenous technological growth.

Experiments reported in *Towards Sustainable Development* show that the implanting of a superior technology in the capitalist sector would make possible its continued participation in production even though wage rates might exceed aggregate labor productivity while reducing technological differentiation between the capitalist and the self-employed modes of production would complement the fiscal policies that may be instituted for reducing the polarization of ownership of resources. Further modeling work we have recently undertaken at AIT, also shows that the superior ability of the capitalist sector to finance technological growth, if an organization for it existed at all, would reduce the effectiveness of the fiscal policies that attempt to reduce polarization in ownership of resources, since these policies would pressure capitalist sector into investing in upgrading its technological ability, which would help to maintain the polarization of ownership. Influencing the inter-sectoral pattern of technological growth would, therefore, offer an additional leverage point for influencing income distribution, if the production units subsumed technological development as an integral part of their activities instead of relying heavily on technology implants from outside. It is observed that for a technology policy to successfully facilitate growth and influence income distribution, it must attempt to promote competition among the monopolistic formal firms in the capitalist sector while providing positive assistance to the competitive informal firms in the self-employed sector [Saeed and Prankprakma 1994]. In operational terms, this translates into putting in place additional discretionary tax and subsidy measures together with the fundamental instruments arrived at in the original model, which assumes technological growth as exogenous in line with the past evidence.

It should be recognized, however, that the first model boundary is pertinent to the many developing countries in earlier stages of growth relying largely on imports of technology embodied in equipment. The second model boundary is relevant to the cases where significant indigenous technological development effort has become instituted as a part

14

of the activities of the production units. In fact, the system boundary could be extended to subsume endogenous technological growth only if it were possible to reform the organization of the production units so they are able to mobilize the innovation potential of the human agents - an alternative approach to economic development which is indeed largely under-utilized except for a few isolated investigations [Westphal 1979, McClelland and Winter 1971]. A preliminary model exploring this approach was reported in a paper on collegial systems that I presented at the '93 conference, but have not yet had the time to pursue further, although I view this to be an important area to work on. Institutional development is now often presented as an important policy option for sustainable economic development, although research into the organizational forms of the institutions which might successfully mobilize human potential for economic development remains sparse. System dynamics can greatly facilitate the exploration of this option.

Other development issues needing examination

Development planning, in general has been driven by situational models rather than by a comprehensive understanding of the complex information relationships formed through the interaction of the concerned organisms. As a result of this, it has often contained contradictions. There have appeared waves and fads in economic development similar to those in business [Saeed 1986, Perrow 1982], but unlike business, the pitfalls of these waves have affected the lives of large cross-sections of people who had no part in the formulation of the policies that affected them.

1960s was a period of indiscriminate expansion in capital that exacerbated an already polarized income distribution pattern, fueling conflict between economic classes. 1970s called for public sector development, which not only created largely inefficient organizations, it also stymied entrepreneurship in the private sector. 1980s advocated export-based development, with disregard to the composition of the trade and its terms, which drained many developing economies and devastated their natural endowments. 1990s are witnessing the advocacy of free enterprise and free world trade with disregard to the polarized control of productive resources existing within as well as between nations. This is accompanied by a drive to privatize public finance, with the question of sustaining welfare often swept under the rug. The 90s have also seen an emphasis on environmental issues, but these remain somewhat disconnected from the other policies.

This progression of policy waves continues to create unforeseen problems which seem to be becoming worse. Foreign assistance over these waves led to staggering debt burdens whose management is a nightmare.

Technology transfers affected created a vulnerable rather than a sustainable production organization that has been unable to find solutions to the problems faced in the course of its operations. The so called comparative advantage in labor cost, actually created stagnation in the local demand in many instances, leading to increased dependence on exports to the industrialized countries. The drive to privatize public finance with disregard of the long term welfare of the population is creating an infrastructure whose burden is regressive and that encourages the development of a centralized economic base. The wide recognition recently accorded to the limitation of the resources shared by the world and the vulnerability of the common environment have invoked only sporadic and piecemeal complements to the policy agenda issued by the popular waves, with doubtful relevance to long term national and global sustainability.

System dynamics offers a powerful means to learn from addressing above problems and I see a great advantage in its being incorporated into the education and research programs on economic development, public policy, regional analysis and infrastructure planning and management dealing with the problems of the developing countries as well as in those dealing with international relations and global agenda.

New discords

As the global economic system becomes highly integrated, concomitant methodological advancements have no doubt also greatly increased our ability to understand the increasingly complex problems of sustainability. There have, however, lately appeared unsavory discords among development scientists on the solutions to these problems. Scientific controversy is not new to System Dynamics. The counter-intuitive nature of the findings of its analyses has drawn raging criticisms from the practitioners of the traditional sciences [Nordhaus 1973, Averch and Levine 1971]. Fortunately, these criticisms have helped us create rigorous and explicit validation procedures, which seem to have greatly eased communication now between system dynamics and the other fields.

The controversy I am referring to is of a different nature in that its roots are in the conflict of interest rather than in the practice of science, yet it is conducted on scientific rather than political fora. Science is repeatedly called upon to support view points of the parties who have locked their horns into a debate on what is an appropriate solution to the global problems, but the logic of the so-called scientific constructs they present often lacks a common denominator. This controversy is now being conducted exceedingly across an intellectual divide that seems to have revived the two decade old North-South doctrine, although this time it concerns the divided intellectual perspectives on the solutions to the global problems. This is an unfortunate trend in a world which is also becoming increasingly integrated in terms of economic relations and a shared common environment. It creates a high potential for global conflict which can impose yet another limit for the sustenance of human society even when the environmental capacity of the world is still adequate [Mesarovic and Pestel 1975].

Four years ago, I came to the fair city of Kyoto to attend a conference on Simulation and Gaming. The keynote address in this conference was given by an eminent scholar of organizational theory from North America whose work on the interpretation of the systems concept I had extensively read and admired although I had never met him. The keynote speech focused on the most serious threats of the century that mankind faced. The keynote speaker made an eloquent case for the three most serious threats to be 1) depletion of resources and degradation of physical environment, 2) proliferation of weapons of mass destruction, and 3) terrorism. However, the solution he suggested to overcome these threats was to create a global organization with the power to enforce regulatory mechanisms and discipline non-complying nations.

I had an opportunity to talk to the keynote speaker during the coffee break following his lecture. I asked him how he saw the composition of his proposed powerful global organization to be in an economically and politically polarized world; and that wouldn't this organization tend to serve power interests rather than sustaining global welfare, and that wouldn't this role fuel global conflict which is a source of the three key problems of mankind he had very eloquently outlined in his lecture? The learned keynote speaker asked my name and my nationality instead of responding to my questions. After I gave this information, he asked me where the exit to the building was. As I pointed to the exit, he walked towards it without pursuing further the conversation I had initiated. This reaction was probably appropriate given the divide, since I seemed clearly to represent south, in terms of appearance, accent, name, country and my questions. I could relate several other episodes re-enacting above experience, but this would be too much of a digression. The point I wish to make is that it has become difficult to even create a dialogue for bridging the North-South intellectual perspectives on solutions to global problems.

The North-South intellectual divide is often reinforced by the presentation of truncated facts and figures used to support already formed perceptions. For example, It has often been argued in a number of studies originating in the North that the fractional rates of growth of industrial production are much higher in the developing countries than in the developed countries, hence, the developing countries should take increasing responsibility for the global environmental degradation. The studies from the South, however, point towards the magnitude and the cumulative impact of the industrial output in the consideration of environmental responsibility. Figure 6 compares the fractional and absolute growth rates posited by the two sides. Figures 7 and 8 compare respectively cumulative changes over 1975-1990 and the absolute levels of production [UNIDO 1992]. Evidently, arguments based only on selected parts of this data would be biased and would inevitably create controversy. Albeit, such divided perceptions now appear routinely in writings in the learned journals and in intellectual fora dealing with the global problems.

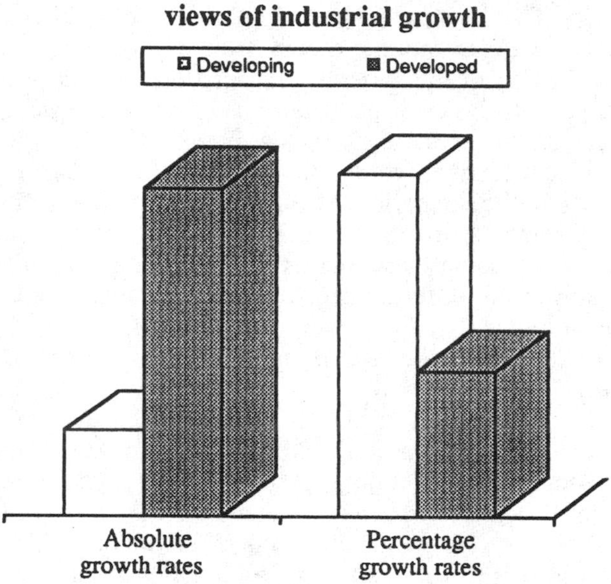

views of industrial growth

Figure 6   **Absolute and fractional rates of growth in world production**
Data source: UNIDO 1992

Arthur Lewis likened the global economic system to an escalator, the rates of ascending of whose riders were intimately linked together due to the interdependence created by the trade flows and their terms, although their respective elevations could vary widely. In this system, it would be impossible to close the gap between the rich and the poor countries unless the former were willing to allow the later a greater share of their markets and also to change the terms of trade in favor of the later. Professor Lewis also observed that what has actually happened is the opposite of this. While the developed countries have attempted to dismantle trade barriers among them, their barriers to a fair trade with the low income countries have progressively increased [Lewis 1984]. There are yet repeated calls from the North reiterating the benefits of a free global market, while the terms of trade for the South have continued to become worse as illustrated in Figure 9 showing the trend of the commodity terms of trade between the developing and the developed countries [Todaro 1994].

cumulative change in production 1975-1990

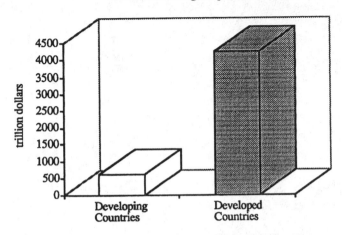

Figure 7   **Estimate of cumulative change in world production 1975-1990**

World Industrial Production

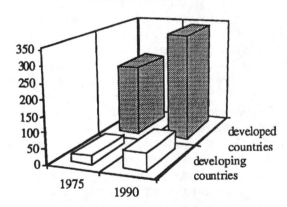

Figure 8   **Developing and developed country shares in world industrial production**
Data source: UNIDO 1992

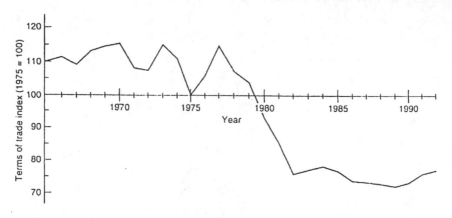

Figure 9   **Trends in North-South terms of trade**
Source: Todaro 1994

While export oriented industrial development has become an important economic strategy, the construction of sophisticated trade instruments have regulated this trade in a way that the developing countries must buy more of high-priced and technologically sophisticated imports while competing intensively to meet the demand of resource intensive and technologically unsophisticated products with low value added content.

This is evident from Figure 10 showing the composition and the growth of the trade flows between the developed trade blocks [USA, EU, Asian Developed countries) and the rest of the Asia and the Pacific region. Figure 10 also registers an alarming increase in the environmentally unfriendly commodities, mostly industrial chemicals and hazardous waste in both directions. Although, desegregate data giving the composition of environmentally unfriendly products traded is not available, there is growing evidence that both hazardous industrial chemical production and the import of hazardous waste are on the rise in the developing countries [Saeed and Acharya 1995]. Either way, the risk of potential environmental damage in the developing countries is rising. Needless to add that some influential economists see this process to be appropriate for achieving economic efficiency on a worldwide scale [Chichilinsky 1994, Economist 92].

An industrial structure responsive to international trade would indeed tend to transfer environmental costs to the countries with lower economic and political muscle, unless a dispassionate analysis of the environmental costs and benefits to the trading partners enters international trade negotiations [Chichilinsky 1994, Copeland and Taylor 1994]. Baron Jakob von Uexkull said at the Rio conference:

20

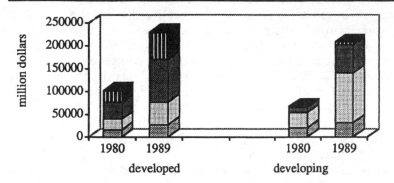

Developed-Developing Country Trade

Resource Intensive ⊠ Low Value Added ■ High Value Added ▣ Envi Unfriendly

Figure 10   **Composition of trade between developed and developing countries**
Source: Saeed and Acharya (1995)

"The present global order appears to recognize only those needs it can satisfy and to see as real only those problems *for which it can offer solutions.* Its amazing shortsightedness is exemplified by the current GATT negotiations, which will create a framework for the global economy – totally at odds with the poor and the environment and designed to circumvent democratic institutions. Laws for the protection of people and environment are to be restricted and localized, while laws for the protection of corporate profit will be globalized. The opportunity to band weak pollution controls and other externalization of environmental causes as unfair trading practices has been missed – thus insuring that any national problems will be globalized and more difficult to repair." [Von Uexkull 1992]

The trend towards global free trade is creating specialization in production among nations in which the North produces high value added equipment while South produces commodities and low value added products [Higgins 1993, Todaro 1994, Saeed and Acharya 1995a]. One manifestation of this specialization appears in the weapons trade. Currently 70% of world exports of weapons originate in the United States. A substantial part of the balance originate in Europe. The magnitude of these exports can be estimated from the fact that the world spends almost a million dollars every minute on weapon purchases [Burns and Hanley 1995]. The price of the military hardware has stayed notoriously high compared with the value of the materials used in their construction. A major buyer of these weapons is the South who must supply raw materials and basic commodities in return. The value transfer in this trade is another issue of controversy between the North and the South.

21

The North-South intellectual divide is similar in many ways to the controversy concerning the situational theories of value. The bargaining power of the various nations is the determinant of the value of what is produced and exchanged at the global level as well as for the responsibility for the damage incurred to the global environment. The related policy issue is not to determine what is fair, but to balance the power that creates value perceptions concerning these issues, which is a complex problem that calls for pursuing a holistic perspective in our analyses to which system dynamics lends itself easily. Policy design addressing global issues must, however, be conceived in terms of the decentralized roles of the actors in the system instead of being seen as a moral issue or the remit of a powerful global organization. I mentioned earlier our efforts to create an operational framework to implement the recommendations of the *Limits* study. Similar efforts would be called for to create the operational means to implement solutions of the impending global problems.

Conclusion

Sustainable development is a familiar turf of System Dynamics, although our exploration of it began at a time when the rest of the world did not recognize the problems we examined, which led to considerable debate. With the greater visibility now of the environmental limits, coming together with global economic integration and the rise in the complexity of the systems we live in, there has lately appeared an urgent need to explore operational policy means for environmental and organizational sustainability all at the global, the national and the regional levels.

As the world becomes highly integrated in terms of its economic relations and a shared common environment, questions concerning economic value and the claims of the various cross-sections of the population to it must also become global. If a political and intellectual divide on these issues is to be avoided, we must learn to resolve them by taking a holistic view of the logic underlying them and creating operational means to implement the solutions so found. System dynamics offers also an important means for achieving this.

Jay Forrester pointed out some eight years ago that system dynamics models represent a logical continuum between the assumptions about the structure of the decisions and the time patterns which result from them. This allows assumptions about the structure to be readily tested, thus facilitating resolution of controversies instead of creating them [Forrester 1987]. The application of system dynamics can help greatly to resolve also the complex policy issues that are renewing a North-South intellectual division about the solutions being proposed to address the global problems of sustainability.

References

Abdel-Hamid, T. and Madnick, S. (1991) *Software Project Dynamics* Englewood Cliffs, NJ: Prentice Hall.

Acharya, S. and Saeed, K. (1995) 'A Search for an Operational Environmental Policy Framework based on the Limits to Growth Study' *Proceedings of the 1995 International System Dynamics Conference* Vol. I Tokyo: System Dynamics Society.

Averch, H. and Levine, R. (1971) 'Two Models of Urban Crisis: An Analytical Essay on Banfield and Forrester' *Policy Sciences* 2(20): 143-158.

Burns, C. and Hanley, C. J. (1995) 'Bargains, Bribes and Rumors Fuel Arms Deals' *Bangkok Post* May 27, 1995.

Chichilinsky, G. (1994) 'North-South Trade and the Global Environment' *American Economic Review* 84(4): 851-874.

Copeland, B. R. and Taylor, M. S. (1994) 'North-South Trade and the Environment' *The Quarterly Journal of Economics* August: 755-787.

Economist Editors (1992) 'Let Them Eat Pollution. News Story on Lawrence Summer's Position in World Bank' *Economist* 8 February.

Forrester, J. W. (1969) *Urban Dynamics* Cambridge, MA: MIT Press.

Forrester, J. W. (1980) 'Information Sources for Modeling the National Economy' *Journal of the American Statistical Association* 75(371): 555-566.

Forrester, J. W. (1987) 'Lessons From System Dynamics Modeling' *System Dynamics Review* 3(2): 136-149.

Forrester, Jay W. and Senge, P. (1980) 'Tests for Building Confidence in System Dynamics Models' in *System Dynamics* A. Legasto, Jr., J. Forrester, J. Lyneis (eds.), Amsterdam: North-Holland.

Herzberg, F. (1966) *Work and Nature of Man* Cleveland, OH: World Publishing Co.

Higgins, B. (1993) *Economic Development, Problems Principles and Policies* London: Norton.

Lewis, W. A. (1984) 'The State of Development Theory' *American Economic Review* 74(1): 1-10.

Mass, N. J. (1975) *Economic Cycles: An Analysis of Underlying Causes* Cambridge, Mass: Wright-Allen Series, MIT Press.

McClelland, D. C. and Winter, D. G. (1971) *Motivating Economic Achievement* New York: The Free Press.

Mesarovic, M. and Pestel, E. (1975) *Mankind at the Turning Point, The Second Report to the Club of Rome* London: Hutchinson.

Mukhia, H. (1981) 'Was There Feudalism in Indian History?' *Journal of Peasant Studies* 8(3): 373-310.

Nordhaus, W. D. (1973) 'World Dynamics: Measurement Without Data' *Economic Journal* 83(332): 1156-1183.

Perrow, C. (1982) 'The Short and Glorious History of Organizational Theory' in *Readings in Organizations* Gibson, J. L., Ivencevich, J. M., Donally, Jr. (eds.), Plano, TX: Business Publications.

Saeed, K. (1986) 'Minds Over Methods' *System Dynamics Review* 2(2).

Saeed, K. (1991) *Towards Sustainable Development, Essays on System Analysis of National Policy* Lahore, Pakistan: Progressive Publishers.

Saeed, K. (1992) 'Slicing a Complex Problem for System Dynamics Modeling' *System Dynamics Review* 8(3): 251-261.

Saeed, K. (1994) *Development Planning and Policy Design, A System Dynamics Approach* Aldershot, England: Avebury Books.

Saeed, K. (1994a) *LAB, The Computer Simulation Program to Accompany Development Planning and Policy Design: A System Dynamics Approach* Bangkok, Thailand: AIT.

Saeed, K. and Acharya, S. (1995) 'The Impending Environmental Repercussions of Industrial Growth in Asia and the Pacific Region' *Working Paper* Bangkok, Thailand: AIT.

Saeed, K. and Prankprakma, P. (1994) 'Technological Development in a Dual Economy: Alternative Policy Levers for Economic Development' *Proceedings of 1994 International System Dynamics Conference* Stirling, Scotland: System Dynamics Society.

Saraffa, P. (1960) *Production of Commodities by Means of Commodities* Cambridge, England: Cambridge University Press.

Schultz, T. (1979) 'The Economics of Being Poor. Nobel Memorial Lecture' in *Economic Sciences, Nobel Lectures 1969-1980* Lindbeck, A. (ed.), Singapore: World Scientific.

Todaro, M. P. (1994) *Economic Development* Fifth Edition. London: Longman.

UNIDO (1992) *World Environment* Ch. 12 New York: United Nations.

Von Uexkull, J. (1992) 'Strategies for Capacity Building' in *Global Environmental Accords: Implications for Technology, Industry and International Relations* N. Choucri (ed.), Cambridge, MA: MIT.

Westphal, L. E. (1979) 'Research on Appropriate Technology' *Industry and Development* 2(1):28-46.

1 Government support for economic agendas in developing countries: a behavioral model[*]

Khalid Saeed

Abstract

A behavioral model of the roles played by the key actors in the political system of a developing country is developed and experimented with to understand circular cause and effect relationships that shape internal trends affecting government commitment for economic development agenda. It is shown that an authoritarian government, whether compassionate or otherwise, will be unable to provide continued support for the economic agenda since its need to increase control will eventually take priority over the need to increase public welfare.

Introduction

This paper examines government's role in supporting economic development agenda with a view to identifying critical mechanisms in the decision structure of the political organization that may significantly affect government's ability to deliver public welfare on a sustained basis. A behavioral model of the pertinent processes in government's functioning is developed and experimented with using computer simulation to understand how organizational conditions affect government commitment to public

* Reprinted from *World Development*, 18(6), Khalid Saeed, Government Support for Economic Agendas in the Developing Countries: A Behavioral Model, pp. 785-801, 1990, with kind permission from Elsevier Science Ltd., The Boulevard, Langford Lane, Kidlington OX5 1GB, UK.

welfare. The model development and interpretation of its behavior is based on the heuristical protocol of system dynamics method suggested by Jay W. Forrester [Forrester 1968, Richardson and Pugh 1981]. The model is implemented on Apple Macintosh personal computer using STELLA software.[1] Mathematical details of the model and its computer versions, which can be implemented on Apple Macintosh personal computer, and also on IBM compatible machines, are available from the author on request.[2]

Experimentation with the model shows that the tendency of an authoritarian government, as its span of control expands, to curtail civil rights and increase the regulation of public life creates powerful feedback loops that interweave to limit government support for public welfare, whether the government is a compassionate one or not. This tendency also results in significant transfer of national resources to the creation of the instruments of control, which include internal security apparatus as well as bureaucratic infrastructure to regulate everyday activity of the public, the consequent scarcity of economic resources not only impairing economic growth, it also fueling dissidence that increasingly pre-occupies the government.

Government's role: expectations and performance

Economic plans for the developing countries invariably designate government as the agency for implementing the various development programs. Most development policies to date also call for rather heavy government intervention and thus further expand governmental control. This makes sense. At least in theory, government is organization legitimately entrusted with the important task of regulating and controlling the actions of the members of a society so that their collective welfare is promoted while their individual prerogatives are preserved [Cypher 1980]. Not designating such an organization to implement development agenda may create anarchy.

In practice, however, a government meeting the theoretical requirements of legitimacy, and able and willing to pursue public interest, may be hard to find in the developing world [Streeten 1979, Ohlin 1979]. And even if a

---

[1] STELLA is available from High Performance Systems, 13 Dartmouth College Highway, Lyme NH 03768, USA. Apple and Macintosh are trademarks of Apple Computer Company.

[2] A menu-driven user-friendly program, which can be implemented on any IBM PC/XT/AT compatible machine is also available on request for further experimentation with the model by those unfamiliar with computer programming. Send requests for technical details and the menu driven program to Khalid Saeed, Social Science and Policy Studies, WPI, Worcester, MA 01609, USA.

government did meet these requirements, an expansion of its control may easily lead to a neglect or rejection of public interest. According to Popper:

".... Interventionism is therefore extremely dangerous. This is not a decisive argument against it; state power must always remain a dangerous though necessary evil. But it should be a warning that if we relax our watchfulness, and if we do not strengthen our democratic institutions while giving more power to the state by interventionist 'planning', then we may lose our freedom. And if freedom is lost, everything is lost, including 'planning'. For why should plans for the welfare of the people be carried out if people have no power to enforce them?" [Popper 1977].

Since direct intervention by a government requires broad governmental authority, development planning might implicitly have encouraged a tendency in the developing countries for the governments to become autocratic. Indeed, the importance of having a "strong" and "stable" government has been emphasized and issues of broader social progress concerning individual rights de-emphasized in many of the treatises on economic development [Friedman 1968, Huntington 1968].

Associations between events taken from historical snapshots have often led to corroboration of above views, although such associations do not imply causality. Morawetz stated over a decade ago:

"The historical experience suggests that political stability, of whatever ilk, and the stability of the 'economic rules of the game' may be an important and under-rated determinant of economic growth. Most of the countries that grew fastest during the period 1950-1975 had such stability. Many of the conspicuous slow growers did not." [Morawetz 1977]

Ironically, Morawetz's list of countries leading in economic performance also included, among others, Venezuela, Argentina, Iran and Mexico, where political unrest and the subsequent breakdown of government control have since disrupted growth. Even El Salvador, which has been touted for some time as a success story has been unable to maintain either the economic progress or the civil rights for its people and is currently experiencing rising levels of insurgence [Smolowe 1988]. It is also interesting to note that, during the period of good economic performance, these countries enjoyed a rather special type of political stability, created by the so-called "strongmen" through military or civilian dictatorships underpinned by considerable natural resources or foreign aid. Experience shows that such political stability often turns out to be fragile.

It is quite true that a welfare-minded strongman may significantly facilitate the development effort since he may be able to take speedy decisions without having to go through a tedious adversarial decision-making process with the various interest groups representing the public. It remains, however, to be seen whether a strongman, however compassionate, can ever continue to support public interest in the face of a

27

more pressing avocation to maintain power, especially when later pursuit may also avoid the rigors of the adversarial decision-making process.

Implemented by authoritarian regimes, economic development programs in many countries have often benefited only the socio-political coalitions which hold the political power, thus creating large differences of income between the rich and the poor and rarely causing any improvement in the economic condition of the general public [White 1974, Griffin 1977, Misra 1981]. A rather poorly documented side effect of such economic development in these countries has been the burgeoning expenditures on national security and defense, euphemistically hidden in the term "public consumption", which has often fueled large national debts [World Development Reports 1980-1987, World Debt Tables 1982-83 and 1986-87].

A disturbing feature of developing countries since the inception of the economic growth effort has been the appearance of active dissident groups, who in many instances are engaged in insurgence against government forces. These dissident groups may state different ideological reasons for their respective fights, but their functioning is made possible only because they are able to elicit support from the public factions who are dissatisfied with the government. The activities of these groups have sometimes created violent political changes in the developing countries that have disrupted economic growth, also destroying life and property.

The apparent political stability provided by authoritarian governments is thus often typified by a concomitant low level of civil rights, considerable dissidence, a continued fight on the part of the government to contain insurgence, a paucity of resources for deployment in the economic sector, and a low priority for the development agenda, irrespective of the stated commitment of the government to public welfare. Such stability is also quit fragile and may often be terminated by violent political change [Saeed 1986].

Research on government's role in the developing countries

There is a considerable casual literature expressing learned opinions on the role of the government in the developing countries. For example, a short article by Professor Becker in a recent issue of *Businessweek* was entitled 'Too Much Government is What Ails the Third World' [Becker 1988]. And Not long ago, *Technology Review* published a short article by Professor Thurow entitled 'Who Said Military Dictatorships are Good for the Economy?' [Thurow 1986]. Similar views routinely also appear in the reporting and editorials of many respectable news magazines. However, concerted efforts to research this issue have been rather few.

A notable analysis is by Huntington who views issues of social justice as a

28

luxury the developing countries cannot afford [Huntington 1968]. There also are a few statistical studies which have attempted to understand government's role in economic development. One of the earliest and better known of these is by Benoit, who reported a positive correlation between military expenditure and economic growth rate, implying that military spending by a government may facilitate economic growth [Benoit 1973, 1978]. Further statistical analyses have, however, failed to confirm Benoit's results [Ball 1983]. In fact, a more recent statistical study by Nabe on 26 African countries found no significant covariance between military expenditure and economic growth. Instead, it found a significant covariance between economic development and social development indicators such as number of teachers and physicians, installed electricity generating capacity, and government expenditure on health and education [Nabe 1983].

Another cross-sectional study by MacKinlay and Cohan employs cluster analysis to understand the differences between the performance of military and non-military regime systems. MacKinlay and Cohan report no significant difference between the economic performance of the two types of regime, although considerable variability exists within each cluster. This may be due to the fact that military are a strong political faction in most developing countries, whether or not they directly control the government. Also, the legitimacy of non-military regimes often lies in the same gray area as that of military regimes, with the two invariably built on similar autocratic lines. The study reports, however, that military regime systems differ from the non-military in imposing substantially greater restrictions on political institutions. The former also undergo a larger number of executive changes than the latter, presumably through military coups, with little change in the nature of their leadership [MacKinlay and Cohan 1976].

A more recent study by Adelman and Hihn formulates and statistically estimates a highly simplified model based on existing political science paradigms. The study concludes that economic and social polarization, which often become a source of political strife, may be difficult to avoid in the process of economic development. It goes on to suggest that the possibility of political instability can be greatly reduced if a government makes a conscious effort to pursue greater social mobility combined with increased political participation [Adelman and Hihn 1984].

Implicitly assuming that the existing conduct of a government is irrational, the various statistical analyses reported above may be used as a basis for issuing normative judgments about how a government should conduct itself. Such advice is, however, of little value in practice since governments might be acting rationally under the conflicting role pressures within the bounded information they have to function with [Simon 1982]. Thus, it is more important to delineate institutional arrangements that may lead a government to remain committed to public welfare than to formulate moral appeals for rational action. Statistical analyses are also an inadequate

29

basis for making any causal conclusions since a correlation does not always represent a causal link. Even if it did, the direction of the causality would be almost impossible to determine [Black 1983, Hendry 1980, Leamer 1983].

Heggen and Cuzan have formulated an interesting micro-political model in which government is viewed as a firm producing "scope" or "control", using legitimacy and/or coercion as production factors. This model serves as a basis to determine expansion paths for socially efficient and socially inefficient governments [Heggen and Cuzan 1981]. However, the model is derived from neo-classical economic theory and incorporates assumptions of perfect information and unlimited rationality with a singular objective, which is inconsistent with the information bounded decisions of the actors in the social systems encountered in reality. Also, the degree of social efficiency of a government is seen by the authors as an exogenously determined precondition whereas in reality it is more likely to be a function of the prevailing institutional arrangements [Myrdal 1978].

The economic theory dominating most of the thinking on economic development has rarely made a distinction between a political system and its actors, thus viewing this system as a well-intentioned individual [Atkinson 1983]. This would seem an unreasonable assumption since the institutional factors and the interests of the actors in the social organization are repeatedly reported as the key determinants of the success or failure of particular development programs [Burki 1971, Alavi 1977, Abeyrama and Saeed 1984].

The role of power groups operating at the national level in the deployment of resources for economic development has also been a subject of much interest to development scientists, although writings on this subject are somewhat informal [Lipton 1977, Furtado 1971]. Political science paradigms on conflict and violence have also been formulated, although these often do not focus on the welfare role of the government or provide adequate experimental explanation of the variety of actual government performance patterns [Schelling 1960, Boulding 1962, Gurr 1979, Honderich 1980]. All things considered, ignorance of the reality of political power, whether deliberate or otherwise, appears to be a significant shortcoming of the formal analyses in economic theory and their applications in development planning [Street 1983, Klien 1980, Dugger 1980].

A behavioral model of the developing country political system

Modeling the political system of a developing country *per se* as an open system, would be a formidable task, although with limited utility. On the other hand, an abstracted closed system consisting of the processes of

30

resource allocation to welfare and control by a government, and the key pressures that affect these processes, can be modeled with relative ease by integrating into a model the locally rational decision components that are widely recognized to be true using the organizing principles of the system dynamics method [Radzicki 1988, Bell and Bell 1980]. Such a model would also have a greater utility with respect to identifying means for realizing an institutional change than a complex model of the government system taken as a whole since the former is not cluttered with irrelevant detail which makes it easier to be understood and applied to thinking for system change [Keyfitz 1979, Baily 1981].

The main actors in the political system modeled are: the government, which holds political power; the dissidents who, in the absence of a due process for political change, wish to overthrow the government and assume power; and the public which seek welfare but often cannot participate in the political decisions that deliver welfare. These actors act upon locally rational criteria in the performance of their respective roles but their interaction may lead to dysfunctional outcomes. A flow diagram created with STELLA software showing information structure of the system is placed at the Appendix. The information relationships incorporated into the model are described below:

a) Creation of social goods and government control

A comparison of the expected inventory of social goods, which is based on the past volumes available, and their current inventory determines perceived goods adequacy. The current inventory of social goods is accumulated through production using economic resources and depleted through consumption proportional to the current inventory. Although there are controversial views existing about the effect of government control over resource management, the model optimistically assumes that the productivity of resources, as well as the rate at which they grow in the economic sector, are enhanced due to increased management efficiency when the government has a large scope. Scope of the government is modeled as a normalized ratio of control to inventory of social goods. Control is modeled as a stock which is increased through creation of control instruments with control resources and depleted at a rate proportional to the existing level of control.

b) Allocation of resources to economic and control sectors

National resources can be transferred from one sector to the other based on the intensity of need in each. Resources placed in the economic sector grow at an exogenously specified net rate and their growth is further facilitated by a high management efficiency made possible by a high government

31

scope. Resources placed in the control sector are consumed at a net rate proportional to their existing level modulated by a measure of their adequacy.

The intensities of need for the transfer of resources between the two sectors are translated in the model into the respective pressures. The pressure for welfare has two components - adversarial pressure which originates from perceived goods adequacy but may surface only when civil rights allowing public groups to censure government exist, and compassionate pressure which arises when a government voluntarily recognizes a lack of adequate welfare for the public even in the face of a rising need for stepping up control.

The pressure for stepping up control arises from the adequacy of resources deployed in the control apparatus - the perceived resource needs to counter insurgence, contain censure, and manage total resources of the nation determining their desired level. There might be some economy of scale possible in the control apparatus needed for the management of an expanded resource base, although the need to contain censure and insurgence would often more than off-set this economy, especially when such need is governed by the powerful feedback loops formed in this systems which are discussed later.

The control resources adequacy not only affects allocation of economic resources to the control sector, but also influences the rate at which control resources are consumed - a shortage of control resources creating a higher rate of consumption. This mechanism also subsumes acts of buying off insurgents which might place insurgency on hold temporarily, although this also steps up the need for control resources.

c) Creation of dissidence and insurgence

Dissidence is assumed to be created by accumulation of un-released censure and ventilated through violent acts. Censure depends on potential censure and the presence of civil rights which allow it to surface. Censure is recognized by the government after a perception delay. Potential censure is created in response to the expansion of control and the size of discrepancy between desired and available social goods.

Numerical values are assigned to the model variables and parameters since the simulation method used requires these. Absolute numerical values have no cardinal meaning but they can be used to make ordinal comparisons of model behavior obtained in the various simulation experiments.

The model is initialized in equilibrium characterized by an absence of dissidence, critically adequate amounts of economic and control resources, and normal values of perceived goods adequacy and censure intensity. This equilibrium is disturbed by stepping up the rate of growth of economic

32

resources, which signifies beginning of the development effort through measures such as increasing saving rate and investment, transfer of technology from the developed countries, increasing exploitation of natural resource base, or provision of foreign assistance.

Many experiments were performed with the model to understand its behavior and the sensitivity of the behavior to parameter changes. The time variant patterns generated by the model appear to be remarkably insensitive to the changes in its parameters, provided its structure representing various pressures and effects is maintained. The simulated behavior of the model with various assumptions concerning government attitudes and organization and its relevance to the real world is discussed in the following section.

Model behavior and explanation of government's support of economic agendas

The compassionate pressure for welfare is neutralized for the base run simulation of the model. This implies that the government would move to increase welfare only under adversarial pressure. Figure 1.1 shows the behavior of the model for this base run. When fractional growth rate of economic resources is stepped up, social goods inventory, perceived goods adequacy and control intensity rise simultaneously. Meanwhile, censure of the government shows an upturn after an initial decline and insurgence recognized by the government steadily rises as total resources of the nation increase. A turning point in these trends is triggered by a decline in total resources caused by poor growth and excessive consumption in the control sector, although social goods inventory is highest at this turning point. A cyclical pattern follows in which both growth and decline phases are accompanied by coterminous changes in control, censure and recognized insurgence.

Figure 1.2 shows the important feedback loops formed by the relationships of the model which lead to the cyclical behavior shown by it. An increase in the total resources of the system caused by economic growth also raises the need for expanding control, as some of the resources must be used to upgrade the system organization. Thus, some increase in control is inevitable when economic growth occurs. However, the proportion of the resources allocated to the economic sector depends not only on total available resources but also on the government's commitment to delivering social goods and its perception of the need for control. The former is kept alive by adversarial activity originating from censure of the government by the public which can surface only when civil rights are maintained. The latter is determined by insurgence which is fueled by dissidence.

Unfortunately, civil rights are progressively reduced as control rises. In

33

the absence of civil rights, adversarial activity creating pressure for welfare wanes while un-vented censure breeds dissidence. The insurgence resulting from dissidence calls for allocating even more resources to the control sector. This allocation process continues until insurgence has risen to a point where it cannot be contained by the existing level of control while so few resources are left in the economic sector that their rate of growth is less than the amount of control resources being consumed, despite the increased management efficiency which is made possible by an increase in the scope of the government.

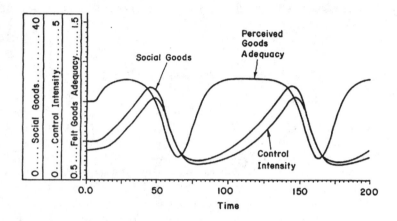

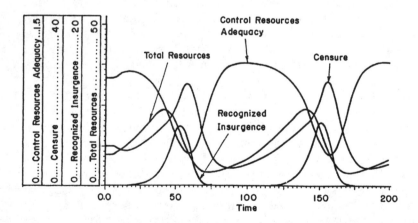

Figure 1.1   **Model behavior in base case showing instability resulting from hypothesized behavioral relationships**

34

At this point, control begins to decay. As control decays, civil rights can no more be curtailed, which causes potential censure to be freely vented. This creates adversarial pressure for stepping up resource allocations to the economic sector although total resources continue to decrease.

A change of regime may occur during this phase and the new regime may even take the credit for increasing support of the economic sector, although it may be responding only to the pressures of the roles vacated by the old regime. Albeit, as soon as the economic trends turn around and positive growth is reinstated, the need to increase control is felt again and the stage is set for repeating the above cycle of events.

The dynamic pattern of behavior exhibited by the model closely resembles the pattern of economic and political changes experienced in many developing countries. The distinguishing features of this pattern are the occurrence of rapid economic growth when government control is rising and the unsustainable nature of this growth which leads to cyclical changes in all variables.

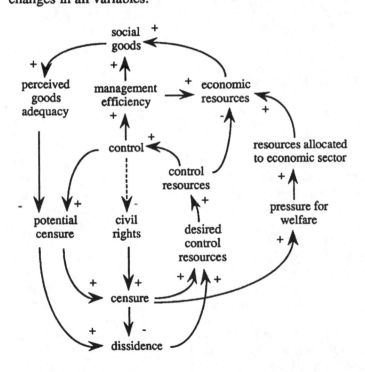

Figure 1.2 **Important feedback loops implicit in the hypothesized behavioral relationships of the model**

35

The cyclical pattern generated by the model also shows an association between economic condition represented by perceived goods adequacy and control intensity over some parts of the cycle. Over other parts, it negates such an association. This rationalizes the conflicting evidence obtained from cross-national studies.

The implication of the unstable behavior of the model which is based on plausible micro-structure is that a government acting rationally under day-to-day pressures to deliver welfare as well as to maintain control, and without willful malafide designs but with freedom to suppress civil rights when its span of control expands, will be unable to support development agenda on a sustained basis. This government profile is more widely applicable to the developing countries than the one modeled by Heggen and Cuzan which incorporates deliberate maximization of scope [Heggen and Cuzan 1981]. The government in the model presented here does expand its scope, but under pressures of its role rather than deliberately. The design problem concerning the role of government in the development process, therefore, is to identify organizational factors which may assure that this role continues be supportive of public welfare on a sustained basis.

The case of compassionate authoritarian government

It is often argued that an authoritarian but compassionate government that is concerned with increasing public welfare can manage national resources judiciously and thus achieve sustainable economic growth. The welfare concern of a regime is incorporated into the model by reactivating the compassionate pressure for welfare which was neutralized for the base run simulation and which acts together with the adversarial pressure to give the net pressure for welfare. This pressure would lead a government to increase allocations to welfare when it is inadequate, even in the face of a heightened demand for control resources.

Simulation of the modified model in Figure 1.3 shows, however, that a compassionate authoritarian government may help only to slightly shorten the periodicity of the cyclical behavior discussed in the previous section. Allocation of resources away from the control sector, when there is already insufficient control, further decreases control resources adequacy. The resulting increase in censure adds to the need for resources in the control sector. Since the government must weigh pressure for control resources adequacy against that for welfare, it may end up allocating resources away from welfare at a faster rate in the subsequent rounds if it has acted compassionately at first.

The impact of improvement in productivity of economic resources

Improving productivity of resources in the economic sector, possibly through technological improvements, along with maintaining a compassionate attitude steps up perceived goods adequacy as shown in Figure 1.4. However, as the need for control also rises concomitantly, resource allocations away from the economic sector soon erode this advantage.

High productivity of economic resources creates a high goods adequacy with fewer resources, which eventually permits increased allocation to the control sector. A high level of control increases potential censure, although, high perceived goods adequacy may off-set this. As a result, both censure and recognized insurgence do not rise as much as in the previous cases. The oscillatory pattern of behavior is maintained, but the amplitude of the oscillations is reduced.

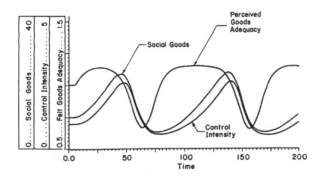

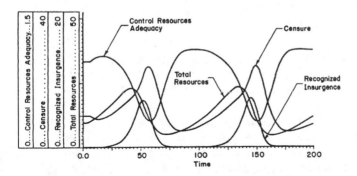

Figure 1.3   **Model behavior when government is assumed to act compassionately**

37

A number of authoritative developing country governments with limited resources appear to have been able to create reasonable growth momentum by adopting high-productivity technologies, although their experiences in maintaining growth differ. On one hand, South Korea, Taiwan and Singapore have maintained rapid growth for extended periods of time. A distinctive characteristic of the governments of these countries has also been economic pragmatism which, possibly, diffused some of the dissidence fueling excessive allocation of resources to control.

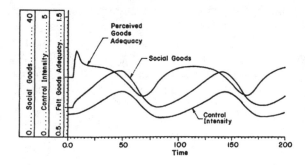

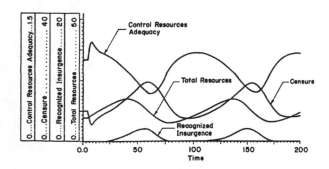

Figure 1.4   **Model behavior with assumptions of compassionate government, and productivity improvement in the economic sector**

On the other hand, ideological and social dogmatisms in many of the Latin American and Asian countries have led to confrontations with dissidents which have rapidly stifled economic progress [Lehman 1985]. The parametric differences in the orientations of the authoritarian governments and their respective performances notwithstanding, experimentation with the model indicates that growth from employment of high productivity technologies may not continue without periodic disruptions due to political conflict.

38

High rate of growth supported by abundant resources or foreign aid

Many developing countries have been able to support a high rate of economic growth either because of access to a plentiful indigenous resource base or massive amounts of foreign aid. Many of these countries have also experienced concomitant growth in dissidence and have been forced to draw large amounts of resources into spending on internal security and defense. Figure 1.5 shows a simulation incorporating a higher economic growth rate in addition to the assumptions of Figure 1.4.

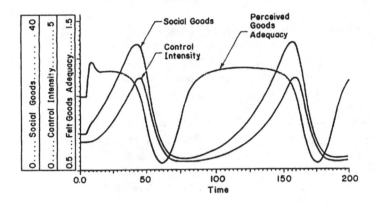

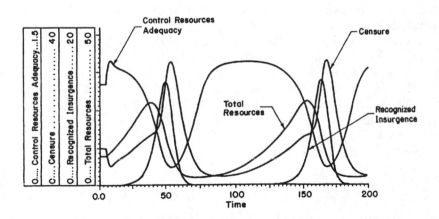

Figure 1.5   Model behavior with assumptions of compassionate government, productivity improvement in the economic sector, and high rate of growth of economic sector

39

It seems from the simulation that such countries may face more violent fluctuations in the economic and control variables than the less endowed ones, although they may achieve higher levels of social goods over the growth phase. This has also been borne out by real cases such as Iran and Argentine where high economic growth was disrupted by violent political changes purging the old guards and replacing them with the new ones. Unfortunately, the new guards may meet the same fate as the old ones unless the structure of the political organization is also changed.

External assistance to facilitate or contain dissidence

Developing country governments have often blamed the growth of dissident movements to foreign interference. Indeed, in some cases like the now Vietnam, Nicaragua, and Afghanistan, dissidents have been openly supported by one super-power or the other. In many other cases, the developing country governments have also been assisted by foreign powers to suppress dissidence.

The effect of external support to dissidence is to facilitate commitment of violent acts against the government by the dissidents. This can be incorporated into the model by increasing the fractional rate at which dissidence is ventilated. Figure 1.6 shows a simulation of the original model used in the base run but with a high rate of ventilation of dissidence, presumably made possible through foreign assistance.

This simulation is no different from the base run except for a slight decrease in the periodicity of the cyclical pattern since no structural change has occurred in the system. External assistance to suppress dissidence, likewise, translates into a decrease in the fractional rate at which dissidence is ventilated. This would only increase the periodicity of the cyclical pattern without changing its fundamental form.

The behavior of the model continues to display the characteristic instability observed in previous simulations. As long as there is a provision for limiting censure, dissidence will be created while subsequent insurgence arising from ventilation of dissidence will continue to increase the need for control which has been identified as the key factor limiting government support of welfare.

A design to improve government support for economic agenda

The analysis of the model has so far established that economic growth is limited when resources are allocated away from the economic sector to meet the increasing need for resources in the control sector. This allocation

40

is stepped up when there is inadequate control to manage resources and to control dissidence and censure, whether or not a government is compassionate. Unfortunately, increased allocations of resources away from the economic sector reduces the quantity of productive resources in the economic sector, which deteriorates overall resource adequacy and this ultimately undermines government control.

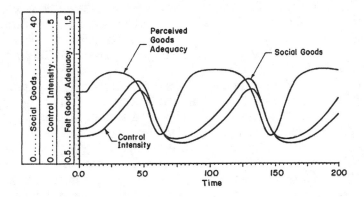

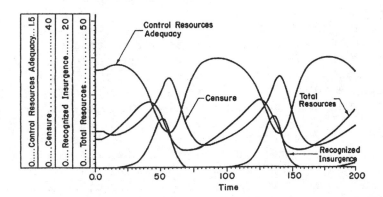

Figure 1.6   **Model behavior with assumptions of base case together with facilitation given to ventilation of dissidence**

A potential for censure exists partly because of inadequacy of social goods compared with expectation for these and partly because of the psychological deprivation experienced due to increase in government control. However, the increase in control may also effectively contain censure through limiting civil rights. The need for expansion of control increases further when the suppressed censure has transformed into

41

dissidence whose ventilation creates insurgence. The urgency of this need wanes government commitment to economic agenda even though it may be genuinely concerned for public welfare.

The need to expand control must somehow be limited to assure that a government remains committed to public welfare. A major component of the need for control arises from insurgence which is fueled by dissidence, while dissidence arises from suppressed censure. A reduction in suppressed censure should limit the need for control, which is possible only when censure is allowed to surface and support adversarial pressure for welfare instead of being suppressed through limiting civil rights. This translates into protecting civil rights through a constitutional guarantee and not allowing these to be limited when control expands.

Many developing country governments provide constitutional protection to civil rights, at least in a limited way. A limited protection of civil rights implies that they may not be freely suppressed, although, increase in control may effectively reduce the communication channels through which censure may surface. Such a policy can be incorporated into the model by reducing the rate at which civil rights are limited in response to the increases in control intensity and also by not allowing the former to be reduced all the way to zero even if the latter is very high. Figure 1.7 shows a simulation of the model with these changes. The assumptions of a compassionate government, high productivity and high rate of growth are also maintained.

Any partial protection of civil rights, therefore, is inadequate to avoid development of conditions which pressure a government to expand control at the cost of undermining welfare. Only when civil rights are completely decoupled from control does a change appear in the model behavior. Figure 1.8 shows a simulation in which civil rights have an iron clad constitutional guarantee and remain fully effective irrespective of the control intensity.

Unlike previous simulations, social goods grow without constraints appearing from the government's excessive need for drawing resources into the control sector. Control intensity also grows but most of the additional control instruments are directed toward management of an expanding resource base. Both, perceived goods and control resources adequacies level off at values greater than unity indicating public and government satisfaction with conditions. Censure grows concomitantly with control, although there is no dissidence. Such a growth in censure should be viewed, however, as a normal part of managing a larger and more complex resource base.

An important observation to be made from above experiments also is that the intensity of the inverse relationship between control and civil rights largely affects the periodicity of the cyclical behavior. Only severing this relationship completely creates un-interrupted growth. Hence, the authoritarian and democratic types of government must be viewed as dichotomous and not as points of a continuum.

There would indeed be other constraints to the growth of social goods determining public welfare which are not incorporated into the model. These may arise from the limitations of resources and technology and from mechanisms of income distribution [Saeed 1985, 1988].

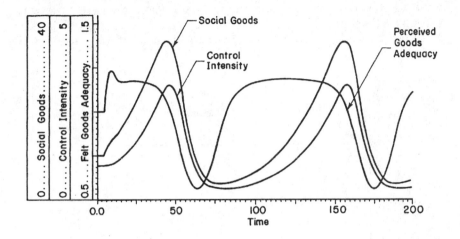

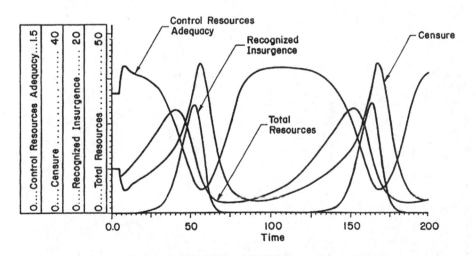

Figure 1.7   Model behavior with assumptions of compassionate government, productivity improvement in the economic sector, high rate of growth of economic sector, and limited protection of civil rights

However, the commitment to implementing policies to overcome those constraints also depends on whether a government is able to support welfare agenda on a continued basis. Therefore, the presence of a political organization that experiences minimal conflict between allocation of resources between social goods production and control, is a key to the development of a nation. Such a political organization must necessarily derive its power from a wide-based electorate whose civil rights it would be motivated to protect, and not from a limited economic or military power faction whose interests may conflict with those of the general public.

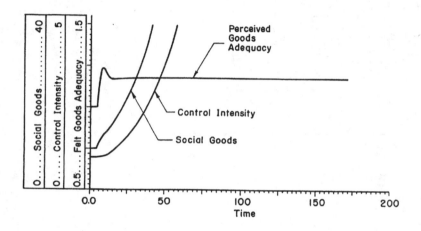

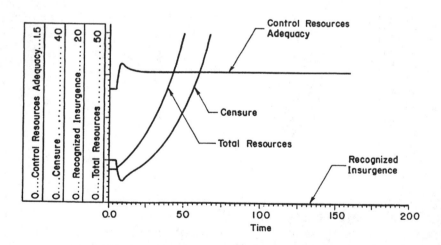

Figure 1.8   **Model behavior with base case assumptions and iron-clad protection of civil rights**

Conclusion

Development plans, however innovative and cognizant of the social, technical, and physical factors affecting the system for which they are prepared, cannot be successfully implemented without the continued support of government. Unfortunately, whether or not a government pays lip service to economic development agenda, its commitment, or otherwise, to promoting public welfare will depend on the role pressures it experiences in conducting its day to day business.

An explicit model of the roles played by the key actors in the political system and their respective motivations to act helps to understand circular cause and effect relationships shaping internal trends affecting government commitment to development agenda. While many circular relationships may potentially exist in the system, only a few of these would play a dominant role in determining its behavior.

An expansion in the authority or the control of the authoritarian government is also linked with a reduction in civil rights. As a result, censure of the government is suppressed although a high potential for such censure may exist. Consequently, any adversarial pressure to support the economic sector weakens while the un-vented censure fuels dissidence, which calls for a further stepping up of control. In this way, an insidious positive feedback loop is created that increases control while at the same time neglecting the economic sector.

An authoritarian government, whether compassionate or otherwise, will be unable to provide continued support to development agenda since its need to increase control will eventually take priority over the need to increase public welfare. The availability of highly productive technologies, abundant resources, foreign economic assistance, and foreign support for or against indigenous dissidence make little, if any, difference to above pattern of behavior. Limited support of civil rights provided in many developing country constitutions also does not affect system trends.

The alternative to authoritarianism is a democratic system in which the expansion in control does not effect civil rights. As a result, censure of the government creating adversarial pressure to maintain support to the economic sector curtails disproportionate allocations to the expansion of control; the resulting improvement in welfare limits censure. Also, since censure can be freely vented, dissidence remains low. Thus, the insidious positive feedback loop creating disproportionately high allocations to the control sector is weakened while a self-correcting negative feedback loop maintaining adequate allocations to the economic sector becomes a dominant force in the system.

The analysis of this paper establishes that contrary to a strong current advocating the presence of an authoritarian government for facilitating economic development, limiting the power of the government so that it is unable to suppress civil rights appears to be the key organizational factor necessary for sustaining its support of the development agenda. The analysis has, however, many limitations. First, it represents largely thought experiments based on integration of theoretical and experiential knowledge of micro-political relationships. Comparison of simulations of the model with reality is informal and further work is needed to soundly establish its relevance to historical experience. Second, economic growth mechanisms incorporated into the model are rather simplistic and do incorporate the details of the information structure underlying saving and investment decisions. Third, income distribution aspects and social class structure have been ignored which may additionally affect system behavior. The paper has, however, attempted to deal with important institutional design agenda which are relevant to economic development but which have been disregarded because they are considered intangible.

References

Abeyrama, T. and Saeed, K. (1984) 'The Gamodaya Mandalaya Scheme in Sri Lanka: Participatory Development or Power Play?' *Community Development Journal* 29(1): 20-31.

Adelman, Irma and Hihn, Jairus M. (1984) 'Crisis Politics in Developing Countries' *Economic Development and Cultural Change* 33(1): 1-22.

Alavi, Hamza (1976) 'The Rural Elite and Agricultural Development in Pakistan in Stevens, et. al. (eds.), *Rural Development in Bangladesh and Pakistan* Honolulu: Hawaii University Press.

Atkinson, Glen W. (1983) 'Political Economy: Public Choice or Collective Action?' *Journal of Economic Issues* 18(4): 1057-1065.

Bailey, Kenneth D. (1981) 'Abstracted vs Concrete Sociological Theory' *Behavioral Science* 26(4): 313-323.

Ball, Nicole (1983) 'Defense and Development: A Critique of the Benoit Study' *Economic Development and Cultural Change* 25(3): 508-523.

Becker, Gary S. (1988) 'Too Much Government is What Ails the Third World' *Businessweek* January 11:10.

Bell, J. A. and Bell, J. F. (1980) 'System Dynamics Modeling and Scientific Method in J. Randers (ed.), *Elements of System Dynamics Method* Cambridge, MA: MIT Press.

Benoit, Emile (1973) *Defense and Economic Growth in Developing Countries* Boston, MA: Lexington Books.

Benoit, Emile (1978) *Growth and Defense in Developing Countries* Economic Development and Cultural Change 20(2): 271-280.

Black, Fischer (1982) 'The Trouble with Econometric Models' *Financial Analysts Journal* 38(1):29-37.

Boulding, Kenneth E. (1962) *Conflict and Defense* New York: Harper and Row.

Burki, S. J. (1971) 'Interest Group Involvement in Pakistan's Rural Works Program' *Public Policy* 19: 167-206.

Cypher, J. M. (1980) 'Relative State Autonomy and National Economic Planning' *Journal of Economic Issues* 14(2): 327-349.

Dugger, W. M. (1980) 'Power: An Institutional Framework of Analysis' *Journal of Economic Issues* 14(4): 897-907.

Forrester, Jay W. (1968) *Principles of Systems* Cambridge, MA: MIT Press, Wright-Allen Series.

Friedman, John (1968) 'The Strategy of Deliberate Urbanization' *Journal of American Institute of Planners* 34(6): 364-373.

Furtado, C. (1971) *Development and Under-development* Los Angeles, CA: University of California Press.

Griffin, Keith (1977) 'Increasing Poverty and Changing Ideas about Development Strategies' *Development and Change* 8: 491-508.

Gurr, Ted Robert (1970) *Why Men Rebel* Princeton, NJ: Princeton University Press.

Heggen, Richard J. and Cuzan, Alfred G. (1981) 'Legitimacy, Coercion, and Scope: An Expansion Path Analysis Applied to Five Central American Countries and Cuba' *Behavioral Science* 26(2): 143-152.

Hendry, David F. (1980) 'Econometrics — Alchemy or Science?' *Economica* 47: 387-406.

Honderich, Ted (1980) *Violence for Equality, Inquiries in Political Philosophy* New York: Penguin Books.

Huntington, S. P. (1968) *Political Order in Changing Societies* New Haven and London: Yale University Press.

Keyfitz, Nathan (1979) 'Understanding World Models' *Behavioral Science* 24(3): 190-199.

Klien, P. A. (1980) 'Confronting Power in Economics: A Pragmatic Evaluation' *Journal of Economic Issues* 14(4): 871-896.

Leamer, Edward E. (1983) 'Let's Take Con out of Econometrics' *American Economic Review* 73(1): 31-43.

Lehmann, Jean-Pierre (1985) 'Dictatorship and Development in Pacific Asia: Wider Implications' *International Affairs* 61: 592-606.

Lipton, Michael A. (1977) *Why Poor People Stay Poor*, Cambridge, MA: Harvard University Press.

MacKinlay, R. D. and Cohan, A. S. (1976) 'Performance in Military and Nonmilitary Regime Systems' *The American Political Science Review* 70: 850-864.

Misra, K. P. (1981) 'The Changing Perception of Development Problems' in *Changing Perception of Development Problems*, Misra and Honjo (eds.), NY: United Nations.

Morawetz, D. (1977) *Twenty-Five Years of Economic Development*, 1950 to 1975, Washington D. C.: World Bank.

Myrdal, Gunar (1978) 'Institutional Economics' *Journal of Economic Issues* 12(4): 771-783.

Nabe, Oumar (1983) 'Military Expenditure and Industrialization in Africa' *Journal of Economic Issues* 17(2): 575-587.

Ohlin, Goran (1979) 'Development in Retrospect' in Albert Hirshman, et. al., *Towards a New Strategy for Development: A Rothko Chapel Colloquium* New York: Pergamon Press.

Popper, Karl R. (1977) *The Open Society and Its Enemies*, Vol. 2, p.130 New York: Routledge.

Radzicki, M. J. (1988) 'Institutional Dynamics: An Extension of the Institutional Approach to Socioeconomic Analysis' *Journal of Economic Issues* 22(3): 633-665.

Richardson, G. and Pugh, A. L. (1981) *Introduction to System Dynamics Modeling with Dynamo* Cambridge, MA: MIT Press.

Saeed, K. (1985) 'An Attempt to Determine Criteria for Sensible Rates of Use of Material Resources' *Technological Forecasting and Social Change* 28(4): 311-323.

Saeed, K. (1986) 'The Dynamics of Economic Growth and Political Instability in the Developing Countries' *System Dynamics Review* 2(1): 20-35.

Saeed, K. (1988) 'Wage Determination, Income Distribution and the Design of Change' *Behavioral Science* 33(3): 161-186.

Schelling, Thomas C. (1960) *The Strategy of Conflict* London: Oxford University Press.

Simon, Herbert A. (1982) *Models of Bounded Rationality* Cambridge, MA: MIT Press.

Smolowe, J. (1988) 'El Salvador: Stricken President Ailing Country' *Time* 131(4) June 13: 26-27.

Street, James H. (1983) 'The Reality of Power and the Poverty of Economic Doctrine' *Journal of Economic Issues* 17(2): 295-311.

Streeten, Paul (1979) 'Development Ideas in Historical Perspective in Albert Hirshman, et. al., *Towards a New Strategy for Development: A Rothko Chapel Colloquium* New York: Pergamon Press.

Thurow, Lester C. (1986) 'Who Says Military Dictatorships are Good for the Economy' *Technology Review* 89(8): 22-23.

White, L. J. (1974) *Industrial Concentration and Economic Power in Pakistan* Princeton NJ: Princeton University Press.

World Bank (1983) *World Debt Tables 1982-83* Washington D. C.: World Bank.

World Bank (1987) *World Debt Tables 1986-87* Washington D. C.: World Bank.

World Bank (1980 through 1987) *World Development Report* 1980 through 1987. Washington D. C.: World Bank.

Appendix
Model flow diagram

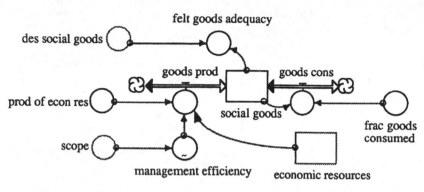

felt goods adequacy

des social goods

goods prod

goods cons

prod of econ res

social goods

frac goods
consumed

scope

management efficiency   economic resources

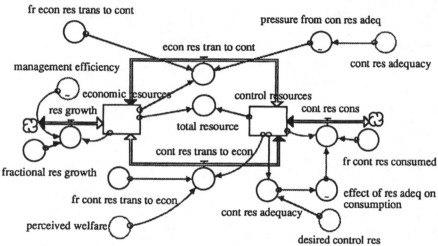

fr econ res trans to cont

pressure from con res adeq

econ res tran to cont

management efficiency

cont res adequacy

economic resources   control resources

res growth

total resource

cont res cons

fr cont res consumed

fractional res growth

cont res trans to econ

effect of res adeq on
consumption

fr cont res trans to econ

cont res adequacy

perceived welfare

desired control res

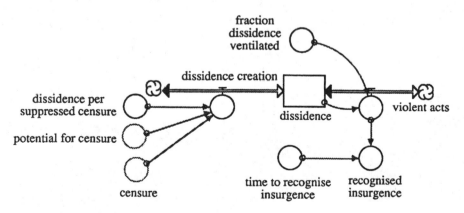

fraction
dissidence
ventilated

dissidence creation

dissidence per
suppressed censure

dissidence

violent acts

potential for censure

censure

time to recognise
insurgence

recognised
insurgence

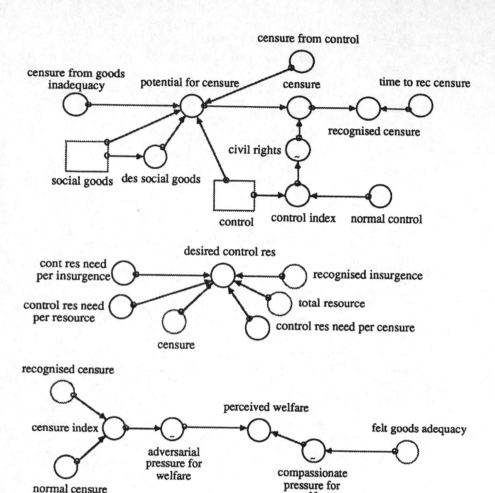

2   Wage determination, income distribution and the design of change[*]

Khalid Saeed

Abstract

Existing alternative models of economic growth, whether based on neo-classical or Marxist thinking, provide an inadequate basis for designing public policies for evolutionary change in wage and income distribution patterns since these models are local to time and geography-specific historical evidence and do not incorporate mechanisms for a possible change from one pattern to another. Hence, both so-called Market and Marxist systems have issued very interventionist designs for economic development. This paper presents a model of an abstracted living system at the societal level which incorporates mechanisms of wage determination and disbursement of income. The behavior of this model is studied through computer simulation. Two potential modes of production are included in the model: formal and self-employed. However, the system thus represented creates a variety of wage and income distribution patterns. The realization of a specific pattern in this model depends not on assumptions about the initial conditions but on the dynamic interaction of the system variables and the social and legal norms concerning renting, financing of investment and choice of technology by the formal and self-employed sectors of the economy. Using this model, the paper explores entry points for evolutionary change in the wage and income distribution patterns currently existing in the developing countries.

[*] Reprinted from *Behavioral Science*, 33(3), Khalid Saeed, Wage determination, income distribution and the design of change, pp. 161-186, 1988, with kind permission from the editor.

51

Introduction

In this paper, I have attempted to reconcile alternative theoretical views and historical patterns concerning wage determination and income distribution using a behavioral model of the information structure underlying the decisions of the various actors in an economic system. This also leads to a search for entry points for evolutionary change in labor-wage rate and income distribution that may not require large-scale direct intervention by a government.

The neo-classical economic theory suggests that in the short run labor-wage rate depends on worker availability while in the long run it is determined by the marginal revenue product of labor. The neo-classical models of economic growth, however, often make the simplifying assumption that an equilibrium continues to prevail in both factor and product markets over the course of growth. Thus, only minor fluctuations may occur in wages, profits and prices in the short run and these can be ignored. The existence of such an equilibrium is justified on the grounds that wages and prices are dictated by long-term considerations concerning wage contracts and production plans and hence these may not respond easily to short-run changes of the market. As a result of the belief in this theory of wage determination, technological choices which increase labor productivity are expected to have a positive effect on wage rate. However, since the neo-classical theory is silent about ownership of capital resources and often assumes them to be widely distributed, labor-wage rate may bear little relationship to the income of households because they are also recipients of profits [Barro 1984, Kindelberger and Harrick 1977].

The Marxist theory of economics, on the other hand, suggests that labor-wage rate is determined by the amount of consumption that is necessary for a worker to support production. The labor-wage rate, therefore, is based on the real value of the commodities needed for a worker to subsist, which is more or less fixed, irrespective of the contribution of labor to the production process. Thus, technological choices which increase labor productivity may only serve to increase the share of the surplus of product per unit of labor appropriated by the capitalist. Labor-wage rate is also a strong determinant of the income of the majority of households since ownership of capital resources is assumed to be concentrated in a minority excluding workers and the majority of households do not receive any part of the profits [Marx 1891, Kaldor 1969, Popper 1977, Pack 1985].

Both neo-classical and Marxist systems can often be corroborated with the help of historical evidence and this has been fully exploited to fuel the debate between their proponents. Interesting artifacts of this debate include the normative theories of value suggested by each system, which have little practical significance for the design of change. This is unfortunate, since contradicting evidence should clearly indicate that some fundamental organizational arrangements exist in the economic system which are capable of creating the multiple behavior patterns on which the two theories are based. Once identified, these mechanisms may serve as entry points for the design of an evolutionary change in an existing pattern [Katz and Kahn 1978].

I propose in this paper a behavioral model of the decision structure underlying wage determination and disbursement of income which subsumes many wage and income distribution patterns. The wage rate in this model depends on the consumption foregone by a worker when he or she leaves self-employment to accept wage-work, which can be interpreted as the opportunity cost of supplying a unit of labor to the formal sector. Since this opportunity cost varies with the amount of capital resources owned by the workers, which may support self-employment, wage rate is strongly affected by the distribution of ownership.

The proposed model does not treat workership and capital-ownership to be either dichotomous or coterminous, as has been assumed implicitly in the alternative economic theories, but allows ownership to change through the normal course of buying and selling transactions based on rational, although, information bounded criteria [Simon 1982]. Using this model, I have attempted to explore entry points into the economic system for evolutionary change in wage and income distribution patterns currently existing in the developing countries.

A behavioral model of wage determination

A behavioral model incorporating the broad decision rules that underlie resource allocation, production, and income disbursement processes of an economic system has been developed, keeping in view the variety of wage and income distribution patterns that have been experienced in history. Capital, labor, and land (which may also be assumed as a proxy for natural resources) are used as production factors. Potential structure is provided for the functioning of two modes of production, commercial, in which resources are employed on the basis of their profitability and which is managed by the formal sector of the economy, and self-employed, in which workers not employed in the commercial mode make a living.

The information structure of this model is based on empirical studies of developing country agricultural economies, most notably by Bardhan (1973) Sen (1966) and Anderson (1968) as well as on my own personal experience of growing up in a developing country undergoing rapid changes and having the opportunity to reflect on this experience while living in a developed country. The latter basis may appear unconventional. It is, nevertheless, a very important input to the modeling process to realize an intimate contact with the system being modeled, since system identification is not possible without such a contact [Popper 1969]. This basis may also be quite inseparable from the modeling process in view of Mannheim's principle, although, if used with a degree of objectivity, it may help to create a realistic model [Landau 1972].

It has been assumed in the model that all workers, whether self-employed using their own or rented capital resources or employed as wage-workers by the formal sector, are members of a homogeneous socio-economic group with a common interest, which is to maximize consumption. This group is also the sole supplier of labor in the economy since the small number of working capitalists is ignored. On the other hand, the formal sector is assumed to maximize profit while it is also the sole wage-employer in the economy. The size of each sector is not specified and is determined endogenously by the model, depending on assumptions about the socio-technical environment in which the system functions.

The changes in the quantities of the production factors owned or employed by each sector are governed by the decisions of the producers and the consumers of output and by the suppliers of the production factors acting rationally according to their respective motivations within the roles defined for them by the system. The value of production is shared by households on the basis of the quantity of the production factors they contribute and the factor prices they can bargain for. Income share of the workers, less any investment needed to maintain self-employment, divided by the total workforce, determines average consumption per worker, which represents the opportunity cost of supplying one unit of labor for wage-employment, and this is the basis for negotiating a wage [Saeed 1980].

It is assumed that formal ownership is protected by law but land and capital assets can be freely bought, sold and rented by their owners. Each buying and selling transaction between the two sectors must be accompanied by a corresponding transfer of the cash value of the assets determined by the going market prices. The financial markets are segmented by sectors and the investment decisions of a sector are not independent of its liquidity position, given by the unspent balance of its savings. The saving propensity of all households is assumed not to be uniform. Since capitalist households receive incomes which are much above subsistence, their saving propensity is stable. On the other hand, the saving propensity of the worker households depends on their need to save to support investment for self-employment and on how their absolute level of income compares with their inflexible consumption [McKinnon 1973, Shaw 1973].

The model also permits the appearance of technological differences between the formal and the self-employed sectors, when more than one type of capital (traditional and modern) is made available and the two sectors cannot employ the preferred type with equal ease. The broad mathematical and behavioral relationships incorporated into the model are described in the Appendix. Further technical documentation and a machine readable listing of the model written in DYNAMO code [Pugh-III 1976] are available from the author on request.

As an arbitrary initial condition, production factors are equally divided between the two sectors and an equilibrium in both product and factor markets is assumed to exist under the conditions of a perfect economic system as described in neo-classical economics. Thus, the marginal revenue products of land and capital are initially assumed to be equal to their respective marginal factor costs determined by an exogenously specified interest rate which represents the general pattern of preference of the community for current as against future consumption [Hershleifer 1976]. The marginal revenue product of workers is equal to wage rate. The market is initially assumed to be clear and there is no surplus of supply or demand.

Analysis of model behavior

In view of its complexity, the behavior of the model proposed here could only be studied through computer simulation using the heuristical protocol of the system dynamics method. This protocol helps an intuitive understanding of the internal dynamics of the model through carefully designed simulation experiments. The design of such experiments requires that a complex model is decomposed into a simpler model and its complicating assumptions. The model is then simulated and its behavior systematically queried with and without its various complicating assumptions. Furthermore, the testing of the sensitivity of the model to changes in its parameters is also necessary, especially, when the parameters used are coarse [Richardson and Pugh 1981, Roberts 1978, Forrester 1961].

The decomposition of the model proposed here essentially entailed simplifying its assumptions on wage determination, renting, self-financing of investment, and the possibility of technological differentiation between the sectors. Many simulation experiments were performed to explain the internal trends of the model and its response to the various parametric and policy changes. The qualitative behavior of the model appears to be relatively insensitive to a wide range of changes in its parameters [Saeed 1980]. Key experiments concerning the subject of this paper are discussed in this section.

Replicating the neo-classical system

This experiment is aimed at understanding internal trends of a much simplified version of the model, where decision structure is consistent with the neo-classical economic theory. To arrive at this version, it is assumed that the production factors employed by each sector are owned by it and no renting practice exists [Barro 1984]. Wage rate is assumed to be determined by the marginal revenue product of workers instead of the opportunity cost of supplying wage labor. Financial markets are assumed to be perfect and investment decisions of the two sectors are uncoupled from their respective liquidity positions. It is also assumed that the technology of production is the same in the two sectors and, in terms of the model, only traditional capital is available to both of them.

The model thus modified stays in equilibrium when simulated as postulated in neo-classical economic theory. When this equilibrium is disturbed by arbitrarily transferring workers from the formal to the self-employed sector, the model tends to restore its equilibrium in a manner similar to that described by the neo-classical economic theory. This is shown in Figure 2.1.

The transfer raises the marginal revenue product of workers in the formal sector, which immediately proceeds to increase its workforce. The transfer also raises the intensity of workers in the self-employed sector as a result of which the marginal revenue products of land and capital in that sector rise. Hence, it proceeds to acquire more land and capital. These activities continue until the marginal.

Note that while the factor proportions and marginal revenue products of the factors are restored by the model to their original values, the absolute amounts of the various factors are different when new equilibrium is reached. There is, however, no difference in endowments per worker between the formal and the self-employed sectors.

Since factor payments are determined purely on the basis of contribution to the production process while the quantities of production factors allocated to each sector depend on economic efficiency, the wages and factor allocations seem to be determined fairly and efficiently, as if by an invisible hand.

Ownership in such a situation can either be communal or very widely distributed among households since otherwise the wage bargaining process will not lead to fair wages. Indeed, ownership is viewed only as a market imperfection by the neo-classists. Renting of production factors among households is irrelevant since transfer to parties who can efficiently employ them is automatic.

Before anything is said about the empirical validity of the simplifying assumptions made in this model, the historical context of these assumptions must be examined carefully. The simplified model is based on Adam Smith's description of an industrial economy observed at the start of the industrial revolution. This economy was run by artisan-turned capitalists and there were many of these capitalists competing with one another, although, none had the financial muscle to outbid the others except through his/her ability to employ resources efficiently [Smith 1974].

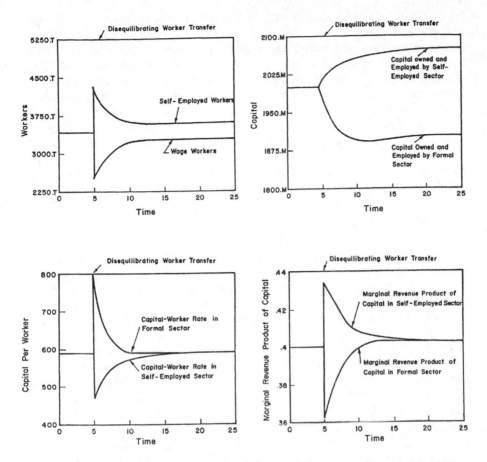

Figure 2.1   **Recovery from disequilibrium in the simplified model**

As far as labor wage rate was concerned, although there were instances of exploitation of workers at a later stage of the industrial revolution, the artisan workers could obtain a wage that was equal to their contribution of labor to the production process, as otherwise they could casily be self-employed since the economy was still quite labor intensive and the tools needed for self-employment may not have cost very much. Also, since ownership of the tools of a trade may have been quite widespread while the contribution of capital resources to the production process was quite small as compared to that of labor, a major part of the income might have accrued to the working households. In such circumstances, the simplifying assumptions of the neo-classical model may appear quite reasonable.

The neo-classical model became irrelevant, however, as the system made progress in the presence of a social organizational framework that legally protected ownership and freely allowed the renting of assets, thus making possible an absentee mode of owning productive resources while technological changes also made the contribution of capital resources to the production process more significant.

Creating an egalitarian system

It is not only methodologically expedient but also pedagogically interesting to explore what ownership and wage patterns might have emerged if labor-wages were determined through bargaining mechanisms incorporated into the model instead of fair payment equal to the marginal revenue product of workers, while all other assumptions of the experiment of section 3.1 were maintained.

Figure 2.2 shows a simulation of the model in which wage rate is determined by the average consumption expenditure per worker (as given in equations 1 and 2 of the model described in the Appendix) while renting of production factors and financial fragmentation of the households are still not allowed. This change in assumptions disturbs the initial market equilibrium in the model thus activating its internal tendency to seek a new equilibrium. No exogenous disequilibrating changes are needed to generate the dynamic behavior in this simulation and in those discussed hereafter.

As a result of this change, the compensation demanded for working in the formal sector becomes much higher than the marginal revenue product of the workers. Thus, wage workers are laid off and accommodated in the self-employed sector. Consequently, the marginal revenue product of land and capital in the self-employed sector increases and its bids for these resources rise. On the other hand, the decrease in the workforce of the formal sector increases its land and capital intensities and hence lowers their marginal revenue products. The falling productivity of these resources increases the opportunity cost of holding them. Hence, the formal sector is persuaded to sell the resources to the self-employed.

As the self-employed sector increases its land and capital holdings, its production rises. When increases in the production of this sector exceed the wage income lost due to decreasing wage disbursements from the formal sector, the net revenue of the workers, and hence their average consumption, rises. The wage rate is thus pushed up further, which

58

necessitates further reductions in wage-workers. These processes spiral into a gradual transfer of all resources to the self-employed sector.

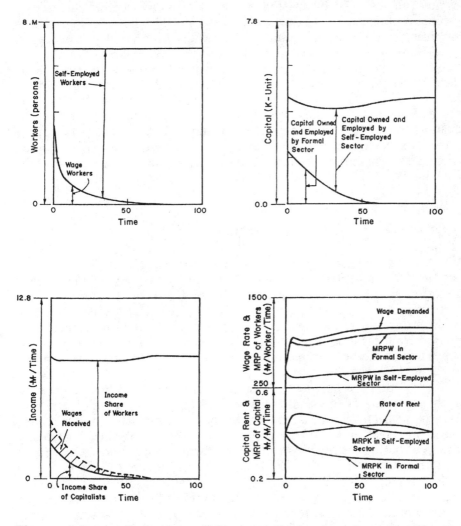

Figure 2.2   **Behavior of the model when wage assumptions are modified**

The marginal revenue products of land and labor in the two sectors tend to equilibrate at different values, but the formal sector exists only in theory because towards the end of the simulation almost all the resources are owned and managed by the self-employed sector. Since no part of the income is obtained by absentee owners, and working households may own and manage resources according to the quantity of labor they can supply, the income distribution may appear to be truly egalitarian.

Even though the above simulation is hypothetical, the wage and income distribution pattern shown by it may be experienced when the separation of resources from the households employing them is socially or legally ruled out and the state allocates capital resources and land according to the quantity and quality of labor supplied by a household. Instances of peasant economies having such characteristics have been recorded in history in tribal cultures and, in a somewhat advanced form, in medieval India [Mukhia 1981].

Appearance of absentee ownership

When ownership of resources is legally protected, whether they are productively employed or owned in absentia, many renting and leasing arrangements may appear which may allow a household to own resources without having to employ them on a commercial basis [Roulet 1976]. This is also exhibited by the simulation in Figure 2.3, in which resources are divided by the formal sector between commercial and renting activities depending on the rates of return in each (see equations 5 and 13 through 24 of the model in the Appendix).

Rents depend on long-term averages of the marginal revenue products of the respective factors and on the demand for renting as compared with the supply of rentable assets. In the new equilibrium reached by the model, the commercial mode of production and wage-employment gradually disappear but a substantial part of the resources continue to be owned by the formal sector which rents these out to the self-employed sector.

Such a pattern develops because of the combined effect of wage and tenure assumptions incorporated into the model. When workers are laid off by the formal sector in response to a high wage rate, the marginal revenue products of land and capital for commercially employing these resources in this sector fall. However, as the laid-off workers are accommodated in the self-employed sector, the marginal revenue products of land and capital, and hence their demand in this sector, rise. Therefore, rents are pushed up and the formal sector is able to get enough return from renting land and capital to justify its investment in these.

Again, the marginal revenue products of the production factors in the commercial mode of production are only hypothetical as that mode is not practiced towards the end of the simulation. The renting mechanism allows the self-employed sector to adjust its factor proportions quickly when it is faced with the accommodation of a large number of workers.

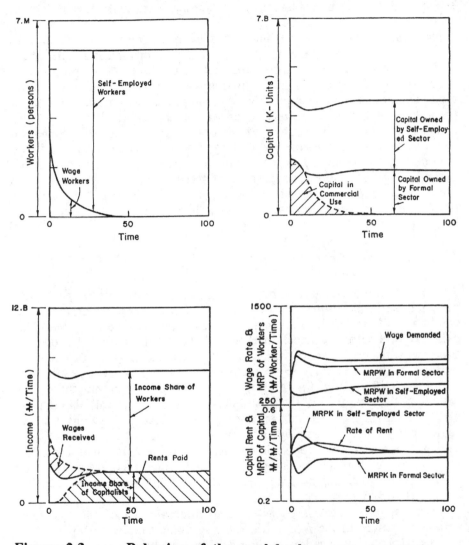

Figure 2.3   **Behavior of the model when wage assumptions are modified and renting is allowed**

When the economy reaches an equilibrium, the marginal rates of return of the production factors in the self-employed sector are the same as those at the beginning of the simulation. But, the wage demanded equilibrates at a level lower than that for the exclusively self-employed economy described in the simulation of Figure 2.2, because a part of the income of the economy is now being obtained by the absentee owners of the formal sector.

Note that, although the total income of the economy falls a little during the transition, it rises back to the original level towards the end equilibrium since the technology is uniform, irrespective of the mode of production. Also note that the end equilibrium distribution of income depends on initial distribution of factors when modifying assumptions are introduced, and on the volume of transfers occurring over the course of transition.

Thus, an unlimited number of income and ownership distribution patterns would be possible depending on initial conditions and the parameters of the model representing the speeds of adjustment of its variables. The common characteristics of these patterns, however, are the presence of absentee ownership, the absence of a commercial mode of production, and a shadow wage that is less than an exclusively self-employed system.

Separation of ownership from workers

The ownership of resources becomes separated from the workers and concentrated in the formal sector in the model, irrespective of the initial conditions of resource distribution, when the assumption about the existence of a perfect financial market is also relaxed. Figure 2.4 shows the ownership and wage pattern which develops when acquisition of resources by the formal and self-employed sectors is made dependent, in addition to their profitability, on the ability to self-finance their purchase (see equations 28 through 35 of the model in the Appendix). Recall also that the ability to self-finance depends on the unspent balance of savings, and the saving rate of the self-employed sector is sensitive both to the utility of saving in this sector to support investment for self-employment and to the rent burden of this sector compared with the factor contribution to its income from land and capital. The saving rate of the formal sector is assumed to be constant.

Such a pattern develops because of an internal goal of the system to employ resources in the most efficient way while the ownership of these resources can only be with the households who have adequate financial ability, which is also not independent of ownership.

The internal goal of a dynamic system represented by a set of non-linear ordinary differential equations is created by the circular information paths or feedback loops formed by the causal relations between its variables implicit in the model structure. These causal relations exist in the state space independently of time (unless time also represents a state of the system). The existence of such feedback loops is widely recognized in Engineering and they are often graphically represented as the so called block and signal flow diagrams [Takahashi, et. al. 1970, Graham 1977].

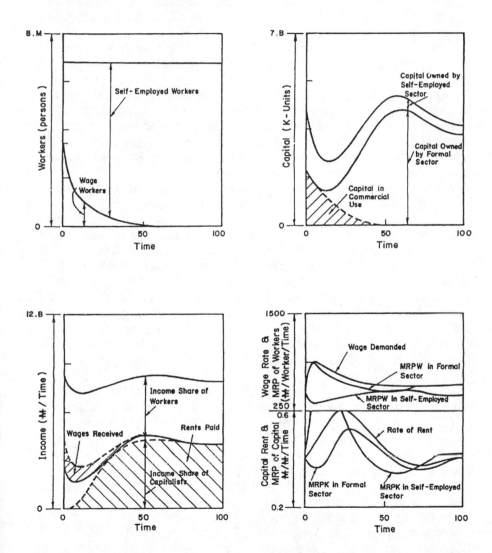

Figure 2.4   Behavior of the model when wage assumptions are modified, renting is allowed, and self-financing of investment is required

63

While many feedback loops may be implicit in the differential equations describing the structure of a system, only a few of these would actively control the system behavior at any time. The nonlinearities existing in the relationships between the state variables determine which of the feedback loops would actively control the system behavior. A change may occur in the internal goals of a system if its existing controlling feedback loops become inactive while simultaneously other feedback loops present in its structure become active. Such a shift in the controlling feedback loops of a system is sometimes called a structural change in the social sciences and it can result both from the dynamic changes occurring over time in the states of the system and from policy intervention. [Richardson 1984, Forrester 1987].

Figure 2.5 describes the feedback loops, formed by the causal relations implicit in the model structure, that appear to govern the peculiar behavior shown in Figure 2.4. Arrows connecting two variables indicate the direction of the causality while positive and negative signs show the slope of the function relating cause to effect. For clarity, only key variables located along each feedback path are shown.

If productive resources can potentially be engaged in commercial or self-employed modes by owners and renters, any autonomous increase in the wage rate would not only decrease the desired capitalist owned resources for commercial employment, it would also concomitantly decrease the utility of investing in resources for self-employment. Thus, while the ownership of resources freed from commercial employment is not transferred to the self-employed sector, the surplus labor released by the commercial sector has to be absorbed in self-employment. As a result, worker income is depressed while the demand for renting rises. Thus, it not only becomes profitable again for the formal sector to hold its investments in land and capital, it also gives this sector a financial edge over the self-employed sector, whose savings continue to decline as its rent burden rises.

These actions spiral into an expansion of ownership of resources by the formal sector even though the commercial mode of production is eliminated due to the high cost of wage labor. This also precipitates a very low wage rate when an equilibrium is reached since a low claim to income of the economy creates low opportunity costs for the self-employed workers for accepting wage-employment.

The existence of a dichotomy between ownership and workership together with a subsistence wage rate represent fundamental assumptions about the existing conditions in the Marxist and revisionist economic descriptions [Marx 1891, White 1974, Lipton 1976, Griffin 1977]. These descriptions are evidently not arbitrary and have an ample empirical basis since feudal social class patterns have existed in history both in agricultural and industrial economies and in developed and developing countries. However, such patterns did not precede the formation of human society but

64

came to be in the course of its existence.

A stable commercially run capital intensive production sector existing together with a self-employed labor intensive sector develops in the model if a technological differentiation is created between the commercial and self-employed sectors. This is shown in the simulation in Figure 2.6, in which an exogenous supply of modern capital is made available after end equilibrium of the simulation in Figure 2.5 is reached.

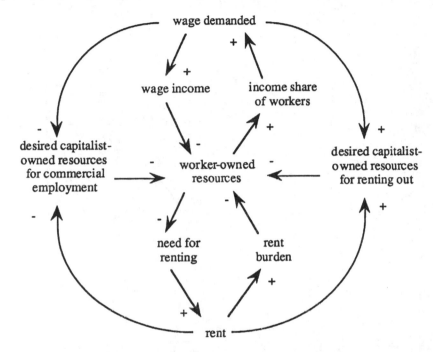

Figure 2.5   **Feedback loops, formed by causal relations between the variables of the model implicit in its structure, which maintain separation of ownership of resources from workers**

Capital differentiation between the two sectors appears since the scale of the self-employed producers does not allow them to adopt modern technologies requiring indivisible capital inputs. The formal sector starts meeting its additional and replacement capital needs by acquiring a mixture of modern and traditional capital inputs while the self-employed sector can use only traditional capital.

However, the capital demand of the formal sector is met by modern capital as much as the fixed supply permits. The balance of its demand is met by acquiring traditional capital. The output elasticity of modern capital is assumed to be higher than that of the traditional capital while the use of the former also allows an autonomous increase in output. The output elasticity of land is assumed to remain constant. The assumption of uniform returns to scale is maintained. Thus, the output elasticity of workers decreases when modern capital is introduced. These assumptions serve to represent the high productivity and labor-saving characteristics of the modern capital.

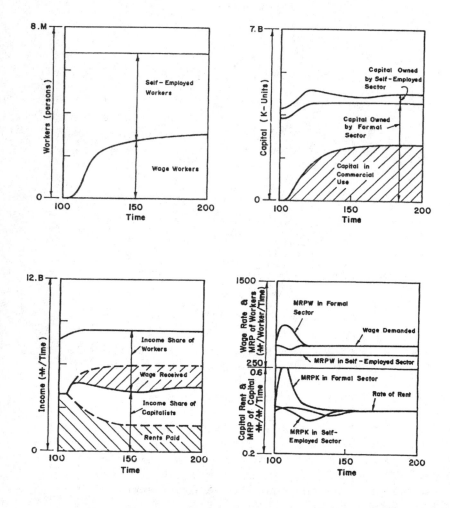

Figure 2.6   **Behavior of the model when technological differentiation is introduced between formal and self-employed sectors in addition to assumptions of Figure 2.4**

As its capital becomes gradually more modern and potentially more productive, the formal sector is able to employ its productive resources with advantage in the commercial mode of production, instead of renting these out, and to employ wage-workers at the going wage rate. The increased productivity and income derived from this make it both economically and financially viable for the formal sector to invest more. Thus, its share of resources, when a new equilibrium is reached, is further increased.

Since the output elasticity of workers falls with the increase in the fraction of modern capital, the marginal revenue product of workers in the commercial mode may not rise much with the increase in its output. At the same time, since resources are being transferred away by the formal sector from renting to commercial employment, the labor intensity and the demand for renting rises in the self-employed sector. Hence rents are bid up and it again becomes profitable for the formal sector to allocate resources to renting. The amount of resources rented out, however, will depend on the degree of technological differentiation that may be created between the two sectors.

The wage rate reaches equilibrium at a lower level and the rents at higher levels than without technological differentiation. Rents, however, equal marginal revenue products of land and capital, which rise in the formal sector because of employing superior technology and in the self-employed sector due to increased labor intensity. Interestingly, dualist patterns appeared in the developing countries only after modern capital inputs became available in limited quantities, particularly in the agricultural sector. Following this introduction, labor-intensive peasant agriculture carried out on leased as well as self-owned land almost always existed side-by-side with the commercially run farms employing wage labor and modern farming equipment and methods. However, worker income, both in wage-employment and peasant farming, remained low [Alavi 1976, Griffin 1979].

The design of change

The analysis in section 3 shows that assumptions made in alternative models of economic growth about wage determination and the prevailing distribution of ownership of resources are linked with the specific historical pattern each model is based on. These patterns, however, represent the various modes of behavior created by a single durable set of decision relationships operating under different legal and technical norms. A model incorporating these relationships would contain policy space for evolutionary change from one pattern to another, while the mutually exclusive theories based on single patterns may only issue interventionist

67

policies for change [Saeed 1987].

The interventionist policies based on any of the mutually exclusive theories may tend to advocate radical changes in the existing, so to speak, dysfunctional system. This is often achieved by designing institutions and laws which increase the direct intervention of the government while limiting voluntary decisions on the part of the public. Such intervention may not only be stressful for the public but may also preoccupy a government with further consolidating its power, which removes it from the goal of delivering welfare [Saeed 1986].

The distribution of ownership is disregarded while its effects are considered benign by the neoclassical theory. However, this theory implicitly assumes that ownership of resources is very widely distributed among households or, in other words, the only type of ownership existing is artisan ownership. The assumption of a perfect financial market further reduces the significance of ownership for the working of the economy. On the other hand, ownership is viewed as a means of exploitation by the Marxist theories, but, their concept of ownership appears to be largely that of absentee ownership.

Both theories are correct in postulating the effects of the specific types of ownership patterns they respectively incorporate although none can propose policy agenda that may change a given pattern without the large scale intervention of the state. However, experimentation with the model I have proposed, a search for the mechanisms that should create an evolutionary change in the ownership and income distribution pattern, leads to the framework discussed now.

According to the analysis in Section 3, the fundamental mechanism which creates the possibility of absentee ownership appears to be renting, while, the financial fragmentation of households and the differences in their saving patterns facilitate its expansion. Technological differences between the formal and self-employed sectors not only make possible the side by side existence of the two modes of production, but also exacerbate the dichotomy between ownership of resources and workership.

Apparently, the policy agenda for changing resource ownership and income distribution patterns should strive to limit renting and should additionally prevent the development of financial fragmentation and technological differentiation between the commercial and self-employed production modes if the objective is to achieve uniform income distribution.

Programs to provide technological, organizational, and financial assistance to the poor have been implemented extensively in the developing countries over the past few decades although they have changed neither income distribution nor wage rate [Griffin and Khan 1978]. This is also borne out by the simulation of the model in Figure 2.7 in which the dualist end equilibrium pattern of Figure 2.6 is used as an initial condition, while the influence of liquidity on investment is made very mild and both sectors are assumed to have similar ability to employ modern capital. These changes translate into building financial institutions to reduce the need to self-finance, and organizing cooperatives and providing appropriate technologies to match scale of production with modern technology in the self-employed sector.

The simulation shows that while there is no perceptible change in the ownership pattern and income shares of capitalists and self-employed, the commercial mode of production is curtailed. This occurs because the increased productivity of the self-employed mode at first pushes up wage rate, thus making renting-out resources more attractive for the formal sector than commercial production. However, the consequent decrease in wage payments and increase in rent payments push down the income share of the workers, which again suppresses the wage they can demand. Thus, wages and rents do not change at all while the commercial mode of production is suppressed.

When growth is also further assisted by an autonomous increase in the productivity of the two sectors, which translates into making available technologically advanced high productivity inputs to the production process (such as high-yielding seed varieties for agriculture, or efficient machinery for industry) ownership only of the formal sector expands. This is shown in the simulation in Figure 2.8, in which wage payments are suppressed while rent payments expand as in the earlier simulation in Figure 2.7. Although, there is a substantial increase in the total income of the economy, wage rate rises only slightly.

Apparently, the programs to assist the poor and to increase productivity through technological development fail to affect income distribution since the mechanism of renting allows the gains of these programs to accrue to the capitalist households. This indicates that influencing the decision to rent-out resources should be the key element of a design for changing wage rate and income distribution.

Renting can be discouraged by imposing a tax on rent income. The results of implementing this additional policy are shown in Figure 2.9. In the face of such a tax, resources which cannot be employed efficiently under the commercial system are offered for sale to the self-employed instead of being leased out to them. Purchase of these resources by the self-employed raises the entitlement of the workers to the income of the economy, which increases the opportunity cost of supplying wage-labor to the commercial sector. This raises wage rate, which makes the commercial mode of production even more uneconomical. Such changes spiral in the long run into a transfer of a substantial amount of resources to the self-employed sector.

Concomitant efforts to decrease the financial fragmentation of households and the technological differentiation between the two modes of production, along with improving productivity, further accelerate these changes.

69

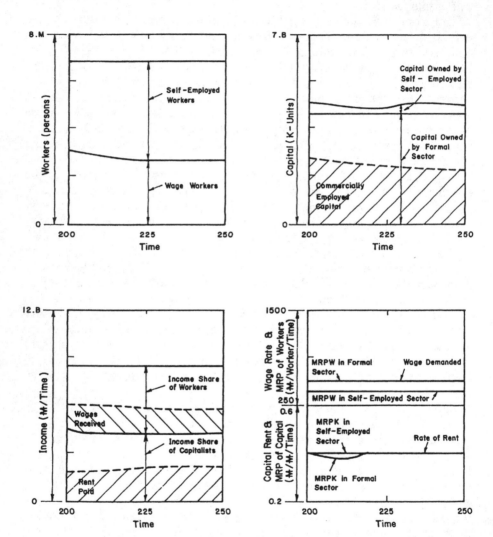

Figure 2.7 **Behavior of the model incorporating introduction of financial, and organizational assistance extended to the self-employed in addition to the assumptions of Figure 2.6**

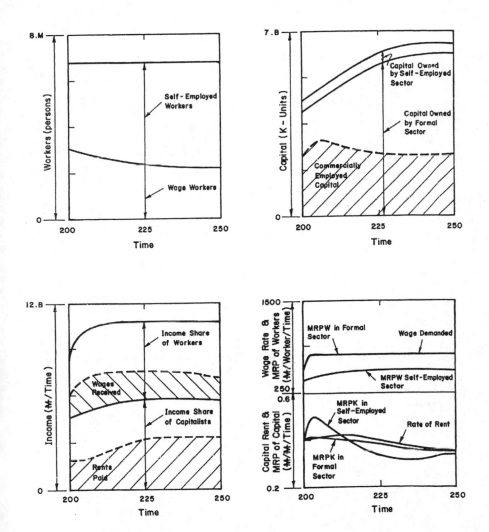

Figure 2.8   Behavior of the model incorporating improved
productivity in addition to the assumptions of
Figure 2.7

71

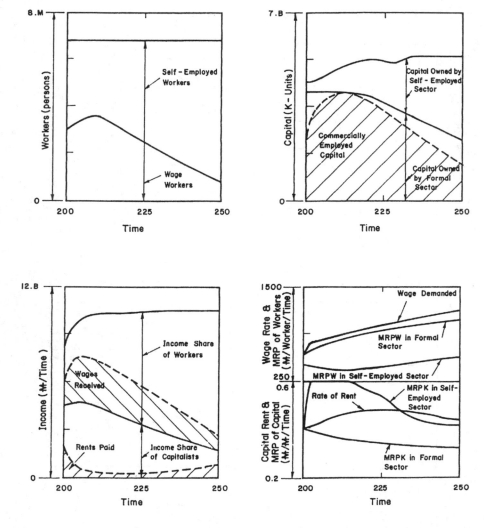

Figure 2.9   **Behavior of the model incorporating a tax on rent income in addition to the assumptions of Figure 2.8**

72

Conclusion

Both neo-classical and Marxist models of economic growth seem to make restricting assumptions about ownership and mechanisms of wage determination, which are linked with specific time and geography related historical evidence. Policies for change based on these models often call for large scale direct government intervention since these models are local to the empirical patterns they are based on and lack entry points for the effecting of evolutionary change in the behavior of the system they represent.

A realistic policy model should be capable of subsuming multiple patterns of wage and income distribution which have existed at various places at various times. Such a model would incorporate a latent information structure which may generate many patterns of behavior. Thus it would offer many points of entry into the system to influence the day to day decisions of its actors to effect evolutionary change from one pattern to another.

This paper has proposed a behavioral model underlying wage and income distribution, in which the opportunity cost of supplying a unit of labor to the formal sector has been used as a basis for negotiating a wage. Neither this opportunity cost nor the ownership pattern are taken as given while the dynamic interaction between the two creates a tendency in the system to generate many wage and income distribution patterns, some of which correspond to those postulated in the neo-classical and Marxist theories of economics. The realization of a specific wage and income distribution pattern depends not on assumptions about initial conditions but on legal and social norms concerning ownership, renting, financing of investment and the state of technology.

Private ownership seems to have two forms, artisan and absentee. Predominance of artisan ownership creates an egalitarian wage and income distribution pattern, but that form of ownership can grow only if the renting of resources can be discouraged. On the other hand, absentee ownership creates a low wage rate and an unequal income distribution, while the growth of this form of ownership is facilitated through the renting mechanism. Potentially, both these forms of ownership can exist in an economic system. The problem, therefore, is not to favor or condemn private ownership *per se* as the alternative theories of economics have often advocated, but to understand the reasons behind the development of a particular ownership pattern and identify human motivational factors that would change an existing pattern into a desirable one.

The analysis in this paper shows that increasing the cost of owning capital resources in absentee form, by imposing a tax on income accrued from such ownership, is vital to promoting artisan ownership and changing an unequal income distribution. Policies aimed at minimizing technological

73

differentiation between the self-employed and commercial modes of production and the presence of a functional financial market further facilitate this change, although, without a rent tax, these policies only suppress the commercial mode of production.

In general, the analysis points towards the need to develop a behavioral approach to the design of change instead of basing it on a controversial body of local theory. This body of theory and its historical contexts can, however, facilitate the development and corroboration of a behavioral model.

References

Alavi, Hamza (1976) 'The Rural Elite and Agricultural Development in Pakistan' in Stevens, et. al. (eds.), *Rural Development in Bangladesh and Pakistan*, Honolulu, Hawaii: Hawaii University Press.

Anderson, K. P. (1968) *Peasant and Capitalist Agriculture in the Developing Country*, unpublished Ph.D. Thesis, Cambridge, MA: MIT.

Bardhan, P. K. (1973) 'A Model of Growth in a Dual Agrarian Economy' in Bhagwati and Eckus (eds.), *Development and Planning: Essays in Honor of Paul Rosenstein-Roden*, New York: George Allen and Unwin Ltd.

Barro, Robert J. (1984) *Macroeconomics*, New York: John Wiley.

Boeke, J. E. (1947) 'Dualist Economics' in *Oriental Economics*, New York: Institute of Pacific Relations.

Elliot, Charles (1975) *Patterns of Poverty in the Third World*, New York: Praeger.

Fie, John C. and Ranis, Gustav (1966) 'Agrarianism, Dualism, and Economic Development' in Adelman and Thorbecke (eds.), *The Theory and Design of Economic Development*, Baltimore, Maryland: Johns Hopkins University Press.

Forrester, Jay W. (1961) 'Industrial Dynamics', Cambridge, MA: MIT Press.

Forrester, Jay W. (1987) 'Nonlinearity in High Order Models of Social Systems', *European Journal of Operational Research*, Vol. 30, No 2.

Forrester, Jay W. and Senge, P. (1980) 'Tests for Building Confidence in System Dynamics Models' in Legasto and Forrester (eds.), *System Dynamics*, Amsterdam: North Holland.

Graham, Alan K. (1977) *Principles of the Relationships Between Structure and Behavior of Dynamic Systems*, Ph.D. Thesis, Cambridge, MA: MIT Press.

Graham, Alan K. (1980) 'Parameter Estimation in System Dynamics Models' in Jorgan Randers (ed.), *Elements of the System Dynamics Method*, Cambridge, MA: MIT Press.

Griffin, Keith (1977) 'Increasing Poverty and Changing Ideas about Development Strategies',*Development and Change*, Vol. 8, pp. 491-508.

Griffin, Keith and Ghose, A. K. (1979) 'Growth and Impoverishment in Rural Areas of Asia'*World Development*, 7(4/5): 361-384.

Griffin, Keith and Khan, A. R. (1978) 'Poverty in the Third World: Ugly Facts and Fancy Models', *World Development*, Vol. 6, No 3.

Heady, Earl O. and Dillon, John L. (1961) *Agricultural Production Functions*, Iowa State University Press.

Hirshliefer, Jack (1976) *Price Theory and Applications*, Englewood Cliffs, NJ, Prentice Hall.

Kaldor, Nicholas (1969) 'Alternative Theories of Distribution' in Stiltz and Ozawa (eds.), *Readings in Modern Theories of Economic Growth*, Cambridge, MA: MIT Press.

Katz, Danial and Kahn, Robert (1978) *The Social Psychology of Organizations 2nd ed*, New York: John Wiley.

Kindelberger, Charles, and Herrick, Bruce (1977) *Economic Development*, Third Edition, New York: McGraw Hill.

Landau, Martin (1972) *Political Theory and Political Science, Studies in the Methodology of a Political Inquiry*, New York: Macmillan.

Lipton, Michael (1976) *Why Poor People Stay Poor*, Cambridge, MA: Harvard University Press.

Marx, Karl (1974) Wage, Labor and Capital (translation of 1891 Edition) Moscow: Progressive Publishers.

McKinnon, Ronald I. (1973) *Money and Capital in Economic Development*, New York: The Brooking Institution.

Mukhia, Harbans (1981) 'Was There Feudalism in Indian History?', *Journal of Peasant Studies*, 8(3): 373-310.

Pack, Spencer J.(1985) *Reconstructing Marxian Economics*, New York: Praeger.

Popper, Karl (1969) *Conjectures and Refutations*, London: Routledge and Kegan Paul.

Popper, Karl (1977) *The Open Society and Its Enemies*, London: Routledge and Kegan Paul.

Pugh III, Alexander L. (1976) *DYNAMO III User's Manual*, Cambridge, MA: MIT Press.

Richardson, George P. (1984) *The Evolution of Feedback Concept in American Social Science*, Ph.D. Thesis, Cambridge, MA: MIT Press.

Richardson, George P. and Pugh III, Alexander L. (1981) *Introduction to System Dynamics Modeling with DYNAMO*, Cambridge, MA: MIT Press.

Roberts, Edward B. (ed.) (1981) *Managerial applications of System Dynamics*, Cambridge, MA: MIT Press.

Roulet, Harry M. (1976) 'The Historical context of Pakistan's Rural Agriculture', in Stevens, et. al. (eds), *Rural Development in Bangladesh and Pakistan*, Honolulu, Hawaii: Hawaii University Press.

Saeed, K. (1980) *Rural Development and Income Distribution, The Case of Pakistan*, Ph.D. Thesis, Cambridge, MA: MIT.

Saeed, K. (1982) 'Economic Development: Phenomenological Models and Irrelevant Controversies', *Dynamica* 8(2).

Saeed, K. (1982a) 'Public Policy and Rural Poverty: A System Dynamics Analysis of A Social Change Effort in Pakistan', *Technological Forecasting and Social Change*, 21: 325-349.

Saeed, K. (1986) 'The Dynamics of Economic Growth and Political Instability in the Developing Countries', *System Dynamics Review*, 2(1): 20-35.

Saeed, K. (1987) 'A Re-Evaluation of the Effort to Alleviate Poverty and Hunger', *Socio-Economic Planning Sciences*, 21(5): 291-304.

Sen, A. K. (1966) 'Peasants and Dualism with or without Surplus Labor', *Journal of Political Economy*, 74(5).

Shaw, Edward (1973) *Financial Deepening in Economic Development*, New York: Oxford University Press.

Simon, Herbert A. (1982) *Models of Bounded Rationality*, Cambridge, MA: MIT Press.

Smith, Adam (1974) *The Wealth of Nations*, New York: Penguin.

Strout, Alan M. (1978) 'Projecting Agricultural Crop Supply from Cross-Country Data', *Working Paper*, Dept. of Urban Studies and Planning, Cambridge, MA: MIT.

Takashi, Yasundo et. al. (1970) *Control and Dynamic Systems*, MA: Addison-Wesley.

White, L. J. (1974) *Industrial Concentration and Economic Power in Pakistan*, Princeton, NJ: Princeton University Press.

Appendix
Model description

Wage rate WR is assumed to adjust over period WRAT towards indicated wage rate IWR.

$$d/dt[WR] \quad = \quad (IWR-WR)/WRAT \tag{1}$$

IWR depends on the wage-bargaining position of the workers, which is determined by their opportunity cost of accepting wage-employment. It is assumed that the opportunity cost of transferring a self-employed worker to wage-work is zero when wage offered is equal to the current consumption expenditure per worker averaged over the whole workforce.

$$IWR \quad = \quad [(R_s*(1-SP_s)+(AS_s/LAS))/TW] \tag{2}$$

where R_s, SP_s and AS_s are, respectively, income share, saving propensity and accumulated unspent savings of the self-employed sector. LAS and TW are, respectively, life of accumulated unspent savings and total workforce. Subscripts s and f designate, respectively, self-employed and formal sectors.

Ownership of land and capital as well as contribution to labor are the bases for claim to income while absentee ownership is possible through leasing arrangements. Thus, R_s is computed by adding together the value of output produced by the self-employed sector VQ_s and the wage payments received by the wage-workers W_f, and subtracting from the sum the rent payments made to the absentee owners. R_f is given by adding together the value of output produced by the formal sector VQ_f and the rent payments it receives from the self-employed sector, and subtracting from the sum the wage-payments it makes.

$$R_s \quad = \quad VQ_s+WR*W_f-LR*RL-KR*RK \tag{3}$$
$$R_f \quad = \quad VQ_f-WR*W_f+LR*RL+KR*RK \tag{4}$$

where LR, RL, KR, and RK, are, respectively, land rent, rented land, capital rent, and rented capital.

KR and LR depend, respectively, on the long-term averages of the marginal revenue products of capital and land (AMRPK and AMRPL) in the economy, and the demand for renting capital and land (RKD and RLD) as compared with the supply of rentable assets (RK and RL). The demand for renting, in turn, depends on the lack of ownership of adequate resources for productively employing the workers in the self-employed sector.

77

$$KR \quad = \quad AMRPK*f_1[RKD/RK]; \ f'_1 > 0 \tag{5}$$
$$RKD \quad = \quad DKE_s\text{-}KO_s \tag{6}$$

where DKE_s is desired capital to be employed in the self-employed sector and KO_s is capital owned by it. Land rent LR and demand for renting land RLD are determined similarly.

The saving propensity of all households in not uniform. Since capitalist households associated with the formal sector receive incomes which are much above subsistence, their saving propensity is stable. On the other hand, the saving propensity of the worker households depends on their need to save for supporting investment for self-employment and on how their absolute level of income compares with their inflexible consumption. Thus, SP_s in the model is determined by the utility of investment in the self-employed sector arising from a comparison of worker productivity in the sector with the wage rate in the formal sector, and the rent burden of this sector compared with the factor contribution to its income from land and capital.

$$SP_s \quad = \quad \mu*f_2[MRPW_s/WR]*f_3[(LR*RL+KR*RK)/$$
$$(VQ_s\text{-}MRPW_s*W_s)] \tag{7}$$
$$SP_f \quad = \quad \mu \tag{8}$$

where $f'_2 > 0$, $f'_3 < 0$, μ is a constant, and MRPW is marginal revenue product of workers.

AS represent the balance of unspent savings, which determine the availability of liquid cash resources for purchase of assets. AS are consumed over their life LAS whether or not any investment expenditure occurs.

$$d/dt[AS_i] \quad = \quad R_i*SP_i\text{-}AS_i/LAS\text{-}LA_i*PL\text{-}\sum_j KA_i{}^j*GPL;$$
$$i = s,f; \ j=m,t \tag{9}$$

where LA, PL, KA, and GPL are, respectively, land acquisitions, price of land, capital acquisitions, and general price level. Subscript i refers to any of the two sectors, self-employed (s) and formal (f) and superscript j to the type of capital, modern (m) or traditional (t). TW is assumed to be fixed, although, relaxing this assumption does not alter the conclusions of this paper [Saeed 1982a].

W_f is assumed to adjust towards indicated workers IW_f given by desired workers DW_f and total workforce TW. All workers who are not wage-employed must be accommodated in self-employment. Thus W_S represents the remaining workers in the economy.

$$d/dt[W_f] \quad = \quad (IW_f\text{-}W_f)/WAT \tag{10}$$
$$IW_f \quad = \quad TW*f_4(DW_f/TW) \tag{11}$$
$$W_S \quad = \quad TW\text{-}W_f \tag{12}$$

where $1 \geq f_4 \geq 0$, and $f'_4 > 0$. WAT is worker adjustment time.

The desired workers in each sector DW_i is determined by equating wage rate with the marginal revenue product of workers. A modified cobb-douglas type production function is used.

$$DW_i \quad = \quad E_i{}^W*VQ_i/WR \tag{13}$$

where $E_i{}^W$ is the elasticity of production of workers in a sector.

Land and capital owned by the formal sector (LO_f and KO_f) are allocated to commercial production (KE_f and LE_f) and renting (RK and RL) activities depending on the desired levels of these factors in each activity. Thus,

$$RK \quad = \quad (DRK/(DRK+DKE_f))*KO_f \tag{14}$$
$$RL \quad = \quad (DRL/(DRL+DLE_f))*LO_f \tag{15}$$
$$Ke_f \quad = \quad KO_f\text{-}RK \tag{16}$$
$$LE_f \quad = \quad LO_f\text{-}RL \tag{17}$$

Capital and land employed by the self-employed sector consist of these production factors owned by them and those rented from the formal sector.

$$KE_S \quad = \quad KO_S+RK \tag{18}$$
$$LE_S \quad = \quad LO_S+RL \tag{19}$$

Desired capital and land to be employed in any sector (DKE_i and DLE_i) are determined on the basis of economic criteria.

$$d/dt(DKE_i)/KE_i = \quad f_6[\ MRPK_i/MFCK] \tag{20}$$
$$d/dt(DLE_i)/LE_i = \quad f_5[\ MRPL_i/MFCL] \tag{21}$$

where f'_5 and $f'_6 > 0$. $MRPL_i$ and $MRPK_i$ are respectively marginal revenue products of land and capital in a sector, and MFCL AND MFCK are respectively marginal factor costs of land and capital.

$$MRPL_i \quad = \quad (E_i{}^l * VQ_i/LE_i) \tag{22}$$

$$MRPK_i \quad = \quad (E_i{}^k * VQ_i/KE_i) \tag{23}$$

$$MFCL \quad = \quad PL * IR \tag{24}$$

$$MFCK \quad = \quad IR + (1/LK) * GPL \tag{25}$$

where $E_i{}^l$ and $E_i{}^k$ are, respectively, elasticities of production of land and capital in a sector. PL is price of land, IR is exogenously defined interest rate, LK is life of capital and GPL is general price level.

Changes in the quantities of capital and land desired to be rented out (DRK and DRL) depend on their respective rents KR and LR compared with their marginal factor costs MFCK and MFCL.

$$d/dt[DRK]/RK \quad = \quad f_7[KR/MFCK]; \; f'_7 > 0 \tag{26}$$

$$d/dt[DRL]/RL \quad = \quad f_8[LR/MFCL]; \; f'_8 > 0 \tag{27}$$

The value of output produced by each sector is given by the product of the quantity it produces Q_i and the general price level GPL.

$$VQ_i \quad = \quad Q_i * GPL \tag{28}$$

$$Q_i \quad = \quad A_i * K_i{}^{E_i{}^k} * L_i{}^{E_i{}^l} * W_i{}^{E_i{}^w} \tag{29}$$

where K_i, L_i, and W_i represent capital, land and workers employed by a sector. A_i represent technology constants, which increase with the use of modern capital.

$$A_i \quad = \quad \mathring{A} * f_9[K_i{}^m/(K_i{}^t + K_i{}^m)] \tag{30}$$

where $f'_9 > 0$ and $\mathring{A}$ is a scaling factor based on initial conditions of inputs and output of the production process.

Ownership is legally protected and the financial market is fragmented by households. Thus, purchase of any productive assets must be self-financed by each sector through cash payments. Land ownership LO_i of each sector changes through acquisitions LA_i from each other. Each sector bids for the available land on the basis of economic criteria, its current holdings, and the sector's liquidity.

$$LA_i \quad = \quad d/dt[LO_i] \tag{31}$$

$$LO_i = (DLO_i/ \Sigma_i DLO_i)*TL \qquad (32)$$

where DLO_i is desired land ownership in a sector and TL is total land which is fixed,

$$DLO_i = LO_i*f_6[MRPL_i/MFCL]*f_{11}[CA_i] \qquad (33)$$

where $f'_{11}[CA_i]$ is > 0, and CA_i is cash adequacy of a sector.

Cash adequacy of a sector CA_i is given by the ratio of its accumulated unspent savings to the desired savings. The latter is computed by multiplying cash needed to finance investment and the traditional rate of consumption of savings in the sector by cash coverage CC.

$$CA_i = AS_i/_i/LAS)+(LA_i*PL)+(\Sigma_j KA_i^j*GPL))*CC \qquad (34)$$

Capital ownership in a sector $KO_i= KO_i^t + KO_i^m$ changes through acquisitions KA_i^j and decay. Although there is a preference for modern capital, its acquisition KA_i^m depends on the ability to accommodate the technology represented by it. Inventory availability of each type of capital KIA^j also limits its purchases.

$$d/dt[KO_i] = \Sigma_j KA_i^j - KO_i/LK \qquad (35)$$
$$KA_i^j = DKA_i^j*KIA^j \qquad (36)$$
$$DKA_i^m = (KO_i/LK)*f_5[MRPK_i/MFCK]*f_{11}[CA_i]*TCF_i \qquad (37)$$
$$DKA_i^t = (KO_i/LK)*f_5[MRPK_i/MFCK]*f_{11}[CA_i]* \\ (1- TCF_i) \qquad (38)$$

where DKA_i are desired capital acquisitions, $f'_{11} \geq 0$, and LK is life of capital. TCF_i represent exogenously defined technological capability. $0 < TCF_i < 1$.

$$KIA^j = f_{12}[KI^j/(\Sigma_i DKA_i^j)*KIC] \qquad (39)$$

where $0 \leq f_{12} \leq 1$, $f'_{12} > 0$, and KIC is capital inventory coverage

$$d/dt[KI^j] = KQ^j - \Sigma_i KA_i^j \qquad (40)$$

where KQ$_j$ represent supply of capital. KQ^m is imported, while KQ^t is created within the economy by allocating a part of the capacity to its production.

$$KQ^t \qquad = \qquad \Sigma Q_i*(\Sigma_i DKA_i^t/TD) \tag{41}$$

The price of land PL is assumed to adjust towards indicated price of land IPL which is given by the economy-wide average of the marginal revenue product of land AMRPL, interest rate IR and the desired land ownership in each sector DLO$_i$.

$$d/dt[PL] \qquad = \qquad (IPL-PL)/LPAT \tag{42}$$
$$IPL \qquad = \qquad (AMRPL/IR)*f_{13}[\Sigma_i DLO_i/TL]; \; f'_{13} > 0 \tag{43}$$

General price level GPL is determined by supply and demand considerations.

$$d/dt[GPL] \qquad = \qquad GPLN*f_{14}[TD/\Sigma_i Q_i] \tag{44}$$

where $f'_{14} > 0$. GPLN is normal value of GPL and TD is total demand for goods and services to be produced within the economy. TD is given by adding up non-food consumption C$_i$, traditional capital acquisition KA$_i^t$ and production of traditional capital for inventory, food demand FD and government spending G which is equal to taxes, if any, collected.

$$TD \qquad = \qquad \Sigma C_i + \Sigma_i DKA_i^t +$$
$$((KIC*\Sigma_i DKA_i^t - KI_j)/IAT) + FD + G \tag{45}$$
$$d/dt(C_i) \qquad = \qquad [(((R_i*(1-SP_i)+AS_i/LAS)/GPL)*$$
$$FNFC_i)-C_i]/CAT \tag{46}$$

where IAT is inventory adjustment time, FNFC$_i$ fraction non-food consumption, and CAT is consumption adjustment time. Food demand FD is given by multiplying population P with normal per capita food demand NFPCD and a function f_{15} representing a weak influence of price.

$$FD \qquad = \qquad P*NFPCD*f_{15}[GPL/GPLN]; \; f'_{15} < 0 \tag{47}$$

where P bears a fixed proportion with total workforce TW.

The elasticity of production of land $E_i{}^l$ is assumed to be constant as is suggested by empirical evidence concerning agricultural economies [Strout 1978, Heady and Dillon 1961]. Elasticity of production of capital $E_i{}^k$ depends on the technology of production which is determined by the proportions of traditional and modern capital employed. Since constant returns to scale are assumed, $E_i{}^w$ is given by equation 47.

$$E_i{}^k \quad = \quad f_{16}[K_i{}^m/(K_i{}^l+K_i{}^m)]; \; f'_{16} > 0 \qquad (48)$$

$$E_i{}^w \quad = \quad 1 - E_i{}^k - E_i{}^l \qquad (49)$$

Behavioral relationships

Sixteen behavioral relationships $[f_1 .... f_{16}]$ have been incorporated into the model. The slope characteristics of these relationships have already been described in above equations. The graphical forms of the functions representing these relationships are shown in Figures A-1 and A-2 placed below. General considerations for specifying such relationships are discussed in Forrester and Senge (1980) Graham (1980) and Richardson and Pugh (1981).

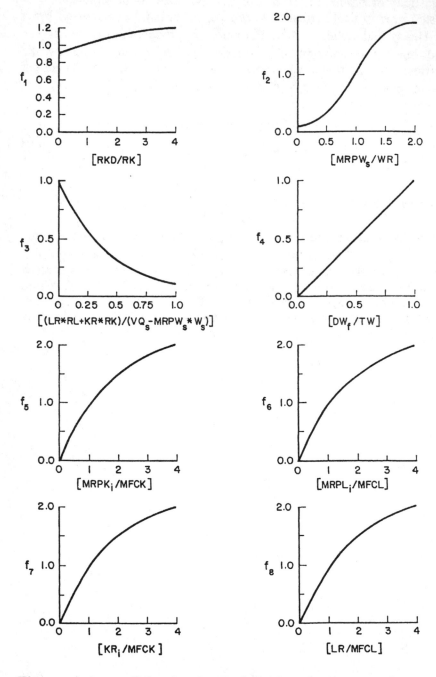

Figure A-1   Behavioral relationships f_1 through f_8

84

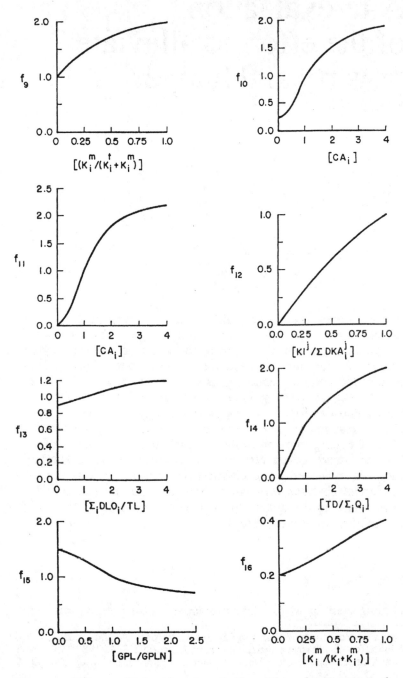

Figure A-2   **Behavioral relationships f_9 through f_{16}**

85

3 A re-evaluation of the effort to alleviate poverty and hunger[*]
Khalid Saeed

Abstract

This paper re-examines the broad public policies implemented in the developing countries to alleviate poverty and hunger. The analysis is carried out through simulation experiments using a generic system dynamics model of an agrarian economy which determines income distribution and food adequacy endogenously but treats government policy as exogenous. It is suggested that policies such as agricultural development, financial and technical assistance for the poor and population control, that directly address the symptoms of the problems of poverty and hunger, may be defeated in the long run since socio-technical arrangements of the system favor persistence of poverty and vulnerability to food shortage. These policies will, however, be successful if concomitant efforts are also made to discourage absentee ownership through fiscal measures and to build up a food slack in the system through adopting staples with a high cereal/edible calories conversion ratios.

Introduction

Poverty and hunger are, perhaps, currently not the most pressing problems

[*] Reprinted from *Socio-Economic Planning Sciences*, 21(5), Khalid Saeed, A re-evaluation of the effort to alleviate poverty and hunger, pp. 291-304, 1987, with kind permission from Elsevier Science Ltd., The Boulevard, Langford Lane, Kidlington OX5 1GB, UK.

of the developing countries. There is an almost worldwide glut of food and massive remittances from expatriate workers seem to have brought affluence to the previously poor households in many developing countries. These conditions, however, might not last since the still growing world population might off-set any surplus in food production while drying up of jobs for the expatriates might take away the temporary affluence the poor are experiencing.

There have, albeit, been instances of temporary relief from poverty and hunger in the past and, to some extent, the credit for this goes to the continued agricultural development effort and programs to help the poor undertaken over the past several decades [FAO 1979, Bhattacharjee 1976]. The problem, perhaps, is their tendency to reappear, not their control on temporary basis [Griffin 1979, Haq 1976, Galbraith 1979].

This study re-examines the broad policies implemented for alleviating poverty and hunger and attempts to explain their inefficacy in terms of the behavioral mechanisms which determine internal trends of the system in which they are implemented. Simulation experiments with a generic system dynamics model of an agricultural economy whose micro-structure incorporates basic mechanisms of production, income disbursement and demographic behavior are used as basis for analysis. The broad mathematical relationships incorporated into this model are described in the Appendix. A non-technical description of the model is given in section 4 of this paper. Further technical details and a machine readable listing are available from the author on request.

The study suggests that the tendency of the system to move towards a goal of mass poverty arises from the ease with which absentee ownership can flourish since this limits the ability of the working households to own productive resources, which reduces the potential of their income from self-employment. Since this potential represents their opportunity cost of accepting wage-employment, it also affects the wage rate and the share of income disbursed as wages. The tendency of the system to move towards a goal of food vulnerability arises from the presence of economical food consumption patterns which increase the facility for the population to grow whenever food availability rises. These mechanisms tend to defeat any direct intervention to facilitate the poor, increase food production, and limit population.

Pattern of poverty and hunger

The countries which have encountered the problems of hunger and mass poverty at one time or another have several common characteristics. These include high birth rates, low life expectancy, wide disparity of income between the rich and the poor, and a concentration of ownership of

87

resources in the hands of a few [Lipton 1977, Griffin 1979]. Also common are chronic food deficits, which may temporarily disappear when there is a good harvest, but which have shown a rising trend despite considerable increases in food production and imports [Siamwalla 1980].

The food consumption habits of the populations of these countries can be described as economical. The staples are cereals rather than animal proteins and the caloric intake needed can be obtained very efficiently from farm production [Simontov 1976]. Most of these countries have a labor surplus with a large under-employed informal sector and a low real wage rate which has persisted in spite of sizable increases in the gross national product [Griffin 1978a].

The pattern described above has been quite resilient, in the long run, to most policy measures adopted in the past, although, short periods of affluence and food adequacy have been experienced by some countries. These measures have included introduction of modern agricultural technology and inputs, use of improved seed varieties, population control programs, organization of cooperatives and extension service for the small farmers, and setting up financial institutions for reducing reliance on household savings for meeting investment needs [Griffin 1978b].

Past intervention and its basis

Although the problems of the developing countries initially received only a cursory treatment from economics, the subject of economic development currently seems to be quite firmly grounded in the economic discipline [Arndt 1973]. Unfortunately, economics has contributed to the discipline little more than a collection of normative theories which appears under the label of development economics, but which bears little relevance to the problems it addresses [Saeed 1982a]. These theories have, nonetheless, been the main basis for the design of economic development policy. This basis has been further supplemented by the humanitarian concerns and moralization, which may be quite well intentioned, although, these have an emotional rather than a logical perspective. All in all, the economic development effort has addressed little more than the symptoms of poverty and hunger and the policies it has issued often require large scale government intervention which has, however, made little impression on the problem itself.

Professor Lewis suggests that attempts to develop theories that exclusively address the problems of developing countries should enable better policy design [Lewis 1984]. Such attempts might, however, only generate models which explain social patterns occurring under very specific conditions but which fail to identify mechanisms of change from one pattern to another. This is because there would be a theory exclusive to

88

each pattern [Katz 1978]. The actual modeling practice in economics has been even more limited as it has largely incorporated mathematical interpretations of the neoclassical economic theory with minor modifications [Leontief 1977]. This has resulted in proliferation of models which have mostly issued stereotype solutions to the problems of poverty and hunger.

The stereotype solutions to poverty often call for increasing economic growth rate, with or without extending direct aid to the poor, and redistributing income. The solutions to hunger call for increasing food production and food aid from abroad, and controlling population. These solutions require enormous amounts of effort by the governments who may be quite genuinely concerned with improving the well being of the public, but are often unable to maintain this commitment due to other political pressures [Saeed 1983a]. Weary of their burden, most developing countries welcome food aid as a way to immediately overcome the problem of hunger, so they may concentrate their effort on other problems of development. Past experience shows, however, that food aid reduces self-reliance and encourages continued dependence on aid while it is often offered on the basis of political rather than need-related criteria [Maxwell 1983].

While the problems of poverty and food shortage and the pros and cons of food aid remain a subject of much debate, there appears to be a general consensus that the problem of food supply can only be solved by raising production and reorganizing distribution within the countries facing the problem. In response to such views, many developing countries have embarked upon programs of agricultural and infrastructure development, which have considerably raised their food production while also improving their distribution facilities [Von Braun 1983, Paarlberg 1975]. However, increases in food supply have often not kept pace with the growth in population. As a result food availability has remained low. Large scale population planning programs have also been undertaken in most poor countries, although, their low effectiveness has raised many doubts about their efficacy.

The design of food policies and the debates about their efficacy has, albeit, disregarded any possible relationship which may exist between population growth rate and food adequacy, although, there is much empirical and anthropological evidence to suggest this. There is also evidence of higher living standards suppressing population growth rates since they permit greater social mobility which makes small family size more desirable [Meadows 1974]. This relationship has been recognized to some extent in the programs which are specifically aimed at improving the lot of the poor. Many such programs have been implemented in the developing countries, although, these have also been quite ineffective in the long run [Morawetz 1977].

A system dynamics model of the social organization underlying poverty and hunger

The developing country economies which have experienced the problems of poverty and hunger are predominantly rural while they also appear to have a dualist structure consisting of a worker hiring or land-leasing capitalist sector and a self-employed peasant sector. It has also been observed that all workers, whether self-employed in tilling their own or rented land or employed as wage-workers, are members of a homogeneous socio-economic group with a common interest, which is to maximize consumption. This group also appears to be the sole supplier of labor in the economy if the small number of working capitalists is neglected. On the other hand, the capitalist sector strives to maximize profit while it is also the sole wage-employer in the economy [Bardhan 1973].

This dualist structure is incorporated into a system dynamics model which is capable of generating many patterns of behavior [Saeed 1980]. The mathematical relationships of this model are described in the Appendix while its main accumulations and flows are shown in Figures 3.1 and 3.2.

Figure 3.1 shows how production factors are allocated between the two sectors of the economy while Figure 3.2 shows how the income of the economy is distributed. The changes in the quantities of the production factors owned or employed by each sector are governed by the decisions of the producers and the consumers of output and by the suppliers of the production factors acting rationally according to their respective motivations within the roles defined for them by the system. The value of production is shared by the households on the basis of the quantity of the production factors they contribute and the factor prices they can bargain for.

The capacity allocated to production of food cereals depends on the demand for food generated by the population less food imports or food aid. Prices of output and production factors are endogenously determined and in turn affect both production and consumption decisions, although, food consumption per capita is relatively inelastic. Food adequacy is determined by the supply of food calories relative to their demand, and in turn, influences birth and death rates. Income share of the workers, less any investment needed to maintain self-employment divided by the total workforce, determines average consumption per worker, which is the basis for negotiating wage rates. Wage rate affects people's standard of living. An improvement in the standard of living reduces both birth and death rates.

The model has been developed and tested in several stages, starting with incorporating in it the substantive assumptions representing the market forces suggested by the neoclassical economic theory and gradually relaxing those assumptions to make the model structure consistent with the

90

actual working of the agricultural economies of the developing countries. The size of each sector is not specified and is determined endogenously by the model depending on the assumptions about the socio-technical environment in which the system operates.

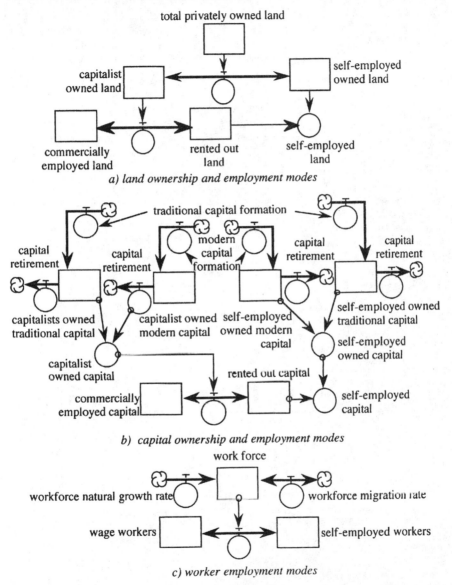

a) land ownership and employment modes

b) capital ownership and employment modes

c) worker employment modes

Figure 3.1   Allocation of production factors in an agrarian economy

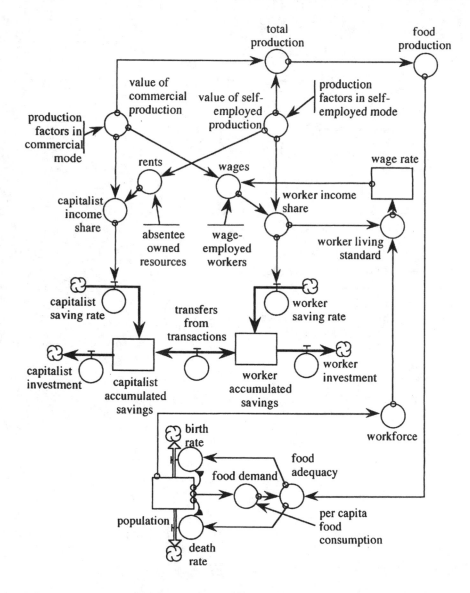

Figure 3.2 **Disbursement of income and changes in population**

The wage and income patterns generated by the model and their relevance to the history of the developing countries is discussed in detail in Saeed (1983b). The following modifications of the neoclassical model are essential to make its decision structure correspond to the actual conditions in the developing countries.

1. Formal ownership is protected by law but land and capital assets can be freely bought, sold and rented by their owners. Each buying and selling transaction between the two sectors must be accompanied by a corresponding transfer of the cash value of the assets. The financial markets are segmented by sectors.
2. Wage rate depends *not* on the marginal productivity of labor as is assumed in many macro-economic models but on economic bargaining position of workers, which is determined by their opportunity cost of supplying an additional unit of labor to the capitalist sector.
3. The saving propensity of all households in not uniform. Since capitalist households receive incomes which are much above subsistence, their saving propensity is stable. On the other hand, the saving propensity of the worker households depends on their need to save for supporting investment for self-employment and on how their absolute level of income compares with their inflexible consumption.

These modifications impart to the model an internal tendency towards concentration of ownership of resources in an absentee ownership mode as shown in the simulation of Figure 3.3 which also assumes a fixed economy. Such a tendency arises out of a goal of the system to employ resources in the most efficient way while the ownership of those resources can only be in the hands of the households which have the best financial ability.

If land can potentially be farmed by owner-cultivators, share-croppers and wage-workers, the presence of wage-employment opportunities offering wages equal to income in self-employment at the start of the simulation (which is characterized by a general market equilibrium) depresses the saving rate of the self employed. In the long run, this also decreases their ability to own land, which decreases their share of income and hence the wage they can demand.

A decrease in ownership of resources by the self-employed, in the face of a decrease in wage-employment opportunities which is caused by high labor costs, also increases demand for renting, which bids up rents. This not only makes it profitable for the capitalist sector to invest in resources for renting them out, it also gives additional financial edge to this sector over the peasant sector whose savings continue to decline as its rent burden rises. Thus, even when commercial farming is eliminated due to an initially high cost of wage-labor, resource ownership by the capitalist sector expands. In the resulting end equilibrium, major share of the resources is owned by an absentee capitalist sector and only a minor share by the self-

93

employed. The results of this simulation are borne out by the pervasive occurrence of resource concentration experienced in most developing countries.

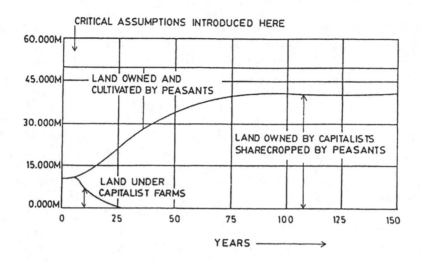

Figure 3.3   **Simulation showing internal tendency of the model towards concentration of resources when critical assumptions are introduced**

When the assumption of a fixed economy is relaxed and birth rate and life expectancy are assumed to be influenced by food adequacy and income level, population change in this system is not significant, although, it is characterized by a high birth rate and a low life expectancy. This is shown in the simulation of Figure 3.4 in which population growth assumptions were introduced after the system settled down with its characteristic resource concentration. The simulation also shows that wage rate and food per capita stay low while the price index rises since any price increase also pushes up factor costs which, in the face of fixed land, perpetuate further price rise.

The stagnant scenario created in the simulation of Figure 3.4 might seem largely hypothetical as most poor countries have also experienced high population growth rates along with the other symptoms shown in the simulation. It, however, quite adequately describes stagnant economies of the poor countries before they engaged in serious development effort. Besides industrialization, this effort has incorporated an increase in the use of modern equipment and inputs for the agricultural sector, which allowed cereal production to rise substantially. This was also accompanied by

94

corresponding increases in population.

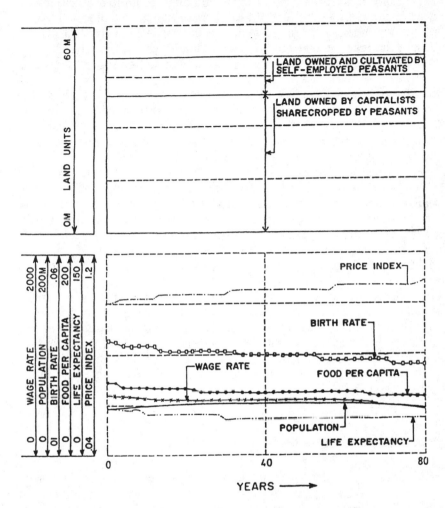

Figure 3.4   Behavior of the model representing the stagnant economies of the developing countries before development effort began

95

Figure 3.5 shows a simulation in which modern capital equipment and inputs are made available to the farmers, although in limited quantities, in an effort to promote agriculture. Most of these inputs are allocated by the model to commercial farming whose scale can be easily adjusted to conform to the level required by modern technology. Thus, a technological differentiation is created between commercial and self-employed modes of farming.

The behavior shown in Figure 3.5 bears a close resemblance to the behavior of the economies of most poor countries where such policies were implemented. The increases in cereal food production are offset by concomitant increases in population. Thus, cereal food per capita (which is a proxy for food adequacy) stays low.

Wage rate also continues to stagnate since it depends on the economic bargaining position of the workers, *not* on labor productivity. The economic bargaining position of the workers stays low since the ownership pattern does not change even though a considerable part of the share-cropped land is converted into commercial farms. Since ownership of resources is a basis for determining income shares, the benefits of increases in production are largely obtained by the capitalist sector, which continues to own a large part of the resources.

The cultivation pattern changes as modern equipment make commercially-run farms profitable. However, since this also creates a shortage of land which is available for rent, renting out land again becomes profitable after some of the share-cropped land has been converted to commercial farms. This results in the side by side existence of share-cropped and commercial farms, which seems to have surprised many observers [Alavi 1976].

Why well-intentioned policies did not work?

The public policies implemented in the developing countries to date have incorporated several measures which were explicitly aimed at alleviating poverty and hunger. Although a very large variety of policies have been proposed, most of these can be placed in three broad categories on the basis of their intent. These are: policies aimed at increasing food production which is, sometimes, also supplemented by food aid and imports; policies aimed at limiting population; and policies which strive to help the poor target groups.

The outcome of the first set of policies is evident in the simulation of Figure 3.5. If food supply were also supplemented by food aid, indigenous food production would decrease, which would allow transfer of the scarce resources to the capital and consumption goods producing sectors, although the increased availability of food would lead to population levels for which indigenous food resources are inadequate. Thus, the dependence on food aid would continue.

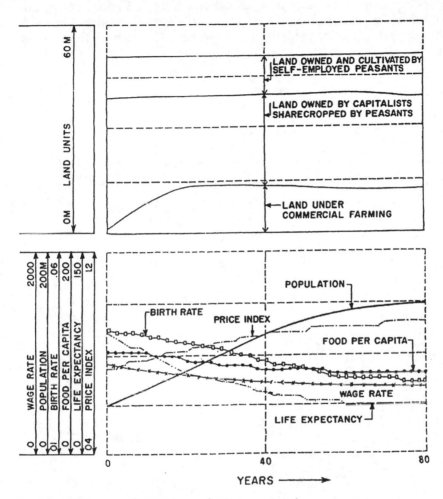

Figure 3.5   Behavior of the model incorporating introduction of labor efficient modern technologies

Birth control programs introduced simultaneously with the policies that increase production are simulated in Figure 3.6. In the short run, this set of policies increases availability of food calories since it limits demand for food. In the long run, however, increased availability of food calories aids birth rate and increases life expectancy, which off-sets the effect of the birth control effort.

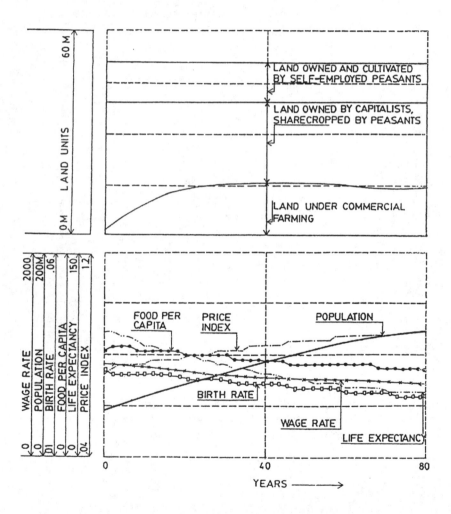

Figure 3.6   **Behavior of the model incorporating introduction of modern technologies and population control**

The resulting increases in population bring down food availability to the old level. Thus, food availability and life expectancy patterns towards the end of the simulation do not differ substantially from those in Figure 3.5. Also since no changes occur in the ownership pattern, wage rate continues to be depressed.

The efforts to assist poor target groups often translate into eliminating the technological and financial differences between the capitalist and the self-employed sectors. These efforts incorporate programs that attempt to organize small farms into cooperatives, introduce small scale technology, deliver extension services, and provide institutionalized financial assistance to the small farmer. It should, however, be borne in mind that the technological differences between the capitalist and the self-employed sectors were initially created when agricultural modernization policies were introduced as a part of the development effort.

It was observed in the simulation of Figure 3.5 that these policies led to a change only in the cropping pattern, without changing appreciably the ownership or the wage rate. Because financial institutions invariably require collateral, while they also need to minimize the risk of a default in the payment of a loan, financial ability cannot be completely decoupled from ownership and household savings. Thus, financial policies may also not radically change ownership patterns.

Figure 3.7 shows a simulation incorporating the technological, organizational and financial policies discussed above in addition to the policies of Figure 3.6. As expected, the only significant change from Figure 3.5 appears in restoration of the earlier cultivation pattern with predominance of share-cropping practice while the rest of the behavior remains unchanged.

The resilience of the system to the well-intentioned policies discussed above is indeed frustrating. The inefficacy of these policies has generated arguments for and against the theories and the data used in policy design. The debate resulting from this has probably been quite interesting, although not very useful from the standpoint of helping policy design.

The advantage of having a model, whose behavior must be interpreted as a logical deduction of its micro-structure, is that the resilience of a policy must be explained in terms of the anatomy of the day-to-day actions in the system instead of being attributed to personal and incidental factors. The source of resistance in the model to well-intentioned policies appears to be its critical assumptions about ownership and wage determination, and the relationship between population growth, food adequacy, and living standards.

When decision making is viewed without reference to the macro-behavior created by it, a debate may arise about the appropriateness of a decision criterion. However, when both micro-structure and macro-behavior are observed, this debate can be readily resolved by selecting a basis for which evidence exists both at micro- and macro- levels.

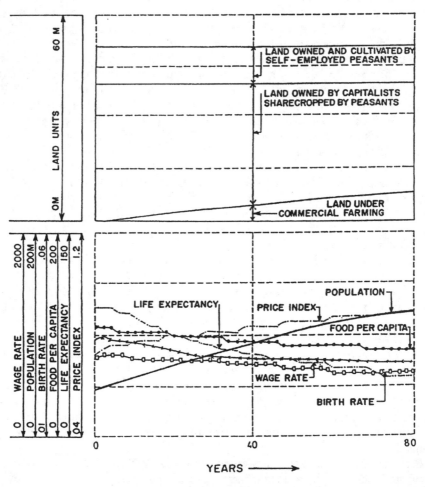

Figure 3.7   Behavior of the model incorporating modern technologies, population control, and programs to help the poor

Thus, the correspondence between the policy resilience of the model is a source of confidence in its structure which was developed on the basis of micro-level evidence. It also calls for redefining the role of public policy, from that of direct intervention to counter macro-behavior, to that of finding appropriate entry points for influencing the day to day decisions of the system.

Identifying entry points into the policy resistant system

Since the internal tendency of a system arises from the powerful feedbacks which dominate the behavior of its actors, the efficacy of a policy depends on how effectively it changes the relative strengths of those feedbacks. Figure 3.8 shows the important feedbacks in the model of this paper. Positive feedbacks, which are self-reinforcing and negative feedbacks, which are self-correcting, are shown separately.

It will be noticed that price is not the only market-clearing mechanism in the system which strives to balance supply and demand. Population changes which are driven by adequacy of food calories and living standards, also strive to achieve this balance.

The internal forces attempting a balance are, thus, embodied in four negative feedback loops, only two of which are recognized in the models treating population exogenously. The remaining two negative feedback loops make it difficult for the system to move away from an internal goal of equilibrating at low levels of wages and food adequacy. The positive feedback loops, which are coupled with these negative feedback loops only speed up the process of adjustment.

Unless the internal goals of the system are changed, any direct effort to increase food supply, change population, or help the poor will be resisted by the forces embodied in the feedback loops of Figure 3.8, although, these policies may create temporary gains. The internal goals of the system may be influenced only by changing income shares of the workers and the ambient cereal food consumption per capita, which emerge as promising entry points for directing efforts to counter poverty and hunger.

Policies for raising incomes of the poor call for a change in the ownership pattern that should allow workers to obtain a larger share of the total income of the economy, which also enhances their wage bargaining position. This, however, may not be achieved through radical means since current ownership patterns are also the result of system's internal tendency. On the other hand, if the cost of being an absentee owner of the resources is increased through fiscal measures such as a heavy tax on rent income, resources which cannot be employed efficiently under the commercial system are offered for sale to the self-employed sector. Purchase of these resources by the self employed raises the entitlement of the worker households to the income of the economy, which increases their opportunity cost of supplying wage labor to the capitalist sector. This raises wage rate, which makes commercial farming even more uneconomical.

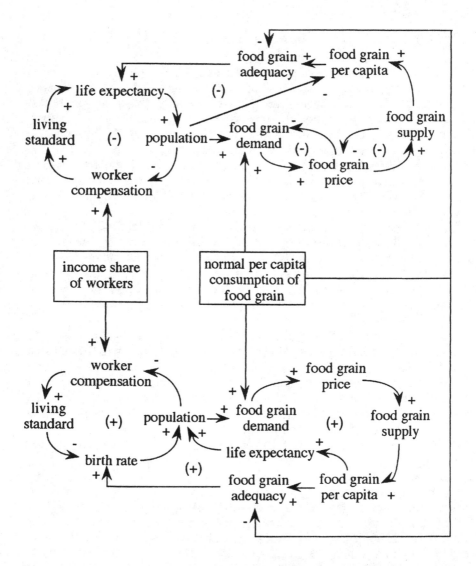

Figure 3.8   **Important feedbacks affecting population, food production, and worker compensation**

Such changes spiral in the long run into transfer of a substantial amount of resources to the self-employed sector. Provision of technological, organizational, and financial assistance to small farmers accelerates this process, although without the fiscal measures which increase the cost of being an absentee owner, such assistance only results in a change in the cultivation pattern. Figure 3.9 shows a simulation of the policy package incorporating taxation of rent income in addition to the policies of Figure 3.7. The scenario generated by the simulation incorporates an increase in the ownership of the resources by the self-employed sector as well as an increase in wage rate.

This policy package does not limit the rise in population, because, even though a higher standard of living has a limiting influence on birth rate, the temporary abundance of cereal food calories offsets this influence. Furthermore, life expectancy rises on account of a better living standard. The quality of life improves because of these changes. There is, however, little change in the trend of cereal food available per capita since food consumption pattern continues to be economical and extra food production only helps to generate additional population. Thus vulnerability to food shortages is not overcome. Since the population goal of the system partly seems to be determined by food availability, a higher level of ambient per capita cereal consumption would limit population in the long run for a given level of cereal production. This policy essentially translates into obtaining food calories from animal proteins instead of cereals, which will limit availability of edible food calories for a given level of cereal production. The writings on hunger often dub this method of generating food calories as uneconomical or even decadent and moralize against it. However, it should be borne in mind that the objective of the policy is not to achieve efficiency in production of edible food calories in the short run, but to provide food security in the long run.

Figure 3.10 shows a simulation which also incorporates a higher per capita cereal consumption as compared to the earlier simulations, in addition to the policy package of Figure 3.9. The results are quite appealing. The birth rate is lowest, and life expectancy and wage rate are highest, of all previous simulations. Increases in population are limited as extra cereal production is used up in generating edible calories uneconomically instead of facilitating population growth. Thus, food cereal production per capita approaches a much higher level and a large slack is created between the cereal food calories produced and edible calories actually consumed, which reduces food vulnerability since in case of a shortage people can always resort to more economical sources of caloric intake.

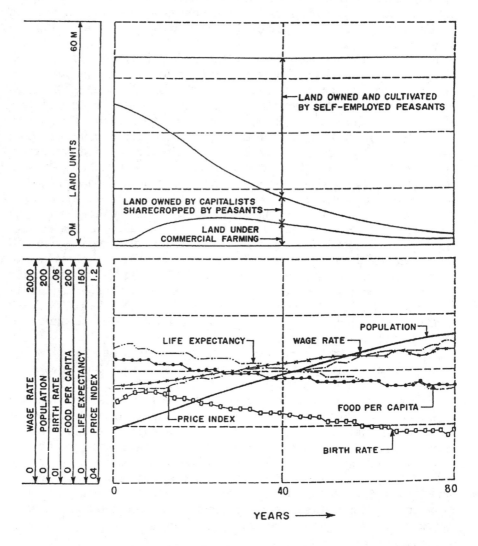

Figure 3.9   Behavior of the model incorporating the policies of Figure 3.6 along with the fiscal measures that discourage absentee ownership

104

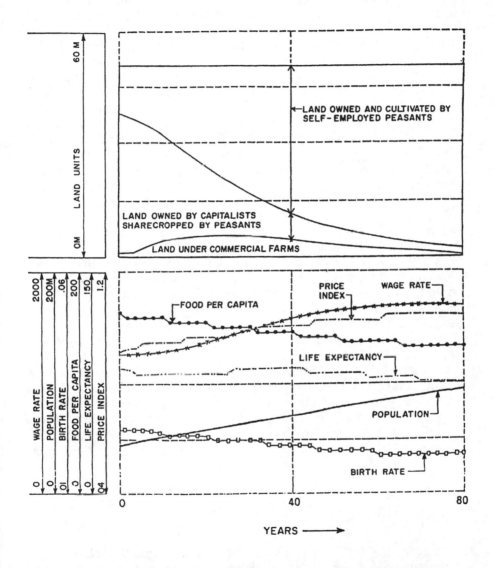

Figure 3.10 Behavior of the model incorporating policies of Figure 3.9 together with adoption of staples with a high cereal/edible calories conversion ratio

Conclusion

This paper has attempted to examine in a holistic framework the various macro-policies that underlie the development programs which have been implemented in the developing countries for alleviating poverty and hunger. When these problems are viewed as manifestations of the powerful feedbacks which govern the behavior of the actors of the system, the inefficacy of the various development programs does not appear surprising.

It would be fair to say that the solutions to hunger and poverty attempted in the past and being proposed now have a phenomenological perspective that addresses the symptoms instead of the organizational arrangements that create those symptoms. Hence, these policies could be easily defeated by the powerful tendencies created by those organizational arrangements which remained intact. The clues to the solutions of problems of poverty and hunger have always existed in the form of the differences in the ownership and income distribution patterns of the rich and the poor countries. The traditional development effort has tried to remove these differences without first understanding their causes. The solution to the problems of poverty and hunger appear to lie neither in providing direct aid to the poor nor in raising food production and introducing population control. These policies are defeated in the long run by the internal goals of the system. However, it appears that the internal goals of the system can be influenced by introducing policies that encourage ownership of resources by the self-employed workers (by taxing rent income) and building up a food slack (by obtaining food calories from cereal production inefficiently).

The analysis of this paper also provides a point of departure from the traditional policy design effort in economic development. A realistic formal model of the system helps one to understand the nature of the problems and identify appropriate points of entry into the system. The solutions suggested require mobilization of the internal forces of the system rather than countering system tendency through direct intervention. Thus, an additional inference to make from this analysis concerns the development role of the governments. It lies in motivating the public instead of engaging in direct action.

References

Alavi, Hamza (1976) 'The Rural Elite and the Agricultural Development in Pakistan' in Stevens et. al. (eds.), *Rural Development in Bangladesh and Pakistan*, Hawaii: Hawaii University Press.

Arndt, H. W. (1973) 'Development Economics Before 1975' in Bhagwati and Eckus (eds.), *Development and Change*, Cambridge: MIT Press.

Bardhan, P. K. (1973) 'A Model of Capitalism in a Rural Agrarian Economy' in Bhagwati and Eckus (eds.), *Development and Planning: Essays in Honor of Paul Rosenstein-Roden*, New York: George Allen and Unwin Ltd.

Bhattacharjee, J. P. (1980) 'Population and Agricultural Development: A Medium Term Review', *Food Policy*.

FAO (1979) *Agriculture: Towards 2000*, Rome.

Galbraith, John Kenneth (1979) *The Nature of Mass Poverty*, Cambridge: Harvard University Press.

Griffin, Keith (1978b) 'Increasing Poverty and Changing Ideas about Development Strategies', *Development and Change*, 8(4): 491-508.

Griffin, Keith and Ghose, A. K. (1979) 'Growth and Impoverishment in the Rural Areas of Asia', *World Development*, 7(4/5): 361-384.

Griffin, Keith and Khan, Azizur Rahman (1978a) 'Poverty in the Third World: Ugly Facts and Fancy Models', *World Development*, 6(3): 295-304.

Haq Mahboobul (1976) *The Poverty Curtain: Choices for the Third World*, New York: Columbia University Press.

Katz, Daniel and Kahn, Robert (1979) *The Social Psychology of Organizations 2nd ed*, New York: John Wiley, pp. 4-9.

Leontief, Wassily (1977) 'Theoretical Assumptions and Non-Observable Facts' in Leontief, *Essays in Economics*, Vol. II, White Plains, NY: M. E. Sharpe.

Lewis, W. Arthur (1974) 'The State of Development Theory', *American Economic Review*, 74(1).

Lipton, Michael A. (1977) *Why Poor People Stay Poor*, Cambridge: Harvard University Press.

Maxwell, H. J. and Singer, H. W. (1983) 'Food Aid to Developing Countries: A Survey', University of Sussex: Institute of Development Studies.

Meadows et. al. (1974) *Dynamics of Growth in A Finite World*, Cambridge: MIT Press, Ch. 2.

Morawitz, David (1977) *Twenty-five Years of Economic Development, 1950-1975*, Washington D.C.: World Bank.

Paarlberg, Don (1975) 'The World Food Situation', *Food Policy*, November.

Saeed, K. (1980) *Rural Development and Income Distribution: The Case of Pakistan*, unpublished Ph.D. Thesis, Cambridge: MIT.

Saeed, K. (1982a) 'Economic Development: Phenomenological Models and Irrelevant Controversies', *Dynamica*, 8(2).

Saeed, K. (1982b) 'Public Policy and Rural Poverty: A System Dynamics Analysis of a Social Change Effort in Pakistan', *Technological Forecasting and Social Change*, 21(Winter).

Saeed, K. (1983a) 'Economic Growth and Political Instability in the Developing Countries: A Systems View', *Proceedings of the System Dynamics Conference*, Boston: System Dynamics Society.

Saeed, K. (1983b) 'Worker Compensation and Income Distribution in the Agrarian Economies: Patterns and the Underlying Organization', *Dynamica*, 9(1).

Siamwala, Ammar and Valdis, Alberto (1980) 'Food Insecurity in the Developing Countries', *Food Policy*, November.

Simontov, A. (1976) 'World Food Consumption: Can We Achieve a Balance', *Food Policy*, May.

Von Braun, Joachim (1983) 'Effects of Food Aid in Recipient Countries', University of Gottinger: Institute of Agricultural Economics.

Yatopolous, Pan A. (1985) 'Middle Income Classes and Food Crisis: "The New Food-Feed" Competition', *Economic Development and Cultural Change*, pp. 463-483.

Appendix
Model description

The following set of relationships describe the broad decision rules incorporated into a model of resource allocation, production, and income distribution processes of an agrarian economic system that may assume many income distribution patterns. Potential structure is provided for the functioning of two modes of production, formal in which resources are employed on the basis of their profitability, and informal in which workers not employed in the formal mode seek self-employment. Ownership of land and capital as well as contribution to labor are the basis for claim to income while absentee ownership is possible through leasing arrangements. Ownership is legally protected and the financial market is fragmented by households. Thus, purchase of any productive assets must be self-financed by each sector through cash payments.

Wage rate depends on the bargaining position of the workers, which depends on their opportunity cost of accepting wage-employment as well as on the absolute availability of wage-workers. Thus, self-employed workers will be available for wage-work when the wage offered is equal to or more than the consumption expenditure per worker averaged over the whole workforce. All workers who are not wage-employed must be accommodated in the informal sector.

$$d/dt[WR] = (IWR-WR)/WRAT \qquad (1)$$

where WR is wage rate, IWR is indicated wage rate and WRAT is wage rate adjustment time.

$$IWR = [(R_p*(1-SP_p)+(AS_p/LAS))/TWF]*f_1[DW_f/W_f] \qquad (2)$$

where $f'_1 > 0$. R, SP, AS, LAS, TWF, DW, and W are, respectively, income share, saving propensity, accumulated savings, life of accumulated savings, total workforce, desired workers (based on economic criteria) and workers. Subscripts p and f designate, respectively, peasant (or self-employed) and formal (or commercial) sectors.

$$R_p = VQ_p+WR*W_f-LR*RL-KR*RK \qquad (3)$$
$$R_f = VQ_f -WR*W_f+LR*RL+KR*RK \qquad (4)$$

where VQ, LR, RL, KR, and RK, are, respectively, value of production, land rent, rented land, capital rent, and rented capital. KR and LR depend, respectively, on the long-term averages of the marginal revenue products

109

of capital and land (MRPK and MRPL) in the economy, and the demand for renting as compared with the supply of rentable assets. The demand for renting in turn depends on the lack of ownership of adequate resources for productively employing the workers in the informal sector.

SP_p depends on the need for investment in the peasant sector arising from the number of workers to be accommodated, and the rent burden of this sector compared with the factor contribution to its income from land and capital.

$$SP_p = f_2[DW_p/W_p]*f_3[(LR*RL+KR*RK)/(VQ_p-MRPW_p*W_p)] \qquad (5)$$

where $f'_2 > 0$, $f'_3 < 0$, and MRPW is marginal revenue product of workers. SP_f is assumed to be stable and constant.

AS represents the balance of unspent savings, which determine the availability of liquid cash resources for purchase of assets.

$$d/dt[AS_i] = R_i*SP_i-AS_i/LAS-LA_i*PL-\Sigma_j KA_i{}^j*GPL; \ i = f,p; \ j=m,t \qquad (6)$$

where LA, PL, KA, and GPL are, respectively, land acquisitions, price of land, capital acquisitions, and general price level. Subscript i refers to any of the two sectors, peasant (p) and formal (f) and superscript j to the type of capital, modern (m) or traditional (t).

$$TWF = P*FAP*FWF \qquad (7)$$

where P is population, FAP is fraction of agricultural population and FWF is fraction of population in the workforce.

$$DW_i = E_i{}^w*VQ_i/WR \qquad (8)$$

where E^w are the elasticities of the production of workers in the two sectors.

$$d/dt[W_f] = (IW_f-W_f)/WAT \qquad (9)$$
$$IW_f = f_4(DW_f/TWF) \qquad (10)$$
$$W_p = TWF-W_f \qquad (11)$$

where $f'_4 > 0$, IW is indicated workers based on economic criteria and absolute availability of workers, and WAT is worker adjustment time.

110

$$d/dt[RK] = RK*f_5[KR/MFCK] \qquad (12)$$
$$d/dt[RL] = RL*f_6[LR/MFCL] \qquad (13)$$

where f'_5 and f'_6 are > 0, MFCK and MFCL are, respectively, marginal factor costs of capital and land.

$$VQ_i = Q_i*GPL \qquad (14)$$
$$Q_i = f_7[K_i, L_i, W_i, E_i^n]*A_i \; ; \; n=l,w,k \qquad (15)$$

where $f'_7[K]$, $f'_7[L]$, $f'_7[W]$, are > 0. Q is output, and K, L, and W represent capital, land and workers employed by a sector. E_i^n are the elasticities of the production factors, land (l) workers (w) and capital (k) in the respective sectors. A represents the number of production cycles in a year, which increase with the use of modern capital. A modified cobb-douglas type production function is used.

$$LA_i = d/dt[LO_i] = LO_i*f_8[MRPL_i/MFCL, CA_i, TL] \qquad (16)$$

where $f'_8[MRPL_i/MFCL]$, $f'_8[CA_i]$, and $f'_8[TL]$ are > 0. LO, CA and TL are, respectively, land ownership, cash adequacy, and total land.

$$d/dt[PL] = (IPL-PL)/LPAT \qquad (17)$$
$$IPL = (AMRPL/IR)*f_9[\Sigma DLO_i/TL] \qquad (18)$$

where $f'_9 > 0$, IPL is the indicated price of land, LPAT is land price adjustment time, AMRPL is the long term average of the marginal revenue product of land, IR is interest rate, and DLO is desired land ownership in each sector.

$$KA_i^j = d/dt[KO_i^j]+KO_i^j/LK$$
$$= KO_i^j*[f_{10}(MRPK_i^j/MFCK; CA_i; KIC^j)+1/LK] \qquad (19)$$

where $f'_{10}[MRPK_i^j/MFCK]$ and $f'_{10}[CA_i] > 0$, and $f'_{10}[KIC^j] \geq 0$. KO, KIC and LK are, respectively, capital ownership, capital inventory coverage and life of capital.

$$d/dt[GPL] = f_{11}[TD/\Sigma Q_i] \qquad (20)$$

111

where $f'_{11} > 0$, and TD is total demand for goods and services.

$$d/dt[P] = P*f_{12}[FPC/FPCD, WR] \tag{21}$$
$$FPC = (FP+FA)/P \tag{22}$$
$$FP = (FD/TD)*\Sigma Q_i \tag{23}$$
$$FD = P*FPCD*f_{13}[GPL]-FA \tag{24}$$

where $f'_{12}[FPC/FPCD] > 0$, $f'_{12}[WR] < 0$, and f_{13} is relatively flat, although $f'_{13} < 0$. FPC, FPCD, FP, FA, and FD are, respectively, food per capita, food per capita demand, food production, food aid, and food demand.

$$E^w = 1-E^k-E^l \tag{25}$$
$$E_i^k = f_{14}[K_i^m/(K_i^l+K_i^m)] \tag{26}$$
$$A_i = f_{15}[K_i^m/(K_i^l+K_i^m)] \tag{27}$$

where E^l is fixed, and f'_{14} and f'_{15} are > 0.

$$K_p = KO_p+RK \tag{28}$$
$$K_f = KO_f-RK \tag{29}$$
$$L_p = LO_p+RL \tag{30}$$
$$L_f = LO_f-RL \tag{31}$$
$$CA_i = AS_i/[(AS_i/LAS)+(LA_i*PL)+(\Sigma_j KA_i^j*GPL)] \tag{32}$$
$$DLO_i = [E_i^l*VQ_i/PL]*f_{16}[CA_i] \tag{33}$$
$$TD = \Sigma C_i+FD+\Sigma KA_i+G \tag{34}$$
$$C_i = [(R_i*(1-SP_i)+AS_i/LAS)/GPL]*FNFC_i \tag{35}$$

where $f'_{16} > 0$, C are sectoral non-food consumption demands, G is government purchases, and FNFC is fraction non-food consumption.

112

4 An attempt to determine criteria for sensible rates of use of material resources[*]

Khalid Saeed

Abstract

This paper uses a systems framework to search for criteria for determining the rates of use of material resources. The existing criteria, which are found in the neo-classical economic theory and the environmental movement, are re-examined and their limitations are discussed. The criteria for material resource use identified by this paper emphasize that resources be selected from the environment on the basis of their regeneration time constant and consumed in a way that should maintain adequate organizational slack in the system. Based on these criteria, geological information about material resources appears to take precedence as basis for determining their rates of use over their economic feasibility and efficiency of use.

Introduction

The criteria for determining appropriate rates of use of material resources are currently found in two conflicting paradigms: The neo-classical economic theory, and the tenets of environmental movement. The former criterion assumes an unlimited future technological capability to utilize materials found on earth, and an almost unlimited supply of these, and

[*] Reprinted by permission of the publisher from An attempt to determine criteria for sensible rates of use of material resources, Khalid Saeed, Technological Forecasting and Social Change, 28(4), pp. 311-323, Copyright 1985 by Elsevier Science, Inc.

attempts to maximize the present value of the ones which can be exploited using current technologies [Nordhaus 1964]. The environmental movement is very concerned about the finiteness of the resource base and about the technological limitations to its exploitation, and advocates conservation, often, irrespective of the societal sacrifices entailed [Meadows, et. al. 1971].

The two models are internally quite consistent but they appear to incorporate bounded information sets which have little overlap. Hence they issue conflicting judgments neither of which may adequately serve the societal interest they ought to further.

This paper examines both views and the consequences of the policy recommendations issued by each with respect to the ability of the resource ecosystem to deliver and that of the human social system to accommodate the content of those recommendations. These factors are, then, the basis for a search for finding guidelines for formulating a sensible policy for managing material resources. The analysis of this paper uses the open system concept as an organizing principle [Katz and Kahn 1978]. A formal system dynamics model of the resource ecosystem is used mainly to facilitate exposition [Richardson and Pugh 1981]. Technical details of this model can be obtained from the author on request.

It is suggested that careful selection of resources from the environment and maintenance of an organizational slack while using those resources are the most important issues concerning the design of a resource use policy. The resource use criteria, therefore, call for selecting resources for use, not on the basis of maximizing their present worth or on the basis of environmental concerns alone, but on considerations of matching their consumption rate with their regeneration rate. It is also observed that increasing efficiency of use offers only a short term solution to a resource shortage problem while it also appears to reduce the organizational slack in the long run that protects society against shocks. Thus, geological information about resources should take precedence over their economic feasibility and efficiency of use as the bases for determining their rates of consumption. With these considerations, various possibilities of intervention into the existing social system are explored.

The neoclassical economic model

While the classical economic theory distinguished between land and capital as surrogates of non-renewable and renewable material resources, modern economic theory tends to treat all such resources as capital [Ricardo 1926, Fisher 1981]. Thus, the neoclassical economic model for exhaustible material resources is based on the valuation of their reserves in the capital markets for determining their rates of extraction. However, since the

114

current and the future rates of consumption of an exhaustible resource have an antagonistic relationship, the neoclassical model uses a mechanism to discount the future utility. The discount rate, together with the interest rate and the extraction cost, act as exogenous influences on the net price, which is endogenously determined by the assets market [Solow 1974]. Later refinements of this model also separately take into account the scarcity rent and the backstop resource production [Nordhaus 1979]. The various endogenous and exogenous factors influencing the production of an exhaustible resource, as incorporated in the neoclassical model, can be interpreted in terms of the feedbacks shown in Figure 4.1.

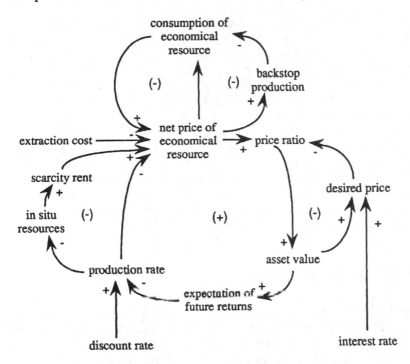

Figure 4.1   Feedbacks implicit in the neo-classical model of resource use

While the criteria for these decisions appear quite rational, they exclude any information about the geological characteristics of the current and the backstop resources, about the finiteness of the resource base, and about technological progress. Depending on the technological factors, the backstop resources replacing the current ones can be richer or poorer in their mineral content, although, the neoclassical model postulates exhaustion of the richer sources of materials first which is possible only if concomitant technological progress supports this pattern [Nordhaus 1979].

Historically, richer minerals seem to have progressively replaced poorer ones as has been correctly observed in the classical model which postulated abandonment of the "less fertile" mines as "more fertile" ones were exploited [Robinson 1980]. Such a historical progression was made possible because of the unique nature of technological development in the past.

The neo-classical model also makes only a passing reference to the finiteness of the resource base. It recognizes the entropic processes of the universe, due to which the degree of disorganization and the quantity of the spent resources in the universe are increasing monotonically, but it does not take those processes seriously as it appears that they will not become effective in the foreseeable future [Solow 1974]. This argument, however, is rather simplistic. The entropic processes in question concern the whole universe, within which, several subsystems exist. These subsystems strive to store negative entropic forces within them, albeit, at a cost to the whole [Bertalanfy 1968]. The sustenance of human society is related more closely to the ability of the resource ecosystem of the earth to renew itself using energic inputs from the sun than to the life of the universe as a whole. An imbalance between consumption and renewal of the resources of the ecosystem could lead to a desperate shortage of resources with disastrous consequences for human society while the rest of the universe lives on. The assumptions of the neoclassical model about the continued availability of resources are indeed heroic, whereas, they also ignore important geological information about the resource ecosystem. Thus, in spite of its internal consistency, the neoclassical economic model is an inadequate basis for formulating a sensible resource use policy.

The environmental movement

The environmental movement appears to base its reasoning on the convictions that the resources of the earth are finite and that their pattern of use is relatively inflexible. Hence, to preserve the consumption pattern in its current form, great social sacrifices are required [Walker 1979]. This movement seems to have gained much momentum from the concerns expressed by Jay W. Forrester in his "World Dynamics" published in the 1960s [Forrester 1971], which were also later reiterated in a detailed study that formed the basis for the publication of the controversial paperback "Limits to Growth" [Meadows 1974, Meadows 1971]. The environmental movement appears to issue mostly normative judgments for the working of human society while it is deeply concerned with preserving the resource environment. Thus, it often appeals to ethical and moral considerations in advocating cutting down on resource consumption, reducing waste, recycling, and increasing the use of renewable resources [Meadows 1974].

Although the environmentalists' model is in conflict with the neo-classical resource use model, the two are similar in that they use a limited information basis for devising criteria for resource use [Morecroft 1983]. The environmental movement appears quite cognizant of the limitations of the resource base but displays little knowledge of the workings of human society. Furthermore, it also appears to impose restrictions on the use of resources without adequately tackling the question of maximizing social utility. Often, in the name of the survival of the human race, the environmentalist resource management policies ignore individual prerogatives and call for enormous amounts of intervention by the state for regulating the use of material resources. This requires that the government of a country will always act in the public interest, which is a questionable assumption [Laszlo 1973].

Most societies consist of many interest groups which strive to uphold their respective short term interests rather than respond to the moral appeals of the environmental movement. If a resource allocation decision is taken by a government under conditions of scarcity, it may invariably compromise the interests of some of the groups and result in some dissidence [Gurr 1970]. Also, an important function of the government is to maintain control and stay in power. Therefore, it must allocate some of the scarce resources it controls to activities directed at overcoming dissidence. Since these resources are taken away from an already limited amount of usable resources, its action would further increase scarcity. Thus, consequent government decisions on resource allocation may result in even greater dissidence. This positive feedback may lead to an increasing use of these scarce resources to maintain political control which, in the long run, may often have a significantly adverse effect on general social welfare [Saeed 1983].

Finally, this growing scarcity of resources within individual nations will also increase international competition for the dwindling global resources. Such competition often leads to serious conflict among nations, which calls for stepping up the allocation of resources to defense. This is realized quite easily if the governments have vast decision powers as advocated in the environmentalist paradigm. However, this not only increases resource scarcity, it also further intensifies international conflict [Schelling 1960]. As a result, social benefits are further limited while an explosive scenario emerges which may bring about the annihilation of mankind even when adequate resources exist for its sustenance.

Resource ecosystem, human society, and the resource use criteria

The resource ecosystem of the earth is a relatively small subsystem within the universe which derives its energic inputs from the environment

117

maintained by a larger subsystem, the sun. The resource ecosystem, in turn, maintains an environment from which the human society - an even smaller subsystem - obtains its energic inputs [Miller 1982]. The hierarchy of these subsystems is shown in Figure 4.2. The throughputs and outputs are not shown as knowledge about those is limited.

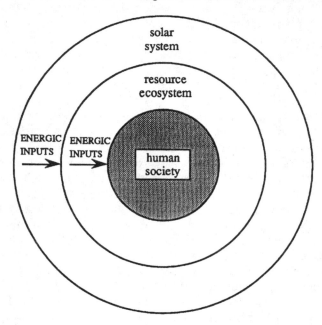

Figure 4.2   **The hierarchy of the resource and human systems**

For all practical purposes, the energic inputs from the sun to the earth's ecosystem can be assumed to remain constant over the entropic life of the sun. However, the energic inputs obtained by human society from the ecosystem will vary depending on the demands made on it and on its ability to deliver. The amount of materials actually obtained from the ecosystem at any time may be different from its sustained ability to deliver since the former depends on the cumulative stock at any time and the latter on the nature's ability to regenerate. With the help of the energic inputs it receives from the sun, the ecosystem is quite capable of regenerating resources from spent form to a usable form.

In fact, given enough time, almost all resources of earth spent over a certain period of time could be regenerated. Articles made from clay break and change back into clay. Metals can either directly be recycled or re-extracted from the oxides which are formed when metals deteriorate. Metal ores are also continuously created and enriched through long term geological processes [Cook 1976]. Plastics and man-made fibers may not be easily biodegradable, but they do not remain stable indefinitely. Eventually, they deteriorate into their simpler components which can be assimilated by nature.

There might remain an unconverted residue in a single regeneration cycle, but in each subsequent cycle, a fraction of the residue remaining from the last cycle would again be regenerated together with a fraction of a more recent batch of spent materials.

Thus, most of the spent materials from a given period may ultimately be regenerated while many vintages of them may be undergoing the process of regeneration at a given time.

Similar regeneration processes also exist for energy sources other than the sun. Felled trees clear space for growing more trees. Residues from burning wood and coal fertilize land. Carbon dioxide and moisture generated from burning are used by growing plants and contribute towards the development of their cellular structure. Coal and oil are formed by nature by the destructive distillation of plant and animal cellulose. Burning of oil also deposits carbon dioxide, moisture, and waste heat in the air that help to nourish plants which, in turn, nourish animals and microbial organisms that provide cellulose for making oil [Ourisson, et. al. 1984]. Radioactive metals can also be regenerated by the tremendous heat and pressure of the earth's inner core. In some of these cases, however, the regeneration process may take an incredibly long time.

The survival of human society, thus, depends not on the life of the universe but on the balancing of the consumption and regeneration of resources. If all resources are converted into the spent form and their regeneration takes a few million years, human society may not live to see the regenerated resources, while the universe lives on.

It may also be recognized that the classification of resources between the renewable and non-renewable categories is quite arbitrary. This is because resources are only transformed between usable and spent forms depending on usage and regeneration rates, and the only difference between the two categories is the length of their regeneration time constant, which is very long for non-renewable resources.

The categorization of resources between usable and spent forms may also seem quite arbitrary for many of the resources when technological factors are taken into account. Future technologies may be able to gainfully employ some of those currently classified as spent and thus it would become possible to reclassify them as usable without having to regenerate them to the currently usable form. Such reclassification would, however, involve significant technological break-throughs. The questions pertinent to the determination of an appropriate resource use policy concern both the resource ecosystem and human society which is sustained by it. Such a policy must incorporate considerations of the boundary interaction between society and its resource environment as well as of throughput and human

119

survivability [Katz and Kahn 1978]. Furthermore, in order to avoid arbitrariness in the design of a resource use policy, antagonistic comparisons of present and future should be avoided and assumptions of technological progress kept modest. To accomplish this, it is necessary to understand the nature of the feedback between the resource environment and the society and to establish rules for boundary interaction and throughput which should assure continued affluence and a sustainable future for society.

A simple model of resource ecosystem

From the point of view of their position in the ecosystem, the resources of the world could be placed in four categories. These are: 1) Usable Resources, which can be expended using currently available technologies; 2) Exploitable Resources, which become usable after they have been exploited; 3) Potentially Usable Undiscovered Resources, which would later become exploitable; and 4) Spent Resources, which must be regenerated by the ecosystem to become potentially usable, or are recycled by man to be directly placed in the usable category again. Figure 4.3 shows these categories and how resources move between them.

The expenditure rate converts usable resources into spent form and is primarily determined by the demand made on the resource ecosystem but is limited by the inventory of the usable resources available. The regeneration rate converts spent resources into the potentially usable form. Regeneration is made possible because of the energic inputs continuously received by the resource ecosystem from the sun, but regeneration time depends on the technology which determines which resources are selected for use. Thus, the aggregate regeneration time that should be applied to this model may range between a few years to millions of years.

The discovery rate allows transfer of potentially usable resources to the exploitable category. Both, discovery and exploitation rates are speeded up if the inventory of usable resources declines below a desirable level as a condition of resource scarcity would raise prices which would draw investment into research and development of resources. A persisting condition of scarcity would also provide motivation for developing technologies for recycling and reclassifying spent resources. Recycling allows a part of the expended resources to be directly transferred to a usable form while reclassification allows a part of the spent resources to be reclassified as exploitable.

When the demand profile is based on criteria exogenous to this model (such as those of the neoclassical economic model, or a simple trend) the resource expenditure patterns produced by it will depend on the assumptions made about technologies that determine the regeneration time of the resource package in use and the rates of recycling and reclassification. Figure 4.4 shows a comparison of the different expenditure patterns generated when the demand profile is a simple trend.

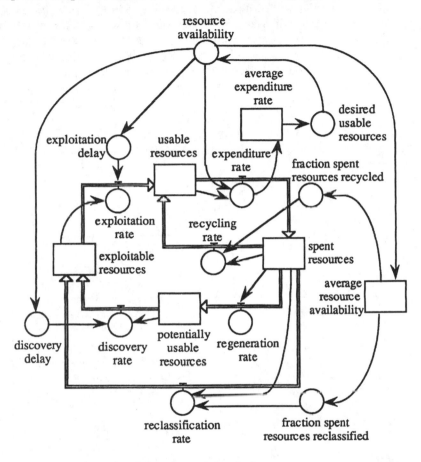

Figure 4.3   **A simple model of the resource ecosystem**

The pattern associated with the pessimistic view results from the assumption that the regeneration time is infinitely long and there is no possibility of recycling or reclassifying spent resources. These assumptions allow a temporary increase in expenditure when demand rises, but this is followed by a catastrophic decline when usable, exploitable, and potentially exploitable resource inventories decline. At the other extreme is the pattern representing the optimistic view which results from the assumption that spent resources may always be reclassified as exploitable ones when demand rises. These two patterns respectively incorporate implicit

121

assumptions of the technological progress made by the environmental and the neo-classical economic models of resource use. In between these lie the patterns corresponding to the revisionist views calling for recycling and for use of fast renewable resources. These strategies result in some increases in the inventory of usable resources and thus help to alleviate a catastrophic decline in their expenditure rate, although, they are unable to match an ever increasing demand trend. Recycling, which cannot be divorced from existing production technologies, is limited to a fraction of the current rate of expenditure. Thus, it can have only a small impact. When usage is confined to fast renewable resources only, the expenditure rate is limited by the quantity and the frequency of resources in circulation. Thus, limiting usage to a narrow group of fast renewable resources may not necessarily allow society to take full advantage of the potential of the resource environment.

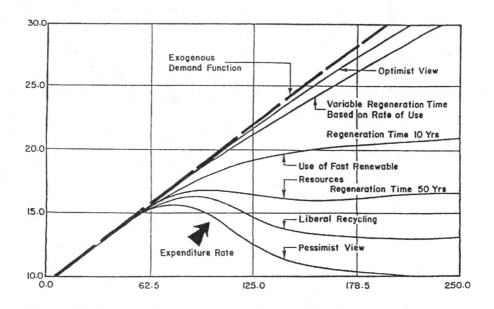

Figure 4.4   **Resource expenditure patterns generated by the resource ecosystem model**

None of the resource use scenarios discussed above appear to be satisfactory. If we expand consumption in the hope that future technologies would always make it possible to reclassify some of the spent resources into usable ones, we would be making heroic assumptions about technology and, possibly, penalizing future generations. If we make conservative assumptions about technology and show an overwhelming concern about the maintenance of the resource ecosystem, we may not only limit the benefits to the human society but also generate much conflict while implementing conservationist policies. What criteria should we base material resource use on if we wish to avoid those anomalies?

The resource ecosystem of the earth contains a very large variety of substances from which we can obtain materials for our consumption. Several sources for a single raw material can often be identified, although, not all of these can be exploited simultaneously since the prevalent economic criteria call for consuming the cheapest source first. The cheapest source to exploit is often the one which is richest in the materials we need for our consumption. Such resources have usually undergone the longest regeneration processing in the resource ecosystem.

If we could wait for nature to complete its regenerative process on materials, it would perhaps make sense to use only the richest sources. However, such consumption could be sustained only as long as expenditure does not exceed regeneration rate. Otherwise, expenditure and regeneration will be separated by delays which human society may not survive. Thus, ideally, we ought to select a resource mix from our environment whose aggregate regeneration rate matches our consumption. When consumption rises, resources with a shorter renewal time should be added to the package in use and those with a longer renewal time dropped. The remaining plot in Figure 4.4 illustrates implications of such a policy. As the stock of usable resources is depleted, more and more materials with a shorter regeneration time are introduced, which increases the aggregate rate of circulation of materials through the regeneration cycle of the resource ecosystem. Consequently, the stock of spent resources is more rapidly converted into the stock of usable resources. Thus, it becomes possible to sustain a higher expenditure rate. Periods of minor shortages may still be experienced, but these shortages also provide the driving force for the resource re-selection process.

An ultimate limit dictated by the absolute amount of resources in the ecosystem and the maximum speed at which these can be circulated would still exist and perhaps some measure for moving towards a *steady state economy* would be in order if this limit is approached [Daly 1974]. There is, however, persuasive evidence to suggest that considerable slack exists between this ultimate limit and the current levels of consumption, provided we are able to take advantage of the variety in the resource base [Brooks and Andrews 1973, Ravelle 1973]. The immediate need, therefore, is to facilitate technological developments which may allow to substitute the resources, which have a long regeneration time constant and which are being currently rapidly exhausted, with those, which are in abundant supply and which also have a shorter regeneration time constant.

Ironically, the opposite of this has taken place in history. As consumption pressures rose, technologies were developed to tap richer

123

geological resources, which continued to increase the aggregate regeneration time of the resource package in use. Such trends even led to the formulation of a very phenomenological classical theory of resource use which postulated abandonment of low quality mines as richer mines were discovered. Since such a historical pattern appeared because of the increasing availability of technologies that economically tapped richer resources rather than those with a faster renewable time, control of the technological progress appears to be an important entry point for implementing a sensible resource use policy.

In view of technology's unique progress in the past, the development of material resources with a shorter regeneration time may often call for reviving and refining technologies from the past when resource expenditure rate rises. Thus, future technological progress should be directed toward making possible utilization of more and more baser metals, clay, coal, firewood, and sun energy instead of more and more precious metals, plastics and radio-active materials. These technological trends may, however, be reversed when adequate stocks of usable resources with a longer regeneration time have been accumulated. Such a resource use pattern may easily be realized without technological miracles, although, it may call for having a better knowledge of our resource ecosystem. Selecting resources for use on the basis of matching their regeneration rate with their consumption rate also dispenses with an antagonistic comparison of the present with the future. Each generation may make the best possible use of the resources available to it without shifting the burden to future generations.

Market clearing and the question of efficiency of resource utilization

For pedagogic reasons the analysis of this paper so far has dealt only with the dynamics of the supply side. The demand for material resources has been assumed to be determined exogenously. When this restriction is removed, the market should clear when increases in price limit the demand for a resource as its availability declines. The market clearing involves two processes. First, an economy may be affected in resource consumption per capita in the short run by raising the efficiency with which natural resources are converted to a usable form. Second, the population of resource users may change in the long run to achieve complementarity with the available resources. These two processes have far greater significance for the welfare of human society than is conveyed by the impersonal view of "market clearing" held in neo-classical economics.

An increase in the efficiency of utilization will alleviate a resource shortage in the short run, but, it will also increase the facility for the user population to grow [Katz and Kahn 1978]. In the resulting equilibrium, the user population will increase to a higher level with fewer resources per capita. The organizational slack will be diminished and society will become more vulnerable to shocks in resource availability [Cyrt and March 1963]. The market will still clear in the long run when there is no change in the efficiency of resource use, but with a lower population and a higher organizational slack.

Figure 4.5 shows changes in usable resources per capita and in population when changes in availability are allowed to affect the demand through an adjustment in the user population, so that, the market clears. The simulation of Figure 4.5 also assumes that the resource re-selection policy suggested above is exercised. The efficiency of resource use is specified exogenously. It will be observed that a higher value of efficiency leads to a lower resource slack in the long run due to concomitant increases in the user population. Thus, the measures to increase efficiency of use of resources appear to provide only short term relief whereas they also seem to make future generations more vulnerable to resource shocks.

It might be argued that increasing efficiency of use at a time when the resource consumption rate is already in excess of the resource regeneration rate would guard against a catastrophic decline in population. This is true, but a policy to re-select carefully resources for use on the basis of matching consumption rate with the regeneration rate would accomplish the same thing without reducing organizational slack.

Consuming end-products extravagantly while increasing efficiency of resource utilization might limit the population of users and should, perhaps, help to raise standard of living and maintain the original level of organizational slack [Saeed 1984]. However, such a policy may still penalize future generations if present consumption of resources exceeds their regeneration rate.

How to intervene?

If human society could be managed through disciplinary regimen alone, it would be quite easy to design idealistic social policies and implement them through a political system which is vested with sufficient authority. This would, however, entail severely limiting individual freedom which people value highly.

Most of the survivalists policy prescriptions for the use of material resources call for expanding the role of government and limiting individual choice, which is justified on moral grounds. Herman Daly even suggests viewing morals as a resource and developing it in a way as to accommodate the imposition of quotas which are determined by a set of public organizations [Daly 1979] Unfortunately, a government which may assume the powerful role of determining a code of conduct and also imposing it may not always be expected to be concerned with public interest. It is also unlikely that such a powerful government would voluntarily subject itself to a democratic electoral process. Instead, it may mainly occupy itself with preserving autocratic control for which it may freely use the resources of the society. According to Popper:

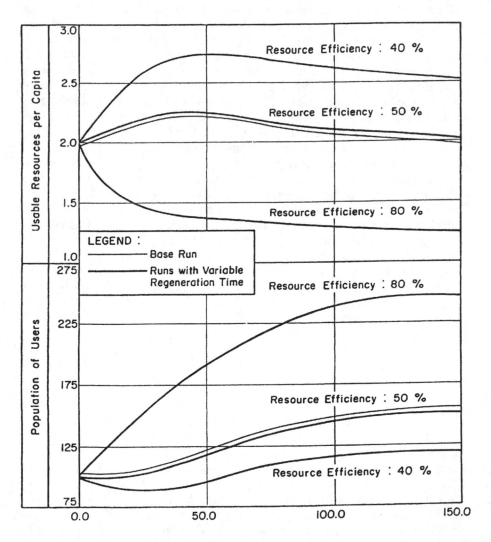

Figure 4.5   Usable resources per capita and user population for different values of efficiency of use when market is allowed to clear

126

".... Interventionism is therefore extremely dangerous. This is not a decisive argument against it; state power must always remain a dangerous though necessary evil. But it should be a warning that if we relax our watchfulness, and if we do not strengthen our democratic institutions while giving more power to the state by interventionist 'planning', then we may loose our freedom. And if freedom is lost, everything is lost, including 'planning'. For why should plans for the welfare of the people be carried out if people have no power to enforce them?" [Popper 1977]

The alternative to direct intervention is to delegate to a government only the power to influence mechanisms of choice through indirect means, such as fiscal measures. From the point of view of obtaining quick and precise results, this form of intervention may be less effective than direct intervention, although, it may also limit the government to assuming a dysfunctional role in relation to power. In fact, indirect intervention has been widely advocated and practiced in many democratically run countries over the past few decades. Unfortunately, it has been based on somewhat simplistic models of economics and hence it has been rather ineffective [Zucker 1985].

In spite of these failures, this author is of the view that indirect intervention continues to be an appropriate form of corrective action that should be undertaken for influencing resource use, provided this action is based on a comprehensive understanding of the resource system. Thus, at the outset, fiscal instruments such as a severance tax suggested by Page [Page 1977] are preferable to fixing depletion quotas and enforcing them by giving the government the power to police as suggested by Daly (1979).

In either case, it will be impossible to achieve exactness in the rates of use of material resources at any time since measurements on which these policies are based will be quite rough anyway. It should, however, be possible to converge to sensible rates of use if the process of design and the implementation of corrective policy is a continuous one. Perhaps, it would be appropriate to set up Natural Resource Boards at the national level that should continuously monitor the consumption and regeneration status of the natural resources and modify the severance tax structure to assure that resource mix in use is continuously adjusted towards achieving a balance between consumption and regeneration rates. This process can be further speeded up if the proceeds from this tax are used to subsidize the cost of appropriate, though, uneconomical resources and to support technological developments that should facilitate substitution.

Conclusion

The controversy about what is an appropriate policy for the use of material resources appears to arise from the comparison of the criteria of the neoclassical and the environmentalist models. They are internally consistent, but otherwise have little overlap. This controversy is of little help in designing a sensible resource use policy. Both neoclassical and environmentalist models of resource use are inadequate bases for formulating a resource use policy because each of these makes unrealistic limiting assumptions.

A sensible resource use policy must incorporate considerations of both the throughput and the boundary interaction of human society with its resource environment. This will be possible only if we move away from the current theoretical controversies and attempt to understand the physics of society and the resource environment viewed together. An open system framework appears to be quite useful for accomplishing this. Based on this framework, a policy to choose a resource mix from the environment that should allow matching of the consumption and regeneration rates appears to be of the highest priority. To implement such a policy, more geological information about resources needs to be gathered. This information should then form the basis for influencing the prices and the course of technological development so that a tendency to select appropriate materials for use is encouraged by the market itself instead of being imposed directly by a government.

The current revolution in information technology makes it quite possible to maintain an extensive base of information on material resources. This information base in itself should make it possible to provide more rational input into resource use decisions than is possible with the limited criteria currently in use. The emphasis on research into resources must also shift to collecting and maintaining an extensive geological data base on resources and to finding ways of influencing technological progress and prices in such a way that continued re-selection of resources for matching their consumption to their regeneration rates is facilitated.

References

Bertalanfy, Ludwig von (1968) *General Systems Theory*, New York: George Braziller.

Brooks, D. B. and Andrews, P. W. (1973) 'World Population and Mineral Resources: Counterintuitive or Not?', *UN Symposium on Population, Resources and Environment*, Stockholm: United Nations.

Cook, Earl (1976) 'Limits to Exploitation of Non-renewable Resources' *Science*, 191(20 February).

Cyert, R. M. and March, J. G. (1963) *A Behavioral Theory of the Firm*, Englewood Cliffs, NJ: Prentice Hall.

Daly, Herman E. (1974) 'The Economics of Steady State', *American Economic Review*, 64(2): 15-21.

Daly, Herman E. (1979) 'Entropy, Growth and Political Economy of Scarcity' in V. Kerry Smith (ed.), *Scarcity and Growth Reconsidered*, Resources for the Future.

Fisher, Anthony C. (1981) *Resource and Environmental Economics*, Cambridge, England: Cambridge University Press.

Forrester, Jay W. (1971) *World Dynamics*, Cambridge, MA: MIT Press.

Gurr, Ted Robert (1970) *Why Men Rebel*, Princeton, NJ: Princeton University Press.

Katz, Daniel and Kahn, Robert (1978) *The Social Psychology of Organizations*, 2nd ed., New York: John Wiley.

Laszlo, Ervin (1973) 'Uses and Misuses of World Models', in Laszlo, Erwin (ed.), *The World System Models, Norms, Applications*, New York: George Braziller.

Meadows, Dennis et. al. (1974) *Dynamics of Growth in a Finite World*, Ch. 2, Cambridge, MA: MIT Press.

Meadows, Donella et. al. (1971) *Limits to Growth, A Report for the Club of Rome's Project on the Predicament of Mankind*, New York: Universe Books.

Miller, J. G. (1982) 'The Earth as a System', *Behavioral Science*, 27(4): 303-322.

Morecroft, John D. W. (1983) 'Rationality and Structure in Behavioral Models of Business Systems', *Proceedings of the International System Dynamics Conference*, Boston: System Dynamics Society.

Nordhaus, William D. (1964) 'Resources as a Constraint', *American Economic Review*, 64(2): 22-26.

Nordhaus, William D. (1979) *The Efficient Use of Energy Resources*, Cowels Foundation, New Haven, CT: Yale University.

Ourisson, Guy et. al. (1984) 'The Microbial Origin of Fossil Fuels', *Scientific American*, 251(2): 34-41.

Page, Talbot (1977) *Conservation and Economic Efficiency: An Approach to Materials Policy*, published for Resources for the Future, Baltimore: Johns Hopkins University Press.

Popper, Karl R. (1977) *The Open Society and Its Enemies (2)*, New York: Routledge.

Ravelle, R. (1973) 'Will Earth's Land and Water Resources be Sufficient for Future Populations?', UN Symposium on Population, Natural Resources and Environment, Stockholm: United Nations.

Ricardo, David (1926) *Principles of Political Economy and Taxation*, 1817, London: Everyman.

Richardson, George and Pugh III, Alexander L. (1981) *Introduction to System Dynamics Modeling with Dynamo*, Cambridge, MA: MIT Press.

Robinson, T. J (1980) 'Classical Foundations of the Contemporary Theory of Renewable Resources', *Resources Policy*, 6(4): 278-289.

Saeed, K. (1983) 'Economic Growth and Political Instability in the Developing Countries: A Systems View', *Proceedings of the International System Dynamics Conference*, Albany, NY: State University of New York.

Saeed, K. (1984) *Poverty, Hunger and Development Policy*, Resource Policy Center, Hanover, NH: Dartmouth College.

Schelling, Thomas C. (1960) *The Strategy of Conflict*, Oxford University Press.

Solow, Robert (1974) 'Economics of Resources or Resources of Economics', *American Economic Review*, 64(2): 1-14.

Walker, K. J. (1979) 'Material Consumption Requirements of a Fully Industrialized World', *Resources Policy*, 5(4): 242-259.

Zucker, Seymore (1985) 'Economists are This Year's Endangered Species', *Businessweek*, January 14.

5 An attempt to operationalize the recommendations of the "limits to growth" study to sustain future of mankind[*]

Surya Raj Acharya and Khalid Saeed

Abstract

Experimenting further with the World3 model, this paper attempts to formulate the operational means to implement the critical recommendations of the "Limits to Growth" study. Using feedback as the organizing principle and the work of Daly (1991) Page (1977) and Saeed (1985) as guidelines, additional policy space was built into the model to accommodate controversial views on resource policy and to self-regulate its critical policy parameters. The policies so created not only appear to lie within the scope of the existing and the potentially feasible regulatory institutions, they are also insensitive to their respective behavioral parameters as well as to the timing of intervention. Furthermore, these policies strive to influence day-by-day actions of the actors in the system instead of imposing a drastic schedule of changes in life-style implicit in the literal interpretation of the broad recommendations of the Limits study. Besides, their implementation appears possible through a national rather than a global order.

[*] Reprinted from *System Dynamics Review*, 12(4), Surya Raj Acharya and Khalid Saeed, An attempt to operationalize the recommendations of the "limits to growth" study to sustain future of mankind, pp.281-304, 1996, with kind permission from John Wiley and Sons, Ltd., Baffins Lane, Chichester, West Sussex PO19 1UD, UK.

Introduction

The environmental issues cut across natural resources, society, economy and technology domains creating some of the most complex abstract systems of the present day world whose management is a challenge. Although generally ignored at the time the "Limits to Growth" study was published, the environmental agenda has lately become an important part of public policy. The Rio conference was a turning point in creating awareness for the environmental issues and giving prominence to environmental policy, which are now considered as important as development policy and have received high attention at all national, regional and global levels.

The policies currently being proposed for abating the environmental problems appear, however, to be often quite superficial and sometimes even vain. Many of these policies have called for powerful exogenous intervention at the global level, although many doubts have been raised about the efficacy of such an approach. Complex systems into which such interventions are made may self-regulate themselves to neutralize any interventions that do not recognize the internal tendencies arising from system structure. Also, the power institutions created to affect an intervention might move away from their original remits and work instead for maintaining their own scope [Saeed 1994].

Although system dynamics modeling is often applied to identify policies that might change system behavior by influencing the day-by-day decisions of the actors, in many cases this might not be attempted and only entry points for policy might be identified, especially when a modeling exercise aims mainly at raising issues rather than designing an operational means for intervention. A case in point is the "Limits to Growth" study, which commissioned a system dynamics model to extrapolate the future consequences of the current economic growth policies, but without specifying an operational policy guideline. When the entry points it suggested are literally translated into policy, they appear to call for a powerful exogenous intervention to limit population, abate pollution and drastically reduce resource use, for which neither an appropriate institutional structure is currently in place nor can it be created without gravely contradicting the existing systems of governance, which might lead to serious global conflict with disastrous consequences [Saeed 1996].

"Beyond the Limits", a sequel to the "Limits to Growth" study, was published in 1992 by the authors of the original study in an attempt to respond to some of the criticisms of the original work [Meadows 1992]. Beyond the Limits makes explicit some of the implicit assumptions of the original model, but focuses mostly on reiterating the concerns of the original study. It also attempts to further expand on the critical policy parameters of the original model in an attempt to devise implementation mechanisms based on feedback, but these mechanisms cannot be intimately linked with an operational framework as the revised model still does not incorporate adequate policy space for this.

We have attempted in this paper to reassess the policy premises adopted in the original Limits study from the point of view of their implementation and to develop guidelines for operationalizing them. We decided to build on the postulates of the original Limits model, World3, rather than on its sequel used in "Beyond the Limits", since the two are similar in terms of their functional assumptions and the policy space they offer while the former is simpler. We slightly revised World3, however, to accommodate the logic of the policy space needed for our extended experimentation. The operational policies we have developed through experimentation with this model mobilize fiscal instruments and service institutions currently existing or potentially feasible. They seek to influence the motivations of the concerned actors on day-by-day basis to achieve a sustainable future rather than call for drastic changes in social behavior which appear to be spelled by a literal interpretation of the policy recommendations of the Limits study and its sequel.

The premises of an operational policy

On the basis of the underlying decision theories, the approaches to policy design can be placed in two broad categories, normative and descriptive. The normative decision theory is concerned with how people should act in order to achieve better results. It provides rules that will improve the consequences of actions. The policies formulated with an orientation of normative decision theory involve an imposition of prescriptions about social behavior decided exogenously, and often without taking into account the compatibility of such prescriptions with the existing circumstances. Due to the very nature of the premises behind the policies of this class, intervening through a power institution is the most common strategy adopted for the implementation of normative policies. The descriptive decision theory, on the other hand, is concerned with how people actually go about handling a problem irrespective of whether the outcomes are admirable or not. This theory describes the patterns of behavior that characterize action, so it provides a simple picture of how organizations works, which is the basis for improving organizational performance [Bauer 1968, Bower 1968].

In either approach, the process of policy formulation involves several distinct steps, such as setting goals, formulating general policy directives and guidelines, identifying appropriate policy leverages and, finally, selecting policy instruments. Although the nature of the formulated policy might depend on its underlying decision theory orientations, if it fails to

133

define operational instruments for affecting the day-by-decisions of the pertinent actors in the system, the implementation of the policy would necessarily require power intervention. Indeed, policy design has traditionally incorporated an interventionist perspective requiring centralization of the power to make decisions by an outside autonomous hand. Unfortunately, such designs invariably fail. Firstly, it is not an easy task to achieve the required level of centralization. Secondly, even when decision making can be centralized, the actors entrusted with making the decisions may not sympathize with the objectives of the design. Finally centralization may conflict with a prevalent management ideology, may be unacceptable to the members of organization in which the design is to be implemented and may invoke much conflict that is destructive [Saeed 1992, 1994].

Saeed (1994) points out that while it is possible to design operational policies by employing the heuristical protocol of system dynamics, this is not attempted in a large number of cases. An operational policy design should aim at mobilizing the internal forces of the system into creating functional patterns and avoiding dysfunction. Such a design can bring about evolutionary change in the system by influencing motivations of the actors that guide their day-by-day decisions. However, if this design is conceived in terms of changing a few sensitive parameters of a system dynamics model that representing social rather than individual behavioral characteristics, its implementation may still require a powerful intervention by the leadership who may often neither have the motivation nor the means to commit to such an intervention, especially when the context is public interest rather than profit motive. Policy design for public agenda must, therefore, be conceived in terms of either new feedback loops that are created to modify the anatomy of critical decisions of the concerned actors or the way the influence structure of the existing feedback loops is changed so that the dominance of insidious mechanisms is minimized and the role of benign mechanisms enhanced. Saeed (1992) also suggests that a model intended for exploring policy options for system change must subsume multiple modes that are separated by time and geography since only then its underlying structure would contain the mechanisms of modal change. This means differing theoretical perspectives that often have local empirical basis should be considered as a part of the modal variety subsumed in a model addressing controversial issues.

The policy prescriptions of the World3 model commissioned by the Limits study are based on sensitive parameters representing social rather than individual behavior, hence their implementation appears to require powerful exogenous intervention. The revised model of its sequel, Beyond the Limits, indeed replaces some of the sensitive parameters with self-regulating feedback structure, but it is still unable to deliver adequately operational policy guidelines since, likewise the original model, it does not consider multiple modes implicit in the contradicting theoretical perspectives on resource policy, which are critical to creating policy space for a productive line of policy experimentation [Saeed 1996].

When run for an extended period of time, both Limits and Beyond the Limits models spell doom even when their policy recommendations are fully implemented. Hayes (1993) simulated the later model (with all prescribed policies) from 1900 through 2400. The policies, which appeared to be effective in ensuring a sustainable world, could only postpone the collapse until the middle of the 22nd century. Both models rule out any energic inputs into the global resource system that may create regeneration of resources or land, hence they cannot accommodate a line of policy experimentation that should create true long run sustainability through increasing the efficacy of the regeneration process. Such regeneration does occur in reality from the energic inputs received from sun, even though very slowly [Cook 1976, Ourisson 1984].

We have attempted in this paper the design of operational environmental policies which build on the entry points identified in the Limits study, but after slightly revising the model to accommodate the modal variety implicit in the competing resource use models. Policy design is then attempted by first setting criteria for the policy goals (which are the same as those of the Limits study) and then creating a feedback structure that may realistically achieve those goals. Thus, the sensitive parameters identified in the original study provide entry points for further policy exploration, but with the possibility of also investigating the efficiency of the regeneration process as a policy lever. Operational interpretation of the policy is then attempted by creating a feedback structure around the sensitive parameters of the original study, creating new role parameters for the actors within existing institutional framework at the level of the individual nations rather than the world at large.

Revision of the World3 model for accommodating multiple perspectives on resource policy

The nature of the policy prescription of the World3 model arises from the way the resource sectors (i.e., natural resources and arable land) have been modeled. The stocks of these resources have only outflows which make the ultimate collapse inevitable since these outflows continue as long as there is any production, which is driven by resources. The model does not consider any possibility of long term sustenance through regeneration which is a widely recognized natural phenomenon, fueled by earth's ecosystem constantly receiving energic inputs from the sun. One could, of course, say that the fixed stocks take into account the ultimate available resources, including the energy received from the sun, but the time frame of such stocks would be very different from the one considered in the Limits study.

135

This characteristic of the model has ruled out consideration of policy options capitalizing on increasing the efficacy of the regeneration process and thus sustaining available stocks in spite of consumption. Figure 5.1 shows how the resource ecosystem works in reality drawing energic inputs from the sun. The total mass of resources in the system represented by the large rectangle might remain constant, but the proportion of usable resources within this stock will depend on the speed of circulation within the resource system, which depends on technological and management practices rather than being given for all times [Abelson and Hammond 1974, Brooks and Andrews 1974].

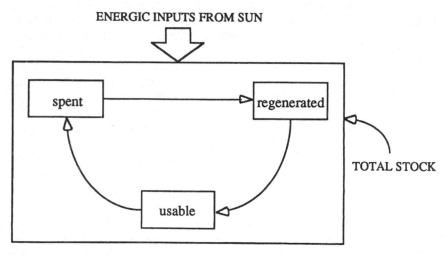

Figure 5.1   **An interpretation of the resource ecosystem within total resource stock suggested by Saeed (1985)**

For this reason, we have revised the base structure of the natural resource and agriculture sectors of World3. Care has been taken, however, to modify the original model minimally so that its original identity is retained. Furthermore, additional information structure is created around the sensitive parameters of the model to Operationalize its key policy recommendations. The revised model also includes variables for the proposed policies with switches which can be activated at any point in time. This was done to experiment with the timing of the proposed policies - to determine their sensitivity to their time of implementation, since the policies of the Limits study are time-sensitive while timing in a system with rough parameters cannot clearly be discerned. Our revision of the World3 model, thus, consisted of two stages - the revision of the base model to accommodate controversial perspectives on resource policy and to create latent structure for a possible equilibrium, and the structural additions representing policy agenda. The revisions made are described in this section while their technical details are placed in the Appendix.

Revision of natural resources sector

Natural resources sector is one of the five principal sectors of World3. Nonrenewable natural resources is the only stock in this sector. The nonrenewable resources are defined as mineral or fossil-fuel commodities essential to industrial production. They are regenerated by nature on a time scale that is long compared with the 200-year time horizon of the model [Meadows et. al. 1974]. The initial value of the natural resources stock is fixed in the original model and the only rate connected to it is the outflowing usage rate, meaning that no part of the resources can be renewed. In terms of the physics of the resources, this really implies that the composition of the resource basket is fixed with the aggregate regeneration time being much longer than the time frame of the model. In reality, however, some of the resources with very short regeneration time (often classified as renewable resources) can be substituted for those with long regeneration time (often classified as nonrenewable resources) hence the aggregate regeneration time in fact can be varied through technology policy [Saeed 1990].

The resource ecosystem of the earth is a relatively small subsystem within the universe which derives its energic inputs from the environment maintained by a larger subsystem - the sun. The resource ecosystem in turn, maintains an environment from which human society - an even smaller subsystem - obtains its energic inputs. With the help of energic inputs it receives from the sun, the ecosystem is quite capable of regenerating resources from an unusable form to a usable form. Given enough time, almost all of earth's spent resources could be regenerated. Thus, the pace of circulation of resources through the resource ecosystem cycle - which determines the availability of resources in a usable form - basically depends on the regeneration time. The aggregate regeneration time of the resource consumption basket can be increased by addition of resources to it with long regeneration time and decreased by addition of resources with a short regeneration time [Saeed 1985]. Thus inclusion of more resources with a short regeneration time in the aggregate resource consumption basket can significantly increase the speed of circulation of the resources in the ecosystem and impact, increasing the proportion available for use. However, at present the priority set for technological development seems not to be cognizant of this fact. For instance, currently, only six percent of public research funds for energy are allocated to renewable sources (with short regeneration time constant) while 60 percent goes for nuclear energy and 15 percent for fossil fuel (with long regeneration time constant) [World Bank 1992].

137

With above considerations, a resource regeneration structure is incorporated into the model in which the regeneration time depends on the composition of the resource basket in use, that in turn is determined by the technological choices made as suggested by Saeed (1985, 1990). These technological choices can be influenced through indirect policy levers. The policy levers affecting the resource basket built into the model are based on the principles of neoclassical economic theory and the physics of the resource ecosystem. The neoclassical economic theory advocates using natural resources to maximize the present utility determined by market situation, discount rates and technology in use. However, the neo-classical economic theory focuses largely on micro issues and lacks a macro dimension [Daly 1991]. In an effort to extend the economic logic driving resource use from micro to macro dimension, Page (1977) suggests that we can think of resource policy at three levels: reactive - responding to immediate pressures, corrective - attempting to improve the working of the markets, and reflective - informed indirect interventions attempting to preserve resources.

Most resource policies currently in use fall in the reactive category. These policies respond to particular pressures and a collection of them may often lack internal consistency. Implementation of reactive policies often requires powerful exogenous intervention. These are not considered in our experimentation.

The corrective policies aimed at improving the market mechanisms attempt to ensure efficient use of resources. As the market becomes a better allocator of resources to various uses, a sustainable balance is expected to be reached. This is also the approach advocated by the resource economics stream of the neoclassical economics, although there exist valid skepticisms about the ability of the market to arrest the increasing trend of erosion of natural resources. Since the original Limits premises lend themselves easily to exploring operational corrective policies, instruments subsuming this level of intervention are experimented with in our study.

The market mechanisms are, however, good only for assuring intra-temporal efficiency of resource use and they cannot address the issue of inter-temporal equity [Pearce, et. al. 1989, Page 1977]. Because, according to the theory of market economy, reserving resources for future use makes sense only when the expected future price of the resources is increasing, at least, at a rate equal to the market rate of interest. However, the market rate of interest generally exceeds the rate at which the society wishes to discount future. Hence, the market mechanisms always favor the present use of resources over the future use, which does not serve the societal interest in terms of inter-temporal equity [Solow 1974]. Also, this approach cannot ensure the maintenance of an adequate level of slack in the resource stocks thereby making the society more vulnerable to shocks, nor can it assure sustenance in the future without heroic assumptions about technological progress.

138

To address the problem of inter-temporal (or inter-generation) distribution of natural resources, Page (1977) suggests moving to the reflective level of policy interventions which basically favor informed government interventions to keep resource base intact. Realizing the fact that even well functioning competitive markets may fail to allocate resources properly over time, Solow (1974) also favors public intervention to slow down and stretch out the exploitation of the resource pool. This level of intervention is further explored in our study.

Figure 5.2 shows the additional information structure added to World3 in our revision of the resource sector. At the outset, a provision for resource regeneration is introduced in the model. Implicit sources of regeneration are the geological processes, recycling, and substitution from the pool of backstop resources, which contrary to their definition are not assumed to be unlimited. The revised structure incorporates active as well as latent feedbacks. First, it has been assumed that market imperfections are removed to enable the market signals to create appropriate feedbacks. The market clearing mechanism has, however, not been explicitly modeled as the level of aggregation of World3 did not allow this. Instead, the price adjustment is assumed to be responsive to resource availability. The price level thus transmits appropriate signals to the technological progress related to substitution, recycling and use of natural resources. The market mechanism assumed here forms part of our revised base model.

The price system discussed above can at best only ensure intra-temporal efficiency of resource allocation. So, to ensure inter-temporal equity, indirect intervention through the provision of a severance taxation system is proposed. Such a severance tax structure must assure that consumption and regeneration rates are matched through an appropriate selection of the resource basket. This requires continuous monitoring of resource use rates and resource stocks to determine coverage time for each stock, which is translated into its availability. The severance tax is, then continuously adjusted in response to resource availability, assuring in the long run that there are no inter-generation transfers of cost.

The severance tax simultaneously influences the recycling rate, the substitution rate (from the stocks of the backstop resources) the efficiency of use, the indicated level of industrial production and the regeneration time constant (determined by the composition of the resource basket in use). The technological dimension is implicitly included in each of these influences. Hence, one of the premises of the revised structure is that technology can be influenced endogenously through severance tax. As all newly created feedback loops are of balancing nature, the advancement in technology is automatically guided towards sensible choices cognizant of environmental considerations.

The severance tax mechanism can also be a useful instrument for the capital sector. In original World3 model's policy package, the desired per capita industrial output was exogenously restricted to 320 units in 1990.

139

With the introduction of the severance tax provision, we can see that the desired industrial output must respond to the level of tax through the pricing mechanism.

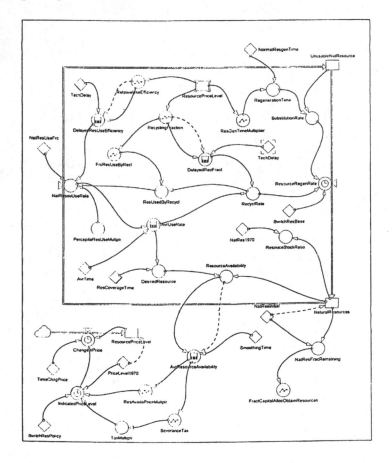

Figure 5.2   Flow diagram showing revisions of the resource sector

Revision of agriculture sector

In the original Limits model, as in the case of natural resource, the arable land has been treated as fixed stock without any possibility of regeneration. It is subjected to continuos erosion even when food production is declining. This structure is responsible for an inevitable decline of food production. The revised model of the Beyond the Limits study also did not make any

140

changes to introduce the structure for land regeneration, which ruled out exploring any policy experimentation concerning land management. In reality, fallow practices have been used for ages to regenerate land fertility. There are also well known land management practices involving crop rotation, planting and soil management methods that facilitate natural soil conservation and regeneration processes. The nomads of Sahel have been able to maintain a reasonable level of soil fertility for an extended period of time even in a precariously balanced desert environment, before, their agricultural system was disturbed through so called development effort [Picardi and Siefert 1976].

Figure 5.3 shows the additional information structure created in our revision of the agricultural sector of World3. As in the case of natural resources, we added structural components to the land stocks to provide for land rehabilitation. This change, on one hand, corresponds to the real world situation as there are cases of rehabilitation of eroded land in the past while on the other it also creates additional space for exploring operational policy. The related policy prescriptions are of reflective category and translate into enhanced efforts for land rehabilitation or regeneration through technological development or extension programs the extent of which is linked with the eroded land fraction.

Revision of other sectors

The only changes made in the other sectors of the model (population, capital and pollution) are in terms of constructing new information links from the respective stocks to the policies based on the information residing in them and connecting those polices to the flows affecting the related stocks.

Population sector determines fertility and life expectancy. The Limits study identifies the desired completed family size as a sensitive policy parameter in this sector. In World3 model this variable is influenced only by industrialization, which is consistent with the classical theory of demographic transition. However, recent work on the political economy of fertility reveals that industrialization was not the sole reason for demographic transition experienced in the industrialized countries. There is substantial historical evidence designating government policy interventions as the primary cause for the fall in fertility rates. The so called "soft" government policy has often governed private micro-level decisions of the reproductively active adults in many of the advanced industrial nations [Ryan 1991]. Demeny (1988) perceives such soft and indirect policies to create a gravitational field of services, incentives, rewards and penalties, that with a minimum of specific intervention would shape individual demographic behavior so as to best harmonize conflicting individual interests.

141

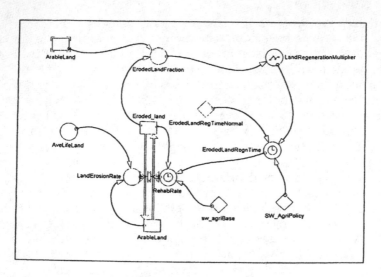

Figure 5.3   **Flow diagram showing revision of the agricultural sector**

Figure 5.4 shows the feedback mechanisms created by our revisions of the population and pollution sectors. In both World3 and its revision used in the Beyond the Limits study, population policy is a function of an exogenously specified critical policy parameter, the desired family size, which is set at two, even though in the later case, this number is achieved through forcing the outcome of a feedback. We have made an attempt to influence this parameter endogenously. Information relationships are added to the model to reflect the effects of industrialization and the level of social service delivery on family size. These policies do not use of any direct instruments, rather they are "soft" in the sense that they create a possibility to indirectly influence individual decisions on desired family size. Thus, government through various means can induce a situation whereby individual fertility decisions would be responsive to income level and social services available. For this purpose costs and rewards could be adopted as policy instruments. These are represented in the model as income and service multipliers, which ultimately determine family size.

In pollution sector, the policy option considered entails the development of pollution abatement technology. An information link has been established between Persistent Pollution Index and Required Level of Pollution Abatement Technology. This structure reflects the need for continuous monitoring of pollution level which is a basis for developing a corresponding level of pollution abatement technology. Needless to add that in reality this would entail development of institutions entrusted with the tasks of monitoring and reflective policy formulation.

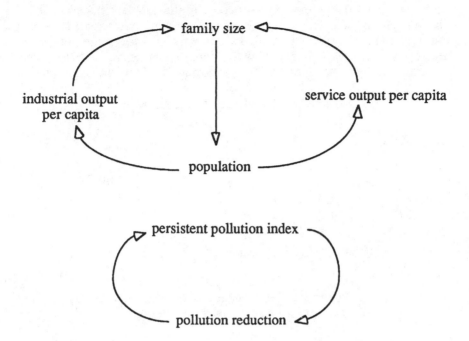

Figure 5.4   **Feedback loops created by the proposed pollution reduction and population planning policies**

Figure 5.5 shows the feedbacks entailed in the revision of the capital sector. The main policy objective in the capital sector is to stabilize industrial growth, which can be accomplished by influencing the decision to invest and which eventually determines the level of industrial output. The condition of natural resources availability and persistent pollution are the key stocks responding to the investment policy. Desired level of industrial investment is also regulated through varying the investment in social services sector. This policy objective can be achieved through indirect government intervention, for example through fiscal instruments influencing the investment decision. The volume of adjustment to be made in the industrial output determines the extent of indirect intervention needed.

We began our experimentation by simulating the revised model without activating any of the policy structure created in our revisions. The policy structure was then activated progressively. Before experimenting with any of the policy options, the factors causing the problem behavior in the revised model were first carefully examined. Following this, a policy or a group of policies likely to correct the problem were activated and the model further experimented with. This process was repeated with different policy options until an improvement occurs in the problem behavior. If an activated policy alleviated the original problem but created others, additional policies were activated. In this way, a wide range of policy alternatives were experimented with. Finally, effective policies were combined into a set that appeared to best correct the problem behavior.

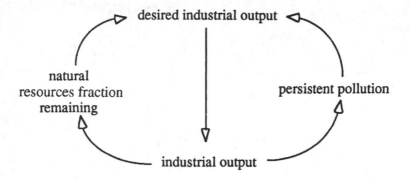

Figure 5.5   **Feedback loops created by the proposed industrial stabilization policies**

Policy experimentation operationalizing recommendations of limits study

Base run with the revised model

Figure 5.6 shows the base run of the revised model which was obtained by activating the revisions made in the base model modifying its natural resources and agriculture sectors in year 1900, but without activating any policy instruments built into it. The system still exhibits the characteristic behavior of overshoot and collapse, although the collapse is deferred for some time. This occurs because the introduction of market mechanisms with a regeneration provision in the resource sector of the model takes the pressure off usable resource stocks to a limited extent. Ultimately, resource base starts dwindling rapidly since regeneration falls much short of consumption. The resulting resource crunch makes the population go down with all indices of standard of living declining. These results show, however, that even if a perfect market is established for the natural resources, it is not possible to alleviate resource scarcity in the long run as widely believed in the postulates of traditional resource economics.

144

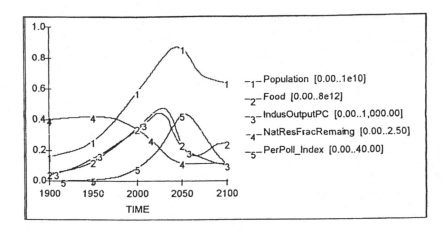

Figure 5.6   Base simulation run of the revised model

Simulation run with severance tax and its influence on technological progress

Figure 5.7 shows the behavior when the model is simulated with the additional policies of clamping severance tax on the scarce resources and making technological progress responsive to resource scarcity as suggested by Saeed (1985). The model structure corresponding to the severance tax and technological policy are activated in the year 1975. The severance tax policy pushes the resources price higher than that determined by the market which simultaneously stimulates substitution, recycling and efficiency of use technology. These policies do not alleviate, however, the problem of collapse, since when resource constraint is removed, the industrial growth is accelerated resulting in excessive pollution. Thus, the excessively high level of pollution created by the accelerated industrial growth (supported by the resources stock) is now responsible for the collapse.

Figure 5.8 shows a simulation run when pollution, industrial output stabilization and population policies were activated in 1975. In order to see the long run effectiveness of policies, simulation was performed until the year 2400. In this run, the problem of excessive pollution seems to have been alleviated by the pollution reduction policy, which was achieved by activating the information link between Persistent Pollution Index and Required Level of Pollution Abatement Technology.

145

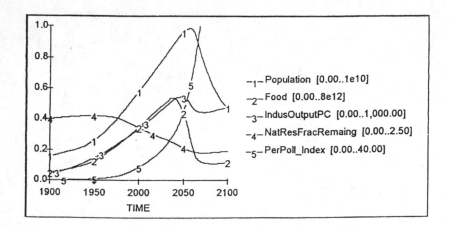

Figure 5.7   Simulation with severance tax and technology policy seeking to adjust regeneration time of the aggregate resource basket in use

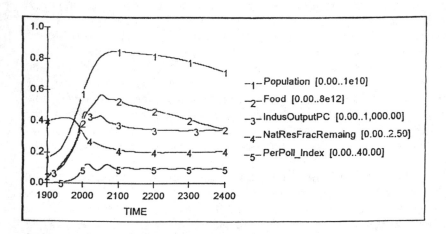

Figure 5.8   Simulation with industrial stabilization, population planning and pollution reduction policies added to the policies of Figure 5.7

Simulation run with pollution, industrial output stabilization and population policies

The industrial output stabilization policy attempts to maintain an indicated level of industrial output by influencing the society's decision on investment for social services. The desired level of industrial output is continuously adjusted in response to the level of persistent pollution and the stock of natural resources through indirect interventions, such as taxation. If the level of industrial output is more than desired, more investment is diverted to social sector and vice-versa. This influences investment trends in the industrial sector and eventually stabilizes the industrial output at around the desired level. This simulation also incorporates the impacts of the level of industrial output and social services on population, that reside in the links created in the revised model from industrial output per capita and service output per capita to desired family size. The model behavior is significantly improved with the introduction of these policies, at least, in the short run. However, if the behavior is carefully scrutinized, it can be seen that the system is not perfectly stabilized. In particular, food production heads for continuous decline, which could cause a collapse in the long run.

Simulation run with land regeneration policy

Finally the model was experimented with land regeneration policy activated, which speeds up the regeneration of eroded land and checks the decline of food production, together with all policies of the previous run activated in 1975. The resulting simulation is shown in Figure 5.9. With this policy package the model is robustly stabilized in the long run.

Time dependence of the proposed policy framework

In the previous simulation experiment a policy package consisting of severance tax, technological progress responsive to resource availability, pollution reduction, land regeneration, industrial output stabilization, and population planning could bring the system into equilibrium when implemented in the year 1975. The same policy framework is now activated in the years 1995 and 2015 in order to observe the time-dependence of the proposed policy framework. Table 5.1 shows the equilibrium value of the key variables with different timings of policy package introduction.

Each of the simulation runs not only exhibit a perfectly stabilized behavior but also yielded no variation in equilibrium value of the key variables. Since an equilibrium goal now exists in the latent structure of the revised model, it should be possible to achieve this goal into the future by activating the necessary feedback elements with a wide range of initial conditions present at the time of policy implementation.

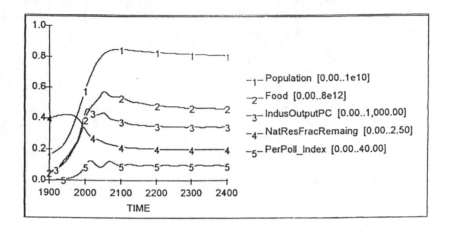

Figure 5.9   Simulation with land erosion control mechanisms added to the policies of Figure 5.8

Table 5.1
Equilibrium values of the key variables when the proposed policy package is implemented at different point in time

Variables Year of policy introduction	End equilibrium values of variables		
	1975	1995	2015
Population	8.0E9	8.2E9	8.85E9
Food	3.7E12	3.7E12	3.7E12
Industrial output per capita	346.5	341.6	336
Resource fraction remaining	0.5	0.5	0.5
Persistent pollution index	3.8	3.9	4.0

A potential equilibrium goal must always be carefully discerned in all models seeking to stabilize the systems they represent. In the absence of such a goal, adequate operational policy space for stabilization will not exist, which has been the limitation of World3 model and its sequel, although these models were quite adequate for understanding the nature of the problem and identifying pressure points for change. Without such a goal, all conceived policies will be time dependent since their impact will be limited to a narrow range of time frames and also sensitive to the starting conditions, as was the case with the World3 model and its sequel.

The implementation process

Sustaining world resources and environment is a global problem, which in common sense perception, should be addressed by a global order. Experience shows, however, that in an economically and politically polarized world, any global order would further power interests rather than promote collective welfare. Hence, solutions for global problems may often not reside in global orders. The Limits study has made a valuable contribution to sustaining mankind by raising issues widely seen today as critical to our existence. It should also be credited with raising those issues almost a quarter of a century ago, when little awareness existed about them. The policy agenda it raised, however, could be considered only in the context of a global order. With a rather conflictful global dialogue about this agenda currently in progress, it is quite evident that a global implementation process might create an enormous conflict which would impose yet another, and perhaps more binding, limit on mankind.

Seeking operational means for the recommendations of the Limits study, as we have attempted in this paper, on the other hand, creates a possibility of global sustenance through local means. The policy package we have developed in the last section can be easily implemented through fiscal instruments and institutions, existing as well as potentially feasible, within the framework of national orders. This means global coercion and its accompanying problems can be avoided. However, in a world intimately connected through information, trade flows and financial interaction, local implementation of our policy recommendations might become rather distorted. There is a need to explore operational means also to sustain global relations, although through local instruments, which is a significant challenge for research on sustainability and a fertile area for system dynamics to pursue further [Saeed 1996, Choucri and Berry 1996].

Conclusion

The Limits to Growth study made a valuable contribution to the knowledge on sustainable development in bringing to fore the implications of indiscriminate growth at a time the environmental capacity was often perceived to be unlimited. It also correctly identified the critical entry points for sustaining mankind in a finite resource environment. Beyond the Limits, a sequel to the Limits study attempted to further enrich the original Limits model by internalizing mechanisms of technological development and also by refining agenda for action proposed by its precursor. The models of the Limits study and its sequel Beyond the Limits were, however, not designed for experimentation to seek operational policy and a verbatim interpretation of their recommendations appears to spell draconian action at the global level, which is seen to be both unfeasible and counter-productive. There has clearly been a need to carefully examine the operational implications of the Limits agenda which we have attempted in this paper.

We modified the Limits model firstly to accommodate the modal variety implicit in the controversial perspectives on natural resource policy, which allowed us to understand the hidden assumptions of each perspective while also offering policy space to seek a pattern change through an operational means. The modified model, albeit, generated behavior similar to the original model under realistic ambient conditions, although it did contain latent structure for arriving at a robust equilibrium state. An attempt was then made to translate the entry points proposed by the Limits study into institutional means using the principle of feedback, which resulted in operational policy guidelines calling for indirect instruments feasible at the national level. These instruments were aimed at influencing motivations of the actors and thereby guiding their day-by-day decisions towards the desired end instead of forcing mankind to make drastic changes in its life-style. It was also found that these feedback-based policies were insensitive to the changes in their respective behavioral parameters as well as to the timing of their implementation since the identified system had latent structure for a robust equilibrium. Furthermore, these could be implemented through a national rather than a global order.

Further refinements of this study must examine regional aspects of the system and the trade relations within and between the regions since inter-regional resource transfers affect sustainability. Also important are the political relations within and between the regions whose dysfunction can result in excessive allocation of scarce resources to the unproductive control activities thus diminishing productivity.

References

Abelson, P. H. and Hammond, A. L. (1974) 'The New World of Materials' *Science*, 191:4228.

Bauer, R. A. (1968) 'The Study of Policy Formation: An Introduction' in Bauer, R. A. and Gergen, K. J. (eds.), *The Study of Policy Formation*, London: The Free Press.

Bower, J. L. (1968) 'Description Decision Theory From The Administrative View Point', in Bauer, R. A. and Gergen, K. J. (eds.), *The Study of Policy Formation*, London: The Free Press.

Brooks, David B. and Andrews, P. W. (1974) 'Mineral Resources, Economic Growth, and World Population', *Science*, 185: 4145.

Choucri, N. and Berry, R. (1996) 'Sustainability and Lateral Issues', *Proceedings of 1995 International System Dynamics Conference*,Tokyo, Japan: System Dynamics Society.

Cook, Earl (1976) 'Limits to Exploitation of Non-renewable Resources', *Science*,191(20).

Daly, Herman E. (1991) 'Elements of Environmental Macroeconomics' in *Ecological Economics*, Robert Costanza (ed.), Columbia University Press: New York.

Demeny, Paul (1988) 'Social Science and Population Policy', *Population and Development Review*, 14(3).

Hayes, Brian (1993) 'Balancing on a Pencil Point', *American Scientist*, 81: 510-516.

Meadows, D.H., Meadows, D.L. and Randers, J. (1992) *Beyond the Limits*, Post Mills, Vermont: Chelsea Green Publishing Company.

Meadows, D.H., Meadows, D.L., Randers, J. and Berhens III, W. W. (1972) *The Limits to Growth*, New York: Universe Books. [Republished by Productivity Press, Portland, OR.]

Meadows, D. L. and Meadows, D. H. (1974) *Dynamics of Growth In A Finite World*, Cambridge, MA: Wright Allen Series (eds.), MIT Press.

Ourisson, G., Albrecht, P. and Rohmer, M. (1984) 'The Microbial Origin of Fossil Fuels', *Scientific American*, 251(2): 34-41.

Page, T. (1977) *Conservation and Economic Efficiency: An Approach To Materials Policy*, Baltimore, Maryland: Johns Hopkins University Press.

Pearce, David W. and Turner, R. Kerry (1990) *Economics of Natural Resources and Environment*, Baltimore: The Johns Hopkins University Press.

Picardi, A. C. and Siefert, W. W. (1976) 'A Tragedy of the Commons in the Sahel', *Technology Review*, 78(6): 1-10.

Ryan, S. (1991) 'Implicit Policy and Fertility During Development', *Population and Development Review*, 17(3), pp. 377-414.

151

Saeed, K. (1985) 'An Attempt To Determine Criteria for Sensible Rates of Use of Material Resources', *Technological Forecasting and Social Change*, 28: 311-323.

Saeed, K. (1990) 'Government Support for Economic Agendas in Developing Countries: A Behavioral Model',*World Development*,18(6): 785-801.

Saeed, K. (1990a) 'Managing Technology for Development: A View from a Systems Perspective', *Socio-Economic Planning Sciences*, 24(3): 217-228.

Saeed, K. (1992) 'Slicing a Complex Problem for System Dynamics Modeling', *System Dynamics Review*, 8(3): 251-261.

Saeed, K. (1994) *Development Planning and Policy Design: A System Dynamics Approach*, Aldershot, England: Avebury.

Saeed, K. (1996) 'Sustainable Development, Old Conundrums, New Discords', *Jay Wright Forrester Award Lecture*, *System Dynamics Review*, 12(1): 59-80.

Solow, R. M. (1974) 'The Economics of The Resources or The Resources of Economics', *The American Economic Review*, 64, 1-14.

World Bank (1992) 'World Development Report 1992: Development and Environment', New York: Oxford University Press.

Appendix A
Equations for revised resources sector

init NaturalResources = NatResInitial
flow NaturalResources = +dt*(ResourceRegenRate)-dt*(NatResouUseRate)
doc NaturalResources = natural resource stock
unit NaturalResources = resource unit
init ResourcePriceLevel = PriceLevel1970
flow ResourcePriceLevel = +dt*(ChangeInPrice)
init UnusableNatResource = 13e12
flow UnusableNatResource = +dt*(NatResouUseRate)-dt*(ResourceRegenRate)
doc UnusableNatResource = unusable natural resources stock
unit UnusableNatResource = natural resource units
aux ChangeInPrice =
  IF(TIME<1970,0,(IndicatedPriceLevelResourcePriceLevel)/TimeChngPrice)
doc ChangeInPrice = fractional change in the resource price level
unit ChangeInPrice = dimensionless
aux NatResouUseRate =Population*PercapitaResUseMultplr*
  NatResUseFrc/DelayedResUseEfficiency+ResUsedByRecycl
doc NatResouUseRate = natural resource use rate
unit NatResouUseRate = resource unit/year
aux ResourceRegenRate = IF(TIME<SwitchResBase,0,RecyclRate+SubstitutionRate)
doc ResourceRegenRate = regeneration rate
unit ResourceRegenRate = resource units/year
aux AvrResourceAvailability = DELAYINF(ResourceAvailability,SmoothingTime,1)
aux AvrUseRate = DELAYINF(NatResouUseRate,AvrTime,1,2.82625E8)
aux DelayedRecFract = DELAYINF(RecyclingFraction,TechDelay,1)
doc DelayedRecFract = delayed recycling fraction
unit DelayedRecFract = dimensionless
aux DelayedResUseEfficiency = DELAYINF(RelativeUseEfficiency,TechDelay,1)
doc DelayedResUseEfficiency = delayed resource use efficiency multiplier
unit DelayedResUseEfficiency = dimensionless
aux DesiredResource = AvrUseRate*ResCoverageTime
doc DesiredResource = resources required to meet demands for indicated coverage time
unit DesiredResource = resource units
aux FractCapitalAllocObtainResources = GRAPH(NatResFracRemaining,0.00,0.10,
  [1,0.9,0.7,0.5,0.2,0.1,0.05,0.05,0.05"Min:0;Max:1"])
doc FractCapitalAllocObtainResources = fraction of capital allocated to obtaining resources
unit FractCapitalAllocObtainResources = dimensionless
aux FrcResUseByRecl = GRAPH(RecyclingFraction,0,0.1,
  [0,0.026,0.057,0.109,0.17,0.248,0.348,0.504,0.684"Min:0;Max:0.7"])
doc FrcResUseByRecl = fraction of resources consumed by recycling
unit FrcResUseByRecl = dimensionless
aux IndicatedPriceLevel = IF(TIME<SwitchResPolicy,ResAvailaPriceMultplr*
  PriceLevel1970,ResAvailaPriceMultplr*PriceLevel1970*TaxMultiplr)
doc IndicatedPriceLevel = indicated resource price level
unit IndicatedPriceLevel = dimensionless
aux NatResFracRemaining = NaturalResources/NatResInitial
aux PercapitaResUseMultplr = GRAPH(IndusOutputPC,0.00,200.00,
  [0,0.85,2.6,4.4,5.4,6.2,6.8,7,7"Min:0;Max:7"])
doc PercapitaResUseMultplr = per capita resource use multiplier
unit PercapitaResUseMultplr = dimensionless
aux RecyclingFraction =GRAPH(ResourcePriceLevel,0.5,0.25,[0,0.016,0.05,
  0.087,0.137,0.19,0.247,0.304,0.3 45,0.379,0.391"Min:0;Max:0.4"])
doc RecyclingFraction = recycling fraction

unit RecyclingFraction = dimensionless
aux RecyclRate = AvrUseRate*DelayedRecFract
doc RecyclRate = recycling rate
unit RecyclRate = resource units/year
aux RegenerationTime = ResGenTimeMultiplier*NormalResgenTime
doc RegenerationTime = regeneration time for the current resource basket
unit RegenerationTime = year
aux RelativeUseEfficiency = GRAPH(ResourcePriceLevel,0.5,0.25,
 [0.56,0.79,1,1.19,1.33,1.46,1.57,1.69,1.8,1.92,2"Min:0.25;Max:2"])
aux ResAvailaPriceMultplr = GRAPH(AvrResourceAvailability,0,0.125,
 [2,1.69,1.48,1.37,1.27,1.18,1.11,1.05,1,0.95,0.91,0.88,0.85"Min:0.75;Max:2"])
doc ResAvailaPriceMultplr = multiplier for resource price from resource   availability
unit ResAvailaPriceMultplr = dimensionless
aux ResGenTimeMultiplier = GRAPH(ResourcePriceLevel,0,0.5,
 [2,1.39,1,0.69,0.5,0.42,0.36,0.31,0.28,0.26,0.25"Min:0;Max:2"])
aux ResouceStockRatio = NaturalResources/NatRes1970
doc ResouceStockRatio = ratio of current stock of natural resources and 1970's stock
unit ResouceStockRatio = dimensionless
aux ResourceAvailability = NaturalResources/DesiredResource
aux ResUsedByRecycl = FrcResUseByRecl*RecyclRate
doc ResUsedByRecycl = resource consumed by recycling process
unit ResUsedByRecycl = resource unit/year
aux SeveranceTax = GRAPH(AvrResourceAvailability,0,0.125,
 [294,171,90,53,34,20,9,3,0"Min:0;Max:300"])
doc SeveranceTax = severance tax (percentage of price)
unit SeveranceTax = dimensionless
aux SubstitutionRate = UnusableNatResource/RegenerationTime
doc SubstitutionRate = substitution rate
unit SubstitutionRate = resource units/year
aux TaxMultiplr = SeveranceTax/100+1
doc TaxMultiplr = price multiplier from severance tax
unit TaxMultiplr = dimensionless
const AvrTime = 5
const NatRes1970 = 8.02E11
doc NatRes1970 = natural resources stock in the year 1970
unit NatRes1970 = natural resource units
const NatResInitial = 8.5e11
const NatResUseFrc = 1
doc NatResUseFrc = natural resource use factor
unit NatResUseFrc = dimensionless
const NormalResgenTime = 8000
doc NormalResgenTime = normal regeneration time for a mix of resource basket
unit NormalResgenTime = years
const PriceLevel1970 = 1
doc PriceLevel1970 = resource price level in the year 1970
unit PriceLevel1970 = dimensionless
const ResCoverageTime = 250
doc ResCoverageTime = resources coverage time
unit ResCoverageTime = year
const SmoothingTime = 10
doc SmoothingTime = smoothing time for resource availability
unit SmoothingTime = years
const SwitchResBase = 1900
doc SwitchResBase = switch for price mechanism in the resources sector
unit SwitchResBase = dimensionless
const SwitchResPolicy = 1975

const TechDelay = 5
doc TechDelay = technology delay
unit TechDelay = year
const TimeChngPrice = 1
doc TimeChngPrice = time for changing resource price
unit TimeChngPrice = years

Appendix B
Equations for revised land regeneration process

init ArableLand = .9E9
flow ArableLand = -dt*(LandErosionRate)+dt*(RehabRate)
doc ArableLand = arable land
init Eroded_land = 100
flow Eroded_land = +dt*(LandErosionRate)-dt*(RehabRate)
aux LandErosionRate = ArableLand/AveLifeLand
doc LandErosionRate = land erosion rate
aux RehabRate = IF(TIME<sw_agriBase,0,Eroded_land/ErodedLandRegnTime)
aux AveLifeLand = AveLifeLandNorml*LandLifeMultplrFromYield
doc AveLifeLand = average life of land
aux ErodedLandFraction = Eroded_land/ArableLand
aux ErodedLandRegnTime = IF(TIME<SW_AgriPolicy,ErodedLandRegTimeNormal,
   ErodedLandRegTimeNormal/LnadRegenerationMultiplier)
aux LnadRegenerationMultiplier = GRAPH(ErodedLandFraction,0,0.05,
   [1,1.16,1.39,1.65,2.04,2.54,3.3,4.04,4.56,4.84,4.98"Min:1;Max:5"])
const ErodedLandRegTimeNormal = 1000
const sw_agriBase = 1900
const SW_AgriPolicy = 1975

Appendix C
Equations for population planning policy

aux DCFS1 = (DesiredComFamilySizeNr*FamilyResponseToSocialNorms
   *SocialFamilySizeNorm)
doc DCFS1 = desired completed family size (before policy intervention)
aux DesiredComplFamilySize = DELAYINF(IndicatedFamilySize,
   AdjustDelay,1,DCFS1)
aux IncomeMultiplier = GRAPH(IndusOutputPC/IOPC1970,1,0.125,
   [1,0.972,0.938,0.904,0.878,0.864,0.856,0.853,0.85"Min:0.85;Max:1"])
doc IncomeMultiplier = family size multiplier from industrial output per capita
aux IndicatedFamilySize = IF(TIME<SwtchPopulatn,DCFS1,
   IncomeMultiplier*ServiceMultiplier*DCFS1970)
doc IndicatedFamilySize = indicated family size
aux IndusOutputPC = IndustrialOutput/Population
doc IndusOutputPC = industrial output per capita
aux ServiceMultiplier = GRAPH(SocialServiceOutputPC/SSPC1970,1,0.25,
   [1,0.991,0.976,0.942,0.888,0.808,0.754,0.722,0.72"Min:0.7;Max:1"])
doc ServiceMultiplier = family size multiplier from services
aux SocialServiceOutputPC = SerOutputPerCapita- HealthServiceAllocatedPerCapita-
   FertControlAllocPerCapita
doc SocialServiceOutputPC = social service output per capita
const AdjustDelay = 5

const DCFS1970 = 3.31
doc DCFS1970 = Desired completed family size (as in World3) in 1970
const IOPC1970 = 218
doc IOPC1970 = Industrial output per capita in 1970
const SSPC1970 = 273
doc SSPC1970 = Social service per capita in 1970
const SwtchPopulatn = 1975

Appendix D
Equations for pollution reduction policy

aux DelayedRedFraction = DELAYINF(PollGenRedFrac,TimeDelay,1)
doc DelayedRedFraction = delayed pollution generation reduction fraction
aux PerPoll_Index = PersistentPollution/PerPoll_In1970
doc PerPoll_Index = persistent pollution index
aux PerPollGenFraction = IF(TIME<SwtPolltn,1,DelayedRedFraction)
doc PerPollGenFraction = persistent pollution generation fraction
aux PollGenRedFrac = GRAPH(PerPoll_Index,0,0.5,
  [1,1,0.99,0.96,0.9,0.83,0.73,0.51,0.39,0.33,0.32,0.31,0.3"Min:0;Max:1"])
doc PollGenRedFrac = pollution generation reduction fraction due to policy reduction
  policies
const SwtPolltn = 1975
const TimeDelay = 5

Appendix E
Equations for industrial output stabilization policy

aux FIOAS = DELAYINF(IndicatedFIOAS,5,1)
aux FIOASmultiplr = GRAPH(IOPCratio,0,0.25,
  [0.05,0.058,0.064,0.08,0.12,0.234,0.364,0.451,0.496"Min:0.05;Max:0.5"])
aux FIOASnormal = GRAPH(SerOutputPerCapita/IndicatedSerOutputPC,0.00,0.50,
  [0.3,0.2,0.1,0.05,0,0,0,0,0"Min:0;Max:0.4"])
doc FIOASnormal = fraction of industrial output allocated to service
aux IndicatedFIOAS = IF(TIME<SwtchCapitlSer,FIOASnormal,FIOASmultiplr)
aux IndusOutputPC = IndustrialOutput/Population
doc IndusOutputPC = industrial output per capita
aux IOPCD = ResMultpIOPCD*PollMultpIOPCD*IndustrialOutputPercapitaNormal
doc IOPCD = industrial output per capita desired
aux IOPCratio = IndusOutputPC/IOPCD
aux NatResFracRemaing = NaturalResources/NatResInitial
aux PerPoll_Index = PersistentPollution/PerPoll_In1970
doc PerPoll_Index = persistent pollution index
aux PollMultpIOPCD = GRAPH(TIME,0,0.5,
  [1,0.991,0.97,0.941,0.893,0.819,0.757,0.721,0.7"Min:0.7;Max:1"])
doc PollMultpIOPCD = multiplier for industrial output per capita desired from   pollution
  index
aux ResMultpIOPCD = GRAPH(NatResFracRemaing,0,0.1,
  [0.307,0.333,0.383,0.446,0.549,0.718,0.843,0.911,0.969,0.988,1"Min:0.3;Max:1"])
doc ResMultpIOPCD = industrial output per capita desired
const IndustrialOutputPercapitaNormal = 600
const SwtchCapitlSer = 1975

6 Technological development in a dual economy: alternative policy levers for economic development[*]

Khalid Saeed and Ponthep Prankprakma

Abstract

Although technological development is widely recognized as a function of human ingenuity and innovation and seen by many development scientists as an important means for achieving economic development, its actual use as a policy lever remains largely underutilized, since the process of its implementation is unclear. This paper attempts to identify operational instruments for supporting technological development so it can be incorporated easily into the development plans. A system dynamics model of a dual economic system incorporating also the behavioral responses of the economic actors to competition and their ability to innovate is developed. This model is used as an experimental apparatus to search for appropriate technological development policies to support economic growth and change income distribution. Policies to promote competition among the monopolistic formal firms while simultaneously providing positive assistance to the competitive informal firms appear to offer promising alternatives to the traditional fiscal policy levers mainly affecting prices and factor costs.

[*] Reprinted from World Development, 25(5), Saeed, K. and Prankprakma, P., Technological Development in a Dual Economy: Alternative Policy Levers for Economic Development, World Development, pp. 695-712, 1997, with kind permission from Elsevier Science Ltd., The Boulevard, Langford Lane, Kidlington OX5 1GB, UK.

157

Introduction

Technological Development has been established as a significant source of economic growth in the analyses concerning the developed countries [Abramovitz 1956, Solow 1957, Denison 1962, Griliches 1963]. Seen as a function of human ingenuity, innovation and entrepreneurship, it is also often seen as powerful means for effecting economic development by the scholars, yet it is seldom explicitly incorporated into the planning policies of the developing countries [Schultz 1979, Hirschman 1958, 1970]. The potential of technological development as a policy lever is often underutilized because the operational means for its implementation are not clear. At the same time, the development planners have come to view technological growth mainly as a function of transfer rather than a process of indigenous development, hence few attempts are made to search for an operational means to promote technological development, even though its efficacy is widely recognized.

Using a formal system dynamics model of a dual economic system also incorporating mechanisms of technological development, this paper explores the possibility of commissioning technology development instruments for effecting economic growth and influencing income distribution. Technical details of the model, including a machine readable listing, for replicating the experiments discussed in this paper and for conducting further experimentation, are available from the authors on request.

The formal model offers an opportunity to experiment with the various technology policies proposed and implemented in the past and to understand their performance under laboratory conditions. This experimentation helps to explain the variability of performance of the technology policy experienced in the past while also pointing toward the critical elements for a successful policy framework. Policy guidelines are outlined for an effective technology-based intervention.

Observed economic and technology patterns

The studies on sources of economic growth conducted in the developed countries show that growth from technological change is significant. For the US economy, the works of Abramovitz (1956) Solow (1957) Denison (1962) Griliches (1963) although different in many ways with respect to time-period, coverage and basic methodology, concur that a large portion of the long-term growth in per capita output is accounted for not by an increasing quantity of capital and labor inputs, but by the rise in productivity attributed to technological change. This broad conclusion was further refined by Denison (1985) who unpacked technological change into a number of components. Denison estimated that only a quarter of the increase in output could be attributed to increased labor input of constant educational level, while another 16 percent was credited to the increased educational qualifications of the average worker. The growth of capital accounted for only 12 percent of the growth of output, which confirmed a similar earlier finding by Solow (1957) 11 percent came from improved allocation of resources, another 11 percent from economies of scale and a hefty 34 percent from the growth of knowledge or technological development in a narrow sense. Although these conclusions should have called for the economic development theories to consider technological development carefully as a policy lever, it has found limited use to date. On the contrary, development planning in the developing countries has mainly sought to transfer technology from the developed countries rather than nurture its indigenous development. A few limited attempts have been made to create a climate conducive to indigenous technological growth and self-reliance, often through building science and technology parks, developing educational and training institutions, building industrial research organizations and providing financial support for the private sector research and development projects, imitating largely similar efforts in the industrialized countries [Choi 1986, 1984, 1989, Chatterji 1990, Subramanian 1987, Celso 1989]. A large variability has been experienced in the performance of such initiatives.

There exist basic differences in the structure of the economies of the developed and the developing countries which makes it difficult to directly transfer strategic instruments or achieve comparable performance when turn-key transfers of technology are made. Thus, policy instruments which work well in the developed countries may not be very effective when implemented in the developing countries. The economic structure of the developing countries is characterized by the side by side existence of two equally significant subeconomies which emerged after organized development effort was undertaken. These include a profit maximizing formal sector and a consumption maximizing informal sector. This classification has been referred to variously in the literature, for example as capitalist and worker sectors [Pasinetti 1989, Dalziel 1991, Fazi and Salvadori 1985], oligopolist and peripheral firms [Gordon 1972, Riech, et al 1973], capitalist and subsistence sectors [Lewis 1954], and modern and traditional subeconomies [Fie and Ranis 1966].

Table 6.1 shows the proportions of the self-employed and wage workers in selected Asian countries. Malaysia lies on one end of the spectrum in this sample in having a predominantly wage employed workforce (62.7%) while Pakistan is on the other end where the majority of the workforce is self-employed (73.4%). For the remaining countries in the sample, the size of the two sectors seems to be comparable [ILO 1990]. It is also widely known that the level of sophistication of technology, discerned in terms of productivity and capital intensity, is much higher in large capitalist firms offering wage employment than in small entrepreneurial firms with self-employed workers, with the former firms also having a higher labor productivity [Lewis 1954, Boeke 1953]. Although the factor proportions as well as the productivity of labor and the capital worker ratio in the two production modes vary from country to country, there appear many similarities in the overall pattern. These similarities manifest in the side by side existence of both production modes with a relatively low productivity in the self-employed sector and a relatively high capital worker ratio in the formal sector.

Table 6.1
Distribution of workers between formal and self-employed sectors in selected Asian countries

Country	Self-employed workers		Wage workers		Total Workers
	(Millions)	(%)	(Millions)	(%)	(Millions)
Bangladesh	17.3	56.7	13.2	43.3	30.5
Korea	7.2	42.6	9.7	57.4	16.9
Malaysia	2.2	37.3	3.7	62.7	5.9
Pakistan	19.9	73.4	7.2	26.6	27.1
Philippines	11.6	54.2	9.8	45.8	21.4
Sri Lanka	2.2	42.3	3.0	57.7	5.2

(Source: ILO 1990)

Prior to the commencement of the economic development effort, the developing country economies were largely closed, with very little inflow of technological information from the developed countries. The production technology was unsophisticated irrespective of the type of firm, with high labor intensity and low productivity. Most production was carried out in small artisan units, both for producing agricultural commodities and other consumer goods. These artisan units often operated in a feudalist environment with a dichotomy between ownership and workership. The mechanism of renting allowed the artisan firms to have access to the absentee-owned land and production capital [Lipton 1977, Samuelson and Nordhaus 1985, Hunt 1989]. These economies opened with respect to trade and capital flows as well as technological information when organized economic development effort was undertaken. Transfer of modern production methods from the industrialized countries allowed the owners of the capital to shift from renting to a formal mode of production, which created large firms. The modern technology used in large firms also made their production more efficient than the small firms, thus allowing them to displace the later. This emergence of large firms is often seen as the expanding capitalist nucleus in the literature on economic development that has led to the creation of the dual economies now pervasive in the

160

developing countries [Lewis 1954, Hunt 1989].

The first system dynamics model incorporating such a classification was proposed by Saeed (1980) to explain the income distribution and wage determination of a rural economy which he extended later to explain the efficacy of development policies used to alleviate poverty and hunger [Saeed 1987], and also to explaining the behavior of the capitalist systems operating under different social and legal norms [Saeed 1988], but without considering the possibility of endogenous technological growth. Saeed found that a fiscal instrument to penalize unearned income, such as taxing rent income, was critical to changing income distribution when technological level was exogenously defined. He also showed that the presence of a technological differential between the formal and self-employed production modes would dilute the effectiveness of the penalty on unearned income [Saeed 1994]. The concept of interaction between technological development and the socio-economic system has appeared more recently as an evolutionary theory of technological change [Freeman 1990, Dosi 1988, Nelson 1987]. This creates an opportunity to further extend Saeed's model to cover this interaction and explore technology-related instruments as alternative levers for economic development, which is attempted in this paper.

Experimentation with the extended model shows that instruments to foster indigenous technological growth are a promising alternative to the traditional development policies which have focused on growth of capital and importation of technologies. However, in a dual economic system, promoting competition among the monopolistic formal firms simultaneously with providing positive assistance to the competitive informal firms is critical to the success of any technology development effort in terms of meeting both growth and equity goals effectively.

A system dynamics model of technological development in a dual economy

The information structure of the proposed model is adapted from a model of wage determination and income distribution developed by Saeed (1980) which he used for experimental evaluation of past and exploratory development policies [Saeed 1987, 1988, 1894]. Saeed's original model draws on neo-classical economics to construct a basic structure for growth and market clearing, and modifies it further by relaxing its simplifying assumptions about aggregation of sub-economies, saving and investment behavior, and wage determination. His model subsumes the concept of economic dualism first recognized by Boeke (1953) and developed further by Lewis (1954) Sen (1966) Bardhan (1973) and others to represent the multiple subeconomies co-existing in the developing countries. The model with its modified assumptions also embodies the behavioral relations concerning saving, consumption, investment, wage determination and disbursement of income recognized in the pioneering works of Kaldor (1956) Kalecki (1965) Wientraub (1956) and Robinson (1978) and developed further by Eichner (1979) Kregel (1973) Davidson (1972) and Marglin (1984).

The model proposed in this study further relaxes the assumption of absence of technological growth used by Saeed. Technological growth in the modified model occurs through investment in technological development motivated by competition between the two production sectors and facilitated by respective financial abilities. The modified model also formalizes the renting process through the introduction of a formal renting sector representing the economy of absentee owners receiving income from renting out capital [Prankprakma 1993]. An overview of this model is shown in Figure 6.1.

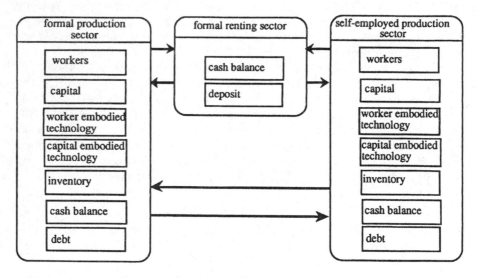

Figure 6.1   An overview of the model

The model incorporates following behavioral assumptions governing the roles of its actors:

Both formal and self-employed production sectors in the model carry out production using capital, workers, technology embodied in capital and technology embodied in workers. Therefore, the capacity of a production sector is determined not only by the capital and labor it employs but also by the level of technology it is able to carry. Capital investment is driven by profitability which is given by the marginal revenue product of capital and the interest rate, as well as by financial capability which is determined by liquidity [McKinnon 1973, Barro 1901] Workers can be wage- or self-employed. Wage workers are hired depending on the marginal revenue product of workers and the average wage rate. Workers unable to find wage employment are absorbed in the self-employed production sector. The average wage rate is set not according to the average marginal revenue product of workers as postulated in the equilibrium models of economic growth, but according to the bargaining power of the workers which depends on the opportunity cost of a worker to leave self-employment, given by the average consumption expenditure per worker [Sraffa 1960, Sen 1966].

Technology embodied in capital is the integration of the technology embodied in each unit of capital employed by a production sector. The technological level of capital of a production sector is calculated by the total amount of technology embodied in its capital divided by the capital. Technology embodied in workers is calculated similarly for each sector. When a worker moves from one sector to the other, the worker embodied technology is concomitantly transferred. Technology embodied in capital and workers can be increased through innovation and learning rates, which are determined by the technological capabilities of the respective sectors and their investment in technology [Dosi 1988, Mansfield 1971]. The pressure to invest in technology is determined by market competition. A firm must innovate to improve its productivity to function in a competitive market. However, when a firm has a monopoly, it does not have to innovate since its profitability is already high [Kamien and Schwartz 1982, Auerbach 1988]. The other factor which greatly affects the investment in technology is the production sector's financial muscle. A high liquidity makes a production enterprise capable of taking the risk involved in investment in technology [Dosi 1988]. The literature on diffusion of innovation also suggests that the size of investment for the adoption of innovations affects the rate at which it diffuses [Mansfield 1971]. This implicitly means that a production enterprise may not be able to adopt an innovation because it does not have enough cash to invest in technology.

Cash balance determines the liquidity of a sector. A shortage in the cash balance of a sector can defer the investment expenditures it might be warranted to make on the basis of economic criteria. Cash balance of each production sector is increased by its revenue and borrowings and decreased by investment, debt payments and consumption of savings. The output of each production sector, determined by the demand and the production capacity, goes to its inventory from which sales are made. The price of output of a production sector depends on goods availability in the economy as well as the quality of the sector's output, which is determined by the technology used in its production [Betz 1987]. All workers, whether self- or wage- employed are assumed to maximize their consumption. On the other hand, the capitalists are assumed to maximize profit [Sen 1966, Averitt 1968, Applebaum, 1979]. In maximizing profit a capitalist can

163

transfer his assets to production or renting activities.

All types of renting are interpreted in the model into equivalent financial terms through borrowing and deposit activities carried out through an invisible bank. The production sectors have debt accounts at the bank while the formal renting sector has a deposit account. Cash balance of the bank is increased by the deposit rate and interest income and decreased by consumption expenditure and withdrawal rate. The renting capitalists can put their excess cash into deposit or can withdraw their deposit when they are short of cash. The bank balances these accounts by setting the interest rate. The bank always balances the debts and deposits and makes no charges, i.e. the total interest payments received from the borrowers are transferred in whole to the depositors. It should be recognized that the model is not concerned with the relationship between the banking system and the creation of money, but rather tracks the net deposits and borrowings of each sector in the economy.

The model incorporating above behavioral relationships was programmed in Vensim software[1] on a 386 type personal computer. The mathematical structure of the model appears in the Appendix. Many simulation experiments were designed and carried out to understand model behavior and its implications for technology policy. Key experiments and the logic of the inferences made from them are discussed in the following sections of this paper.

Model behavior and the history of technological performance of developing countries

The historical analysis of the model behavior consists of two parts. The first part explains the occurrence of feudalism, which prevailed in the history of most developing countries when modern technologies were not available. In the second part, the model is used to replicate the behavior of the present-day technological and economic systems this study is concerned with.

a) Economy with no modern technology: the occurrence of feudalism

Before modern technologies became available to the developing countries, their economies were predominantly feudalist with most of the resources owned by a small number of capitalists. Most production was carried out by self-employed workers who had to rent resources from the capitalists. The distribution of income in such economies was highly unequal. In order to see how the model can generate such economic conditions, the following

---

[1] Available from Ventana Systems, Inc., 149 Waverly Street, Belmont MA 02178, USA.

164

simulation experiment was set up.

A neoclassical equilibrium was created in the model with the assumptions that the economy is fixed and without technological differentiation between the two sectors, wage rate is determined by the marginal revenue product of workers, renting is not allowed so that the initial values of deposit and debt are zero. This equilibrium also requires that the marginal revenue products of capital and worker be the same in the two production sectors and equal to their corresponding factor costs. Further, the total demand for production of output must equal the production capacity of the economy and all revenues and expenditures should be in balance. As an arbitrary initial condition, the two production sectors were allowed to have an equal share in the production of the economy. The equilibrium of the model was disturbed by modifying the wage and rent assumptions at year 5. The wage rate was switched to be determined by the average consumption expenditure per worker and renting was allowed. The results of the simulation with these modifications are shown in Figure 6.2. After the wage and rent assumptions are modified, the formal production sector gradually shrinks in size while the formal renting sector expands. In the final equilibrium, all production of the economy is carried out by the self-employed using rented resources.

Figure 6.3 shows the feedback processes arising out of the information relationships of the model that create above behavior. Since average consumption expenditure of workers includes entitlements both from value additions by labor and capital, a wage based on it exceeds the marginal revenue product of workers in the formal production sector when wage and rent assumptions are modified. This causes a decrease in the profitability of workers in this sector, prompting it to lay off workers, who are accommodated in the self-employed production sector.

However, as the profitability of production activity decreases due to the decrease in the rate of return in the formal production mode, the profitability of renting activity increases in the capitalist sector since the increase in the workforce of the self-employed sector generates an increasing demand for renting resources, this also causing an increase in the interest rate. Therefore, the capitalists transfer their investment from production activity to renting activity, which appears in the model as deposits available for lending.

Since an increase in production caused by the expanding self-employed workforce inflates the marginal revenue product of capital, the need for capital in the self-employed sector rises, which necessitates borrowing as the cash resources of this sector are limited. Thus, the debt of the self-employed sector increases.

These spiraling actions allow gradual adjustment of workers, capital and debt of the two production sectors, and the deposit of the formal renting sector. In the long run, the formal production mode dies out. However, since renting is allowed, the production capitalists in the formal production

165

sector transfer all their assets to the renting activity.

From the above explanation it can be seen that feudalism emerges due to the distortion in the labor market arising from the way the wage rate is determined by the average consumption expenditure per worker, the requirement of self-finance for investment and the availability of renting activity which creates a profitable alternative investment portfolio for the capitalist sector, when production activity becomes unprofitable.

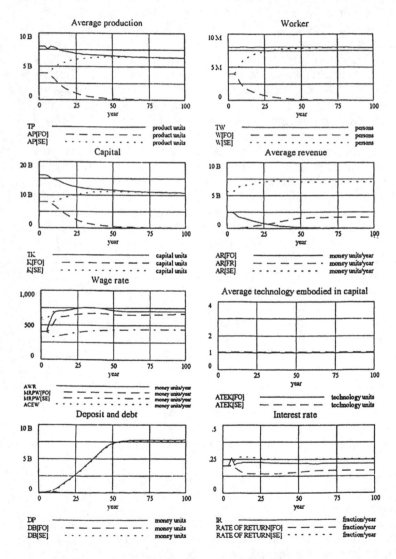

Figure 6.2   Occurrence of feudalism

166

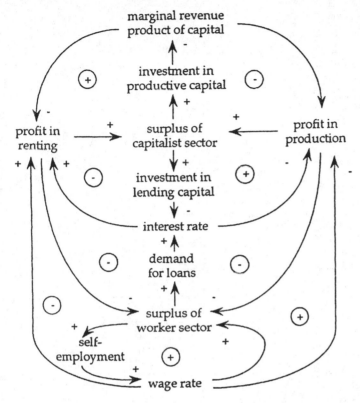

Figure 6.3   **Feedback processes in the information relationships of the model creating feudalism**

b) Economy with modern technology: the appearance of dualism

In this experiment the model is used to replicate the development of the dual technological and economic systems widely experienced in the developing countries after economic development effort began. The simulation of the base case is generated by stepping up the ambient level of technology in the formal production sector while also allowing the population to grow after the end conditions of the simulation of Figure 6.2 have been reached, and simulating further. The formal production sector is also assumed to have a higher capability to innovate than the self-employed sector on account of its better resource position. These changes represent introduction of modern technologies for the formal production mode. All other parameters and behavioral relationships remain unchanged. The results of this simulation are shown in Figure 6.4.

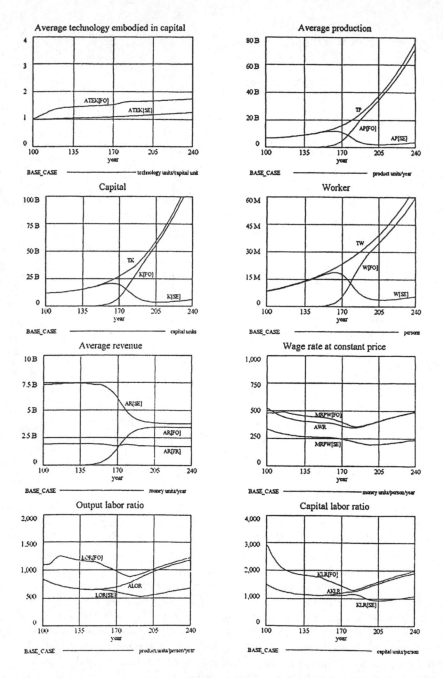

Figure 6.4   **The emergence of a dual economy: the base case**

168

The total output of the economy rises, although the average technology embodied in capital stagnates in both production sectors. Also, the relative size of the formal production sector expands while that of the self-employed sector is reduced. The availability of modern technology offers an opportunity to both sectors to improve their productivity. The formal production sector, which has a high pressure to innovate due to the prevailing unprofitability, affects an increase in the average technology embodied in its capital and also in its workers. The self-employed production sector also attempts to upgrade its technology but is limited both by its ambient poor technological capability and financial constraints.

Figure 6.5 shows the information relationships governing technological development in the two sectors. For the formal production sector, the increase in the average technology embodied in the capital causes an increase in both the marginal revenue product of workers and capital, which causes its size to expand. The increase in the technology of the formal production sector also induces an increase in the profitability of the production activity compared to the renting activity so the capitalists in the formal renting sector tend to transfer more resources to invest in the formal production mode.

For the self-employed production sector, the rate of increase in the average technology embodied in capital is slow compared to the formal production sector. Therefore, its production efficiency and quality are also low. The marginal revenue products of workers and capital in this sector decrease, which causes its size to decline, also further decreasing its liquidity. The decrease in the liquidity cannot be checked by borrowing since the size of the available collateral also declines, which suppresses its investment in technology and hence its innovation rate. Thus, the average technology embodied in the capital of the self-employed sector will further lag behind that of the formal production sector.

The decrease in the production output of the self-employed also decreases the income share of the workers which reduces the average consumption per worker. This suppresses wage rate also in the formal sector.

Both the decrease in the wage rate and the increase in the average technology embodied in the capital of the formal production sector fuel expansion in the production of the formal sector. The spiraling action of these changes allows gradual adjustment of the workers, the capital, the debt of the two production sectors and the deposit of the formal renting sector in a way that the formal production mode expands, while the self-employed mode declines. However, as the profitability in the formal production sector rises, the pressure to innovate declines and the investment in technology is neglected. In the self-employed sector the investment in technology is low any way due to the constraint from its liquidity position. Hence, the aggregate technological capability is also restricted.

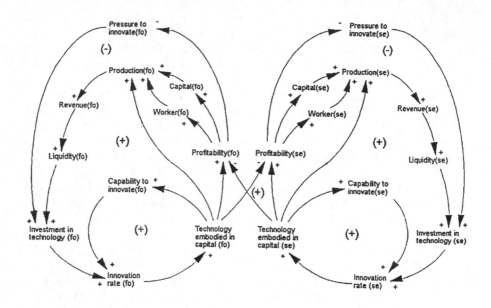

Figure 6.5   **Information relationships governing technological development in the two sectors**

To assure that the qualitative patterns of behavior generated by the model are independent of its numerical parameters and the slopes of the behavioral relationships used in it, a sensitivity analysis was carried out. Figure 6.6 shows the aggregate patterns of behavior assembled for the various sensitivity runs indicating that the qualitative patterns created are relatively independent of the parameter changes.

The model creates patterns representing the behavior of the technological and economic systems in most developing countries. Before modern technology became available, the developing country economies were dominated by feudalism. Only after modern technology became available could the capitalist production mode expand displacing artisan production [Lipton 1977, Samuelson and Nordhaus 1985]. In the dual economies that subsequently emerged, the technologies used in the formal production sector were generally more sophisticated than those used in the self-employed production. The growth of the economy, which occurred from both capital accumulation and increase in productivity from using sophisticated technologies has not increased the consumption level for the majority of the people. The real average wage rate has only slightly increased, and in some cases, has even decreased [Morawetz, 1977, Lipton 1977].

Furthermore, the rate of improvement of the technology used in production by small entrepreneurs remains low due to the limits imposed by their ambient technological capability and liquidity [Technonet Asia 1983, Sharma 1979, Uddin 1989, Bhatt 1988]. The large firms have no constraints on their liquidity while they also enjoy higher technological capability compared with the self-employed. However, their innovation rate, remains low because there is little incentive for them to invest in technology improvement due to a lack of competition in a highly monopolistic market [Auerbach 1988, Hunt 1989].

The policies proposed to address technological and economic stagnation in the developing countries fall into three broad categories: 1) Building institutions and infrastructure to upgrade technological ability of production units; 2) Mobilizing funds for technology-related investments; and 3) Creating indirect incentives for upgrading technology in the production units [Choi 1984, 1986, 1989, Chatterji 1990, Celso 1989]. These policies have often not differentiated between the two production sectors suggested in the model, which could be one of the reasons why their performance is varied. The experiments in this sections of the paper attempt to understand the variability of the performance of these policies, also attempting to identify guidelines for an effective technological development plan that should serve as an alternative to the traditional direct and indirect instruments for economic development.

The efficacy of each tested policy is evaluated by comparing its results with the base case in Figure 6.2. The criteria for this comparison are the output labor ratio, the average production, the average revenue share of the self-employed production sector, and the average wage rate at constant prices compared at the end of the simulation. The first two criteria represent growth in technology and production of the overall economy, the remaining two indicate how evenly the growth is distributed. Table 2 summarizes the results of the experimentation.

Policy runs 1 and 2, the policies to upgrade technological capability of the formal and self-employed production sectors, represent strategies for human resources development often sought through technical education, training and technological infrastructure development attempted through private and public sector institution building for assisting production units in adopting sophisticated technologies. These policies are simulated by stepping up the normal fractional innovation rate and the normal fractional worker learning rate in the respective production sector after the system has settled into a dual mode.

171

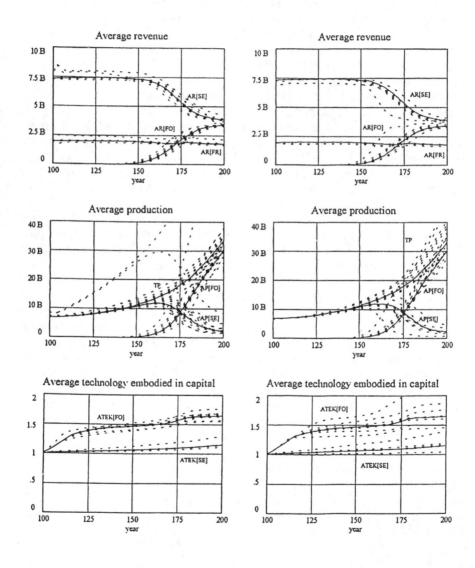

Figure 6.6 **Sensitivity of model behavior to the changes in parameters**

Technology policy as an alternative lever for economic development

Policy runs 3 and 4, the policies for mobilizing funds for technology-related investments, translate into providing loans for technological investment through special banks and financial institutions and mobilizing venture capital. This policy is simulated in the model by relaxing liquidity constraints on technological investments of the respective production sectors.

Policy runs 5 and 6, the policies to increase pressure on the two production sectors to improve technology, represent measures to promote market competition. In practice, this is accomplished by facilitating market entry through investment promotion in certain industries, providing market information to the consumers and educating consumers on product specification. These policies can increase the pressure on the production sectors to improve their technology, for which they must increase their investment in technological activities. This policy is simulated in the model by increasing the pressure to innovate and the pressure on worker learning rate of each production sector.

Policy runs 7, 8 and 9, the policies to levy taxes, represent fiscal instruments found critical to changing income distribution in Saeed (1988). These include taxation of rent income, with and without applying the collection to the worker-run activities. The rent income tax policy is simulated in the model by deducting a tax equal to 20 % of the rent income from the revenue of the formal renting sector, which reduces the rate of return on renting activity.

Policy run 10 combines the policy to tax rent income with the financing of the technological investment and upgrading technological capability of the self-employed production sector. Finally, policy run 11 simulates the financing of the technological investment and upgrading technological capability of the self-employed production sector through an income rather than a rent tax in an effort to explore the efficacy of selective technology development policy without penalizing unearned income.

The figures in Table 2 show the results of the above policy runs compared at the end of each simulation (at time 240) with the base run of Figure 6.2. Many of the policies experimented with do not cause much improvement by the defined criteria when compared to the base case. The ineffective policies include attempts to upgrade technological capability of either production sector (1 and 2) mobilization of funds for technology-related investment for the formal production sector (3) increasing inducement for the self-employed production sector to improve technology (6) taxing rent income (7) and taxing rent income and transferring it to the self-employed (8).

173

Table 6.2
Policy runs compared to the base case

Policy run	Output labor ratio units/person/year (fo)	(se)	Capital labor ratio units/person (fo)	(se)	Self-employed workers	Wage rate	Average production billion units/year (fo)	(se)	(Total)	Worker income share
Base case	1.00	1.00	1.00	1.00	1.00	1.00	1.00	1.0	1.00	1.00
1. Upgrading technological capability of formal production sector	1.08	0.97	1.06	0.95	0.88	1.07	1.09	0.78	1.08	0.98
2. Upgrading technological capability of self-employed production sector	1.06	1.31	1.05	1.30	1.88	1.05	0.98	2.28	1.04	1.05
3. Mobilizing fund for technology related investment of formal production sector	1.01	0.99	1.01	0.99	1.00	1.00	1.01	0.97	1.01	.98
4. Mobilizing fund for technology related investment of self-employed production sector	1.55	2.19	1.45	2.19	4.00	1.53	1.13	8.39	1.48	1.20
5. Increase pressure to improve technology of formal production sector	3.37	0.57	2.73	0.55	0.38	3.16	3.47	0.22	3.32	0.98
6. Increase pressure to improve technology of self-employed production sector	1.00	1.00	1.00	1.00	1.00	0.99	1.00	1.00	1.00	1.00
7. Taxing rent income	1.08	0.95	1.08	0.94	0.88	1.08	1.10	2.78	1.08	1.02
8. Taxing rent income and giving the tax collected to the workers	1.29	1.00	1.29	0.97	2.75	1.30	1.10	2.64	1.17	1.12
9. Taxing rent income and financing the technological investment of the self-employed production sector	1.59	2.17	1.50	2.17	3.88	1.61	1.16	8.14	1.50	1.21
10. Combination of policies: Taxing rent income and financing the technological investment of the self-employed production sector and increasing the technological capability of the sector	4.26	6.25	3.81	5.75	9.50	4.74	1.10	55.0	3.69	1.67
11. Combination of policies: Taxing all income and financing the technological investment of the self-employed production sector and increasing the technological capability of the sector	3.93	5.97	3.48	5.52	10.8	4.06	0.67	53.3	3.44	1.71

The comparison of Table 2 shows that the output labor ratio, the average production, the worker income share, and the wage rate are not improved much in these cases except in policy run (8) that creates some rise in the wage rate and in the income share of the workers, although with a stagnating output.

Attempts to increase the technological ability (1 and 2) are defeated for the formal production sector by its lack of competitiveness and for the self-employed sector due to its financial constraints. Since, liquidity is not a constraint for the formal sector, financial assistance for its technological activity (3) does not accomplish much. Likewise, since self-employed lack finance rather than motivation to fuel technological activity, inducing them further to invest in technology (6) is pointless. Taxing rent income appeared to be critical to changing income distribution in Saeed's original model in which he defined the technological differential between the two sectors exogenously but its effect is much diluted in policy run (7) of the modified model which endogenizes technological growth process. This is not surprising in view of Saeed's extended experimentation with the parameters representing technological differential between the two sectors which appeared to dilute the impact of this policy on income distribution [Saeed 1994].

When technological development is endogenized, penalizing unearned income will cause adjustment in the technological differential between the two sectors while maintaining status quo in income distribution. The policy to tax rent income and subsidize the workers with the collection (8) increases liquidity of the self-employed production sector, but cannot fuel technological development substantially since that sector has a priority for maximizing consumption rather than making technological investments.

The promising policies include mobilization of funds for technology-related investment of the self-employed production sector (4)   increasing inducement for the formal production sector to improve technology (5) and taxing rent income and using the collection to finance the technological investment of the self-employed production sector (9). These policies result in significant improvements in all criteria, namely output-labor ratio, average production, wage rate and worker revenue share, except in policy run 5 where the worker revenue share is slightly decreased when compared to the base case run.

The policy to mobilize funds for technology related investment of the self-employed production sector (4) is effective since it relaxes the financial constraint on the technological activity of the competitive sector. The resulting increase in the productivity of the self-employed sector also gives the workers a greater bargaining power which leads to an increase in the wage rate. At the same time, an increase in the technology used by the self-employed also increases the competitive pressure on the formal production sector to innovate and improve the technology used in its own production. In the end, labor productivity and capital intensity rise in both

175

sectors.

The policy to increase pressure on the formal production sector to improve its technology (5) significantly improves all criteria except the worker income share since it largely stimulates the growth of the formal sector, without affecting wage rate, ownership distribution or worker income share.

The policy to tax rent income and finance the technological investment of the self-employed production sector (9) significantly affects both economic growth and income distribution by increasing competitiveness as well as changing income distribution.

Policy run 10, which combines policy runs 2 (increasing technological ability of the self-employed sector) and 9 (financing technological investment of the self-employed sector) shows that the former policy further facilitates the changes set into motion by the later although by itself, policy 2 is ineffective. An increased inducement for the self-employed to innovate in the presence of reduced financial constraints on technological investment yields significant improvements. It is noticed that while total production increases 3.69 fold, the share of the self-employed sector increases 55 fold while the number of self-employment workers increases 9.5 fold. These high numbers appear since the contribution of the self-employed sector is transformed from a minor to a significant level. This means the self-employed sector assumes a leading rather than a lagging role.

The taxation of rent income alone (7) did not appear to be effective for redistributing ownership in the extended model since adjustments in technological differential were able to maintain existing ownership pattern, while instruments providing preferential incentives and facilitation for technological development created the primary forces for change. This led to experimenting with policy package 11 which is similar to policy package 10 except that it finances the self-employed through a tax on aggregate income instead of one penalizing unearned income.

The performance of policy package 11 is almost as good as policy package 10, which confirms that technology policy instruments might be as effective as fiscal incentives and disincentives for affecting changes in income distribution. It should be added that there might appear considerable resistance to implementation of fiscal instruments selectively penalizing economic actors in view of the interest group involvement in the decision process [Burki 1971, Alavi 1976, Abeyrama and Saeed 1984]. On the other hand, technology-related instruments may not arouse as much adversarial response since these may not be seen to be directly linked with the various forms of income generation activities.

176

Conclusion

The developing country economies have been observed to incorporate two equally significant production modes: a profit maximizing formal sector and a consumption maximizing self-employed sector. Yet, only their formal sectors have been targeted for much of the economic and technological development effort. On the other hand, although the developed country economies consist predominantly of profit maximizing firms but their small self-employed sectors are often targeted for assistance for technological development.

Having accounted for a significant part of economic growth in the industrialized countries, technological development instruments offer a good promise also for the developing countries for accelerating economic growth and affecting income distribution. These instruments, however, remain underutilized. Even when used, they often disregards the dual structure of the developing country economies whose relations must be understood for creating any effective policy designs.

This paper has attempted to explore the efficacy of technology policy for the developing countries using a system dynamics model of economic growth, income distribution and technological growth building on an earlier model developed by Saeed. Experimentation with this model shows that technological development related instruments might offer a promising alternative to the traditional direct and indirect policy levers used for fostering economic growth and influencing income distribution.

It is observed, however, that for a technological development initiative to successfully facilitate growth and influence income distribution, it must attempt to promote competition among the monopolistic formal firms while providing positive assistance to the competitive informal firms.

While our analysis evidently deals with economic duality in the industrial sector, our conclusions and their policy implications can be extended to other contexts of economic duality, e. g., in the agricultural sector, between agricultural and industrial sectors, between leading and lagging regions and between industrialized and developing countries. The underlying structure in those other forms of duality is not different from the one elaborated in our model. In fact, Saeed's original model modified for our analysis addressed primarily the agricultural sector [Saeed 1980]. Also, in a recent re-interpretation of this model, Saeed (1996) views the global economic structure to have the characteristics of a dual economy in which free movement of production factors and commodities might be poised to create global feudalism. Use of technological policy levers in those contexts needs to be explored further.

References

Abeyrama, T. and Saeed, K. (1984) 'The Gramodaya Mandalaya Scheme in Sri Lanka: Participatory Development or Power Play?', *Community Development Journal*, 29(1): 20-31.

Abramovitz, M. (1956) 'Resource and Output Trends in United States Since 1870', *American Economic Review*, 46, May: 5-23.

Alavi, H. (1976) 'The Rural Elite and Agricultural Development in Pakistan' in Steven et. al. (eds.), *Rural Development in Bangladesh and Pakistan*, Honolulu, Hawaii: Hawaii University Press.

Applebaum, E. (1979) 'The Labor Market' in A. Eichner (ed.), *A Guide to Post-Keynesian Economics*, White Plains, New York: M. E. Sharpe.

Auerbach, P.(1988) *Competition: The Economics of Industrial Change*, Oxford, England: Basil Blackwell.

Averitt, R. T. (1988) *The Dual Economy: The Dynamics of American Industry Structure*, London: Norton.

Bardhan, P. K. (1973) 'A Model of Growth in a Dual Agrarian Economy' in G. Bhagwati and R. Eckus (eds.), *Development and Planning: Essays in Honor of Paul Rosenstein-Roden*, New York: George Allen and Unwin.

Barro, R. J. (1984) *Macroeconomics*, New York: John Wiley.

Betz, F. (1987) *Managing Technology*, New Jersey: Prentice-Hall Inc.

Bhatt, V. V. (1988) 'Financial Institutions and Technical Consultancy Services: The Indian Experiment in Small-Enterprise Promotion', *Journal of Development Planning*, 18: 63-82.

Boeke, J. H. (1953) 'Economics and Economic Policy of Dual Societies', Mimeo, Institute of Pacific Relations, New York, in G. M. Meier (ed.), *Leading Issues in Economic Development*, 3rd Edition, New York: Oxford University Press, 1976, pp. 130-131.

Burki, S. J. (1971) 'Interest Group Involvement in Pakistan's Rural Works Program', *Public Policy*, Vol. 19, pp. 167-206.

Celso, F. (1989) 'Technology Policy in Newly Industrialized Countries: A Brazilian Perspective', *Science and Public Policy*, 16(3): 167-175.

Chatterji, M. (1990) *Technology Transfer in the Developing Countries*, Hong Kong: MacMillan Press.

Choi, H. S. (1984) *Industrial Research in the Less Developed Countries*, Bangalore, India: Regional Center For Technology Transfer.

Choi, H. S. (1986) *Technology Development in Developing Countries*, Tokyo: Asian Productivity Organization.

Choi, H. S. (1989) 'Springboard Measures for Becoming Highly Industrialized Society', Mimeo: APCTT/UN- ESCAP.

Dalziel, P. (1991) 'A Generalization and Simplification of the Cambridge Theorem with Budget Deficits', *Cambridge Journal of Economics*, 15: 287-300.

Davidson, P. (1972) *Money and the Real World*, London: MacMillan.

Dennison, E. (1962) 'United States Economic Growth', *Journal of Business* (April): 109-121.

Dennison, E. (1985) *Trends in American Economic Growth, 1929-1982*, Washington, D. C.: The Brookings Institution.

Dosi, G. (1988) 'Sources, Procedures and Microeconomic Effects of Innovation', *Journal of Economic Literature*, 26: 1120-1171.

Eichner, A. (1979) *A Guide To Post-Keynesian Economics*, White Plains, New York: M. E. Sharpe.

Fazi, E. and Salvadori, N. (1985) 'The Existence of Two-Class Economy in a General Cambridge Model of Growth and Distribution', *Cambridge Journal of Economics*, 9: 155-164.

Fie, J. C. and Ranis, G. (1966) 'Agrarianism, Dualism, and Economic Development', in Adelman and Thorbecke (eds.), *The Theory and Design Of Economic Development*, Baltimore, MD: John Hopkins University Press.

Freeman, C. (1990) *The Economics of Innovation*, Aldershot, England: Edward Elgar.

Gordon, D. M. (1972) *Economic Theories of Poverty and Underemployment*, London: D. C. Heath.

Griliches, Z. (1963) 'The Source of Measured Productivity Growth: United States Agriculture, 1940-60', *Journal of Political Economy*, 55 (August): 331-346.

Hirshman, A. O. (1958) *The Strategy of Economic Development*, New Haven, CT: Yale University Press.

Hirshman, A. O. (1970) *Exit, Voice and Loyalty: Responses to Decline in Firms, Organizations, and States*, Cambridge, MA: Harvard University Press.

Hunt, D. (1989) *Economic Theories of Development: An Analysis of Competing Paradigms*, London: Harvester Wheatsheaf.

ILO (1990) *Statistical Yearbook*, Geneva: International Labor Organization.

Kaldor, N. (1956) 'Alternative Theories of Distribution', *Review of Economic Studies*, 23:83-100.

Kalecki, M. (1965) *Theory of Economic Dynamics*, London: George Allen and Unwin.

Kamien, M. I. and Schwartz, N. L. (1982) *Market Structure and Innovation*, Cambridge, England: Cambridge University Press.

Kregel, J. (1973) *The Reconstruction of Political Economy: An Introduction to Post-Keynesian Economics*, New York: John Wiley.

Lewis, A. (1958) 'Economic Development With Unlimited Supplies of Labor', Mimeo, Manchester School (May 1954); reprinted in A. Argarwala and S. Singh (eds.), *The Economics of Underdevelopment*, London: Oxford University Press.

179

Lipton, M. (1977) *Why Poor People Stay Poor*, Cambridge, MA: Harvard University Press.

Mansfield, E. (1971) *Technological Change*, New York: W. W. Norton.

Marglin, S. A. (1984) *Growth Distribution and Prices*, Cambridge, MA: Harvard University Press.

McKinnon, R. I. (1973) *Money and Capital in Economic Development*, Washington, D. C.: The Brookings Institution.

Morawetz, D. (1977) *Twenty-Five Years of Economic Development 1950 To 1975*, Baltimore, MD: John Hopkins University Press.

Nelson, R. R. (1987) *Understanding Technical Change as an Evolutionary Process*, Amsterdam, Netherlands: Elsevier Science.

Pasinetti, L. L. (1989) 'Ricardian Debt/Taxation Equivalence in the Kaldor Theory of Profits and Income Distribution', *Cambridge Journal of Economics*, 13: 25-36.

Prankprakma, P. (1993) 'A System Dynamics Model to Explore Macro-Policy Instruments for Technological Development to Influence Economic Growth and Income Distribution', Ph.D. Dissertation # IE94-2, Bangkok, Thailand: AIT.

Richardson, G. P. and Pugh III, A. L. (1981) *Introduction To System Dynamics Modeling With DYNAMO*, Cambridge, MA: MIT Press.

Riech, M., Gordon, D. and Edwards, R. (1973) 'A Theory of Labor Market Segmentation', *American Economic Review*, 63.

Robinson, J. (1978) *Contributions To Modern Economics*, Basil Blackwell, Oxford.

Saeed, K. (1980) *Rural Development and Income Distribution: The Case of Pakistan*, Ph.D. Dissertation, Cambridge, MA: MIT.

Saeed, K. (1987) 'A Re-evaluation of the Effort to Alleviate Poverty and Hunger', *Socio Economic Planning Sciences*, 21(5): 291-304.

Saeed, K. (1988) 'Wage Determination, Income Distribution and the Design of Change', *Behavioral Science*, 33(3): 161-186.

Saeed, K. (1994) *Development Planning and Policy Design: A System Dynamics Approach*, Aldershot, England: Avebury Books.

Saeed, K. (1996) 'Trade Relations in a Dualist Global Economy', paper presented at the Symposium on Global Accords on Sustainable Development, Cambridge, MA: MIT.

Samuelson. P. A. and Nordhaus, W. D. (1985) *Economics*, New York: McGraw-Hill.

Schultz, T. (1979) 'The Economics of Being Poor', Nobel Memorial Lecture in A. Lindbeck (ed.), *Economic Sciences, Nobel Lectures 1969-1980*, Singapore: World Scientific.

Sen, A. K. (1966) 'Peasants and Dualism With or Without Surplus Labor', *Journal of Political Economy*, 75(5).

Sharma, S. V. S. (1979) *Small Entrepreneurial Development in Some Asian Countries: A Comparative Study*, New Delhi: Light and Life.

180

Solow, R. (1957) 'Technical Change and the Aggregate Production Function', *Review of Economics and Statistics*, 34 (August): 312-320.

Sraffa, P. (1960) *Production of Commodities By Means of Commodities*, Cambridge, England: Cambridge University Press.

Subramanian, S. K. (1987) 'Planning Science and Technology For National Development: The Indian Experience', *Technological Forecasting and Social Change* (31): 87-101.

Technonet Asia (1983) 'Small Enterprise and Entrepreneurship Development in Eleven Asian-Pacific Countries' in *Proceedings of A Workshop in Pattaya, Thailand*, Singapore: Canadian International Development Agency.

Uddin, S. (1989) *Entrepreneurship Development in India*, Delhi, India: Mittal Publications.

Wientraub, S. (1956) 'A Macro-Economic Approach To Theory of Wages', *American Economic Review*, 46 (December).

7 The dynamics of collegial systems in the developing countries*

Khalid Saeed

Abstract

This paper develops a conceptual model of a collegial system working without external adjudication or an institutional charter governing the conduct of its operations. The model is applicable to many of the academic and research organizations established in the developing countries, which have attempted to emulate the equivalent professional organizations in the advanced industrial countries but have achieved low efficacy. The analysis suggests that an unadjudicated collegial system is not sustainable, for it will tend to create an authoritarian administration which will impair the collegial norms and misallocate scarce resources to the activities fueling bureaucratization and expansion of administrative scope, while professional autonomy, innovativeness and self-actualized behavior are suppressed. Professional conduct tends to be more value- rational than the bureaucracy since it is subject to reviews by external peers. Thus, legitimization of referent power is essential to creating value-rational decisions which assure a balanced resource allocation that sustains a collegial system. Limiting scope of the administration through an external scrutiny of its conduct or a charter appears to facilitate this process.

---

* Reprinted from Higher Education Policy, the Quarterly Journal of the International Association of Universities, 9(1), Khalid Saeed, The dynamics of collegial systems in the developing countries, pp. 75-86, Copyright 1996, with kind permission of the editor.

Introduction

A heavy emphasis has lately been placed on higher education, research and development in the developing countries. Many universities, institutes and research and development organizations attempting to emulate similar institutions in the advanced industrial countries have been established at national, non-government and multilateral levels. Many more are being planned. The efficacy of these organizations is, however, generally low since they often are unable to maintain collegial values essential to professional performance.

Often, collegial organizations deteriorate from the development of a power struggle between the instrumental and value-rational interests over which collegiality deteriorates. In particular, institutions that are located in a monopolistic market or a non-competing environment that create internal rather than external terms of reference and those cut off from adjudication by professional peers through limiting referent power of the professionals, whose performance is subject to review by the external peers, may rarely be able to maintain collegial values that sustain them in the long run. Such organizations run high risk of failure.

This paper attempts to understand the processes creating decay in professional organizations using a formal model of the decision relationships underlying the main functions of a collegial system. The fragmented information concerning the behavioral relationships found in the literature serves as a basis for constructing a formal model using system dynamics method (Forrester 1980, Saeed 1991). The model can be generalized to subsume institutions employing professionals and engaged in the production of intangible services. It incorporates three types of decision processes existing in a collegial system: those governing resource allocation, production, and value creation. Experimentation with this model helps to understand the nature of the internal trends potentially existing in a collegial system. Extended experimentation also helps to identify appropriate entry points for maintaining professional health in collegial systems.

The study suggests that the absence of an organizational norm, a charter or a means of adjudication by external peers, that should curtail administrative scope and protect the prerogatives of the professionals to referent power, a collegial organization would tend to centralize operations over the course of its growth and pursue instrumental rather than value-rational interests, which not only makes it difficult to maintain a healthy professional environment but also misallocates resources to unproductive activities that may eventually lead to a closure due to economic reasons.

The performance of collegial organizations

Collegial organizations consist of groups of professionals creating intangible products or services. Institutional norms governing the conduct of the actors in collegial organizations develop out of a balance between the referent power of the externally adjudicated professionals that upholds value-rationalism and the manifest power of the largely unadjudicated administrators subscribing to instrumentalism. A university is a typical example of a collegial system where the referent power of the faculty must maintain a value-rational decision process so instrumental interests are kept at bay and a high degree of professional health is maintained. Collegiality is thus an organizational value rationalizing referent power. Max Weber defined many organizational arrangements under which the monocratic character of authority is limited by the principle of collegiality (Weber 1978).

The literature on the performance of the collegial organizations is fragmented and provides static views of the organizational processes rather than a coherent theory that may explain the diversity of the patterns experienced. Gouldner's seminal work on manifest and latent roles in collegial systems identified two important latent role models, cosmopolitans and locals, which seemed to influence the performance and the inner coherence of an organization (Gouldner 1957). Gouldner did not, however, analyze the dynamics of interaction between those latent roles and how this might affect the economic and professional health of the collegial system in the long run. In a more recent study, Benvensite (1987) has emphasized the need to cultivate cosmopolitan professional roles to maintain innovation in an organization. He does not, however, clearly identify an organizational process that should accomplish this, but seems to leave intervention to leadership. Unfortunately, intervention by leadership often requires centralization of decision-making and concentration of power that will often create ruthless pursuit of instrumental interests which is further intensified in the presence of machiavellian attitudes (Jennings 1960).

The consequences of the loss of collegiality in a university manifest both in the economic and value-related indicators. Indeed, the studies on the mortality of the university have focused both on economic and value related attributes, although separately and using a variety of measures. The economic attitudes addressed include shrinking student enrollment (Freeman and Hannan 1975) and shrinking revenues (Cameron 1983). The value related attitudes addressed are the maladaptation to a shrinking environmental niche (Greenhalgh 1983) professional stagnation (Whetten 1987) loss of legitimacy (Benson 1973) and deteriorating and unsatisfactory organizational performance that causes members and clients to become disgruntled (Hirshman 1970).

Zammuto (1982) has examined changes in the population of US colleges and universities that occurred between the early 1970s and the early 1980s. He suggests that the decline and failure rates are strongly associated with the institutional environment. Other investigators of the causes of decline have addressed the internal forces that may explain the onset of a downturn. Since academic institutions produce an intangible product, their economic and value-related attributes may be strongly intertwined. Truly, the propositions concerning the internal causes of success or failure of a collegial system often attribute the loss of value-rationalism, which eventually results in the loss of a collegial culture, to bureaucratization and centralization processes that precipitate economic conditions causing decline (Waters 1989). In general, the fallibility of centralizing the decision process in professional organizations is quite widely recognized. Clark (1990) suggests that in order to sustain a productive academic environment, officially mandated orders should be avoided and both strategic and operational decision making decentralized to the point where the responsibility for institutional advancement is largely localized.

A formal analysis of the value processes that affect economic growth in the developing countries through changes in the commitment of a government to public welfare and consolidation of its own power appears in Saeed (1990). Saeed's model focuses on the allocation of resources to the production and control activities and on the consequences of the functioning of the political system under such allocation for the subsequent rounds of resource allocation. These processes entail strong feedbacks affecting the value orientation of a government. These feedbacks can create functional or dysfunctional outcomes depending on the decision structure of the government organization. An attempt is made in this paper to apply the concepts underlying the resource allocation and value maintenance processes developed in Saeed (1990) to a formal collegial organization.

The formal collegial organization: a system dynamics model

A collegial system involves both production and value maintenance processes, although their performance cannot be measured on a cardinal scale (Weber 1978). The cause and effect relationships governing these processes may be identified on the basis of the existing theoretical and empirical information, which exits in fragmented form. A formal system dynamics model of these processes is developed in this section for experimentation to understand the dynamics of a collegial system. Following the flow diagramming convention of the system dynamics method, the rectangles represent stocks, the valve symbols flows and the circles intermediate computations. The circles containing a ~ represent nonlinear behavioral relationships (Richardson and Pugh 1981, Richmond et. al. 1987, Saeed 1991). This model is implemented on an Apple

Macintosh personal computer using iTHINK software.[1]

Three main decision systems discussed below are covered by the model. These are: resource allocation between professional and administrative activities, production and organizational health, and value creation. Technical details and a computer program listing can be obtained from the author on request.

a) Resource allocation between professional and administrative activities

Figure 7.1 shows the processes allocating resource between administrative and professional activities in a collegial organization. The allocation of the total budget between the two activities depends on economic health, value rational pressures and instrumental pressures. When perceived economic health is good, administrative activities tend to expand in preparation for a larger expected size. When economic health is bad, administration may be reduced, although, not directly in proportion to economic health (Katz and Kahn 1978).

The instrumental pressures increase allocations to administration, while value rational pressures tend to limit this allocation in an effort to maintain the support for the professional activities. The total budget of the organization adjusts towards a potential budget after a delay representing time elapsed between sales effort and its fruition. Potential budget is determined in the first instance by production. However, administrative expediency representing marketing or fund-raising effort will increase the production to potential budget yield, while a lack of innovativeness in the institution will reduce market appeal thus limiting the effectiveness of the sales effort. Expediency depends on the size of the administrative resources.

b) Production and organizational health

Figure 7.2 shows the processes underlying production and the determination of organizational health. Professional resources represent the production workforce of the collegial system. Production, although difficult to measure in any tangible terms, can be assumed to depend on the professional resources and their productivity.

Productivity is a function of innovativeness and organizational citizenship - values depending respectively on professional health and authoritarianism experienced in the organization. Organizational citizenship, an indicator of the employee altruism for the organization contributes to improving the productivity. Citizenship is suppressed by the

---

[1] iTHINK is a trade mark of High Performance Systems, 45 Lyme Road Suite 300, Hanover, NH 03755, U.S.A.

practice of authoritarianism manifest in a large administrative scope since it limits the opportunities for self-determination (Organ 1988). Economic health is the ratio between the actual and the expected levels of production. After a certain recognition delay, the economic health comes to influence the budget allocation decisions as described in section (a) above.

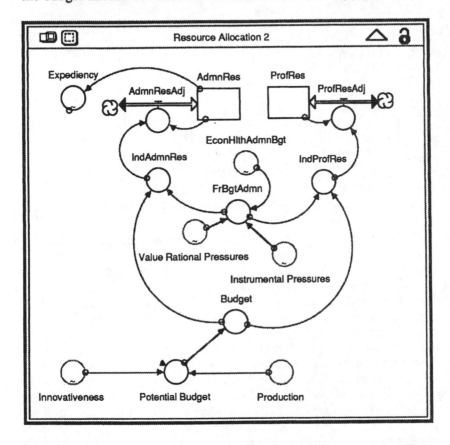

Figure 7.1   **Resource allocation in a collegial system**

c) *Value creation*

In addition to production, collegial organizations must also support a value system that maintains a collegial culture allowing referent power of the professionals to prevail upon the manifest administrative authority. A strengthening of the collegial culture will promote value rationalism in the organization which will tend to give priority to the professional agenda.

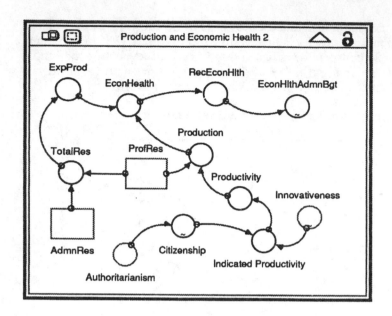

Figure 7.2   Production process and organizational health

A weakening of the collegial culture will create instrumentalism that will lead to an increased emphasis on control while also suppressing self-actualized behavior and thus alienating professionals (Benvensite 1987, Waters 1989). Figure 7.3 shows the relationships underlying the value creation and maintenance processes.

Values and attitudes in an organization must be constantly reinforced as otherwise they are susceptible to decay. Collegiality is a value created through the free interaction of the professionals, which is made possible when a reasonable degree of autonomy exists while the organizational environment also supports the self-actualization processes driving professional effort. However, the rigidities created by a high degree of bureaucratization limit autonomy and the alienation of the professionals from the decision process created by an authoritarian administration suppresses self-actualized behavior. Collegiality maintains referent power that generates value rational pressures. It also breeds professional health necessary for preserving innovativeness in the organization.

Authoritarianism is bred by scope which represents the extent to which the administrative processes govern professional functions. Once created, authoritarianism leads to instrumental pressures while also suppressing self-actualized behavior. Scope is created through the mobilization of the administrative resources when the administrative functions of the organization are unadjudicated by an organizational charter or censure by external peers.

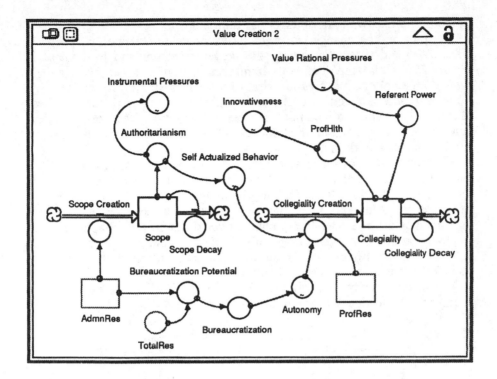

Figure 7.3 The value creation and maintenance system

The dynamics of the unadjudicated collegial system

The model of the last section is parameterized in a way that an equilibrium exists in all stocks. The initial values of collegiality scope and bureaucratization thus issued are assumed to be moderate and are scaled at unity. The total amount of initial resources is assumed to be 10 units. 80% of these resources are allocated to professional activities and only 20% to administration. The system is disturbed by stepping up the ambient production to budget ratio implying stepping up of the fund raising or marketing effort or its yield from a change in the environmental support.

Figure 7.4 shows a simulation of the model over a hypothetical 32 year period starting in equilibrium in year 1968 and stepping up the production to budget ratio by 20% in year 1972. There is a healthy increase in budget from 10 in the year 1972 to about 30 in year 1990, but thereafter, a rapid downturn is experienced. Scope and collegiality change very little until year 1980, after which, scope rises rapidly while collegiality decays. Scope

189

continues to rise even after budget has turned down.

The plots of the changes in other facets of value orientation appear in Figure 7.5 and those concerning the power structure and healthiness in Figure 7.6. It is seen that both bureaucratization and authoritarianism, which stifle collegiality creation rise while values supporting collegiality, autonomy and self actualized behavior, decline. The net effect of these changes in value orientation is devastating for the organization. Innovativeness and autonomy plunge. while both economic health and professional health decay.

Expediency rises as much as it can, but is unable to sustain budget since productivity is curtailed by falling innovativeness and impoverished citizenship behavior. The decline in budget eventually atrophies the organization. Although such dynamics may often be attributed to the personalities of the leadership in charge over different parts of the pattern, it should be noted that the model only displays a continuation of the long term trends arising out of its durable decision structure that does not include any personality-related changes.

The pattern exhibited in Figures 7.4, 7.5 and 7.6 can be explained by examining the feedback loops in the system shown in Figure 7.7.

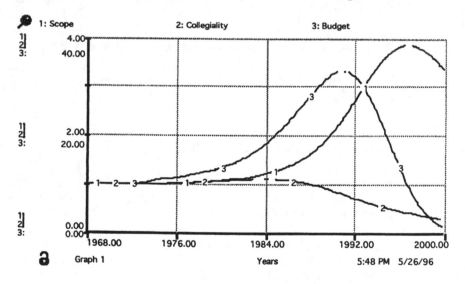

Figure 7.4 Key economic and value related indicators over the life cycle of the unadjudicated collegial system

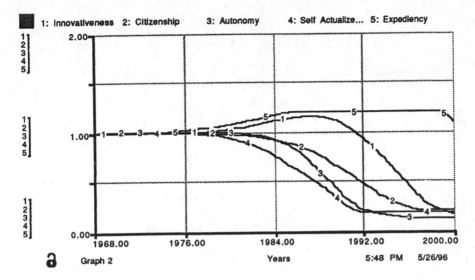

Figure 7.5   Changes in selected value indicators

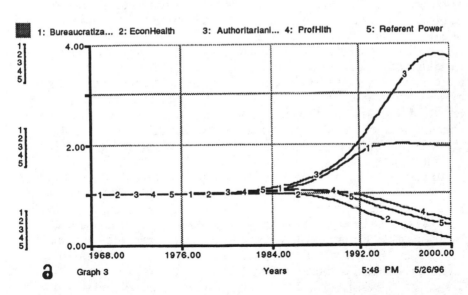

Figure 7.6   Changes in power structure and healthiness

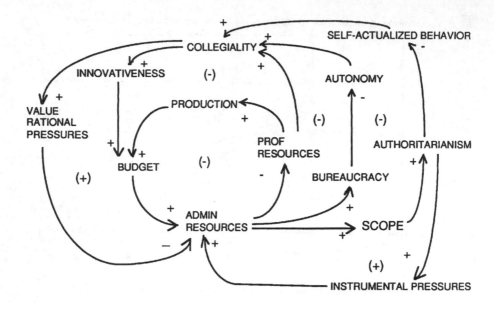

Figure 7.7   **Feedback processes in the collegial system**

The limits to growth arise at the outset due to a rising allocation of resources to the administrative activities over periods of good economic health and the reluctance to cut down administrative budget during periods of poor health. These limits are further accentuated due to the rigidities created by the expanding bureaucracy which reduces autonomy, thus curtailing the development of collegiality and the ensuing commitment to value-rationalism. Furthermore, in the absence of a charter or a tradition of peer audit providing adjudication of the organization's activities, the increased bureaucratization fuels the creation of scope which allows operations to be centralized into an authoritarian working mode. This alienates professionals, inhibiting self-actualized behavior and further stifling the creation of collegiality.

Authoritarianism also promotes instrumentalism and an emphasis on control. These developments not only reduce productive resources, but also limit their yield. A downturn is precipitated when budget begins to decline due to a low level of production and poor professional health and innovativeness that attracts fewer and fewer resources to the organization. Expediency will rise with the increase in scope creating much promotional effort but its yield is limited by the falling production and innovativeness. These processes snowball due to the positive feedback loops shown in Figure 7.7.

What sustains collegial systems?

Many experiments were performed with the model to identify a critical element in the decision structure that should sustain a collegial system both professionally and economically. A complete documentation of all the experiments would be cumbersome. It is discovered that there exist two powerful insidious positive feedback loops shown in Figure 7.7 created due to the ease with which administrative resources can be used to yield an expansion in scope. These feedback loops can function only when the administrative actions are not subject to adjudication through an organizational charter or external peer audit, which is often possible in autonomous non-government organizations located in monopolistic markets and not having a well developed collegial tradition of legitimizing the referent power of the externally reviewed professionals. The presence of multi-ethnic and multi-cultural variety in the membership of the organization may often make it further difficult to adhere to a generally accepted collegial order, which may further facilitate the expansion of scope.

The presence of an institutional charter and adjudication of the services produced as well as the organizational norms and practices by external peers would imply that the relationship between scope creation and administrative resources is severed.

Figures 7.8, 7.9, 7.10 show simulations of the model with this change. It is observed that the organization experiences sustained growth with a value system conducive to professionalism, a balanced power structure and robust levels of economic and professional health. The change basically helps to maintain an input into the decision process from the value rational pressures which preserves a balanced allocation of the resources between professional and administrative sectors of the organization. There indeed would be other constraints to growth due to the processes not covered by the model but the catastrophic decline arising from misallocation of resources and the stifling of collegial values shown in the earlier set of simulations is eliminated.

It should be recognized that a change in the administrative structure of an unadjudicated collegial organization may not be possible without a large scale change in the leadership and the administrative coalition it has formed. When its power is limited, an existing administrative coalition will fear much animus from the professionals because of the past hostilities between the two groups which are bound to develop under an authoritarian administrative role. This coalition will strongly resist any decentralization drive, although it might give this move a lip service.

Additionally, limiting tenure of the senior administrators and making it mandatory for their key rule-making and norm-setting decisions to be approved by a plenary professional committee would help to create a

193

tradition of internal adjudication of the administrative decisions that is linked with the outside peers through the professional review process.

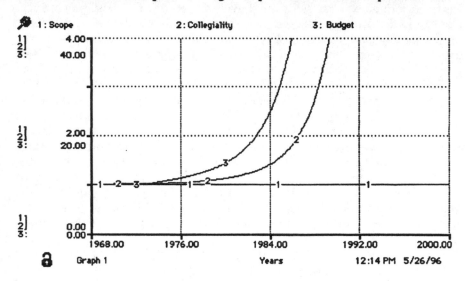

Figure 7.8   **Key economic and value-related variables in the revised system**

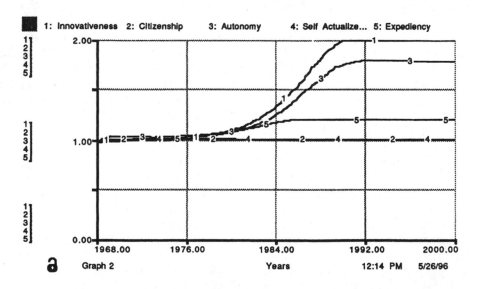

Figure 7.9   **Organizational values in the revised system**

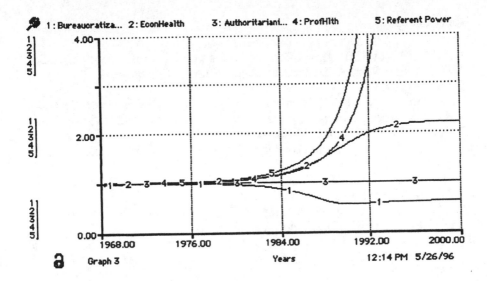

Figure 7.10   Power structure in the revised system

Frequent comparisons with the administrative norms in well-balanced collegial organizations should further help to maintain a value-rational decision-making process.

Conclusion

This paper has attempted to explain the dynamics of growth in an unadjudicated collegial system. This pattern is characterized by a decay of collegiality over the course of growth which is accompanied by the creation of a highly centralized bureaucracy.

The analysis shows that the use of administrative resources to create scope is a key factor creating the characteristic growth pattern, which is unsustainable. Adherence to an institutional charter or peer audit limiting administrative powers and supporting the exercise of referent professional power is the key to the health of a collegial system. Implementation of such a structural change in an existing unadjudicated organization may, however, pose difficulties due to the resistance from the power coalitions. This, a large scale personnel change should probably accompany implementation of a structural change.

References

Benson, J. K. (1973) 'The Analysis of Bureaucratic-Professional Conflict: Functional Versus Dialectical Approaches', *Sociological Quarterly*, 14:376-394.

Benvensite, Guy (1987) *Professionalizing an Organization, Reducing Bureaucracy to Enhance Effectiveness*, London: Jossey-Bass Publishers.

Cameron, Kim S. and David Whetten (1983) 'Models of the Organizational Life Cycle: Applications to Higher Education', *Rev. Higher Educ.* 6(4): 269-299.

Clark, Burton R. (1990) 'The Organizational Dynamics of the American Research University', *Higher Education Policy* 3(2) 31-35.

Freeman, John and Hannan, Michael (1975) 'Growth and Decline Processes in Organizations', *Am. Sociol. Rev.* 40: 215-228.

Forrester, Jay, W. (1980) 'Information Sources for Modeling the National Economy', *Journal of the American Statistical Association* 75(371): 555-569.

Gouldner, Alvin (1957) 'Cosmopolitans and Locals: Towards an Analysis of Latent Social Roles — I', *Administrative Science Quarterly* 2: 281-306.

Greenhalgh, Leonard and Rosenblatt, Zehava (1984) 'Job Insecurity: Toward Conceptual Clarity', *Academy of Management Review* 9.

Hannan, Michael and Freeman, John (1984) 'Structural Inertia and Organizational Change', *American Sociol. Review* 29: 149-164.

Hirshman, A. O. (1970) 'Exit', *Voice and Loyalty: Responses to Decline in Firms, Organizations and States*, Cambridge, MA: Harvard University Press.

Jennings, Eugene E. (1960) *An Anatomy of Leadership, princes, heroes, supermen, New York*: McGraw Hill Book Company.

Katz, Daniel and Kahn, Robert L. (1978) *The Social Psychology of Organizations' second edition*, New York: John Wiley.

Organ, D. W. (1988) *Organizational Citizenship Behavior*, Lexington, Mass: D. C. Heath and Company.

Richardson, George and Pugh, Alexander (1981) *Introduction to System Dynamics Modeling with DYNAMO*, Cambridge, MA: MIT Press.

Richmond, Barry, et. al. (1987) *An Academic User's Guide to STELLA*, Hanover, NH: High Performance Systems.

Saeed, K. (1990) 'Government Support of Economic Agendas in Developing Countries: A Behavioral Model', *World Development*, 18(6).

Saeed, K. (1992) 'Slicing a Complex Problem for System Dynamics Modeling', *System Dynamics Review* 8(3).

Waters, Malcolm (1989) 'Collegiality, Bureaucratization and Professionalization: A Weberian Analysis', *American Journal of Sociology*, 94(5):945-972.

Weber, Max (1978) *Economy and Society*, Berkeley, CA: University of California Press.

Whetten, David A. (1987) 'Organizational Growth and Decline Processes', *Annual Review of Sociology*.

Zammuto, R. F. (1982) *Assessing Organizational Effectiveness*, Albany, NY: State University of New York Press.

Part II: Concepts Extended

8 The world hunger problem, do we really understand it?[*]

Khalid Saeed

Abstract

The problem of world hunger is redefined from a feedback system perspective. It is suggested that occurrence of hunger is not an act of fate but a phenomenon which arises from an atrophying of the slack in the system that normally should absorb shocks in food availability. Research on this problem must aim at properly managing this slack and not merely on increasing food supply or limiting population.

Introduction

The problem of hunger and its occurrence in the developing countries are probably some of the most extensively studied issues of modern times, as is evidenced in the profusion of the printed word on this subject. Yet hunger has eluded almost all learned analyses and well-intentioned solutions. Large populations continue to starve while many moral statements are made about the gravity of the problem of hunger and the responsibility of the world to feed its hungry.

With some variations on this theme, most learned views expressed about hunger attribute it either to a shortage of cereal food production in the

* Reprinted from *System Dynamics Review*, 3(1), Khalid Saeed, The world hunger problem, do we really understand it?, pp. 36-44,1987, with kind permission from John Wiley and Sons, Ltd., Baffins Lane, Chichester, West Sussex PO19 1UD, UK.

countries where it occurs, or to a rapid growth in population, or both. The solutions suggested vary from a 'triage' strategy, according to which all nations must be left to their own fate, to a warm-hearted sharing of food among nations, which requires either voluntary cooperation at the global level or the presence of a world order. Most of these solutions appear to issue moral appeals rather than any viable strategies of implementation. What is rarely considered in the analysis of the problem and its solutions is the dynamic interaction of forces that create hunger in a nation in the first place. Nor is any effort made to find pressure points to change the dynamics of the system.

The analysis of this paper is built on the premise that the phenomenon of hunger does not appear in a certain society as a natural calamity but arises from the feedback mechanisms that create a tendency in the system to move towards a hunger prone condition. This condition is characterized by the decaying of the system slack. The solution to this problem, therefore, does not lie in exogenous interventions to increase food supply or limit population, whether at global or national levels, but in regulating the system forces in a way that an appropriate level of slack is always maintained.

The well-known hunger problem

According to well informed sources, almost half a billion individuals received inadequate nutritional energy in 1970 and their number has since been increasing [FAO 1981]. The World Bank estimate of hungry population in 1980 was one billion [World Bank 1981].

Most of the hungry population resides in the developing countries where average food calories available per capita are only 70% of those in the developed countries. When the composition of these calories is also considered, the differences in food supply between the two categories of countries further increase. Most of the edible calories in the developing countries are obtained directly from food cereals while 70% of those in the developed countries come from animal proteins that require twice (for poultry) to seven times (for red beef) cereal feed inputs as compared with their caloric yield. In fact, 83% of the cereal food production is consumed by 26% of the world population, mostly in the form of feed for producing animal proteins. Only 17% is available to the remaining 74% population who consume most of it directly [Bhattacharjee 1976, Yatopoulous 1985].

The world food situation has not been static. The growth rate of food production since 1950 has ranged between 2.8% and 3.1% both in the developing and the developed countries. However, while there has been a steady decline in the growth rate of population in the developed countries, the populations of the developing countries have grown almost at the same rates as their food production. Thus, food adequacy in these developing countries has not improved, even though total world supply of food calories currently exceeds demand [Bhattacharjee 1976].

It has also been reported that due to a steady worldwide rise in per capita income over the past few decades, the demand for edible calories in the form of animal proteins has increased which has further depressed food availability among the low income cross-sections of the populations of developing countries [Yatopoulous 1985].

The global picture of food availability described above has been interpreted in many ways to define the hunger problem. The popular perceptions about this problem are summarized below [Paarlberg 1975, Haru 1984]:

a) Nature has endowed different nations differently. A given country's hunger problems are essentially due to internal deficiencies of the country. Some countries are deficient beyond help. Others can survive with some assistance.

b) Due to uncertain weather conditions and poor market incentives, poor countries have been unable to produce enough food for themselves. Improved farming practices and better management of the market can help to increase food production.

c) Population in the poor countries has expanded beyond their resource base. In some cases, little can be done to alleviate this problem. Albeit, population planning is a must.

d) The character of a country's development status is strongly conditioned by its position within the structure of the global economy. The world economy's exchange mechanisms are not working properly which creates pockets of hunger even when adequate food is available at the global level.

e) The hunger problem cannot be addressed at national levels. There is widespread decadence in food consumption in the rich countries while there is hunger in the poor ones. A global food management strategy is needed to assure an equal distribution of food.

These perceptions may vary with respect to the moral values they express, but they all arise from a common underlying view about the nature of the problem. This view is a static one which does not consider the history, but takes the problem as given, as if it were created by an act of fate. When we attempt to integrate these perceptions, their common underlying basis can be clearly seen. This basis is illustrated in Figure 8.1.

The extent of hunger is measured in terms of edible food calories available per capita which depends on total edible food calories available and population. The edible calories available depend on the cereal and raw food supply in terms of local production as well as international transfers and its mode of consumption. When cereals are directly consumed as a staple, the efficiency of converting cereals into food calories is very high. On the other hand, when animal proteins are the staple, most of the cereals are used as animal feeds, which results in a very low conversion efficiency. Cereal and raw food supply consist of local production and international transfers through free trade or aid. Finally, the local food production depends on resource endowments in the form of land, water, and soil fertility, and the technology used to tap these resources.

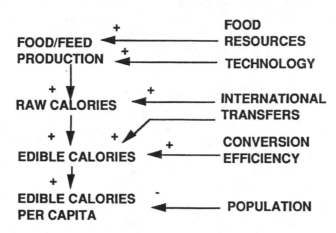

Figure 8.1   **Popular perceptions about the hunger problem**

At the outset, a nation would face the hunger problem when the edible food calories available to it fall short of the nutritional needs of the population. Thus, according to this model, both shortage of edible food calories and excess of population are to be blamed for creating hunger, although views on which is more important may vary [Hardin 1985].

The supply of edible food calories depends on cereal food production, international transfers through trade flows and aid, and the efficiency with which cereals are converted into edible calories. Limitations in the supply of cereals to a nation can be attributed to inadequate production on account of limited resource endowments in terms of land, water and soil fertility, and use of inefficient agricultural technologies [paarlberg 1975], to international trade barriers which restrict the flow of food across national boundaries [Siamwalla and Valdès 1980], to insufficient flow of aid from food-surplus to hunger-ridden nations and its poor use within the recipient nations [Maxwell and Singer 1983]. Edible calories are further limited due to decadent consumption patterns of the rich countries and the rich cross-sections of the populations of the poor countries [Yatopoulous 1985, Lipton 1975].

The well-known solutions

The solutions to the hunger problem proposed on the basis of the above perceptions appear in the form of appeals to national governments and the world conscience that incorporate different shades of a common moral rhetoric. This moral rhetoric calls for various degrees of warm-hearted intervention (or cold-hearted acquiescence) by the national governments or the world community, all of whom are expected to feel for the plight of the hungry.

At the national level, this intervention is to be aimed at increasing food production by effective use of agricultural resources and employment of improved seed varieties, fertilizers, pesticides and farming equipment. Attention is also to be paid to improving transportation facilities to help improve distribution of food to rural areas. Waste is to be discouraged and a search made to identify the most economical sources of edible calories [Lipton 1975]. Family planning effort to limit population has lately also gained prominence as an important measure at national level, although it has not received an adequate degree of emphasis in the past [Hardin 1985].

At the global level, two opposite views have been aired. The first of these is the triage strategy which has the implicit assumption that global resources are inadequate to feed the world population. According to this strategy, the countries in a position to help a hungry nation, materially or in the form of transfer of knowledge, are not morally obligated to do so. Their first obligation is to maintain an affluent environment for their own people. Some countries are beyond help and must be written off. Compulsive sharing in the face of inadequate global resources will make everybody starve. The realities of surviving should take precedent over any arbitrary moral values about warm-hearted sharing [Hardin 1976].

The second view, which is an antithesis to the triage strategy, assumes that there are enough global resources to feed everybody and only their unequal distribution has created pockets of hunger. Sharing of these resources and the knowledge to exploit them with the poor is, therefore, a moral obligation of the rich who must also cut down on their own decadence to assure that hunger is eradicated from the world.

Three types of mechanisms have been proposed to facilitate global sharing of resources. The simplest one consists of making moral appeals to the world conscience soliciting voluntary sharing [Aiken 1977, Maxwell and Singer 1983]. At a more involved level, the unfair international transfers and trade practices of the past are seen as causes of the current inequality. Therefore, it is considered a moral obligation of the rich nations to give up such practices while they also genuinely attempt to give back to the poor some of the wealth transferred away from them in the past [O'Neill 1977]. Finally, there are the appeals for introducing an international global order that should replace the existing world market structure, since the latter lacks a built in purpose of meeting human needs [Bhagwatti 1972, Menon 1977].

Why well-known solutions are fallible?

Since a world level organization does not currently exist, nor are there any chances of arriving at a consensus to create one, the global perspectives on solving the hunger problem can achieve little more than merely moralizing about its importance. Such perspectives have generated much rhetoric to date without providing any hope for overcoming world hunger.

A nation continues to be the largest organizational unit which can be managed from within with any success. However, direct intervention by the national governments is not a panacea that should alleviate all ills. Firstly, if the forces creating the problem are not adequately understood, much of the government effort is used up in fighting these forces without creating any positive results [Saeed 1986a]. This is quite evident from the widespread failures of the food production and population control programs to alleviate hunger.

Secondly, the very prerogative to intervene often removes the government from a mandate to deliver welfare to the public which makes it indifferent to their problems [Popper 1977]. Indeed, the growing tendency of governments of the poor countries to ignore the welfare of their people and spend large fractions of national resources on the purchase of military arsenals is a proof of the fallibility of the interventionist paradigm [Nabe 1983, Saeed 1986b].

In view of these facts, any attempts to solve the hunger problem must take the following into consideration. First, the problem must not be taken as given but its causes, particularly those involving self-regulating feedbacks, which create an internal tendency in the system to move towards a goal of realizing a hunger ridden scenario, must be clearly understood. Second, the possibility of a global level solution to this problem is a mirage and it is pointless to waste any time on the debate between the triage and the sharing strategies. Third, at the national level, any policy design to alleviate hunger should aim at minimizing instruments that require large scale intervention by the government which increases its control and detaches it from the mandate of delivering welfare to the public.

The anatomy of the hunger problem

The area currently worst hit by the hunger problem lies in the Sahel region in Africa which was the recipient of much development aid a few decades ago. This area is repeatedly hit by droughts during which its population faces conditions of famine whose severity has increased over the years. During good years, there is usually enough food for the population but bad years reoccur. This region is mostly a desert with a precariously balanced environment that has a limited carrying capacity. Another well known hunger prone region of the world is Bangladesh which is endowed with fertile lands and adequate water but faces food shortages because of its burgeoning population.

In both these regions, extensive government and international effort has been undertaken to provide food relief and develop local resources. This effort has been aimed at interjecting new technologies that, at least temporarily, increase food production but often at the cost of consuming the natural resources which provided the precarious environmental balance. The consequences of this have been quite disastrous for Sahel [Picardi 1976], although, in the case of Bangladesh, no serious environmental damage has so far been reported. The population growth in both regions has, however, outstripped any gains in the supply of food.

The food shortage problem for both of the above as well as for the other less seriously affected nations has been seen to be a problem of short term variability which calls for quick relief through interventionist means. Food security is often defined as the ability of the food deficit countries and regions to meet target levels of consumption on a *yearly* basis, while targets are to be fixed by the planners, not determined endogenously by the system [Siamwalla and Valdés 1980].

What is ignored in this view is that the vulnerability to short term variability in food supply arises from the absence of a slack in the system that should absorb periodic shocks without causing hunger and that the long run system goals can be vastly different from any exogenously determined targets. Indeed, there has been some recognition of the problems created by the concomitant growth of both the supply and the demand for food. Garrett Hardin suggests:

"To avoid disasters, keep supply greater than demand. When demand outruns supply, two alternatives are available: reduce demand (by keeping birth rate below death rate) or increase supply (of food, energy, and so forth)." [Hardin 1985]

However, according to this recipe, the sources of the coterminous growth in food and population are assumed to lie outside the system while the balance between the food and population must also be kept through exogenous intervention. Even though there is ample empirical evidence that points towards a tendency for populations to achieve a complementarity between food and population in the long run, while anthropological theories that explain this complementarity in terms of cause and effect relationships also exist, the analyses on food policy have shied away from considering these [Meadows, et. al. 1971]. Figure 8.2 illustrates two important self-regulating feedbacks concerning, respectively, resource

207

endowments and population carrying capacity, which can easily defeat any policies based on the static model of Figure 8.1.

The negative feedback between food resources and food/feed production maintains a given level of slack in the supply of food which depend on the choice of technology. The negative feedback between population growth rate and edible calories per capita maintains another given level of slack in the demand of food which depends on the conversion efficiency of raw food calories to edible ones. Both these slacks may be drawn upon in times of crisis. The recognition of these feedbacks completely changes the perception of the hunger problem as well as the nature of the policy design necessary for alleviating this problem.

The slack in the supply of food is greatly affected by the characteristics of the technologies employed to produce food from the resource endowments. Agricultural production in the United States expanded primarily by consuming a part of an enormous surplus of non-renewable resources such as ground water, soil fertility and energy [Peterson 1983, Le Riche 1985]. There is little justification for applying these technologies for increasing food production in regions which have a precariously balanced resource environment with almost no surplus of non-renewable resources.

On the contrary, technologies that tap renewable or new but plentiful food resources and improve the rates at which current resources can be renewed must be explored [Saeed 1985]. For reducing vulnerability to hunger, increasing slack in the supply of food must take precedence over increasing raw food production. The former would reduce vulnerability to food shocks while the latter might increase this vulnerability if it has been realized by consuming scarce but non-renewable agricultural resources.

The slack in the supply of food can be increased by using technologies that nurture the regenerative mechanisms of nature not the ones which strain them in the process of achieving a temporary growth in food supply. Thus, indiscriminate use of high-yielding seed varieties, pesticides, and fertilizers which may adversely affect soil texture, energy intensive farming techniques, and pumping water out of limited but non-renewable aquifers, which are often seen as green revolution technologies, may only qualify as slack consuming technologies. On the other hand, crop planting techniques that limit soil erosion, measures that limit wastage of water through evaporation and make use of it to the optimum, crop rotation patterns that maintain fertility of soil, and energy efficient farming methods may help improve the slack in the supply of food even if they do not increase yield. A search for such agricultural techniques would go a long way to reducing vulnerability to hunger.

The slack in the demand of food is determined by the difference between the availability of raw calories in the form of cereals and animal feeds, and edible calories. When this difference is large, variation in raw calories can be easily absorbed by slight changes in the composition of the edible

208

calories. Consumption of unprocessed cereals can be increased in time of a shortage while animal proteins form the bulk of consumption in time of abundance. It may be noted that this type of slack is possible to realize only when the normal efficiency of conversion from raw to edible calories is quite low.

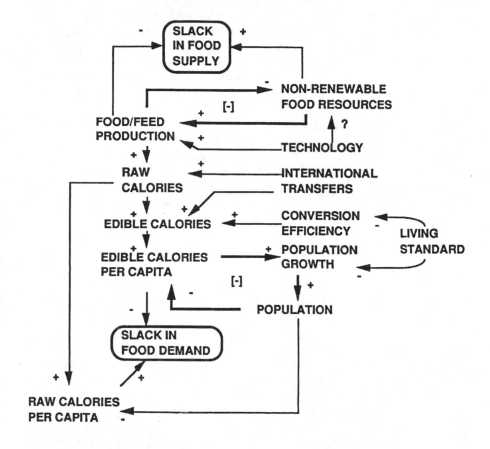

Figure 8.2   Revised view of the hunger problem

An obvious implication of the importance of the slack in food demand is that moralistic judgments about the decadence in consumption of food by the rich nations and the rich cross-sections of population in the poor nations appear quite ludicrous. Such decadence, evidently, provides for a flexibility in food demand which is a security against hunger.

It should be noted that any efforts by a government to increase the supply of edible calories and limit population may contribute little to increasing food security since the negative feedback affecting food supply and population attempts to achieve a complementarity between the two without affecting level of the slack in food demand. These measures, therefore, may only provide temporary relief from hunger while they contribute little to the ability to cope with shocks in food supply.

Even though linking hunger with poverty is an old fashioned proposition [Sen 1981], according to the model in Figure 8.2, poor societies may appear to have a greater tendency to move towards a goal of a lower food slack than the affluent societies. An empirical study by Yatopoulous indicates that the use of cereals as feed for producing animal proteins in the developing countries has been rising with the increases in their GNP per capita [Yatopoulous 1985]. Although, he is dismayed at this trend, it may have contributed to increasing the slack in the food demand.

There also exist empirical evidence as well as theories of demographic transition that link population growth rates with living standard [Chenery and Syrquin 1975]. A rise in the living standard of population should, therefore, limit population while it also reduces the efficiency of conversion from raw cereals to edible calories. These forces acting together would further improve food slack. Thus, alleviating poverty appears to be an essential pre-requisite for alleviating hunger.

Conclusion

The analysis of this paper portrays hunger not as a short term calamity but a problem whose roots lie in the long term forces affecting the resource system and consumption pattern. This problem cannot be solved by using the widely advocated short term measures.

The problem of hunger must be viewed in terms of the feedbacks which create a tendency in the system to come to rest with a low level of food slack if a lasting solution to it is to be found. The food slack can be drawn upon when a temporary shortage occurs. Thus it is a source of food security. The use of direct interventionist policies, warm hearted or otherwise, that are implemented without regard to environmental and social factors that determine the slack goal of the system, cannot provide a lasting solution to the hunger problem. Such policies assume that the intervening organizations are always committed to deliver welfare to the people, which is a false assumption.

A global level organization does not currently exist nor are there any chances of one coming into being. Therefore, a global strategy to solve the hunger problem is ruled out. The solution to the hunger problem appears to lie in improving the slack in resources and edible food calories available in the system. However, a government will be unable to affect any changes in this slack through merely issuing a decree. Moralistic campaigns or coercive regulations would only create resentment which would shift the attention of the government from managing resources to fighting dissidence, also consuming scarce resources in the process [Saeed 1986b]. Intervention, therefore, continues to be a complicated matter even though a theoretical solution to the problem can be found. Research on the hunger problem needs to be aimed at finding pressure points into the system that maintains a poor resource slack and effectively managing its human and ecological actors to improve this slack.

References

Aiken, W. (1977) 'The Right to be Saved from Starvation' in Aiken, W. and La Follette (eds.), *World Hunger and Moral Obligations*, Prentice Hall.

Bhagwatti, Jagdish N. (1972) 'Economic and World Order, The 1970's to 1990's: The Key Issues', in Bhagwatti (ed.), *Economics and World Order*, MacMillan.

Bhattacharjee, J. P. (1976) 'Population, Food and Agricultural Development: A Medium Term Review', *Food Policy*, May.

Chenery, Hollis and Syrquin, Moises (1975) *Patterns of Development 1950-1970*, Oxford University Press.

FAO (1981) *Agriculture: Toward 2000*, Rome.

Hardin, C. (1977) 'Life Boat Ethics: The Case Against Helping the Poor' in Aiken, W. and La Follette (eds.), *World Hunger and Moral Obligations*, Prentice Hall.

Hardin, Garrett (1985) 'Preventing Famine', letter in *Science*, March 15.

Haru, T. (1984) 'Moral Obligation and Conceptions of World Hunger: On the Need to Justify Correct Action', *Journal of Applied Behavioral Science*, 20(4): 363-368.

Le Riche, W. Harding (1985) 'High-Technology Agriculture', letter in *Science*, 26 April: 392.

Lipton, Michael (1975) 'Urban Bias and Food Policy in Poor Countries', *Food Policy*, 1(4): 41-52.

Maxwell, H. J. and Singer, H. W. (1983) 'Food Aid to Developing Countries: A survey', *Institute of Development Studies*, University of Sussex.

Meadows, Dennis et. al. (1974) 'Population Sector', *Dynamics of Growth in a Finite World*, MA: MIT Press.

Menon, Bhaskar P. (1977) *Global Dialogue: The New International Order*, New York: Pergamon.

Nabe, Oumar (1983) 'Military Expenditure and Industrialization in Africa', *Journal of Economic Issues*, 17(2): 575-587.

O'Neill, O. (1977) 'Lifeboat Earth', in Aiken, W. and La Follette (eds.), *World Hunger and Moral Obligations*, Englewood Cliffs, NJ: Prentice Hall.

Paarlberg, Don (1975) 'The World Food Situation: A Consensus View', *Food Policy*, 1(4): 15-22.

Peterson, Steven O. (1983) *Soil Dynamics*, unpublished M. Sc. Thesis, Thayer School of Engineering, Dartmouth College, June.

Picardi, Anthony C. and Siefert, William W. (1976) 'The Tragedy of Commons in Sahel', *Technology Review*, 76(6): 1-10.

Popper, Karl R. (1977) *The Open Society and Its Enemies*, New York: Routledge, Vol. 2, p.130.

Saeed, K. (1982) 'Public Policy and Rural Poverty: a System Dynamics Analysis of a Social Change Effort in Pakistan', *Technological Forecasting and Social Change*, Vol. 21, Winter.

Saeed, K. (1985) 'An Attempt to Determine Criteria for Sensible Rates of Use of Material Resources', *Technological Forecasting and Social Change*, 28(4): 311-323.

Saeed, K. (1986) 'Dynamics of Economic Growth and Political Instability in the Developing Countries', *System Dynamics Review*, 2(1): 20-35.

Saeed, K. (1986) 'Limits to National Development: Resources or Resource Allocation Processes?', *Proceedings of the 1986 International Conference of the System Dynamics Society*, Seville, Spain.

Sen, A. K. (1981) *Poverty and Famines: An Essay on Entitlement and Deprivation*, Oxford: Clarendon for ILO.

Siamwalla, Ammar and Valdès, Alberto (1975) 'Food Insecurity in the Developing Countries', *Food Policy*, 5(4): 258-272.

World Bank (1981) *World Development Report 1981*, Oxford University Press.

Yatopoulous, Pan A. (1985) 'Middle Income Classes and Food Crisis: The "New" Food-Feed Competition', *Economic Development and Cultural Change*, 33(3): 463-483.

9 Managing technology for development: a systems perspective[*]

Khalid Saeed

Abstract

This paper re-examines, from a system perspective, criteria for the selection and implementation of technologies appropriate to developing countries. Viewed so, the efficacy of a technology and the distribution of its benefits do not appear to depend on the technology *per se*, but are seen as aspects of the management of technology. Thus, development plans must provide means for both making an appropriate technological choice and generating a suitable management strategy to obtain maximum and widespread benefit from that choice, while avoiding creation of dysfunctional social or environmental conditions. An appropriate technological choice should be based on considerations of efficiency and sustenance, while a concomitantly implemented organizational plan addresses the problems of adoption of efficient production methods, resource allocation between production and control activities, and spread of benefits.

Introduction

New technologies, of many ilks, have been introduced in a number of

[*] Reprinted from *Socio-Economic Planning Sciences*, 23(4), Khalid Saeed, A re-evaluation of the effort to alleviate poverty and hunger, pp. 217-228, Copyright 1990, with kind permission from Elsevier Science Ltd., The Boulevard, Langford Lane, Kidlington OX5 1GB, UK.

213

developing countries for increasing productivity. These include high-yielding seed varieties, synthetic fertilizers, pesticides and improved cropping practices in the agricultural sector, the use of capital intensive mass production techniques in the industrial sector, and those implements and inputs which are affordable by the poorer target groups in both sectors. These technologies have been successfully adopted in many developing countries, making a significant contribution to precipitating a green revolution in the agricultural sector while also creating a large-scale manufacturing sector.

In the agricultural sector, the use of productivity-improvement technologies has been fairly widespread. In the industrial sector, their application has been limited to relatively large-scale operations. The improvements in productivity have not, however, improved the living conditions for most people in either sector. In some instances, the introduction of low and intermediate technologies affordable by the poor have also exacerbated the dualities existing in the system instead of creating any significant benefit for the poor [Griffin and Ghose 1979, Lipton 1976].

The diverse experiences of performance of new technologies have been evaluated in the literature from many different vantage points. The variety of opinions thus generated has led to much debate on what might be an appropriate technological choice, although the variously prescribed choices are often based on different considerations with limited common ground. Table 1 shows some of the terms used to qualify technological choices and their respective contexts (which are often implicit). Technologies described as high, low or intermediate, capital or labor intensive, efficient, biased, discriminating, modern, traditional, or only vaguely, as appropriate or inappropriate, have little common basis for comparison.

High, low, and intermediate labels describe production processes at the micro-level without considering their overall societal context. Labor- or capital-intensive classifications pertain to aggregate economic measurements without considering distributional aspects and the technical details of the production process, while appropriate technologies often imply production processes that acquiesce with existing social structure without considering overall system efficiency and sustenance. Since none of the vantage points prescribing these technological choices gives an adequate view of the system to which the technology is to be applied, the choices they issue incorporate many blind spots, which predisposes them to unpredictable performance [Adelman and Morris 1973, Saeed 1990].

This essay re-examines, from a system perspective, the issues of choice and the problems of management and implementation of technologies for developing countries, moving away from the debate on appropriate technology and attempting to understand the performance of a technology in relation to the information relationships that precipitate performance. The framework issued has important implications for policy design since it requires exploring ways to influence the information relationships to obtain

214

reliable performance instead of imposing choices through large scale direct intervention [Forrester 1979].

Table 9.1
Technological choice labels and their respective contexts

Contexts	Technological choice labels
Resource Environment	Consuming, Polluting, Sustaining, Resource Efficient, Energy-based
Social Class Structure	Biased, Inappropriate, Appropriate Dysfunctional, Disruptive
Factors Market	Economically Efficient, Labor Intensive, Capital Intensive
Industrial Relations	Labor Substituting, Employment Generating
Production Process	High Tech, Low Tech, Intermediate Tech, Efficient, High Productivity

Notwithstanding the many interpretations of the term system, a somewhat pragmatic view is adopted for defining a system boundary as advocated by Antol Rapoport, Talcott Parsons and Jay Forrester [Parsons 1980, Rapoport 1980, Forrester 1968]. A system, according to this view, incorporates information relationships relevant to well-recognized processes, although it may not strictly qualify as an open system as defined by Bertalanffy and Miller [Bertalanffy 1968, Miller 1975]. Such systems are sometimes described as abstracted, although they may have relatively permanent boundaries and decision structure [Bertalanffy 1968, Miller 1975, Baily 1981].

It is suggested here that the criteria for selection of a technology should be concerned with the issues of efficiency of production and the sustenance of the resource environment. At the same time, design of the related management strategy must aim at achieving a proper balance between economic and control activities by the government, facilitating wide-spread distribution of benefits by the economic system, and realizing trouble-free operation in the production units. In this regard, an attempt is made to

215

identify broad principles of an effective policy framework to meet the above requirements.

Ad hoc considerations for technological choices

Technology has often been viewed by economists as a recipe for combining production factors in given proportions to generate output. In a static sense, these proportions can be interpreted to be what Leontief defines as technical coefficients which remain fixed in an input-output model [Leontief 1966]. Neo-classical micro-economic theory also postulates that the proportions in which production factors may be combined depend on the incremental revenue generated by each factor compared with its incremental cost. Any changes in the relative costs and productivities of the factors will create a need to combine them in different proportions, thus precipitating technological change [Hirshliefer 1976]. Furthermore, technical coefficients will change with respect to output as increases in productivity are obtained through innovative use of existing machinery, equipment and methods of production, with improved labor skills creating several facets of what has been classified as technological progress [Kendrick 1961, Solow 1957, Diwan and Livingstone 1979].

Initial statements about the application of technology in the context of development implicitly assumed that given techniques of production could be applied anywhere, leading to the notion of technology import and transfer. Capital-intensive technologies giving high levels of output per worker were seen to be ideal for economic development. Experience showed, however, that such production methods and processes transplanted through imports from developed countries were not always successful either in terms of improved productivity or the spread of benefit across all social classes [Diwan 1979].

Implementation of capital-intensive technologies led to the creation of what was first recognized by Boeke as economic dualism, which manifested in the side by side existence of a modern and apparently efficient capital-intensive sector with a traditional and apparently inefficient labor-intensive sector [Boeke 1976]. However, when the apparently efficient modern sector was encouraged to expand, the interdependence between the two sectors often increased surplus labor in the traditional sector. Hence, revisionist ideas concerning the choice of technology were formulated which emphasized the need for labor-intensive technologies to alleviate unemployment and for the so-called intermediate technologies to improve productivity of the traditional sector, as against the earlier emphasis on selecting technologies for improving productivity of the capital-intensive sector [Griffin and Ghose 1979, Lipton 1976].

The recent realization of impressive economic growth propelled by

216

exports in some developing countries has (understandably) led several governments to seek the establishment of industry producing mainly for export and employing highly sophisticated production techniques. However, the efficacy of such policies has been variable in terms of relevance to efficient utilization of national resources and the ability to sustain high-tech production within a developing country environment [Malecki 1987, Siddiqi 1990, Misra 1988].

Diverse experiences in implementing various technological choices has apparently led to a rather vague definition of technology deemed suitable for developing countries. This definition calls for a panacea to integrate techniques of production and consumption with the culture of the society. The historical process through which technology and culture develop hand in hand has generated a new term - appropriate technology. There has since been a variety of views on what might be considered an appropriate technology [Dunn 1978, Schumacher 1973] Most of these are ad hoc and often unclear both about their objectives and about integration with the culture. The panacea is apparently still not in sight.

The attempt to identify a technology in accord with culture has often led to the creation of unsophisticated production methods which can neither cause nor facilitate a change in the economic well-being of a society, but rather which often acquiesce with society's existing cultural, income, and resource profiles. This has generally led to an inability of the population to make capital investments, the concentration of ownership of capital resources in the hands of a few, and low compensation for labor. Additionally, a high population growth rate, together with an unequal distribution of income, has tended to maintain a low standard of living for most people even when output of the economy is expanding. In addition, inadequate slack in resource systems created high susceptibility to natural disasters [Chenery 1975, Saeed 1987].

A vague expectation also expressed in the writings on economic development and technology has been that the benefits of a highly productive technology might diffuse on their own to reach all the people [Diwan 1979, Myrdal 1957]. Unfortunately, the social system is not structured like the molecules of a gas through which the type of diffusion postulated in the models of technological change can occur. Rather the distribution of benefits of a technology must occur through information relationships underlying the behavior of the economic and political actors in the system [Myrdal 1957, Ardnt 1983]. These relationships need to be clearly understood and, if necessary, simultaneously influenced if a technological choice is to be successfully implemented in engineering a change for the better.

217

Systems criteria for designing a technology policy

A technology must function within the information relationships and the knowledge base underlying the decision rules exercised in an organizational system [Ayres 1988]. These information relationships and decision rules make possible sustenance of the organization in its environment, as well as the production of the throughput for its maintenance and growth. Any reasonable definition of technology must thus subsume the technical and managerial processes involved in selecting inputs from, and outputs to the environment as well as the creation of throughput for the organization and its application to overcoming entropy, sustaining membership, and propelling growth [Katz and Kahn 1978, Rifkin 1981]. This model can be easily extended to apply to a developing nation which is essentially an organization concerned with increasing welfare for its members while also trying to maintain organizational integrity in the face of disruptive forces and exploiting its natural endowments cleverly to sustain itself in its physical environment [Miller 1975]. However, the functions required to be performed in this model relate not to a single organizational unit but to actors at the levels of 1) the political system , 2) the economic system, 3) the production units and 4) the resource system, which form a hierarchy as shown in Figure 9.1. The political system dictates rules of conduct that control the economic system. The economic system, in turn, creates an environment in which the production units operate. The material inputs for production are obtained from the resource system whose sustenance determines the ultimate conditions of survival.

The abstract system to be constructed for addressing the issues of choice and management of technology must integrate the relevant functions of these systems, even though they operate at various levels of the hierarchy. These functions include

1) the creation of an incentive system by the government that determines technological choices leading to the selection of appropriate materials from the resource environment;
2) the allocation of resources (by the government) between economic activities and instruments of control in an effort to maximize welfare while also overcoming political conflict;
3) the efficient transformation of resources into throughput (products, services, energy) by smooth and trouble-free adoption of the selected technologies; and
4) the equitable distribution of income through transactions occurring between the economic actors of the system and the regeneration of waste materials in the resource system.

Figure 9.2 shows how these four functions, residing in the four

218

subsystems represented in Figure 9.1, may interact in relation to the choice of technology and its management. The numbers in the various boxes refer to the sub-systems of Figure 9.1 incorporating the respective functions. Usable resources are selected from those in place in the resource system (4). This depends on the technological choices as determined by incentives created by the government (1) and the dictates of the economic system (2). Usable resources are also created through investment activity of the production units (3). The government (1) effects a broad allocation of usable resources between economic activity and the instruments of control, depending upon the need for each activity. This is accomplished directly or through a system of taxes and subsidies. The resources allocated to economic activity are converted by the production units (3) into throughput, a part of which is reinvested; the rest is distributed through the transactions of the economic system (2). Resources consumed by the various social classes and the instruments of control form waste, which is slowly regenerated by the resource system (4) into exploitable resources or exploited commercially by the production units (3) if available technology permits this.

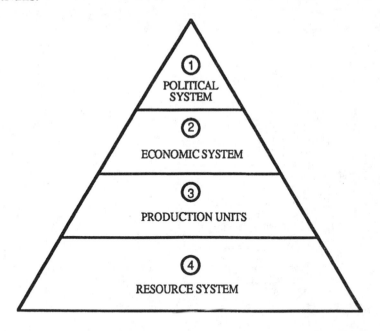

Figure 9.1   **Functional systems concerned with choice of technology and its management**

Given acceptance of the proposed organizational model, there appear to be four fundamental requirements that a technology policy must meet if it is to facilitate change for the betterment of a society. First, the technological choice must be able to effect as much increase as possible in throughput in the form of goods and services available to its members, while not indiscriminately consuming all the natural endowments of society. It should, however, help to maintain a reasonable level of slack in the resource system to serve as "insurance" against environmental shocks. Second, it should cause as little increase as possible in the need for exercising government control, so that the additional throughput created does not have to be consumed in proliferation of the instruments of control. Third, the benefits of the increase in throughput should not be limited to a small group of people but rather should accrue to a wide-cross section of the population. This will tend to minimize any conflict and dysfunctional motivational patterns. Finally, the production units should function so as to allow for trouble-free implementation of the new efficient production methods that might otherwise be abandoned due to organizationally-related problems [Katz and Kahn 1978]. These requirements do not necessarily preclude the transplantation of efficient technologies from developed countries. They do, however, make it necessary to integrate organizational and technological instruments in preparing a comprehensive design for change.

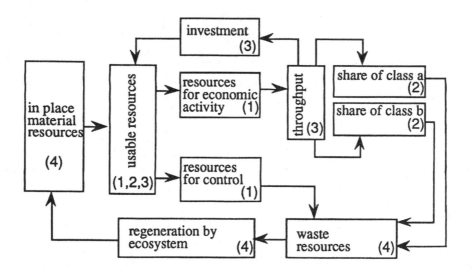

Figure 9.2   **Abstracted system integrating relevant processes from the various functional systems**

220

Broad principles for the design of a technology policy

When viewed as a whole, the abstracted system represented in Figure 9.2 appears much too complex to be tractable. It can, however, be partitioned into subsystems that have specific organizational contexts as well as relatively permanent boundaries and decision structures. Each of these partitions could thus be examined separately in an effort to identify broad principles for the design of a technology policy [Baily 1981, Keyfitz 1979].

A framework is now presented for generating technological and organizational policies relevant to performance of the four subsystems concerned with, respectively, the selection of material resources, the allocations to various activities by the government, the distribution of benefit and production. Each subsystem is discussed in turn.

Selection of materials from the resource system

Technological developments in the West have often been based on consuming the resource slack present either in the well-endowed territory from which the technology emerged or on resource availability through transfers from colonized lands. Application of technologies based on such criteria in the precariously balanced resource environment of a developing country possessing little slack can be quite disastrous [Hardin 1985, Picardi and Siefert 1976].

The earth's resource ecosystem contains a very large variety of substances from which we can obtain materials for our consumption. Several sources for a single raw material can often be identified, although not all of these can be exploited simultaneously since the prevalent economic criteria call for the consumption of the cheapest source first. The cheapest source to exploit is often the one which is richest in the materials we need for our consumption. Such resources have usually undergone the longest regeneration process in the resource ecosystem.

Figure 9.3 shows feedback loops in a resource use policy that may reduce the slack in the system. When technological developments strive to tap low-cost rich minerals as consumption rises, regeneration time rises while the slack in the system is consumed. If such a consumption pattern continues, a catastrophic decline in resource use must follow unless there are significant technological breakthroughs that allow reclassification of some of the spent resources as usable. Such breakthroughs are often not easy to realize. Thus, ideally, we should select a resource mix from our environment whose aggregate regeneration rate matches that of our consumption. When consumption rises, resources with a shorter renewal time should be added to the package in use while those with a longer renewal time should be dropped [Page 1977, Saeed 1985].

Ironically, history has generally seen the opposite situation take place.

Thus, as consumption pressures have risen, technologies have been developed to tap richer geological resources. This, in turn, has increased the aggregate regeneration time of the resource package in use. Such trends have even led to the formulation of a very phenomenological classical theory of resource use which postulates the abandonment of low quality mines as richer mines are discovered [Robinson 1980]. This pattern is due to the increasing availability of technologies that tap richer resources rather than those with a faster renewable time. Control of technological progress thus appears to be an important entry point for implementing a sensible resource use policy. In this regards, resource use should apparently be based on geological information rather than on economic criteria. This implies a need to investigate ways and means of influencing technological progress that would help balance resource consumption and regeneration rates.

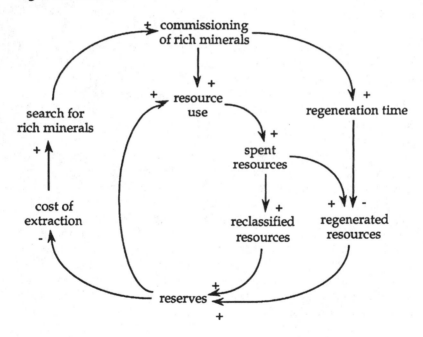

Figure 9.3   **Feedback loops in the resource subsystem concerned with maintenance of a slack**

Maintenance of government control

One reason for the failure to obtain, through improved productivity, a sustained rise in the standard of living of poor people in developing countries has been a tremendous increase in the proportion of national resources channeled by governments into instruments of control for the regulation of public life and the maintenance of national security. Sometimes an expansion in government control may occur as a result of an outside intervention or threat about which little can be done. More often, however, it arises from endogenous causes and is often justified on the basis of: 1) an increase in the size of the economy to be managed; 2) enlargement of the interventionist role of the government, or 3) the need to cope with dissidence experienced over the course of development [37-39]. Indeed, the coterminous expansion of government's role and economic growth has sometimes given the impression that the former is necessary to achieve the latter [Benoit 1978, Morawetz 1977]. In fact, the excessive allocation of a nation's resources to control activities may partly arise from implementation of overly interventionist policies and be further exacerbated by the feedback loops underlying the political system.

Figure 9.4 shows feedback loops that may lead a typical developing country government, which is often autocratic, to occupy itself with expanding control at the cost of undermining public welfare. When introduction of productive technologies raises the level of economic resources, a need to expand system organization is simultaneously created. Thus, some increase in the control function of government is inevitable when new technology creates economic growth. However, the proportion of total resources allocated in the next round to the economic sector depends not only on total available resources but also on government's commitment to delivering social goods and its perception of the need for control. The commitment to delivering social goods is kept alive by adversarial activity originating from censure of the government by the public. The perception of the need for control is determined by the volume of resources to be managed, the scope of government intervention and, most importantly, by the rise in insurgence which is fueled by dissidence.

Dissidence arises from unvented censure. Potential censure can be vented only if adequate civil rights exist. Unfortunately, civil rights are often progressively reduced as government control rises. In the absence of civil rights, unvented censure breeds dissidence. The insurgence resulting from dissidence calls for allocating even more resources to the instruments of control. Thus, allocation of resources to control activities can far exceed the organizational needs of the enlarged economy [Saeed 1986].

To avoid excessive allocation of resources to control activities and to limit increase in dissidence, it is necessary to maintain a democratic process through which the government remains accountable to the people and committed to improving their welfare, instead of concentrating on increasing its control. Developing countries have mostly failed on this count. Authoritative governments, whose commitment is to increasing their control and not to improving the welfare of the public, have been bred through the design of interventionist development strategies. Government management practice, therefore, must change from powerful direct

223

intervention to influencing motivational patterns in the system to effect a change. The technologies selected must be implementable without powerful intervention by the government. Management instruments supporting a technology must also not require the government to assume direct responsibility for implementation but should instead clearly indicate indirect policy measures needed to change the existing motivational patterns [Popper 1977].

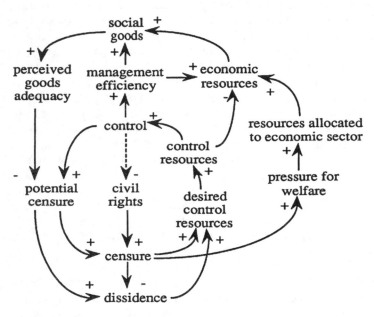

Figure 9.4   **Feedback loops in the government management subsystem concerned with allocation of resources to welfare and control activities**

The feedback structure of Figure 9.4 indicates that severing the relationship between control and civil rights would maintain censure and decrease dissidence, which should lead to a balanced allocation of resources between social goods and control. Thus, maintenance of civil rights appears to be a significant principle to be upheld in organizational designs for governing systems for developing countries. Further research is needed on delineating the structure of a governing system that should assure government commitment to a welfare agenda over the course of a technological change and on devising a technology policy that can be implemented without direct intervention.

The impact of improved productivity on the people's standard of living is limited by the social relations of production and distribution. It should be recognized that the distribution of benefits from improved productivity depends on social arrangements and not on the selected technology *per se*. Depending on these arrangements, a technology may benefit a majority and/or a minority of the population [Schumpeter 1950]. When a highly productive technology appears to benefit only a minor cross-section of society, the answer is not to discard the technology in favor of a less productive one (which might benefit a wider cross-section) but rather to influence the social arrangements responsible for the distribution of benefits.

The gains from improvements in productivity are distributed through claims to income on the basis of ownership of productive resources as well as on the contribution of labor.

However, in a dual economic system the ability of a worker to negotiate a high wage depends on his opportunity cost of leaving wage-employment, which is generally low if he does not own the resources for engaging in self-employment. In such a system, an autonomous increase in productivity may stimulate considerable further investment and create the subsequent multiplier effects, although it may not lead to expansion of workers' resource ownership [Bardhan 1973, Anderson 1968, Sen 1975].

Figure 9.5 shows the feedback loops present in the relationships of social exchange that restrain the transfer of benefits of improved productivity to workers. When productive resources can potentially be engaged in both commercial and self-employed modes, an autonomous increase in productivity of capital resources in the commercial mode would draw resources away from workers' ownership, thus reducing their opportunity cost of wage-work.

On the other hand, an increase in the productivity of capital resources owned by the workers may only bid up rents since a change in ownership is not necessary for expanding resource employment in the self-employed mode; resources vacated by the less-productive commercial sector will be offered for renting to the self-employed. At the same time, the surplus labor released by the commercial sector has to be absorbed in self-employment. Worker income is thus depressed whether the application of a new technology improves productivity in the commercial sector or in self-employment [Saeed 1988].

Apparently, it is important to introduce instruments that help redistribute the ownership of resources together with the technology that improves productivity. Since direct intervention may expand the scope of the government, which may create a dysfunctional role for it with respect to power, only indirect instruments creating an evolutionary change should be considered. For example, introduction of a fiscal policy to discourage the renting of resources may help to transfer ownership of absentee-owned resources to the self-employed and thus improve the distribution of the benefits of high productivity. Future research should seek to identify innovative incentive schemes that influence income distribution patterns rather than pursuing technologies that are in accord with existing patterns.

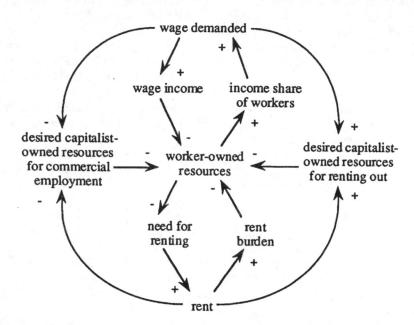

Figure 9.5 **Feedback loops in the economic subsystem concerned with distribution of capital resources and income**

Smooth functioning of the production units

The ability of a technology to perform reliably is not necessarily only a function of its design. The use of a new technology must pass through a learning phase during which the user must become familiar with its idiosyncrasies and understand its managerial requirements. Many technologies may not successfully pass this phase thus limiting the performance of the production units.

A variety of normative models have been proposed to explain the process of technology adoption. Unfortunately, the structure of these models is often highly abstract and difficult to utilize in real world applications. Hence, they may have had little significance from the point-of-view of policy design, although they are sometimes used for forecasting [Mahajan 1985, Sharif and Kabir 1976, Sharif and Ramanathan 1982].

The important feedback loops underlying the problem of new technology adoption in a production organization are shown in Figure 9.6. As a new technology is adopted, a backlog of unsolved problems associated with its functioning begins to build up. These problems can be solved only when an adequate number of professionally competent people are available, failing which a backlog of problems can discourage further adoption while actually encouraging abandonment by existing adopters [Homer 1987 and Ambali 1987].

At the outset, the remedy for this problem might appear to be ensurance that an adequate number of professionals are on hand to attend to technology-related problems. Indeed, developing country governments have instituted many training programs for the public while setting up extension services and community development organizations. Unfortunately, these programs often become victims of political maneuvers and fail in their objective to provide professional assistance to the community [Alavi 1976, Abeyrama and Saeed 1984].

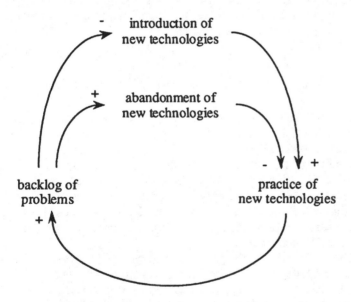

Figure 9.6   **Feedback loops in the implementation process limiting spreading of new technologies for the production of throughput**

I am of the view that politicization of these programs stems from the widespread organizational tradition of placing a high value on loyalty and a low value on professionalism which is pervasive in developing countries.

227

The colonial experience, during which local artisanship was suppressed and loyalty to authority of the ruler was rewarded, might have contributed to the nurturing of such a value system.

Not surprisingly, most developing country governments continue to be run on colonial lines with an emphasis on loyalty to authority. These governments have attempted to organize much of their development efforts under the umbrella of their own bureaucratic system which is often times not conducive to professionalism [Streeten 1979]. Because of such value systems, the key to advancement within an organization is often loyalty to authority rather than professional competence, leaving little incentive to professionalism [Gouldener 1957-58]. Widespread illiteracy in some of developing countries might further reinforce the lack of emphasis on professionalism.

It is not a simple matter to find an entry point for changing the value system of a society. A concerted effort to eradicate illiteracy might be a reasonable starting point for inducing change. An expanded role for the private sector, which generally places a high value on professionalism, might further facilitate the nurturing of a professionally oriented corporate culture [Benvensite 1987]. Understanding these institutional dynamics in delineating viable implementation strategies for a technological choice is clearly an important research agenda to pursue.

Implications for development policy and planning education

Development plans for developing countries often blindly specify targets for change. They also implicitly assume that the (relevant) system is static and not self-regulating. It should thus be possible for an outside hand to change existing conditions and create a higher level of prosperity. A common feature of these plans has been the considerable government intervention they require. Not surprisingly then, the role of government and the scale of the resources allocated to constructing and operating instruments of control often increase concomitantly with the implementation of development plans.

Current approaches to national planning and policy design often entail fragmented efforts undertaken in the compartmentalized wings of government. These efforts may ultimately assembled be into a statement of targets by a central planning organization. Such a process can rarely identify organizational mechanisms for effectively creating change. Sometimes, impromptu agendas originating at the top also determine directions of the effort. The systems view advocated in this paper would require a reorganization of the planning activity and designing organizational instruments of change along with the statement of targets. This would certainly require some restructuring of relevant planning institutions and new ideas for education in socio-economic planning.

In general, it is necessary to construct the organizational means for understanding the dynamics of an existing system before developing an appropriate policy framework. The resulting framework must help identify mechanisms to produce healthy growth within the system. Without an attempt to understand the social organization in which development is to occur, planning is reduced to only wishful thinking or moral statement-making. It is noteworthy that such uncontextualized thinking has been widely practiced in preparing development plans.

There exist fundamental impediments, however, to adopting a systems perspective. First, professional specializations create conceptual filters that confine thinking process to only our well-known turfs. Second, living close to the events taking place within the system, it becomes difficult to step back in time and space so as to obtain a detached and holistic view of those processes causing the various events we experience. Finally, a systems view calls for policy considerations with a time frame that is often too long for the political considerations of the actors concerned with implementation. It may not, therefore, be sufficiently appealing for a professional to strongly pursue long-term issues [Beer 1980, Richmond 1987, Schön 1983].

The most important requirement for improving design of a technology policy appears to be an overcoming of the fundamental conceptual barriers through interdisciplinary cooperation and cultivation of systems thinking. This may not be easy to accomplish due to past and current compartmentalization of university curricula into narrow areas of specialization. Further, practitioners may only rely on prior specializations in their practice or base their work on short term pressures experienced in their respective roles.

Perhaps education in socio-economic planning should aim at cultivating what Schön labels "reflective practicum", which should allow practitioners to engage in a meaningful dialogue with self while preparing a policy design. In some professions such as architecture and music, this might be possible to accomplish by learning to critically examine the outcomes of initial designs as these can be quickly translated into visual or aural media [Schon 1987, Forrester 1968]. However, any reflective practice in planning would require experimenting with those perceived behavioral relationships forming part of a design. This has not been possible except in a limited way due largely to constraints imposed by the methodological vehicles available for such experimentation, namely qualitative reasoning and formal mathematical logic. The former, being inexact, is unable to assist the reflective process in a reliable way. The later can handle only a very limited level of complexity while its application requires specialized skills.

The study of organizing principles of systems, together with the ability to simulate, on a computer, the outcome of hypothesized systems relationships, provide easy-to-use means for experimentation with social systems [Simon 1969, Richmond 1987]. The widespread availability of low-cost computing and user-friendly software such as STELLA and DYNAMO bring the ability to experiment with relationships to a large cross-section of professionals [Richardson 1981]. Active use of these tools, together with heuristics of scientific practice should help to cultivate a much-needed reflective practicum in planning both in the classroom and in professional practice. Future research agendas should, therefore, be most concerned with curriculum innovations relevant to educational and professional development.

Conclusion

Technology policy in developing countries has in general been based on *ad hoc* considerations, ranging from creation of economic efficiency to helping certain target groups maintain existing social relations. The adoption of technologies based on these types of considerations has generated a wide variety of performance patterns thus confusing the issue of what might be an appropriate choice of technology.

The efficacy of a technology and the distribution of its benefits do not, however, depend on the technology *per se*, but are instead problems of the management of technology. A successful design of change in developing countries should thus require making both an appropriate technological choice and seeking an effective management strategy.

The problems of choice of technology and its implementation must be examined in view of the dynamic political and social organizations (systems) and the resource environment in which a selected technology must function. Viewed so, a technology policy must provide a basis for selecting appropriate materials from the resource environment, creating the means for obtaining adequate throughput for the members of society, minimizing entropy, and creating an equitable distribution of benefits.

An appropriate basis for selection of materials from the environment requires the balancing of aggregate regeneration rates with consumption, using geological information instead of the prevalent economic criteria. The production of adequate throughput requires creating the organizational means for successful implementation of production methods and technologies. The reduction of entropic forces entails creating a democratic process of government which functions with minimal conflict and frugal instruments of control. Creating equitable distribution requires introduction of fiscal measures that help to redistribute the ownership of resources together with technology that is capable of improving productivity.

The design of a technology policy based on these considerations requires a moving away from current planning practices in developing countries. These practices often entail the stating of targets on the basis of fragmented

230

projections carried out in compartmentalized organizations or of impromptu agendas originating at higher levels of the organization. What is needed is an accounting of relevant systems relationships. There exist, however, conceptual barriers to adopting systems thinking. Thus, reforming education in socio-economic planning and creating organizational means for effective of planning and implementation of constitute important research issues for the future.

References

Abeyrama, T. and Saeed, K. (1984) 'The Gamodaya Mandalaya Scheme in Sri Lanka: Participatory Development or Power Play?', *Community Development Journal*, 29(1): 20-31.

Adelman, I. and Hihn, J. M. (1984) 'Crisis Politics in Developing Countries', *Economic Development and Cultural Change*, 33(1): 1-22.

Adelman, I. and Morris, C. T. (1973) *Economic Growth and Social Equity in the Developing Countries*, Stanford University Press, Stanford, CA.

Alavi, H. (1976) 'The Rural Elite and Agricultural Development in Pakistan in Stevens et. al. (eds.), *Rural Development in Bangladesh and Pakistan*, Honolulu, Hawaii: Hawaii University Press, 317-353.

Ambali, J. (1987) *Dynamics of Innovation Implementation, The Case of Quality Control Circles*, Bangkok, Thailand: AIT.

Anderson, K. P. (1968) *Peasant and Capitalist Agriculture in the Developing Country*, unpublished Ph.D. Thesis, Cambridge, MA: MIT Press.

Ardnt, H. W. (1983) 'The Trickle Down Myth', *Economic Development and Cultural Change* 32(1): 1-10.

Ayres, R. U. (1988) 'Technology: The Wealth of Nations', *Technological Forecasting and Social Change*, 33(3): 189-201.

Baily, K. D. (1981) 'Abstracted vs Concrete Sociological Theory', *Behavioral Science*, 26(4): 313-323.

Bardhan, P. K. (1973) 'A Model of Growth in a Dual Agrarian Economy' in Bhagwati, J. and Eckus, R. (eds.), *Development and Planning: Essays in Honor of Paul Rosenstein-Roden*, George Allen and Unwin Ltd., London, 109-117.

Beer, S. (1981) 'Death is Equifinal', *Behavioral Science*, 26(3):185-196.

Benoit, E. (1978) 'Growth and Defense in Developing Countries', *Economic Development and Cultural Change*, 20(2): 271-280.

Benvensite, G. (1987) *Professionalizing the Organization, Reducing Bureaucracy to Enhance Effectiveness*, London: Jossey - Bass Publishers.

Bertalanffy, L. V. (1968) *General Systems Theory*, New York: George Braziller.

Boeke, J. H. (1976) 'Economics and Economic Policy of Dual Societies, Institute of Pacific Relations, New York (1953)' in G. M. Meier (ed.), *Leading Issues in Economic Development*, 3rd ed., Oxford University Press, New York, 130-131.

Chenery, H. and Serquin, M. (1975) *Patterns of Development, 1950-1970*, London: Oxford University Press for World Bank.

Denison, E. F. (1967) *Why Growth Rates Differ*, Washington D.C.: Brookings Institution.

Diwan, R. K. and Livingstone, D. (1979) *Alternate Development Strategies and Appropriate Technology: Science Policy for an Equitable World Order*, New York, NY: Pergamon Press.

Dunn, P. D. (1978) *Appropriate Technology, Technology with a Human Face*, New York: MacMillan Press.

Forrester, J. W. (1968) *Principles of Systems*, Cambridge, MA: MIT Press, Wright-Allen Series.

Forrester, J. W. (1979) 'An Alternative Approach to Economic Policy: Macrobehavior from Microstructure', in Karmany, N. M. and Day, R. (eds.), *Economic Issues of the Eighties*, Johns Hopkins University Press, Baltimore, 80-108.

Gouldener, A. (1957-58) 'Cosmopolitans and Locals: Towards An Analysis of Latent Social Roles', *Administrative Science Quarterly*, 2: 281-306.

Griffin, K. and Ghose, A. K. (1979) 'Growth and Impoverishment in Rural Areas of Asia', *World Development*, 7(4/5): 361-384.

Hardin, G. (1985) *Filters Against Folly, How to Survive Despite Economists, Ecologists, and the Merely Eloquent*, New York: Penguin Books.

Heggen, R. J. and Cuzan, A. G. (1981) 'Legitimacy, Coercion and Scope: An Expansion Path Analysis Applied to Five Central American Countries and Cuba', *Behavioral Science*, 26(2): 143-152.

Hirshliefer, J. (1976) *Price Theory and Applications*, Prentice Hall, Englewood Cliffs, NJ.

Homer, J. A. (1987) 'Diffusion Model with Application to Evolving Medical Technologies', *Technological Forecasting and Social Change*, 1(3): 197-218.

Katz, D. and Kahn, R. (1978) *The Social Psychology of Organizations*, 2nd ed., New York: John Wiley.

Kendrick, J. W. (1961) *Productivity Trends in the United States*, Princeton University Press, NJ.

Keyfitz, N. (1979) 'Understanding World Models', *Behavioral Science*, 24(3): 190-199.

Leontief, W. (1966) *Input-Output Economics*, Oxford University Press, London.

Lipton, M. (1976) *Why Poor People Stay Poor*, Cambridge, MA: Harvard University Press.

Mahajan, V. and Peterson, R. A. (1985) *Models for Innovation Diffusion*, London: Sage Publications.

Malecki, E. J. (1987) 'Hope or Hyperbole? High Tech and Economic Development', *Technology Review* 90(7): 44-51.

Meadows, Donella (1980) 'The Unavoidable A Priori', in Jorgan Randers (ed.), *Elements of System Dynamics Method*, Cambridge, MA: MIT Press, 23-57.

Miller, J. G. (1975) 'The Nature of Living Systems', *Behavioral Science*, 20(6); 343-365.

Misra, R. P. (1988) 'Role of High Technology in Productivity for Improvement of Quality and Reliability in Developing Countries', *International Seminar on Technology Transfer and the Developing Countries*, Bangkok: Asian Institute of Technology.

Morawetz, D. (1977) *Twenty-Five Years of Economic Development, 1950 to 1975*, Washington D.C.: World Bank.

Myrdal, G. (1957) *Economic Theory and Under-developed Regions*, Gerald Duckworth Ltd., London.

Nabe, O. (1983) 'Military Expenditure and Industrialization in Africa', *Journal of Economic Issues*, 17(2): 575-587.

Page, T. (1977) *Conservation and Economic Efficiency: An Approach to Materials Policy*, Baltimore: Johns Hopkins University Press.

Parsons, T. (1980) 'Concrete Systems vs Abstracted Systems', *Behavioral Science*, 25(1): 46-55.

Picardi, A. and Siefert, W. (1976) 'A Tragedy of Commons in the Sahel', *Technology Review*, 76, 1-10.

Popper, K. (1977) *The Open Society and its Enemies*, Vol. 2, Routledge and Kegan Paul Ltd., Boston.

Rapoport, A. (1980) 'Philosophical Perspectives on Living Systems', *Behavioral Science*, 25(1): 56-64.

Richardson, G. P. and Pugh, A. L. (1981) *Introduction to System Dynamics Modeling with DYNAMO*, Cambridge, MA: MIT Press.

Richmond, B. (1987) *Systems Thinking: Four Key Questions*, Hanover, NH: High Performance Systems.

Richmond, B. et. al. (1987) *An Academic User's Guide to STELLA*, Hanover, NH: High Performance Systems.

Rifkin, J. (1981) *Entropy: A New World View*, New York: Bantam Books.

Robinson, T. J. C. (1980) 'Classical Foundations of the Contemporary Theory of Renewable Resources', *Resources Policy*, 6(4): 278-289.

Saeed, K. (1985) 'An Attempt to Determine Criteria for Sensible Rates of Use of Material Resources', *Technological Forecasting and Social Change*, 28: 311-323.

Saeed, K. (1986) 'The Dynamics of Economic Growth and Political Instability in the Developing Countries', *System Dynamics Review*, 2(1): 20-35.

Saeed, K. (1987) 'A Re-Evaluation of the Effort to Alleviate Poverty and Hunger', *Socio-Economic Planning Sciences*, 21(5): 291-304.

Saeed, K. (1988) 'Wage Determination, Income Distribution, and the Design of Change', *Behavioral Science*, 33(3): 161-186.

Saeed, K. (1990) 'Prevention of Dysfunctional Environmental and Social Conditions in Technology Transfer', in Chatterji, M. (ed.), *Technology Transfer and Development*, MacMillan, London 129-139.

Schön, D. (1983) *The Reflective Practitioner*, New York: Basic Books.

Schön, D. (1987) *Educating the Reflective Practitioner*, San Francisco: Jossey-Bass Publishers.

Schumacher, E. F. (1973) *Small is Beautiful*, London: Blond and Briggs Ltd.

Schumpeter, J. A. (1950) *Capitalism, Socialism and Democracy*, New York: Harper and Row, 156-161, reprinted as Schumpeter on the Disintegration of Bourgeois Family, Archives, *Population and Development Review*, 14(3): 499-507.

Sen, A. K. (1975) *Employment, Technology and Development*, Clarendon, Oxford.

Sharif, M. N. and Kabir, C. (1976) 'System Dynamics Modeling for Forecasting Multi-level Technological Substitution', *Technological Forecasting and Social Change*, 9, 89-112.

Sharif, M. N. and Ramanathan, K. (1982) 'Polynomial Innovation Diffusion Models', *Technological Forecasting and Social Change*, 21: 301-323.

Siddiqi, T. A. (1990) 'Factors Influencing the Transfer of High Technology to the Developing Countries', in Chatterji, M. (ed.), *Technology Transfer and Development*, MacMillan, London, 152-165.

Simon, H. (1969) *Sciences of the Artificial*, Cambridge, MA: MIT Press.

Solow, R. (1957) 'Technology Change and the Aggregate Production Function', *Review of Economics and Statistics*, 39: 312-320.

Streeten, P. (1979) 'Development Ideas in Historical Perspective' in Albert Hirschman et. al., *Towards a New Strategy for Development: A Rothko Chapel Colloquium*, New York: Pergamon Press, 21-52.

10 Entrepreneurship and innovation: a search for an appropriate model for developing countries[*]

Khalid Saeed

Abstract

This paper analyses the various situational views found in the literature concerning entrepreneurship, and the participation of the various income, gender and age groups in it, to arrive at a framework suitable for designing an entrepreneurship policy to facilitate economic development in the developing countries. This framework emphasizes the role of the small family enterprise or the shophouse in leading entrepreneurial activity, creating innovation and economic growth. Motivational, organizational and infrastructure-related factors for stimulating and supporting entrepreneurship are identified and their contributions to increasing participation and improving performance are discussed.

Introduction

This paper reviews diverse evidence and theoretical perceptions to suggest guidelines for an entrepreneurship development policy for the developing countries. Particular attention is given to women and youth participation in entrepreneurial activity, taking a positive view of the increased overall energy of the process, rather than a standpoint on equity, or gender and age-group participation.

The term entrepreneurship, in everyday use, is associated with pursuing

---

[*] This paper is based on a presentation made by the author at the Third Beijing International Conference on Science and Technology, May 1990.

risky economic ventures for profit, although scholars concerned with the concept often differ with this view and with each other. According to Hoselitz:

"A study of the economists' opinions on entrepreneurship leads to strange and sometimes contradictory results. Some writers have identified entrepreneurship with the function of uncertainty-bearing, others with the coordination of productive resources, others with the introduction of innovation, and still others with the provision of capital." [Hoselitz 1952]

An entrepreneur working in a market may perform all of the above functions, provided positive opportunities exist to channel his/her energies. In the absence of these opportunities, entrepreneurial energies may also find outlet in dysfunctional activities. Indeed, in common usage, the term entrepreneurship may imply asocial behavior when mentioned in the context of scholarship, professionalism, or group values. Unregulated entrepreneurship may even create a proliferation of activities in which individual gains are obtained at a cost to the commons; these may even consume the commons in the long run [Hardin 1985, 1968].

Even when applied to socially beneficial processes, entrepreneurship is only one of the important ingredients fueling economic activity. It may contribute to economic performance only if an appropriate economic and opportunity environment exists. Growth orientation and innovation potential will often be facilitated by entrepreneurship, provided the trends for them already exist. The absence of these ingredients may either stifle entrepreneurship or divert entrepreneurial energies into asocial activity. Thus, depending on individual motivation, organizational structure and the existing infrastructure, varying entrepreneurial performance patterns may be experienced at different geographic locations and at various times [D. Young 1983, Maidique 1980].

Entrepreneurship patterns and performance have been widely studied, which has led to many situational views of the process, although it is difficult to transfer experiences from one situation to another. A comparative study of the diverse performance patterns and the situational views arising from them is necessary to identify a general framework for an effective policy intervention, which is attempted in this paper [Saeed 1988a]. It appears that the performance of a large part of the widely-applied policy instruments aimed at encouraging entrepreneurship and innovation, which often call for building the needed infrastructure, depends on the presence or absence of a few fundamental social and organizational factors. The participation of women and youth in entrepreneurial activity also suffers from a lack of institutional support for the informal family-run production units. Such a pattern implies that social reform and institutional development must go hand in hand with infrastructure development for the success of the later.

Entrepreneurship patterns and performance

The decade of the 1980s has brought contrasting experiences in terms of economic performance and the emergence of new products and technologies. On one hand, most industrialized countries faced a prolonged economic stagnation, while a small number of newly industrialized countries saw unprecedented growth. On the other, many innovative technological developments, particularly in the areas of computers, communications, materials, biotechnology, medicine and service industries, emerged from the industrialized countries and made a significant impact at the environment of the workplace and the home. Interestingly, a number of the new products and services from the industrialized countries were created by small entrepreneurial firms. The economic growth in the newly industrialized countries was, however, largely based on technologies transferred from the industrialized countries through large conglomerates and multinational organizations.

In the case of Europe and North America, the 1980s can also be truly called the decade of women and youth entrepreneurs. During this period, an increasing number of women left their traditional roles as mothers, housewives and workers in low paid routine jobs and launched themselves into self-supported entrepreneurial careers. The proportion of the firms owned and managed by women in the USA increased from 7% in the 1970s to 28% in the 1980s. Many of these firms became models of innovation both in terms of their management style and the products and services they provided [McDermot 1985, White 1984]. During the same period, small firms formed by young entrepreneurs, some of them women, became the single most important source of innovation, creating a revolution in the computer industry [Berney 1988].

Innovation and technological development have been hard to come by in many of the developing countries, on the other hand, irrespective of gender and age group, in spite of the significant economic growth achieved by some of the newly industrialized countries. Also, in most cases the economic activity has been dominated by men. The role of women has been limited to motherhood or to routine repetitive jobs, and although the average age of the population is low, the young continue to be viewed as a disruptive force [G. Young 1984, Jones 1988]. Many forms of government intervention have been suggested to create an environment conducive to innovation, but the results of such interventions have been patchy [Westphal 1987, McClleland and Winter 1971]. The varied experience of the performance of the widely-used policies to develop entrepreneurship and create innovation, and the participation of women and youth in these activities, is summarized below.

a) Education

The effect of education on economic performance is widely recognized [Schultz 1961, Becker 1975]. As for its specific impact on entrepreneurship, the evidence is fragmented and modulated by personal biases, although invariably supporting a positive association between education and entrepreneurial performance [McClelland and Winter 1971]. Recent studies on women entrepreneurs, which can be generalized to some extent to the other gender, also show that entrepreneurial firms perform consistently better when run by educated people [Scott 1986]. A strong educational system emphasizing elementary and vocational education helped industrial progress in Japan [Uchida 1981]. Empirical studies also show that the education of women, whether they are actively involved in business or not, positively contributes to the performance of the small family enterprise [Wong 1986].

An appropriate educational curriculum not only upgrades technical know-how, it should also create an ability to carefully reflect over truisms and rules of the thumb. In this way, it would cultivate a sharpened common sense to face the unforeseen circumstances often encountered in the operation of a business. There is a need to prepare innovative designs of education to effectively cultivate reflective faculties instead of confining one only to situational inferences and theory [Schon 1987, Saeed 1987, Saeed 1989].

b) Physical infrastructure

Access to roads, electricity, gas, telephone, major transportation systems, and the availability of service firms facilitates the establishment and progress of small firms started by enterprising individuals [Eisener 1989]. Poor infrastructure may often stand against the realization of full entrepreneurial potential in many developing countries. The development of physical infrastructure has been reported to be a key facilitating factor in the industrial progress of Japan [Inukai 1981]. However, the construction of physical infrastructure alone may not always create entrepreneurship and innovation.

c) Clustering

Schumpeter pointed out that innovations are not evenly distributed over the whole economic system but tend to concentrate in certain sectors and their surroundings [Schumpeter 1939]. Recent studies show that deliberately breeding innovation clusters also facilitates technological development. Such clustering may involve the promotion of a certain family of technologies or a network of innovating firms and industries [Deberesson

1989]. Examples of natural clustering appear in the Technologies Highway in Massachusetts, Silicon Valley in California, and in many unplanned industrial clusters in the developing countries. Planned clustering may, however, not always be successful, especially when some of the motivational and organizational ingredients discussed in sections 2.1 and 2.2 are absent [Malecki 1987].

d) Technical facilitation and "incubation"

Many developing countries have embarked upon expensive programs to establish research and development institutes to facilitate indigenous development and transfer from abroad and the adaptation of technology. These programs often give mixed results.

The clustering of high-tech entrepreneurial activity in the vicinity of many universities possibly led to the concept of "incubators", which are business parks constructed around or within university campuses that allow free interaction between the firms and the university personnel. This may substantially facilitate entrepreneurial activity. Experience, however, shows that such planned incubation also gives mixed results, possibly depending on the presence of the necessary motivational and organizational ingredients [Malecki 1987].

e) Communication

Innovation is essentially a human and a social process. Innovation, entrepreneurial investment, and economic development do not happen unless there is a social environment of attitudes and mechanisms encouraging the giving and receiving of information and the stimulation of creativity in others. In R and D laboratories, where sometimes 50-75% of the time is spent on communication, productivity has been observed to be critically affected by the communication networks existing. It is, therefore, considered important to design channels for effective communication [Tushman 1979].

The innovation potential of a geographic region may also depend, among other factors, on the richness of its information environment made up of networks, formal as well as informal, internal as well as external to the firm. It is, therefore, very important to create "technical cultures" that allow easy communication between the entrepreneurs and the facilitating personnel [Sweeny 1987].

f) Management training

Besides education, prior management experience in a job has been seen to help in overcoming routine problems encountered in the establishment of a business [Scott 1986]. A high degree of mobility between jobs may often facilitate the move from salaried to self-employed modes of work, thus taking advantage of the managerial experience gained in the salaried job. Training to associate achievement correctly with the critical parameters of effort is useful in cultivating entrepreneurial qualities. Many training programs have been designed and implemented, both in the developing and the developed countries, but results are mixed [Technonet Asia 1981, ESCAP undated].

g) Institutional finance

Many entrepreneurs, irrespective of gender and age group, consider the availability of start-up and running capital as a significant bottleneck in their respective pursuits of innovation. The existence of institutions providing finance to the entrepreneurs may facilitate new ventures, although, the collateral requirements of the banking system have a built-in bias against new and un-established firms. Even when institutional finance is available, women and the young find it difficult to obtain because of a bias against them [Macgrath 1987, Byrne 1985].

h) Women and youth participation

The participation of women in the entrepreneurial activity is a relatively new phenomenon in the developed countries; it seems to have been facilitated by a social transformation that has liberated women from their traditional roles of housewife and mother in the nuclear family. It is further propelled by the economic need created by the emergence of many single-parent families headed by women [Scott 1986].

The participation of youth appeared as a strong trend in the developed countries only after the personal computer and its software made its entry, and the young whiz kids clearly proved their superiority. In other businesses, youth still face credibility problems since tradition favors experience and maturity, which are often measured in terms of age rather than on a profession-related scale [Byrne 1985].

Both, women and youth entrepreneurs, continue to be viewed with some reservation. Even when this reservation is set aside, a bias against employing women in managerial positions exists due to their high turnover precipitated by personal agenda and the long maternity leaves they need [Schwartz 1989]. While in some cases the novelty of seeing a woman in a leadership position has helped women in the discharge of their responsibility, systematic discrimination by financial institutions, and sometimes by the clientele is frequently reported [Correa, et. al. 1988, McGrath 1987].

240

Youth has always been viewed by sociologists as a period of problematic transition, although its energy and potential are acknowledged [Jones 1988]. As a result, young people do not realize their limits, although they work extremely hard and pay meticulous attention to technique [Aldrich 1986]. The computer-related industry is probably an exception where youth are well-accepted having proved their mettle beyond any doubt.

The participation of the various gender and age groups in economic activity has been advocated in the context of the developing countries largely from the stand point of social justice and equity, although such concerns are often manifest in the employment of women and youth in routine jobs where they are unable to realize their innovation potential [G. Young 1984]. In addition, the traditional patriarchal value system places much emphasis on the duties of women as mothers, while emphasis on the precedence of age often suppresses youth.

The evidence of the impact of infrastructure facilities on entrepreneurship may appear contradictory if it is not viewed against the backdrop of the fundamental sources of motivation and the organizational environment. The role of infrastructure in fostering entrepreneurial activity is similar to those of the hygienes delineated by Herzberg in connection with the motivational patterns and performance in a firm [Herzberg 1966]. Given the fundamental motivators, and an organizational environment conducive to innovation, the availability of an appropriate infrastructure may considerably facilitate entrepreneurial activity.

It is also very difficult to draw a definite conclusion that the participation of women and youth is productive to the growth of the economic activity. In spite of Japan's remarkable industrial and technological progress, the role of women in management positions in Japan is almost non-existent [Phalon 1988]. Until recently, the woman's role has also been confined to routine work in the western countries. The change in this, propelled possibly by further disintegration of the family, may have had a positive impact on economic performance, but this experience may be difficult to transfer to the developing countries which still have a strong family tradition. It is therefore necessary to search for alternative models of entrepreneurship development that are unbiased against certain genders and age groups and are also relevant to the existing social norms of the developing countries.

Organizational factors determining performance

Information relationships existing within a firm and between the firm and its outside environment greatly effect performance [Katz and Kahn 1979]. Small companies have been observed to possess the energy, flair and flexibility to keep a steady flow of new ideas coming to market. Small

241

companies, however, need freedom of enterprise, a variety of marketing opportunities possible in a horizontally integrated production system, and political stability in the country, to be able to reliably assess and manage the risk associated with enterprise. These factors are discussed below.

a) Firm size

Informally-managed small firms established by enterprising individuals have been a most significant factor contributing to the development of new technologies, products and services, at almost all times, both in the industrialized and the developing countries [Quinn 1979]. The celebrity they have been accorded has, however, varied over time. In the case of the industrialized countries, small firms have been credited with providing the engine of growth over the industrial revolution of the eighteenth century and the continuing developments thereafter. However, prominent economic thought emphasizes the role of large firms and economies of scale over the early part of the twentieth century, while in the latter part, small firm again start to be viewed as the centers of innovation [Harrison 1989].

In the case of the developing countries, small enterprise was dismissed as a facet of the inefficient informal sector, and the development of a large-scale formal sector was emphasized at the start of the organized development effort in the 1940s and 50s [Boeke 1947]. Technological developments realized in the formal sector were expected to trickle down to the rest of the economy [Ardnt 1983]. When this did not occur, attention shifted to the small firm [Schumacher 1973, McClelland and Winter 1971].

The fact remains that the informal organization of the small firm which is free of bureaucratic ropes is conducive to creating innovation. Small companies, often headed by youthful entrepreneurs and sometimes by women, have produced some of the best ideas often stolen by some of the giant companies in the USA [Rowland 1988]. Often, large organizations form RandD units mimicking the informal information relationships in the small firms to facilitate innovation [Quinn 1985].

b) Freedom of enterprise

Entrepreneurial activity has been seen to flourish in an environment of free enterprise and minimal interference from the regulating authority of the government, and to be stifled by strong government interference [Rydenfelt 1984]. It is also a well-known fact that the absence of economic restrictions or regulatory measures led to unprecedented growth of the entrepreneurial activity in eighteenth century England, giving a substantial lead over France, which was infested with cumbersome bureaucratic regulations, although the latter was ahead in terms of the fundamental scientific discoveries underlying much of the technical advance achieved over the course of the industrial revolution [Boswell 1972].

This does not imply, however, that all forms of government intervention are dysfunctional. Some intervention is necessary to deliver social justice and to protect the rights and prerogatives of the various sectors of society. Some forms of indirect government intervention may also help influence the market in a way to facilitate growth of healthy economic activity [Popper 1977].

c) Horizontal integration of firms

Vertically integrated high-tech industry in the developing countries tends to remain isolated from the rest of the economy. The establishment of large-scale public sector industry dealing in high technology and making strategic products has also created a technological duality that works against the small entrepreneur. Large vertically integrated firms wield much influence and are able to lobby successfully for special privileges from the government, from which small enterprise is barred. On the other hand, the horizontal integration of production provides many business opportunities for start-up firms. The industrial interdependence resulting from this not only promotes cooperation among firms and fosters healthy competition, but also increases the synergy of the industrial system. Industrial interdependence resulting from the horizontal integration of firms cultivated what has been termed "organized entrepreneurship" in Japan, which has precipitated unprecedented economic and technological dynamism [Nakagava 1981].

d) Political stability

Stablity in the political environment of a country is extremely important to entrepreneurship. Strong economic take-offs were precipitated in many developing countries including, Pakistan, Sri Lanka, and the Philippines in the early 1960s and 1970s but further progress was blocked by the many political upheavals that followed. Political instability creates uncertainty about the future, which increases the risk in business beyond what an entrepreneur may be able to manage. Strong authoritarian governments existing in many developing countries may provide an illusion of stability while concomitantly destroying the very institutions that assure stability of the rules of conduct. The stability created by authoritarian governments is therefore often quite fragile. A democratic tradition, although giving only limited authority to the government, may help to provide long-term stability and continued commitment to the economic agenda [Saeed 1986, 1990].

The presence of above organizational mechanisms would often create an environment that allows to realize a considerable part of the potential of

243

the entrepreneurial activity, provided fundamental motivational ingredients already exist to draw participation in it.

Fundamental requirements for participation

The most fundamental requirement for entrepreneurship to exist is the presence of highly motivated individuals capable of producing innovative ideas and assuming the risk necessary to commercialize them. Four basic conditions must be met to assure that an adequate number of enterprising individuals initiate entrepreneurial activity. These are, the presence of the opportunity to participate, the individual drive, the access to capital resources, and the presence of marketing opportunities.

a) The opportunity to participate

Innovation occurs in a probabilistic setting and its chances of success are increased if it is attempted by many individuals and firms [Quinn 1985]. To be able to take advantage of naturally endowed human talent, which is distributed very widely, the opportunity to participate in the entrepreneurial activity must be freely available and not limited to certain cross-sections differentiated by income, social class, gender or age group.

Experience shows that young people are often hardworking and idealistic; in recent years, many successful entrepreneurs in the US have been under 30 years of age. Their success often comes from their almost militant determination to succeed, their attention to technique, their ability to take risk and work extremely hard [Aldrich 1986]. Likewise, many women and members of socially disadvantaged minority groups entering self-employment in the US have discovered their new potential as successful and innovative entrepreneurs [Stevenson 1986].

There exist, however, barriers in many societies that restrict choice of work for certain social and ethnic groups. Also, the potential of young people and women is often not realized, especially in the patriarchal societies placing heavy emphasis on the precedence of age and gender.

b) Individual drive

Many views have been expressed about what makes an entrepreneur tick. The profile of an entrepreneur has often been observed to include a passion to prove oneself, an attachment to a certain service or product, past economic deprivation and frustration with the status-quo [Boswell 1972]. These elements may, however, have different origins. According to Schumpeter, the self-interest of entrepreneurs may not originate from the rational self-interest of a detached individual, but from that of a family. Indeed, during the industrial revolution of the eighteenth century, family and family home were the mainsprings of the profit motive [Schumpeter 1950]. More recently, however, many entrepreneurs in the western countries, particularly the women and the youth, started businesses to fulfill psychological and economic needs created by the further disintegration of the family unit and because of the opportunity arising out of the changing attitudes about their roles [Scott 1986]. In all cases, a strong personal motivation has been a necessary element for launching oneself into an entrepreneurial career.

c) Access to capital resources

A shortage of capital resources significantly restricts entrepreneurial activity even if participation is freely permitted and the potential participants are highly motivated. A common solution to this problem is to set up a banking system that provides venture capital for the new enterprise. A banking system must, however, mobilize household savings, and the availability of these savings will remain limited if the existing distribution of wealth allows only some households to save. Also, most banking systems create rationing in favor of a small rich section of households because of collateral requirements. Thus, the distribution of wealth is a fundamental determinant of the access to capital resources while the banking system may only exacerbate an existing pattern of access.

Widespread availability of capital resources can occur only when wealth and income are not confined to a small group, as has been the case in most developing countries. Most models addressing distributional issues imply atomistic households in a classless society, whereas in reality the lack of capital is closely associated with landless labor, plantation workers and village artisans [Griffin and Khan 1978]. The association between class structure and income distribution calls for a reconsideration of the policy agenda for distributional issues.

d) Marketing opportunities

Marketing opportunities must exist for entrepreneurship to succeed. An absence of marketing opportunities would stifle entrepreneurial initiative. The existence of the potential buyers of an innovation depends mainly on the disposable income of the households and to some extent also on the presence of industrial users. Thus, the market demand may be strongly linked with income distribution and horizontal integration of firms in the industrial sector. Economic growth with income concentrated in a few households often creates stagnation, since disposable income remains limited [ESCAP 1989]. The development of a vertically integrated modern

245

sector also provides few opportunities for small entrepreneurs to act as vendors. According to some observers, industrial interdependence was a key factor in the remarkable economic progress of Japan [Nakagava 1981].

It might be argued that in an open economy, opportunities to export would always exist in the absence of a domestic market. Indeed, export-oriented development is a well-known model, successfully been adopted by many developing countries. Firms participating in export are, however, predominantly large; the export market is subject to many influences which make it too risky to attract small investors [ESCAP 1989]. Export-oriented development, therefore, may exacerbate income differences already existing, thus further reducing the access to capital resources of the small self-employed innovator, which would severely limit his progress.

Any policy initiative to expand entrepreneurial activity across social classes and gender and age groups must take into consideration above fundamental sources of motivation, together with the critical organizational requirements. Without these elements, the impact of the infrastructure-related facilities or special encouragement accorded to specific target groups may be severely limited.

A search for an appropriate entrepreneurship model

The macro and micro level analyses in the literature appear to be linked with time and geography specific empirical evidence. Both Adam Smith and Karl Marx considered technological innovation in their original models, although in different ways. Smith viewed it as an entrepreneurial quality in an economic system, consisting of infinitely many artisan owners of the production units that created gains in productivity as well as a large variety of goods and services [Skinner/Smith 1974]. Marx viewed it as a facet of the capitalist institution, consisting largely of the absentee owners, that aided exploitation of the workers by creating labor-saving capital [Marx 1891, Pack 1985].

The two views of the innovation process, although poles apart, nevertheless took into account the empirical evidence in the respective scenarios considered by the two social philosophers. Adam Smith based his postulates on the experience of the newly- created artisan economy that emerged at the start of the industrial revolution, whereas Karl Marx was evidently influenced by the feudal agricultural system in which ownership was separated from the workers and concentrated in a small feudal sector. As postulated in neoclassical macro-economic theory, technological innovations will indeed be directed at increasing productivity in an artisan factory setting and creating new goods and services that fill newly-identified market niches for the small entrepreneur, when capital ownership is widely distributed. However, when capital ownership is separated from the workers, the technological developments would be directed at creating labor-saving capital to further increase profit, as postulated by the Marxist analyses [Saeed 1988].

Unfortunately, the sterile mathematical formulations of the latter theories of economics, although having their roots in the philosophies of Smith and Marx, completely ignored the concept of innovation until the 1950s, when Robert Solow found that steady-state growth rates were independent of investment quotas. This called for a reconsideration of the role of technological progress and on-job-innovation, which were introduced into the growth model by Solow as the concepts of embodied and disembodied technological development, although in too abstract a form to be of much value in formulating any policy agenda for technological progress and innovation [Solow 1988, 1957].

At the micro-level, many insights have been provided into the understanding of the process of innovation by the behavioral scientists, who have continued to explore ways and means to facilitate this process in a variety of organizational settings. It is generally recognized that the entrepreneur is the central figure in technological innovation, whether in large or small firms [Roberts 1969], and that national wealth is derived from technological innovation, rather than from resources [Ayres 1988]. These insights, together with a comparative study of the macro-level analyses are the bases for identifying an appropriate entrepreneurship development model for the developing countries that should help entrepreneurship to flourish by eliciting maximum participation from all population cross-sections.

Most entrepreneurship models are designed to capture the underlying drives motivating the variety of individuals who are likely to become involved in significant entrepreneurial activity. These models also indicate how much risk such individuals may be willing to take to achieve their basic goals. However, the facilitation of risk management alone may not yield increases of any order of magnitude in entrepreneurship participation unless the fundamental motivational and organizational conditions discussed in section 2 are satisfied. The risk management models of entrepreneurship are, therefore, an inadequate basis for developing an effective policy framework to promote entrepreneurial activity.

Influenced by the prevailing entrepreneurship development models, great emphasis has been placed in the developing countries on upgrading the various types of infrastructure to facilitate entrepreneurial activity. The results of these efforts vary greatly, depending on whether basic motivational and organizational requirements were met or not. The success of women and youth participation in forming entrepreneurial firms in the western countries has also created a desire to transfer this phenomenon to the developing countries, although the family structure and the social roles of women currently existing in the developing countries differ greatly from those in the west, which makes it difficult to re-enact the western

247

experience.

Fortunately, social systems exhibit the property of equifinality, which allows for the existence of multiple paths leading to a given end [Bertalanffy 1968]. Thus, an effective strategy for entrepreneurship development for the developing countries, also eliciting the participation of women and youth, may not necessarily imitate the recent experience of the industrialized world. Rather, it must recognize the existing social and cultural norms that determine opportunity, individual initiative, the extent of capital availability and marketing opportunity. It must also attempt to create the organizational ingredients to facilitate innovation. The development of infrastructure would also help, provided the fundamental motivational and organizational mechanisms already exist.

There are basic differences between the industrialized and the developing countries in the origins of the fundamental motivational and organizational mechanisms creating entrepreneurship. In the case of the western countries, individual initiative may contribute greatly to the creation of an opportunity, while individual motivation may be shaped by frustrations in the family relationships and an urge to prove oneself. Furthermore, because most venture capital comes from institutional sources, capital availability may depend on the discriminating behavior of the financial institutions. Finally, marketing opportunities may be created with relative ease by introducing new products and advertising since the disposable income of households is much above subsistence level.

In the developing countries, the opportunity is often linked with the social class and the family linkages, while the motivation for entrepreneurship may stem from a commitment to support the extended family. The investments are financed largely through household savings, and marketing opportunities are closely linked to the disposable income of the households, both depending on the distribution of income and wealth [McKinnon 1973, ESCAP 1989]. The strong hold of the bureaucracy in the developing countries, whose members often have family links with the wealthy, has also led to a systematic discrimination against the average-income household from where entrepreneurial activity may originate [White 1981]. Last but not least, the pre-occupation of authoritarian governments in dealing with their adversaries and the political instability resulting from it create much risk, which discourages entrepreneurial ventures [Saeed 1986, 1990].

There exists a promising institution in most developing countries, however, which has great potential as a focal point of entrepreneurial activity. This institution is the small family enterprise, which may take the form of a shop-house or an artisan manufacturing firm in the urban sector or a peasant farm in the rural sector. It allows participation from all members of the family, including the youth and the women, while also providing the informal small-group organization considered conducive to innovation in many studies. Its members are highly motivated to work hard and assume the risk of enterprise because of their commitment to support the extended family. This enterprise is somewhat similar to the small manufacturing units that created the industrial revolution in England in the early nineteenth century. It has also been observed that the small family enterprise tends to maximize consumption, hence its income significantly affects demand, which creates new marketing opportunities [Bardhan 1973, Sen 1966]. Unfortunately, this enterprise has been systematically suppressed and discriminated against in favor of the large-scale formal sector. Even its output remains largely unaccounted for in the national accounting systems of most countries [Hicks 1940, Eisener 1989].

The small family enterprise, which elicits participation from all age and gender groups, is proposed as an appropriate entrepreneurship model for the developing countries. The following section discusses a policy framework for reviving and facilitating this sector.

Recommended policy framework

The small family enterprise, variously described as the informal, labor-intensive, traditional, peasant, and sometimes inefficient sector in the developing countries has been stifled in the first instance by a set of social and legal norms through which the wealth has become concentrated in an absentee ownership mode. Working households are mostly poor and own few assets [Griffin and Khan 1978]. The prosperity of these households will not only provide the much needed financial resources for entrepreneurial activity, their capacity to spend will also create many marketing opportunities for the potential entrepreneur. Thus, influencing income distribution ranks first on the agenda for designing a policy framework for change. Secondly, the family enterprise, even when financially viable, needs a non-interfering and stable political environment to operate in. This requires a democratic and stable political system. Finally, the activity of the family enterprise will be greatly facilitated by developing basic infrastructure and services, and also creating technical institutions incorporating communication channels to interact with the family enterprise. The details of this policy framework are discussed below:

a) Influencing income distribution

In an economic system where production is divided both on the basis of the ownership of capital assets and the contribution of labor, ownership of capital assets by workers would have a significant effect on income distribution since it would provide them the means for self-employment, which is an alternative to wage work. This alternative source of income would create high opportunity costs of providing labor to the formal sector thus also affecting wage-rates.

Private ownership has, however, two forms: artisan and absentee. The predominance of artisan ownership would create an egalitarian wage and income distribution pattern, while absentee ownership would lead to a low wage rate and an unequal income distribution. Figure 10.1 shows the feedback loops present in the relationships of social exchange that may limit artisan ownership of capital resources while concentrating them in the absentee mode.

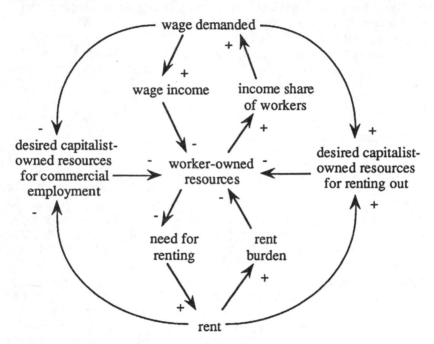

Figure 10.1   **Behavioral relationships working against widespread ownership of capital assets by the self-employed family**

When productive resources can potentially be engaged both in commercial and self-employed modes, an autonomous increase in productivity of capital resources in the commercial mode would draw resources away from ownership of the self-employed sector, thus reducing their opportunity cost of wage-work. On the other hand, an increase in the productivity of capital resources owned by the workers may only bid up rents, since a change in ownership is not necessary for expanding resource employment in the self-employed mode; resources vacated by the less productive commercial mode will be offered for rent to the self-employed and thus employed in the absentee mode. At the same time, the surplus labor released by the commercial mode will have to be absorbed in self-employment, which will further depress the artisan sector financially.

Ironically, the fine distinction between the artisan and absentee types of ownership is not recognized in the political systems based on the competing neoclassical and Marxist economic paradigms. The former protects both types of ownership, the latter prohibits both. None creates a feasible environment in which a functional form of ownership may help to capture the entrepreneurial energy of the family enterprise.

The author has proposed elsewhere a behavioral model underlying wage and income distribution, in which the opportunity cost of supplying a unit of labor to the formal sector has been postulated as a basis for negotiating a wage. Neither this opportunity cost nor the ownership pattern are taken as given while the dynamic interaction between the two creates a tendency in the system to generate many wage and income distribution patterns, some of which correspond to those postulated in the neoclassical and Marxist theories of economics. The realization of a specific wage and income distribution pattern depends not on assumptions about initial conditions but on legal and social norms concerning ownership, renting, financing of investment and the state of technology.

Increasing the cost of owning capital resources in absentee form, by imposing a tax on income accrued from such ownership, appears to be vital to promoting artisan ownership and changing an unequal income distribution. Policies aimed at minimizing technological differentiation between the self-employed and commercial modes of production and the presence of a functional financial market act as hygienes further facilitating this change, although without a rent tax, these policies only suppress the commercial mode of production [Saeed 1987a, 1988].

b) Creating a non-interfering and stable political environment

In theory, government is the organization legitimately entrusted with the important task of regulating and controlling the actions of the members of a society so that their collective welfare is promoted while their individual prerogatives are preserved [Cypher 1980]. In practice, however, a government meeting the theoretical requirements of legitimacy, and able and willing to pursue public interest, may be hard to find in the developing world [Streeten 1979, Ohlin 1979]. And even if a government did meet these requirements, an expansion of its control may easily lead to a neglect or rejection of public interest [Popper 1977].

Since direct intervention by a government requires broad governmental authority, development planning might implicitly have encouraged a tendency in the developing countries for the governments to become authoritarian, although both excessive intervention and authoritarianism may create a political environment in which entrepreneurial activity is

251

stifled. The former limits free enterprise, and the latter creates the dissidence which often preoccupies developing country governments, periodically also leading to their purge. Figure 10.2 shows the important causal relationships governing the conduct of an authoritarian government that lead to the creation of an environment of low freedom and high instability.

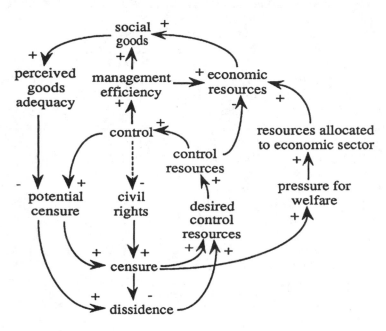

Figure 10.2   Causal relationships in the working of an authoritarian government creating political instability

An expansion in the authority or the control of the authoritarian government is also linked with a reduction in civil rights. As a result, censure of the government is suppressed although a high potential for such censure may exist. Consequently, any adversarial pressure to support the economic sector weakens while the un-vented censure fuels dissidence, which calls for a further stepping up of control. In this way, an insidious positive feedback loop is created that increases control while at the same time neglecting the economic sector. If allowed to continue, this process may generate enough dissidence to overthrow the regime.

The alternative to authoritarianism is a democratic system in which the expansion in control does not effect civil rights. As a result, censure of the government creating adversarial pressure to maintain support to the economic sector curtails disproportionate allocations to the expansion of control; the resulting improvement in welfare limits censure. Also, since censure can be freely vented, dissidence remains low. Thus, the insidious positive feedback loop creating disproportionately high allocations to the control sector is weakened while a self-correcting negative feedback loop maintaining adequate allocations to the economic sector becomes a dominant force in the system. The result is a relatively non-interfering and stable political environment that may be able to nourish entrepreneurial activity [Saeed 1990].

c) Development of infrastructure and facilitating institutions

When the motivational and organization elements to invoke entrepreneurship have been brought together, there is a good chance that wide participation from all age and gender groups will occur and this will create innovation. However, the full potential of this participation can be realized only when adequate technical facilities and infrastructure are also present. Thus, the infrastructure discussed in section 2.3 provides productive agenda for a welfare-oriented government to pursue, although it will be limited by financial resources, and a clear view of priorities.

Development of a physical infrastructure such as roads, communication, utilities and services has an undoubtedly high priority since these help the entrepreneurial firm to operate smoothly. Institutional finance and subsidization often appear productive in theory, although the experience of their efficacy is varied. Many developing country governments have also instituted training programs for the public while also setting up extension service and community development organizations to assist small entrepreneurs in urban and rural sectors. These programs often become victims of political maneuvers, failing in their objective to provide professional assistance to the community whenever social structure allowed discriminatory treatment of the various social classes [Alavi 1976, Abeyrama and Saeed 1983].

Many developing countries have also established RandD organizations to facilitate new enterprise. Their impact is often limited due to the absence of an appropriate communication system and linkages [TDRI 1985]. Figure. 10.3 shows how key supporting institutions might productively interact if appropriate communication channels exist. RandD activity is expected to occur both in public sector organizations and private firms, but the motivation in both cases must come from the entrepreneurial firm. Thus, legislative and procedural obstacles limiting communication between universities, public RandD institutions, financial institutions, and entrepreneurial firms need to be carefully considered and removed when the supporting institutions are planned. The nature of these obstacles may vary from country to country depending on the local legal norms, procedures and practices.

253

The above guidelines notwithstanding, there are fundamental impediments to adopting the recommended policy framework. Firstly, an already existing authoritative government may be unwilling to limit its scope and become responsive to public opinion. Secondly, the policy instruments for facilitating the self-employed to acquire a greater share of income may be in direct conflict with the influential power factions. Finally, the financial resources of the country may be committed to defense or internal security to an extent that very little is available for investment in the infrastructure and institutional development programs [Saeed 1986,1990].

It should be recognized that the root cause of all of the above impediments is the absence of a democratic system of government denied to the public in many developing countries by military dictators and strongmen. A change in this attitude is necessary for creating any efficacy in the development effort.

Conclusion

The entrepreneur is the central figure in technological innovation, whether in large or small firms. However, entrepreneurship patterns experienced in various the countries and over various periods of history differ widely. Many motivational, organizational and infrastructure-related factors seem to affect entrepreneurial activity, although to varying degrees and in a hierarchical fashion.

Four fundamental conditions must be met to assure that an adequate number of enterprising individuals initiate entrepreneurial activity. These are: the presence of the opportunity to participate, the individual drive, the access to capital resources, and the presence of marketing opportunities. Once initiated, entrepreneurial activity is facilitated by the flexibility of a small firm, the presence of freedom of enterprise, a horizontal integration of firms, and political stability in the country. The availability of certain elements of infrastructure may further help to realize the full potential of the process. These include education, physical infrastructure, clustering of inter-related activities, technical facilitation, communication, management training, and institutional finance.

The participation of woman and youth in entrepreneurial activity is a relatively new phenomenon in the western countries that seems to have considerably increased the energy of the process. This participation seems to have originated from the further break down of the family, which has created the financial and psychological need for women to start their own businesses.

Small entrepreneurs and indigenous technological innovation seem to have played a limited role in the economic progress of developing countries, which is dominated by relatively large firms and technology transfer from abroad. The role of women and youth in this process has been particularly limited. Also, given the existence of strong family ties, the motivation for the participation of women and youth on the lines of the western countries may be difficult to realize.

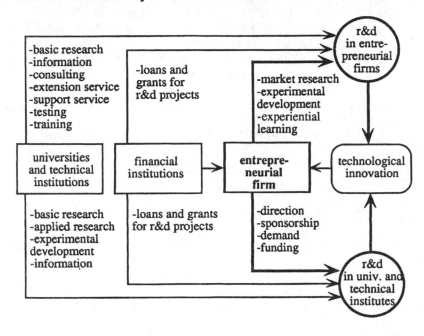

Figure 10.3   Information channels necessary for effective working of institutions supporting technological innovation

There exists in most developing countries, however, a promising organization in the form of the shophouse or small family-enterprise eliciting participation from all members of the family, which can be developed as the focal point for the entrepreneurial activity. The most important reforms needed at the government level to facilitate the small family enterprise are the discouragement of absentee ownership of capital assets, which would create a wider distribution of wealth, and the creation of a stable and non-interfering democratic political tradition, which would allow freedom of enterprise with an assessable and manageable amount of risk for the potential entrepreneurs. When these fundamental reforms can be implemented, the development of an infrastructure to realize the full potential of the entrepreneurial process would also help; otherwise, it will often remain inefficiently utilized.

References

Abeyrama, T. and Saeed, K. (1984) 'The Gamodaya Mandalaya Scheme in Sri Lanka: Participatory Development or Power Play?', *Community Development Journal* 29(1): 20-31.

Alavi, Hamza (1976) 'The Rural Elite and Agricultural Development in Pakistan', in Stevens et. al. (eds.), *Rural Development in Bangladesh and Pakistan*, Honolulu: Hawaii University Press.

Aldrich, N. W. Jr. (1986) *Young Founders*, Inc. 8(8): 63-65.

Ardnt, H. W. (1983) 'The Trickle-Down Myth', *Economic Development and Cultural Change*, 32(1): 1-10.

Ayres, T. U. (1988) 'Technology: The Wealth of Nations', *Technological Forecasting and Social Change*, 33: 189-201.

Bardhan, P. K. (1973) 'A Model of Growth in a Dual Agrarian Economy', in Bhagwati and Eckus (eds.), *Development and Planning: Essays in Honor of Paul Rosenstein-Roden*, New York: George Allen and Unwin.

Becker, G. S. (1964) *Human Capital*, New York: Columbia University Press.

Berney, K. (1988) 'Where Women are Welcome', *Nation's Business*, 6(8): 26R-27R.

Bertalanffy, L. V. (1968) *General Systems Theory*, New York: George Braziller.

Boeke, J. E. (1947) 'Dualist Economics', in *Oriental Economics*, New York: Institute of Pacific Relations.

Boswell, J. (1972) *The Rise and Decline of Small Firms*, London: George Allen and Unwin.

Byrne, J. A. (1985) 'Careers: Pity and the Poor Phenoms', *Forbes*, 135(7): 148,150.

Correa, M. E. et. al. (1988) 'Reactions to Women in Authority: The Impact of Learning in Group Relations Conferences', *Applied Behavioral Science*, 24(3): 219-233.

Cypher, J. M. (1980) 'Relative State Autonomy and National Economic Planning', *Journal of Economic Issues*, 14(2): 327-349.

Deberesson, C. (1989) 'Breeding Innovation Clusters: A Source of Dynamic Development', *World Development*, 17(1): 1-16.

Eisner, R. (1989) 'Divergences of Measurement Theory and Some Implications for Economic Policy', *American Economic Review*, 79(1): 1-13.

ESCAP (1989) *Restructuring the Developing Economies of Asia and Pacific in the 1990s*, 45th Session of Economic and Social Commission for Asia and Pacific, Bangkok: United Nations.

ESCAP (undated) *Training Manual on the Transfer of Technology Among Rural Women*, Bangkok: United Nations.

Griffin, K. and Khan, A. R. (1978) 'Poverty in the Third World: Ugly Facts and Fancy Models', *World Development*, 6(3): 295-304.

Hardin, G. (1968) 'The Tragedy of Commons', *Science*, 162 (December 13): 1243-1248.

Hardin, G. (1985) *Filters against Folly, How to Survive Despite Economists, Ecologists, and the Merely Eloquent*, New York: Penguin Books.

Harrison, B. (1989) 'Who Innovates?', *Technology Review*, 92(3): 15-77.

Herzberg, F. (1966) *Work and Nature of Man*, Cleveland: World Publishing Co.

Hicks, J. (1940) 'The Valuation of the Social Income', *Economica*, 7 (May): 163-172.

Hoselitz, B. F. (1952) 'Entrepreneurship and Economic Growth', *American Journal of Economic Sociology*, 12.

Inukai, I. (1981) 'Experience in Technology Transfer from the West, Lessons from False Starts', in Nagamine, H. (ed.), *Nation Building and Regional Development: The Japanese Experience*, Nagoya, Japan: United Nations Center for Regional Development.

Jones, G. (1988) 'Integrating Process and Structure in the Concept of Youth: A Case for Secondary Analysis', *Sociological Review*, 36(4): 706-732.

Katz, D. and Kahn, R. (1978) *Social Psychology of Organizations*, 2nd ed., New York: John Wiley.

MacGrath, R. E. (1987) 'Women Business Owners: Do They Have Special Needs?', *Buyouts and Acquisitions*, 5(2): 43-44.

Maidique, M. (1980) 'Entrepreneurs, Champions, and Technological Innovation', *Sloan Management Review*, 30 (Winter): 59-76.

Malecki, E. J. (1987) 'Hope or Hyperbole? High Tech and Economic Development', *Technology Review*, 90(7): 44-51.

Marx, K. (1974) *Wage, Labor and Capital* (English Translation of 1891 edition) Moscow: Progressive Publishers.

McClelland, D. C. and Winter, D. G. (1971) *Motivating Economic Achievement*, New York: The Free Press.

McDermot, K. (1985) 'The '80s: Decade of Women Entrepreneurs', *D and B Reports*, 33(4): 14-16,34.

McKinnon, R. I. (1973) *Money and Capital in Economic Development*, New York: The Brookings Institution.

Nakagava, K. (1981) 'Organized Entrepreneurship in the Course of the Industrialization of Prewar Japan', in Nagamine, H. (ed.), *Nation Building and Regional Development: The Japanese Experience*, Nagoya, Japan: United Nations Center for Regional Development.

Ohlin, G. (1979) 'Development in Retrospect', in Albert Hirshman et. al.,*Towards a New Strategy for Development: A Rothko Chapel Colloquium*, New York: Pergamon Press.

Pack, S. J. (1985) *Reconstructing Marxian Economics*, New York: Praeger.

Phalon, R. (1988) 'I am a Business Person', *Forbes*, 142(3): 54,56.

Popper, Karl R. (1977) *The Open Society and Its Enemies, Vol. 2*, p.130, New York: Routledge.

Quinn, J. B. (1979) 'Technological Innovation, Entrepreneurship, and Strategy', *Sloan Management Review*, 21(Spring): 19-30.

Quinn, J. B. (1985) 'Managing Innovation: Controlled Chaos', *Harvard Business Review*, 85(3): 73-84.

Roberts, E. B. (1969) 'Entrepreneurship and Technology', in W. H. Gruber and D. G. Marquis (eds.), *The Factors in the Transfer of Technology*, Cambridge, MA: MIT Press.

Rowland, M. (1988) 'Tales of Triumph', *Working Women*, 13(2): 76-79.

Rydenfelt, S. (1984) *A Pattern for Failure*, Orlando, Florida: Harcourt, Brace, Jovanovich.

Saeed, K. (1986) 'The Dynamics of Economic Growth and Political Instability in the Developing Countries', *System Dynamics Review*, 2(1): 20-35.

Saeed, K. (1987) 'Minds over Methods', *System Dynamics Review*, 2(2): 150-156.

Saeed, K. (1987a) 'A Re-Evaluation of the Effort to Alleviate Poverty and Hunger', *Socio-Economic Policy Sciences*, 21(5): 291-304.

Saeed, K. (1988) 'Wage Determination, Income Distribution and the Design of Change', *Behavioral Science*, 33(3): 161-186.

Saeed, K. (1988a) 'System Dynamics Modeling for the Design of Change', *Conference of the System Dynamics Society*, La Jolla, CA: July 1988.

Saeed, K. (1989) 'Cultivating Reflective Practice with the System Dynamics Method', *29th Conference of The Institute of Management Sciences*, Osaka: July 1989.

Saeed, K. (1990) 'Government Support for Economic Agendas in Developing Countries', *World Development*, 18(6).

Schön, D. (1987) *Educating the Reflective Practitioner*, San Francisco: Jossey-Bass Publishers.

Schultz, T. W. (1961) 'Investment in Human Capital', *American Economic Review*, 51(1): 1-17.

Schumacher, E. F. (1973) *Small is Beautiful*, London: Blond and Briggs Ltd.

Schumpeter, J. (1939) *Business Cycles: A Theoretical, Historical and Statistical Analysis of the Capitalist Process*, New York: McGraw-Hill.

Schumpeter, J. A. (1950) 'Capitalism, Socialism and Democracy', New York: Harper and Row, 156-161, reprinted as Schumpeter on the Disintegration of Bourgeois Family, Archives, *Population and Development Review*, 14(3): 499-507.

Schwartz, F. N. (1989) 'Management Women and the New Facts of Life', *Harvard Business Review*, 89(1): 57-76.

Scott, C. E. (1986) 'Why More Women Are Becoming Entrepreneurs?', *Journal of Small Business Management*, 24(4) October.

Sen, A. K. (1966) 'Peasants and Dualism With or Without Surplus Labor', *Journal of Political Economy*, 75(5).

Skinner, A. (ed.) (1974) 'Adam Smith', *The Wealth of Nations*, Middlesex: Penguin Books.

Solow, R. (1957) 'Technology Change and the Aggregate Production Function', *Review of Economics and Statistics*, 39: 312-320.

Solow, R. (1988) 'Growth Theory and After', *American Economic Review*, 78(3): 307-317.

Stevenson, L. A. (1986) 'Against all Odds', *Journal of Small Business Management*, 24(4): 30-36.

Streeten, Paul (1979) 'Development Ideas in Historical Perspective', in Albert Hirshman et. al., *Towards a New Strategy for Development: A Rothko Chapel Colloquium*, New York: Pergamon Press.

Sweeny, G. P. (1987) *Innovation, Entrepreneurs and Regional Development*, London: Frances Pinter.

TDRI (1985) *Policy Review Framework for Scientific and Technological Development of Thailand*, Bangkok: Thai Development Research Institute Report # PO 493-0309-0-00-5012-00.

Technonet Asia (1981) *Trainer's Manual on Entrepreneurship Development*, Singapore: Technonet Asia.

Tushman, M. L. (1979) 'Managing Communication Networks in RandD Laboratories', *Sloan Management Review*, 21(Winter): 37-49.

Uchida, T. (1981) 'Building a Modern Education System: Focus on Elementary and Vocational Education' in Nagamine, H. (ed.), *Nation Building and Regional Development: The Japanese Experience*, Nagoya, Japan: United Nations Center for Regional Development.

White, J. (1984) 'The Rise of Female Capitalism - Women as Entrepreneurs', *Business Quarterly* (Canada), 49(1): 133-136.

White, L. J. (1974) *Industrial Concentration and Economic Power in Pakistan*, Princeton, NJ: Princeton University Press.

Wong, Y. (1986) 'Entrepreneurship, Marriage, and Earnings', *Review of Economics and Statistics*, 68(4): 693-699.

Young, D. R. (1983) *If Not For Profit, For What?*, Lexington, MA: D. C. Heath Co., Lexington Books.

Young, G. (1984) 'Women, Development, and Human Rights: Issues in Integrated Transnational Production', *Journal of Applied Behavioral Science*, 20(4): 383-401.

Part III: Case Studies

11 Public policy and rural poverty: a system dynamics analysis of a social change effort in Pakistan*

Khalid Saeed

Abstract

This paper attempts to explain why public policies that were expected to alleviate rural poverty in Pakistan have not worked. The analysis is based on a system dynamics model that incorporates the income distribution processes of a typical developing country agrarian economy consisting of a capitalist and a self-employed sector. Only the economic factors arising out of the rational decisions of the two sectors regarding production and disbursement of income have been taken into account. These factors are considered adequate for explaining the persistence of rural poverty, although the role of social and political factors is acknowledged.

The study suggests that the absence of an economic force that should encourage land ownership by its cultivators is a key factor responsible for the poor economic condition of the working rural households that form the majority of the rural population. Land is easily separated from cultivators and is concentrated among the few capitalist households. This concentration significantly reduces income in self-employment and thus leaves the cultivators with very little bargaining power for negotiating compensation for their labor. Thus development policies striving to increase productivity may only serve to increase the claim to income of the few capitalist households, leaving incomes of the majority of the households unchanged while also assuring continuation of low worker compensation.

The study indicates that a development policy for alleviating poverty should simultaneously incorporate fiscal instruments to encourage transfer of land ownership to its cultivators and measures that help increase the productivity of land.

Introduction

Mass poverty and inequality of income are important social issues facing most developing countries. Public policy being an instrument of governments for affecting social change, a number of policies introduced in the developing countries over the past few decades have been aimed at alleviating poverty, with or without equalizing income. Unfortunately, the efficacy of the public policies implemented for this purpose has been quite low [Galbraith 1979, Griffin 1977, Haq 1976, Lipton 1977]. The failure of public policy is often attributed to the unforeseen events that occur over the course of implementation of a development program. Failure may be justifiable because social systems are complex and their behavior cannot be easily predicted by using traditional analytical tools. However, technological progress in computers has also made it possible to experiment with the relatively complex models of social systems and to understand their behavior even if these models are not amenable to analysis using traditional methods [Forrester 1971].

This paper presents a computer simulation model of the income distribution system of a developing country and attempts to use this model for understanding the impact of the public policies aimed at alleviating poverty. The mechanics of the method of analysis used conform to the framework suggested by Forrester [1968] and Saeed [1981]. Pakistan is used as a case study to provide empirical validation for the analysis. The technical details of the model presented are discussed elsewhere [Saeed 1980, 1983]. Documentation of these details and machine-readable copy of the model are available from the author on request. This paper delineates the broad structure and the hierarchy of the income and resource streams of the model and describes the key decisions endogenous to the income distribution system affecting those streams.

It is suggested that the conditions of persistent poverty arise out of the absence of an economic force to act against the separation of the means of production from the cultivators. The absence of this force also makes income distribution resilient to most public policy instruments and thus assures the persistence of poverty.

While the importance of social, cultural, and political factors in affecting incomes of the various cross-sections of rural households is acknowledged, only economic factors are used in this study because they adequately explain the resilience of the income distribution system to change.

Rural poverty as an income distribution problem

The majority of rural households in Pakistan receive incomes much lower than what is reflected in per capita income figures [Griffin and Ghose 1979]. Per capita income has been quite low by western standards, but it has been rising steadily both in real and money terms over the past three decades [Government of Pakistan 1979]. However, poor households have experienced little change in their standard of living, which has declined in some cases [Griffin and Ghose 1979], in spite of the several rural development policies specifically aimed at the poor. Apparently no dent can be made in the poverty problem by stimulating production unless the mechanisms of income distribution are concomitantly influenced. Therefore the focus of this analysis is income distribution.

The pattern of rural income distribution in Pakistan is characterized by wide disparities in income between the capitalist and the cultivator classes, whereas within each class the members enjoy relatively uniform incomes and life-styles. The capitalist class consists of absentee landlords, who rent their land to sharecroppers, and commercial farmers who employ wage labor to cultivate their land. The cultivator class consists of self-employed peasants tilling their own land and/or sharecropping on rented land and wage workers [Alavi 1976].

Based on the size of land owned and the pattern of farm management according to farm size in the 1950s, it can be easily shown that capitalist households constituted about 3% of rural households in the early part of that decade. However, they owned about 70% of the land and obtained about 50% of the rural income. The remaining 97% of the households consisted of cultivators who owned 30% of the land and shared about 50% of the rural income among themselves [Saeed 1980].

Since the 1950s, a number of development programs have been implemented in Pakistan. Most of these programs can be placed in the framework of a small number of macro policies that have a mixed set of economic and social objectives. The policies with economic objectives include the provision of mechanical implements, green revolution inputs, institutional credit, and industrialization of the urban sector [Stern and Falcon 1971]. Policies with social objectives include land reforms, community development efforts, and family planning. Policies with economic objectives have apparently helped to increase significantly land productivity and agricultural output, although the incomes of the poor are unaffected. Social reforms have usually been introduced on a limited scale and have had little effect on the incomes of the poor [Papanek 1977].

265

Historical tendency of the income distribution system

"Historical tendency" is used as a reference condition for testing the hypotheses advanced in this study as compared with "historical behavior" because of the lack of data providing a substantive basis for measuring historical behavior. The historical tendency serving as reference mode is abstracted from various pieces of historical evidence. This tendency encompasses the aspects of history that determine the shares of the various claimants to rural income. These   aspects are land ownership, land management, and worker compensation.

Before the nineteenth century, agricultural land ownership rights did not exist in the region that is now Pakistan. All farming was carried out by self-employed cultivators who traditionally lived on the land they tilled. The size of a land tract often depended on the size of the family cultivating it and the produce of the land was claimed by its cultivators after a share representing land revenue was given to the representatives of the ruler [Roulet 1976].

In the 1900s a new land tenure system was introduced by the colonial British government under which land ownership rights were formalized and land could be bought, sold, mortgaged, and rented like any other commodity. Simultaneously, marginal lands were irrigated and large land tracts were granted to the subjects of the crown as well as to prospective commercial farmers [Roulet 1976].

In the following period not only did commercial farming gradually disappear but cultivators also lost most of their land holdings to the big, and often absentee, landowners. Sharecropping emerged as the dominant land management practice, while land rents rose and worker compensation declined. Thus over the course of these changes, the economic condition of cultivators continuously deteriorated. These changes eventually led to the stagnant pattern of land ownership, land management, and income distribution that was prevalent in the 1950s [Roulet 1976].

A significant effect of the rural development programs introduced after the 1950s was a change in the land management pattern. Over this period, commercial farming became quite popular and a large part of the sharecropped land was converted by its owners to commercial farms [Alavi 1976]. This change is reported to have also further decreased cultivators' land holdings and depressed worker compensation [Burki 1976].

Structure of the rural income distribution system

Ownership of land and farm capital and labor input into the production process are the bases of claim to the farm income. However, the income shares of the various claimants are determined not on the basis of the productivity of the factors contributed by the claimants but by their respective bargaining positions [Andersen 1968, Bardhan 1973], although in the long run the factor proportions are adjusted in such a way that the marginal revenue product of the factors equals their respective wages. Thus even though a correlation may appear between factor productivity and factor wage, the causal relations between the two are far more complex. This is an important premise for understanding the income distribution system. The mechanisms of bargaining and the feedbacks these create are discussed later in this paper.

The prevalent patterns of farm management indicate that the agrarian economy is distinctly dualist (i.e., consisting of a worker-hiring and/or land-leasing capitalist sector and a self-employed peasant sector). Furthermore, all workers, whether self-employed in tilling their own or rented land or employed as wage workers, belong to a homogeneous socioeconomic group. This group has a common interest – to maximize its consumption. This group is also the sole supplier of labor in the economy. On the other hand, the capitalist sector strives to maximize profit while it is also the sole wage employer in the economy [Bardhan 1973].

As the tenure system protects the ownership rights of farmers and absentee landlords alike while it also warrants easy and un-cumbersome land transactions, production resources may be owned by one sector and employed by the other. Ownership of resources by a sector depends on its financial ability, while the amount of resources employed by a sector depends on its production efficiency. Figure 11.1 illustrates the broad accumulation processes and the rates of change related to the allocation of land between the sectors for ownership and for farming.

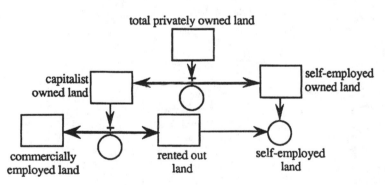

Figure 11.1   Allocation of land between sectors

The total land available for cultivation is divided between the capitalist and self-employed sector. The land owned by each sector changes as the two sectors buy and sell land between them. Land in the capitalist sector is either commercially farmed or rented, according to which is the more profitable method. Land farmed by the self-employed sector consists of land owned by workers as well as land rented from the capitalist sector.

The rural work force is divided between wage-employment and self-employment sectors, as shown in Figure 11.2. The capitalist sector hires as many workers as it needs at a wage determined by the collective bargaining position of the workers. The remaining workers are accommodated in the peasant sector.

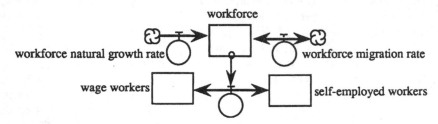

Figure 11.2   Allocation of workers between sectors

Capital is allocated between the sectors in the same way as land. But traditional capital can be created on farms by diverting some of the production capacity for producing it, whereas modern capital is imported from the industrial sector. Each type of capital is available to the two sectors as shown in Figure 11.3 and is acquired by the two sectors depending on their utility for capital and their financial resources.

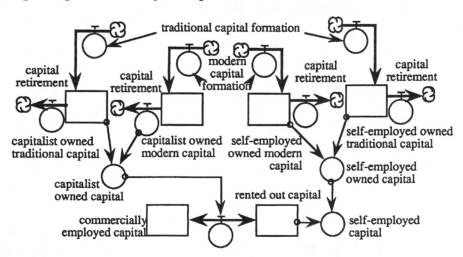

Figure 11.3   Allocation of capital between sectors

Figure 11.4 shows how capitalist and worker shares of income are determined. Part of the value of production of the capitalist sector is paid out as wages, and the rest is added to the revenue of the sector. The other component of the revenue of the capitalist sector is rent payments received from the self-employed sector for the production factors rented out to it. A part of the production of the self-employed sector is disbursed as these rent payments. The rest is added to the revenue of the workers. Wage payments received from the capitalist sector for labor provided also add to the revenue of the workers.

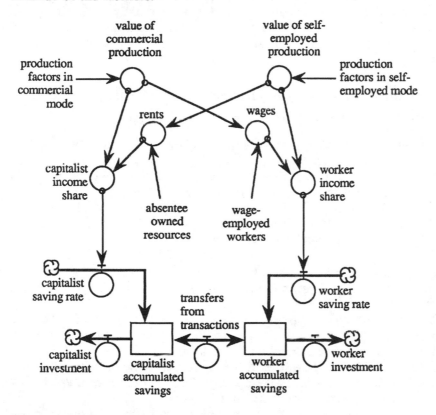

Figure 11.4   Disbursement of rural income

A part of the income in both sectors is consumed. The unconsumed parts of the incomes flow into the respective accumulated savings. Accumulated savings are spent by each sector on the acquisition of land and capital or are eventually consumed. When any assets are liquidated by a sector, funds equal to the money value of the liquidated assets flow into the accumulated savings. Thus as land is bought and sold between the sectors, savings representing the money value of the transacted assets are at the same time

269

transferred between them.

The value of farm capital produced by a sector is included in the value of its production. Thus for accounting purposes, when a sector invests in farm capital, whether this capital is acquired from the sources indigenous to the rural sector of from the industrial sector, the money value of the acquired capital flows out of that sector's accumulated savings.

The resource and income streams of the rural economy discussed in this section are governed by the feedbacks arising out of the economic decisions of the two sectors. These feedbacks are responsible for a tendency of the income distribution system to move toward an internally determined goal that assures low incomes for the cultivators. Key feedback mechanisms in the system are included in the next section.

Key mechanisms underlying production and income distribution decisions

At the outset, the resource and income streams discussed above may be assumed to be governed by the mechanisms of a perfect market in which both capitalist and self-employed sectors are price-takers and are perfectly competitive. Further, the simplifying assumptions of homogeneous technology and output, fixed economy, and employment of all resources available to each sector are made. These assumptions also impose on the model the following unrealistic restrictions:

1. All production factors including labor are paid according to their respective marginal revenue products averaged over the whole of the economy.
2. The issue of ownership of resources is not clear. In default, the resources employed by a sector can be assumed to be owned by it. Renting of resources, therefore, is irrelevant.
3. As resources easily flow toward the sector where they can be efficiently employed, the financial markets are perfect, and the investment ability of a sector is independent of its saving ability.
4. For accounting purposes, the savings of a sector should in the long run equal its investment. Therefore the saving habits of both sectors must be similar and stable (i.e., the marginal propensity to save in each case is the same and, for simplification, fixed).

In view of the structure of the dual economy described above, only one feature differs in the resource allocation decisions of the two sectors: While the capitalist sector adjusts the number of workers it employs on the basis of their cost relative to their benefit, the peasant sector absorbs all residual workers after the capitalist sector has met its worker needs.

A system dynamics model of the income distribution processes in a dualist rural economy embodying the above assumptions was formulated. The resources were arbitrarily equally distributed between the two sectors and the model was initialized in a state of "market equilibrium", which persisted when the model was simulated.

Next, the equilibrium was disturbed by taking away a fraction of the workers from the capitalist sector and placing them in the self-employed sector, and the model was again simulated. The transfer raised the marginal productivity of workers in the capitalist sector, which immediately proceeded to increase its work force.

The transfer also increased the intensity of cultivation in the self-employed sector, as a result of which the marginal productivities of land and capital in that sector rose; hence it proceeded to acquire more land and capital. Worker hiring by the capitalist sector and land and capital acquisition by the self-employed sector continued until marginal revenue products of factors and their proportions were the same in both sectors.

Figures 11.5: a and b illustrate how the two sectors proceeded in the simulation to equalize proportions and the marginal revenue products of factors in response to the exogenous transfer of workers. It may, however, be noted that the new equilibrium manifests a different distribution of land and worker between sectors than that of the original equilibrium. This should be expected, as both sectors are concerned with maintaining efficient factor proportions and are not committed to having an absolute amount of any one factor.

Also, as long as the wage rate is based on the aggregate marginal revenue product of workers, the equilibrium proportion of workers with respect to other factors will be the same in both sectors, even though the peasant sector does not have any hiring or firing ability. The tendency of the capitalist sector to equate marginal productivity of workers to their wage rate assures that the worker intensity is the same in both sectors.

The income share of the workers is not adversely affected by the arbitrary transfer of workers to the self-employed sector. The loss in wages of the workers is adequately compensated for by increases in production of the self-employed sector when it acquires additional resources. The average consumption per worker suffers when wage income is lost but recovers to a higher level as the workers start receiving additional income from the newly acquired resources.

The behavior of the model incorporating assumptions of a perfect market is quite consistent with what is manifested in the neoclassical economic literature, although this behavior is empirically invalid. Evidently the unrealistic limitations stated at the outset contradict what takes place in the real world. The suppliers of the production factors are paid according to their respective bargaining positions and not on the basis of the productivities of the production factors they supply.

A formal framework of ownership of land and capital exists and is

271

protected by law in most nonsocialist countries including Pakistan. Both land and capital can be freely bought, sold, mortgaged, and rented by their owners. Often production resources are owned by one sector and employed by the other, while rural financial markets are invariably segmented where all economic units are confined to self-finance and a complementarity exists between the saving ability of a household and its investment ability [McKinnon 1973].

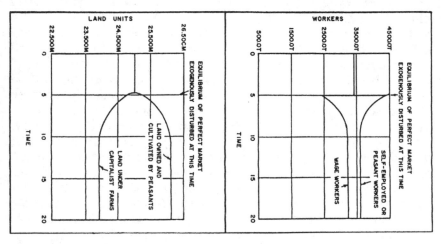

a) *Land and worker distribution*

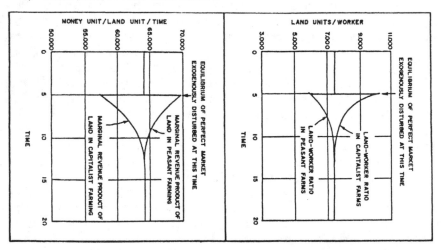

b) *Land-worker ratio and marginal revenue product of land*

Figure 11.5   **Recovery from disequilibrium in a dual economy with perfect market assumptions**

272

Furthermore, the savings patterns of the capitalist and cultivator households differ widely. The former, having incomes much above subsistence, show stable saving propensities. The saving propensity of the latter is very sensitive to the availability of wage employment opportunities that decrease the need to save for supporting investment for self-employment, and to decreases in the absolute level of their income in the face of inflexible subsistence consumption that limits their savings rate even when investment for self-employment is necessary [Mellor 1959].

The implications of relaxing each of the above limitations of the model are discussed in detail in Saeed [1980]. It suffices here to say that these limitations must be relaxed *en bloc* to achieve consistency between the structure of the income distribution system and the model. If these limitations are relaxed, the model displays the income distribution tendency shown in the historical evidence about the behavior of Pakistan's rural income distribution system. Furthermore, the income distribution goal of the model is independent if its initial conditions as illustrated in Figure 11.6, which compares the land ownership behavior of the model with different initial conditions.

In both cases shown, the model was in equilibrium with perfect market assumptions before its modifying assumptions were activated. The model strives to reach a new equilibrium that is the same irrespective of the initial equilibrium. The equilibrium goal of the model shows that most of the land is owned by the capitalist sector, that commercial farming is almost eliminated, and that sharecropping emerges as the leading land management practice.

Figure 11.7 shows the end equilibrium income shares of capitalists and workers. Even when the capitalist sector's share of income is small initially, toward the end about 50% of the income falls to that sector. Capitalist households being a very small fraction of total households, worker compensation equilibrates at a low level.

The income distribution system modeled exhibits an internal tendency toward separation of the means of production from the workers. Ownership of resources tends to concentrate in the sector with a stable savings ability while ownership does not bind this sector to cultivate the land, which is rented to the self-employed sector.

When the wage rate or, in the case of self-employment, the claim to income on the basis of labor input is determined independently of land ownership, the separation of ownership from cultivators may not necessarily lead to reduction in worker compensation. However, when income is divided between its claimants through mutual agreement, the share obtained by each is strongly influenced by the collective bargaining position of the claimants.

If workers can afford a high level of consumption by being self-employed on a family farm, their opportunity cost of becoming wage workers will be high. When self-employed workers own little land and mostly sharecrop, not only is their share of income claimed on the basis of ownership small, but the level of consumption available to them, and consequently their opportunity cost of becoming wage workers, are also low. Thus the concentration of land ownership in the capitalist sector undermines the collective bargaining position of the cultivators and causes worker compensation to decline.

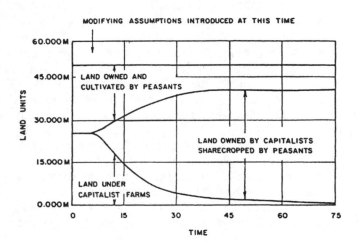

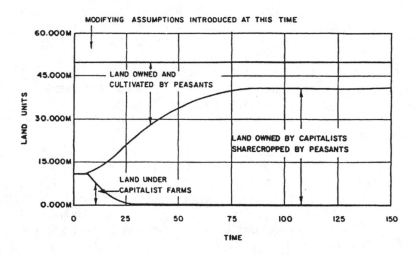

Figure 11.6   **Internal tendency for the land distribution of the complete model, various initial conditions**

274

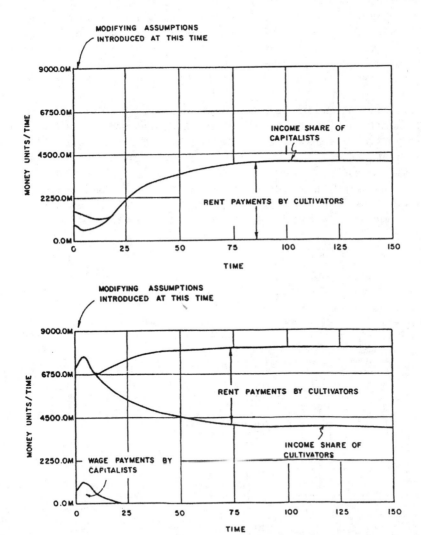

Figure 11.7   **Internal tendency for the income distribution of the complete model**

275

It should be interesting to note here that the model behavior exhibits a high positive correlation between wage rate and the marginal revenue product of workers (see Figure 11.8) that is in agreement with the economic belief that production factors are paid according to their incremental contribution to production. However, the model does not incorporate in its structure a corresponding causal relation.

Figure 11.9 represents a much simplified causal diagram showing important negative feedbacks affecting wage rate and marginal productivity of wage workers. Wage rate, a function of the bargaining position of the workers, depends on how much of the resources workers own. Because the savings and investment abilities of the parties are complementary, worker ownership of resources is positively affected by their own savings ability, whereas it is negatively affected by the savings ability of the capitalist sector.

Everything else remaining unchanged, worker savings ability will be negatively affected by the number of workers being accommodated in self-employed workers increases when fewer wage workers are hired by the capitalist sector, whereas the decision to hire workers depends on the wage rate. The savings and ownership ability of the capitalist sector depends on the volume of its profits. These profits are positively related to the productivity of the wage workers, which is negatively related to the number of wage workers, and this number depends on the wage rate.

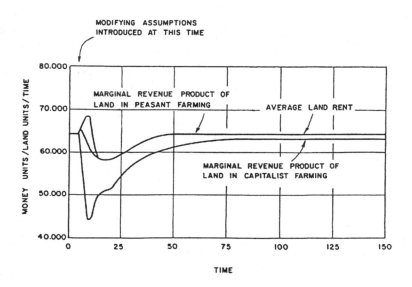

Figure 11.8   Wage rate and marginal revenue product of workers

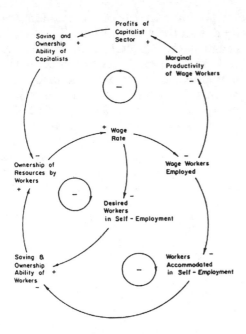

Figure 11.9   Simplified causal diagram showing negative feedbacks affecting worker compensation and income distribution

Another negative feedback loop affecting the wage rate arises out of the consumption-maximizing behavior of the workers. When the wage rate is high, the self-employed sector would encourage some of its members to accept wage employment, so that it becomes possible to expand consumption by not having to save for supporting self-employment facilities for these workers. In the long run, however, the diminished savings rate decreases the ownership ability of the workers, and this suppresses their bargaining ability and thus the wage rate.

A further examination of Figure 11.9 reveals that in terms of causations, wage worker productivity negatively affects the wage rate, whereas the wage rate positively affects wage worker productivity. The two would eventually move toward the same goal and might have a positive correlation but this correlation is not guaranteed by the structural relationships between them.

When both capitalist and self-employed sectors use the same technology, and the opportunity cost of capital investment is uniform everywhere, the marginal revenue product of workers must become the same in the two sectors. However, as wage rate depends on the total income claimed by the workers less their cost of investment in self-employment, the wage rate cannot become equal to the marginal productivity of workers unless the workers' claim to income is primarily due to their labor input. Thus if the capitalist sector is to exist at all, a high degree of dichotomy must arise between the owners and the cultivators of resources. The existence of the capitalist sector is assured because it is possible to practice sharecropping that allows capitalist households to obtain a profitable return on land owned by them without having to hire wage workers for cultivating it. Thus low worker compensation with accompanying accumulation of income in the capitalist households is assured.

There are also several positive feedbacks in the system coupled with the negative feedbacks described above. These feedbacks further facilitate separation of the means of production from the workers. Figure 11.10 shows the key positive feedbacks.

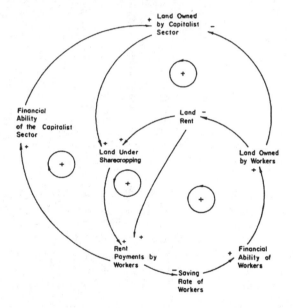

Figure 11.10   Simplified causal diagram showing positive feedbacks affecting worker compensation and income distribution

These feedbacks arise out of the strong coupling between the two sectors in terms of sharing resources and income and from the zero-sum nature of the economy. Rent payments by cultivators strengthen the financial ability of the capitalist sector but weaken that of the cultivators. Since financial ability affects the ability to own land, the sector with increasing savings ability will end up owning the most land. Furthermore, as ability to own land in the peasant sector decreases, land rents are bid up, which further increases rent payments while also encouraging the capitalist sector to rent out more land. Thus separation of land from the cultivators is speeded up.

Population growth in such an economy will worsen income distribution and further suppress worker compensation even though the accompanying increase in the work force raises the intensity of cultivation and total output. As increased intensity of cultivation increases productivities of land and capital, rents are bid up. Consequently, the capitalist sector's share of total rural income absorbs a substantial part of the increase in output, while the remaining output has to be divided among an increasing number of workers. Therefore the average consumption level of workers and their wage bargaining position declines. Thus the burden of population increase is largely borne by the workers.

The behavior of the model quite accurately represents the internal tendency of Pakistan's rural income distribution system, while the micro structure of the model also embodies the typical characteristics of the system. Furthermore, the qualitative behavior of the model is quite insensitive to changes in its parameters that appear to affect largely the speed of adjustment of the system. Details of the model parameters and their sensitivity are described in Saeed [1980]. Further discussion will be aimed at studying implications of the various development policies, past and exploratory, with a view to further increasing our understanding of the nature of the forces responsible for making the income distribution system resilient to policy changes and to identifying policies that can affect change.

Development policy and poverty

The emphasis of development policy in Pakistan has varied over the past few decades. During the 1950s, industrialization was promoted almost exclusively [Falcon and Stern 1970]. In the mid-1950s and early 1960s extension services in rural areas were also introduced [Galbraith 1979]. In the mid-1960s and 1970s, agricultural modernization, rural credit, and promotion of agricultural cooperatives were pushed as key policy instruments [Burki 1976]. Some effort was also made at redistributing land through the land reform acts of 1958 and 1971 [Haider 1975]. Industrialization was expected to absorb the surplus rural labor in addition to causing an increase in the aggregate income. Rural extension service programs attempted to help farmers by making available to them agricultural technicians. Agricultural development programs were aimed at increasing the income of the rural population. Land reform represented explicit efforts to redistribute rural income. The failure of these policies to make a dent in the poverty problem is amply documented [Alavi 1976, Griffin and Ghose 1979, Mizrow 1963, Nutley 1962].

In an income distribution system, where land ownership not only entitles a party to a share of income but also determines the level of compensation for the labor input to production, any development programs aimed primarily at increasing productivity and aggregate income may only increase the income shares of the parties owning most of the productive resources. Additionally, the dependence of investment on internal savings allows parties with rising incomes to expand their ownership further. Thus growth-oriented development programs not providing for land redistribution may worsen rural income distribution and draw down the compensation of rural workers. This has been amply demonstrated by the outcome of the development programs in Pakistan. The key macro policies implemented and their implications are discussed below.

Modernizing agricultural technology

There have been numerous arguments about the scale of technology that has been applied to modernizing agriculture. While large-scale technologies give economies of scale, the small farmer can often not use these and as such productivity of small farms cannot be enhanced. Thus divisibility of technologies has lately been emphasized. However, this debate appears irrelevant to the poverty issue when viewed in the context of the dynamics of income distribution.

Figure 11.11 compares two simulation runs showing changes in land ownership and land management patterns in response to the introduction of large- and small-scale modernizing technologies. In both cases, it is assumed that application of modernizing technology will increase the output elasticity of capital while simultaneously decreasing the output elasticity of labor. Furthermore, this application is assumed to make the sowing and harvesting processes faster, thus permitting multiple cropping, which increases yearly production in proportion to the intensity of application. The technological inputs are available in small quantities and are rationed between the two sectors according to their respective demands.

Finally, to assure a high degree of access to the technological inputs for the small-scale farming sector, financial constraints on investment are reduced, that can be translated into provision of institutional credit to farmers. The initial condition parameters for these simulations are comparable to the corresponding conditions in Pakistan in the 1950s. Additionally, a fixed population growth rate of about 2% per year is assumed.

The two simulation runs exhibit more or less similar land ownership patterns although different land management patterns. When the applications of technology produces high capital differentiation, a rapid increase in capitalist farming is shown, whereas when technology produces low capital differentiation, sharecropping continues to be the dominant land management practice.

280

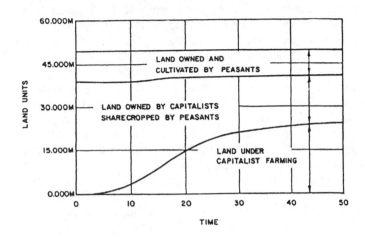

a) *Large scale technological inputs made available only to capitalist sector*

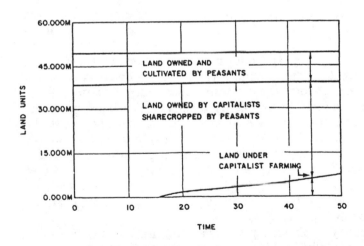

b) *Technological inputs available to both sectors*

Figure 11.11   Modernizing agriculture: land ownership and land management patterns

In the first case, capitalist farming expands because the productivity of land where modern inputs are applied is higher than the land rent available in sharecropping. However, the conversion of sharecropped land into capitalist-farmed land displaces more self-employed labor than the wage labor it employs. Consequently, the shortage of rentable land pushes up land rents. Also, as the self-employed sector absorbs the surplus labor in the economy, its cultivation intensity increases, which raises its productivity to the level of that of commercial farms. At this point, the conversion of sharecropped land to commercial farms stops.

When modernizing technology is almost equally available to both sectors and the capital differentiation between the two is small, productivity in the two sectors is comparable. Therefore rents remain high and sharecropping remains competitive with commercial farming for the capitalist sector. Thus the land management pattern does not deviate substantially from the case when modernizing technology is not applied at all.

The worker compensation will be quite comparable in both cases discussed above as these incorporate similar ownership patterns, which as pointed out earlier, determine workers' wage bargaining position. Thus low worker compensation and concentration of income in the capitalist households will persist.

Radical land reform

Land redistribution is recognized as an important income redistributing factor. However, radical land reform policies incorporating instantaneous transfers of land form the capitalist owners to the self-employed peasants are not only difficult to implement but may also be quite ineffective in the long run.

In Pakistan two rounds of land reform have been implemented over a little more than a decade. Both were on a trivial scale but were concomitant with the mechanization effort. These reforms reportedly   started a chain of private transfers, largely to the family members of a big landowners. The purpose of these transfers was to make per capita land ownership conform to the official ceilings but to retain ownership within the family. But land reform did little to change the land holding distribution pattern. In fact, small peasant farmers were reported to have lost 7 to 12% of their holdings over the decade following the 1959 land reform. Over the same period, the holdings of the big landlords engaged in commercial farming expanded considerably [4].

Land reform policy is simulated by arbitrarily transferring a million acres of land from capitalist landowners to peasants while at the same time modern technology is made available to the capitalist sector as was the case in Pakistan.

Figure 11.12 shows the changes in distribution of land resulting from the

282

combined effects of mechanization and land reform policies. Although peasant land holdings increase when land reforms are introduced, by the end of the simulation, a large fraction of peasant holdings have been lost to the capitalist owners.

Transfer of land to the cultivators, at the outset, reduces their rent burden while also raising their claim to income on the basis of ownership. The ensuing increase in the incomes of the self-employed not only stimulates worker consumption but also bids up wage rates in the capitalist sector. This has two effects: first, the utility of savings for investment in the self-employed sector goes down; second, the number of workers desired to be employed in the capitalist sector decreases. As a result, a large number of workers have to be accommodated in the self-employed sector, which in turn depresses this sector's consumption as well as savings. Thus the savings ability of the cultivators and their internal cash balances may not rise with the increase in their land holdings, At the same time, the capitalist share of income is only marginally affected. Capitalists can easily increase the intensity of modern technologies in commercial farming, hire fewer workers, and generate enough savings to bid the self-employed out of their land holdings. As cultivator land holdings decline, income in self-employment decreases, which causes the wage rate to decline rapidly.

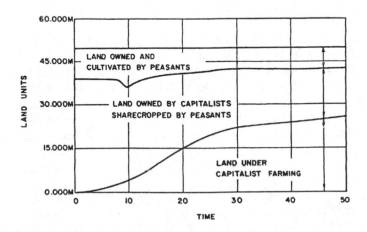

Figure 11.12   Changes in land distribution: radical land reform

283

Radical land reform may thus bring only temporary relief to cultivators. Such reforms may have to be periodically repeated if their equity objectives are to be realized. Recognizing that land reform is a politically and administratively difficult policy to implement, a continuous program of land redistribution is practically impossible.

Migration

Migration out of a poor region is often seen by planners as a way of relieving pressure of the region's overburdened resources. But migration also decreases the labor resources of the donor region and thus diminishes its production ability [Lipton 1977]. Population redistribution policies therefore are a subject of much controversy and debate.

In Pakistan migration from rural areas followed an ambitious industrial development program implemented in the urban sector during the 1950s and early 1960s. The relative expansion of the urban sector over the past three decades (from 15% to over 30%) indicates that the volume of rural emigration has been quite high. The persistence of rural poverty also shows that the emigration has not helped the rural poor. Lately, however, remittances from the emigrants to the Middle East seem to have increased money incomes of many rural households, but this has also fueled inflation in the absence of corresponding increases in the availability of goods and services.

Migration policy is simulated by activating a rate of rural emigration of people in the model that depends on urban-rural wage differentials. The urban wage rate is assumed to be fixed at a higher level than the rural wage rate at the beginning of the simulation. The resulting distribution of land is shown in Figure 11.13.

Migration seems to have no effect on the ownership of land, though it causes the land under commercial farming to rise at a faster rate and to a higher level than before in response to the accompanying modernization effort. Furthermore, because of the attrition of labor resources from the rural sector, the total income of the agricultural economy will grow at a much slower rate with migration than without, but the share of the capitalists will be only slightly decreased owing to the continuing land ownership pattern and an increase in the labor-intensive capitalist farming. Thus most of the loss in production is absorbed by the workers' share of income.

In the long run, migration tends to balance the compensation of rural workers with that of their urban counterparts, but at the cost of a decrease in rural production and without changing the rural land ownership and income distribution pattern. If the wage rate is determined by the economy-wide collective bargaining position of all workers, and the bulk of the workers are from the rural sector, the urban wage rate may not be

284

expected to be much different from the rural wage rate, In such a case, population growth rates and the rates of relative expansion of the urban and rural economic bases will determine migration. The changes in worker compensation and income distribution in such a system are outside the scope of this analysis.

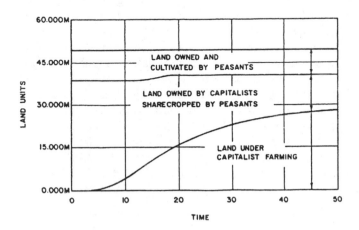

Figure 11.13   Changes in land distribution: migration policy

Fiscal policies

The key factor responsible for creating a dichotomy between landowning and land cultivating classes and the income differentials between them appears to be the absence of a force that should assure ownership of land by its cultivators. Apparently the ease with which land can be profitably rented out by owners allows its employment in the sector that efficiently uses it as a production factor.

The transfer of ownership, however, is relatively difficult because it involves a concurrent financial transaction. Accordingly, the ownership of land by a party is not coterminous with the land cultivated by that party. Because ownership is an important basis for claim to income, cultivators often have to give up a substantial share of their production to the owners.

As the renting practice appears to serve as a means to separate owners from cultivators, renting in all forms needs to be discouraged. An administrative ban on renting can not only be impossible to implement, but can also be ineffective if imposed in an economic environment where renting is seen as an efficient and convenient practice both by the renters and the rentees. A simple fiscal policy such as taxing rent income is much simpler to implement while also being very effective.

A rent income tax may be quite difficult to collect. Nonetheless, even if the collection of such a tax is inefficient, the presence of the tax should discourage land-renting and sharecropping practices. The amount of tax needed to be collected may diminish over time and when the practice of renting has ceased, no tax will have to be collected.

It should be recognized that when a fiscal instrument discouraging renting is introduced at the same time as labor-saving technology in an environment where sharecropping dominates, a wave of evictions of sharecroppers from land that is rapidly converted into commercial farm may follow. But these evictions will also increase labor intensity on the peasant farms that absorb the surplus workers. The productivity of peasant farms and their bids for land therefore will rise, which will also increase the opportunity costs of owning land by the relatively less productive capitalist sector. The policy of taxing rent income is simulated by subtracting a constant fraction of all rent income from the revenue of the capitalist sector. It is assumed that the rent burden cannot be directly passed on to the rentees as this would limit their demand for renting land. The changes in the distribution of land caused by the policy are shown in Figure 11.14.

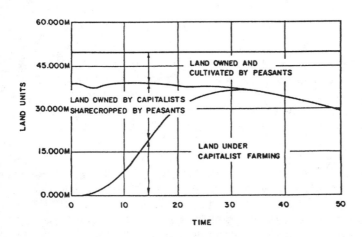

Figure 11.14   Changes in land distribution: taxation of rent income

Sharecropped land is either rapidly converted to commercial farms or sold after the policy is in effect, but holdings of commercial farmers continue to decline as land prices are pushed up by the intensive peasant cultivation and as the opportunity costs of maintaining investment in commercial farms rise.

The final distribution of land between the peasant and commercial sectors depends on the degree of capital differentiation between the two sectors permitted by the available supply of mechanized implements exclusively available to commercial farmers. The greater the supply of those implements, the higher the profits in commercial farming, and the greater the area of land under commercial farms. But if mechanized inputs are equally accessible to both sectors and there is no capital differentiation, the capitalist farming mode will eventually disappear.

Policies for alleviating poverty

Public policy aimed at improving the well-being of the people should incorporate objectives of both growth and equity. None of the policies discussed so far appear satisfactory for realizing those objectives when implemented alone. Also, if all policies are introduced together without knowing how they interact with one another, some of them may counteract the others and thus make the outcome of a development program uncertain. Consequently it is important to have knowledge of the individual characteristics of various policies for delineating a set that must underlie a welfare-oriented rural development program.

The first and foremost requirement of a policy set aimed at alleviating widespread poverty and low worker compensation is that it should encourage land ownership by its cultivators so that cultivators obtain a greater share of the income, which also enhances their wage bargaining position. Thus taxation of rent incomes appears to be the most important instrument for a welfare-minded rural reform. Second, for stimulating growth in rural production, it seems necessary to provide modern technological inputs. However, if these technological inputs are available only to the large scale commercial sector, this sector will enjoy an advantage over the small-scale self-employed sector, and the degree of land redistribution achieved will depend on the quantity of modern technological inputs made available.

This problem can be overcome by emphasizing the divisibility of modern technology and by encouraging the organization of peasant cooperatives able to make use of relatively large-scale technologies. Finally, the ability of the self-employed sector to invest in modern technologies may be limited owing to the low level of its internal savings. This handicap can be overcome by organizing rural financial markets that

287

should decouple the investment ability of a sector from its savings ability. Policies such as radical land reform appear to be ineffective in the long run, whereas policies causing emigration from the rural areas can greatly reduce the level of rural production.

Figure 11.15 shows the changes in the distribution of land ownership when the set of policies delineated above is simulated. Most of the land continues to be farmed by the self-employed sector, but the ownership pattern changes significantly. As sharecropping declines in response to taxation of rent incomes, it is not replaced by commercial farming, but the land taken away from sharecropping is sold to the peasants and is cultivated by self-employed workers.

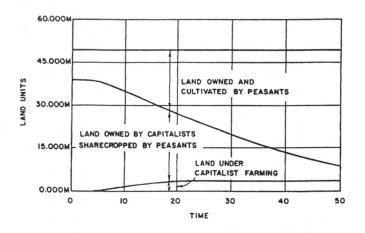

Figure 11.15   Changes in land distribution: suggested policy framework

Figure 11.16 shows the income shares of capitalists and peasants and wages and rents. The overall income grows significantly because of the application of modern technological inputs, although most of the increases occur in the income share of cultivators. Land rent rises at a fast rate as productivity of land rises, but as the amount of land under sharecropping diminishes, the rent burden of the cultivators decreases. The rising income of cultivators allows significant increases in average income per worker even though population is assumed to be growing exponentially.

288

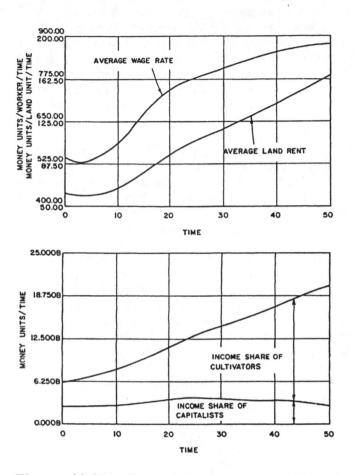

Figure 11.16   Income shares, wages and rents: suggested policy framework

Conclusion

The analysis of this paper suggests that the rural poverty problem is strongly linked with the internal tendency of the rural income distribution system to move toward a state of inequality. This tendency arises at the outset because of the determination of the shares of the claimants to income on the basis of their respective bargaining positions that, in turn, depend on ownership of resources by each claimant. Ownership is easily separated from cultivators in a system where resource ownership must rest with households having high savings ability while cultivation is carried out by households who are able to employ these resources efficiently. A high degree of dichotomy between land ownership and land cultivation appears as workers try to maximize consumption while capitalists maximize profit. Separation of resources from the workers diminishes their claim to income while also undermining their bargaining position; thus it is an important cause of their impoverishment. In such an income distribution system, growth-oriented development programs not providing for the redistribution of resource ownership may worsen income distribution and further draw down worker compensation.

Radical land redistribution policies are both difficult to implement and inadequate in their ability to achieve a lasting resource redistribution. On the other hand, fiscal instruments increasing the cost of separation of ownership from the workers appear to be quite promising for bringing about a change in the ownership pattern. Such instruments must form an important part of any rural development program aimed at alleviating poverty.

Several simplifying assumptions limit the scope of this study. The model does not incorporate mechanisms for endogenously determining the rate of population growth, which in the real world is postulated to depend on several factors. Also, the role of the urban economy is not endogenized in the model, whereas strong links exist between urban and rural sectors that govern their relative growth rates and income transfers between them. The demand for agricultural products is also not adequately related to the income and to the manufacturing base. Additional work is needed for relaxing those simplifying assumptions and expanding the scope of the study to both urban and rural sectors of the income distribution system.

References

Alavi, H. (1976) 'The Rural Elite and Agricultural Development in Pakistan', in Stevens, et. al. (eds.), *Rural Development in Bangladesh and Pakistan*, Honolulu, Hawaii: Hawaii University Press.

Andersen, K. P. (1968) *Peasant and Capitalist Agriculture in the Developing Country*, unpublished Ph.D. Thesis, Cambridge, MA: MIT.

Bardhan, P. K. (1973) 'A Model of Growth in a Dual Agrarian Economy', in Bhagwati and Eckus (eds.), *Development and Planning: Essays in Honor of Paul Rosenstein-Roden*, New York: George Allen and Unwin Ltd.

Burki, S. J. (1976) 'The Development of Pakistan's Agriculture: An Inter-Disciplinary Explanation', in Stevens, et. al. (eds.), *Rural Development in Bangladesh and Pakistan*, Honolulu: Hawaii University Press.

Falcon, W. P. and Stern, J. (1970) *Growth and Development in Pakistan*, Center for International Affairs, Harvard University Press, Cambridge, MA.

Forrester, J. W. (1968) *Principles of Systems*, Cambridge, MA: MIT Press, Wright-Allen Series.

Forrester, J. W. (1971) 'Counterintuitive Behavior of Social Systems', *Technology Review*, 73(3): 52-68.

Galbraith, J. K. (1979) *The Nature of Mass Poverty*, Cambridge, MA: Harvard University Press.

Government of Pakistan (1979) *Pakistan Economic Survey, 1977-78*, pp. 8-13.

Griffin, K. (1977) 'Increasing Poverty and Changing Ideas about Development Strategies', *Development and Change*, 8: 491-508.

Griffin, K. and Ghose, A. K. (1979) 'Growth and Impoverishment in Rural Areas of Asia', *World Development*, 7(4/5): 361-384.

Haider, Azimushan (1975) *Economic History of the Region Constituting Pakistan, 1825-1974*, Karachi.

Haq, Mahboobul (1976) *The Poverty Curtain: Choices for the Third World*, New York: Columbia University Press.

Khan, S. S. (1976) 'Rural Development Experience in Pakistan' in *Policy and Practice in Rural Development*, Hunter et. al. (eds.), Overseas Development Institution.

Lipton, Michael A. (1977) *Why Poor People Stay Poor?*, Cambridge, MA: Harvard University Press.

McKinnon, R. I. (1973) *Money and Capital in Economic Development*, New York: The Brookings Institution.

Mellor, John W. (1959) 'The Subsistence Farmer in the Traditional Economics' in *Subsistence Agriculture and Economic Development*, Wharton Jr., C. R. (ed.), Chicago: Aldine Publishing Co.

Mizrow, John D. (1963) *Dynamics of Community Development*, Scarecrow Press.

Nutley, Lesley (1962) *The Green Revolution in Pakistan: Implications of Technical Change*, New York: Praeger.

Papanek, Gustav F. (1977) 'Economic Development Theory, The Earnest Search for a Mirage' in *Essays on Economic Development and Cultural Change in Honor of Bert F. Hostlitz*, Nash, M. (ed.), Chicago: University of Chicago Press.

Roulet, Harry M. (1976) 'The Historical context of Pakistan's Rural Agriculture' in Stevens, et. al. (eds.), *Rural Development in Bangladesh and Pakistan*, Honolulu, Hawaii: Hawaii University Press.

Saeed, K. (1980) *Rural Development and Income Distribution: The Case of Pakistan*, Ph.D. Thesis, Cambridge, MA: MIT.

291

Saeed, K. (1981) 'Mechanics of the System Dynamics Method', *Proceedings of the International Conference on Systems Theory and Applications*, Ludhiana, India.

Saeed, K. (1983) 'Worker Compensation and Income Distribution in Agrarian Economies: Patterns and the Underlying Organization', *Dynamica*, 9(1): 20-32.

Stern, J. and Falcon, W. P. (1971) 'Pakistan's Development: An Introductory Perspective' in *Development Policy II – The Pakistan Experience*, Falcon and Papanek (eds.), Cambridge, MA: Harvard University Press.

12 The role of credit in a rural economy: the case of Thailand*

Jayaprakashan Ambali and Khalid Saeed

Abstract

Rural credit schemes have formed an essential part of the rural development programs implemented in the developing countries over the past few decades, although a high default rate has made it difficult to continue to support them. This paper analyzes the high loan default rate in the rural areas of Thailand and attributes the problem to the distribution pattern of land ownership. The availability of credit may help to fuel investments into farm inputs which increase land productivity. However, when most of the land is absentee-owned, a large share of the benefits of improved productivity is siphoned away by the landlords while the farmers are left with the responsibility of servicing the loan. Since the farmers' financial capacity is limited, a high rate of loan repayment default results. The analysis of the paper is based on a system dynamics model of a dual rural economic system, often encountered in the developing countries. It is shown that the lack of credit facilities is not a fundamental impediment to rural development.

* Reprinted from *System Dynamics Review*, 2(2), Jayaprakashan Ambali and Khalid Saeed, The role of credit in a rural economy: the case of Thailand, pp.126-137, 1986, with kind permission from John Wiley and Sons, Ltd., Baffins Lane, Chichester, West Sussex PO19 1UD, UK.

293

Introduction

Since the early sixties, the diffusion of high-yielding varieties of seeds, pesticides, chemical fertilizers, and modern methods of irrigation and cultivation have played an important part in the design of policies for rural growth in the poor countries. These developments have required relatively costly farm inputs which have necessitated high capital investment in farming operations that only rich farmers have been able to afford. To make these technological advances available to a wider cross section of the rural population, some form of financial assistance to the farmers has been considered imperative. Thus, the extension of credit facilities in the rural areas has become an essential component of rural development programs. Unfortunately, government efforts to provide credit through commercial banks, cooperatives, rural credit banks, and other financial institutions have been frustrated because of the high rate of loan repayment default by the peasants.

This paper attempts to analyze the rural credit system of a developing country and explain its dysfunctional outcomes namely the increasing rural indebtedness and loan repayment default by the peasants, in terms of the organizational arrangements of the system. Since the system under study is complex and does not lend itself easily to a formal mathematical modeling protocol, the heuristic system dynamics approach is used for analyzing it. The analysis makes use of a modified version of a generic system dynamics model of the rural economy, originally developed by Saeed (1983). This model divides the rural economy into two broad production sectors - formal (capitalist) and informal (peasant) - and explicitly represents the economic transactions occurring between them. Data for the central region of Thailand are applied to empirically substantiate the analysis.

The modified model used in the present analysis incorporates an explicit credit sector whereas the credit transactions are implicitly incorporated into the renting of capital in the original model. An outline of the original model and a somewhat more detailed description of the credit sector added to it are given later in the paper. Further technical details of these models are reported elsewhere (Saeed 1980; Ambali 1983). A machine-readable listing of the model written in DYNAMO can be obtained from the authors on request.

An attempt is made to provide a causal explanation for increasing rural indebtedness and loan repayment default by the peasants. It is shown that the availability of credit to the peasants does not substantially alter the pattern of changes in the rural economy.

The credit situation in Thailand

Since the early 1960s there has been active government intervention in the development of agriculture in Thailand, mediated through the National Economic and Social Development Plans of the Royal Thai Government. These plans have focused on the expansion and diversification of crops to meet export demands and on the construction of infrastructure facilities such as roads, communication links, irrigation facilities, and so forth (March 1974).

High-yielding varieties of seeds (HYV seeds) fertilizers, and modern farm machinery have also been introduced to enhance the productivity of farms (Ng 1979). Since these inputs require substantial investment by the farmers, the demand for credit in the rural areas has increased. It has been estimated that the rural credit need has increased from 9.1 billion Baht in 1963 to 25.1 billion Baht in 1977 (Onchan 1984). This, however, does not include the credit needs for consumption as well as the long-term credit needs for land development.

In 1962/63, 90 percent of rural credit was supplied by informal moneylenders (Onchan 1984). These moneylenders, mostly traders, accepted standing crop as security for the loans, on the condition that the farmers sell their crop to the moneylender at a predetermined price. This practice, known as rice baiting, is considered one of the most exploitative forms of money-lending in Thailand, since it deprives the farmers of receiving the market price (Rozental 1970).

The formation of the Bank of Agriculture and Agricultural Cooperatives in 1966 and the issue of a directive from the Bank of Thailand to all commercial banks to advance 13 percent of their total deposits as rural credit have, however, helped to replace a sizable portion of such money lending with formal credit. According to estimates, 60 percent of the total farm credit was provided by the formal sector in 1982/83 (Onchan 1984).

The central region of Thailand, which is considered to be the rice granary of the country, has been the focal point of the agricultural policy that has emphasized green-revolution inputs and farm mechanization. A 1982 survey by the International Labor Organization reports that the buffalo as a drought animal has completely vanished from the central region, and mentions the extensive use of chemical fertilizers and HYV seeds (Pongpaichit 1982).

These changes have been followed by concomitant changes in the land ownership, income distribution, and employment structure in the region. As a result, the distribution of operational land holdings has become highly skewed; the number of agricultural wage workers has increased; and rural income distribution has worsened (Senarak 1976). This pattern of changes is similar to that experienced in several other developing countries that have experimented with the green-revolution strategy (Griffin 1979).

The salient features of the rural debt situation in the four regions of Thailand are summarized in Table 12.1. The table shows that the percentage of the households indebted in the central region of Thailand is considerably higher than in the other regions and also that the amount of debt is more than twice that of the next highly indebted region. A sample survey in the central region indicates that the ratio of debt to total annual income is 38.4 percent while the country-wide average is 16.9 percent (Onchan 1984). This debt pattern indicates that the credit needs are higher in regions where green-revolution inputs have been introduced and where the rural economy is in a state of transition. The failure of the credit system to benefit the small farmer is, however, largely unexplained.

Table 12.1
Rural debt in Thailand

Region	% of total households in debt (1977)	Average debt/ household(1977) (Baht)
Central	78	7786
North	53	3290
South	67	3323
Northeast	60	2552

1 US dollar = 23 Baht
Source: Onchan 1984

Historical role of rural credit: some theories

The need for credit is usually quite low in a traditional rural economy working with an unchanging technology. This is because over the years, the cultivators have acquired the necessary amount of capital adequate for the technology they use and for the size of their holdings (World Bank 1974). In such a setting, the need for credit usually arises only when there is a crop failure or some expenditure related to family ceremonies such as birth, death, or marriage. Some poor farmers also use credit to meet their consumption needs, especially during the pre-harvest season (World Bank 1974). Loans of this nature usually are obtained from informal sources such as friends, neighbors, and relatives. These loans usually are unsecured and involve high risk, and, when taken from a moneylender, involve a high interest rate (Bhisalbutra 1984).

It has been argued, however, that the credit is used for more productive purposes in an environment of technological change than in the case of an economy with stagnant technology. The modern technological inputs of high-yielding varieties of seeds, fertilizers, pesticides, and irrigation equipment (also referred to as inputs of the green revolution) need more capital outlays than the traditional inputs. Furthermore, in a modernizing environment, loans are less likely to be available from other farmers, since in all likelihood they will be using whatever surplus they have to finance their own investments. Hence the institutional sources of credit become very important for facilitating modernization.

In a modernizing rural economy it has been found that the landlords and the traders take on additional roles as moneylenders and provide the much-needed capital though at very high interest rates (Rozental 1970). These informal financial intermediaries have often been denounced as usurers and exploiters even though there have been views to the contrary (Demsetz 1971; Adams 1984). This debate notwithstanding, the stated objectives of the government's intervention in the rural financial markets is to provide low-interest loans to farmers and to displace the informal intermediaries from the system.

To this end, several countries have instituted agricultural cooperatives, rural credit banks, and legal directives to commercial banks to advance a certain percentage of their lending to the farmers. These methods have been viewed as the easiest way to move money to the rural areas to provide an impetus for agricultural modernization. Low interest rates have been justified on the grounds that they offset other price distortions introduced by duties on imported farm inputs, farm product price ceilings, over-valued exchange rates, and a lack of public investment in rural areas (Belshaw 1959).

Implementation of development programs incorporating green-revolution strategies, together with credit facilities, was intended to herald an era of modernization in the rural sectors of the developing countries. However, these have worsened the problem of income distribution (Ladejinsky 1976). The availability of farm machinery has displaced labor, and mechanized commercial farming has displaced tenancy arrangements. In many areas landlessness has increased (Griffin 1979). These anomalous results can be understood only if the role of credit, which is seen as an instrument of modernization, is analyzed in relation to the structural changes which are brought about by the modernization process itself.

A system dynamics model of the rural credit sector

The model of the rural economy has two sectors: capitalist (formal) and peasant (informal). The formal sector is characterized by its option to rent out the land or to resort to commercial farming by employing wage-labor. The peasants till their own land, along with that rented from the formal sector. They also provide wage-labor to the formal sector. Those who cannot find wage-labor are absorbed into the farming activity of the peasants. The ability to acquire land and capital depends on the financial capacity of each sector, which, in turn, depends on its accumulated savings. However, the amount of resources employed by a sector depends on its production efficiency. Thus land and capital owned by the formal sector can be employed by the peasants.

The formal sector is modeled as a profit maximizer while the peasant sector is a consumption maximizer. An important assumption of the model is that the wage rate is determined by the bargaining position of the peasants. Thus, the wage rate is the average consumption expenditure of the peasants, which is further modified by the availability of the wage-workers. Land is owned by the capitalists and the peasants, with buying and selling taking place between them at prices determined by the average marginal revenue product of land and the supply-demand ratio. The peasants cultivate their own land along with that rented out by the capitalists. The land liquidated to recover the bad debt of the peasants is bought by the capitalists. These transactions are shown in Figure 12.1a. Transactions relating to capital are shown Figure 12.1b and to modes of employment in Figure 12.1c.

Modern capital is supplied from outside the rural economy and can be owned by the capitalists as well as by the peasants. Traditional capital is produced within the rural economy and allocated according to the demand from the two sections. The peasants use the capital owned by them along with that rented out by the formal sector. Modern capital liquidated to recover the bad debt of the peasants is bought by the capitalists.

Details of the income streams that determine the accumulated savings of the two sectors are shown in Figure 12.2. Income share of the capitalists is the sum of value of production from their own commercial farming operations and rent receipts from the peasants. Income share of the peasants is the sum of wage payments received from capitalists and the value of production from self-employed farming less rent payments made to the capitalists. Purchase of land and capital, and consumption, deplete the accumulated savings of the two sectors. The saving rate of the peasants is depressed by high land rent and is stimulated by the need to support many workers in self-employment. The saving propensity of capitalists is assumed to be stable and constant. The output of the rural production process meets the demands of agricultural production, traditional capital, and consumption goods. The rural population is assumed to increase at a net rate of 2 percent per year, which may include births, deaths, and migration. Social factors such as demographic transition and value change are ignored, and environmental conditions outside the rural economy are assumed to remain constant.

Income streams relating to the operation of an explicit credit sector are shown in bold lines in Figure 12.2. Borrowings by the peasants flow into their accumulated savings while the debt repayments flow out of it. These two streams, simultaneously, affect the accumulated debt. Peasants' bad debts are recovered by selling their assets to the formal sector, causing a corresponding reduction in the accumulated savings of the formal sector as well as in the debt of the peasants.

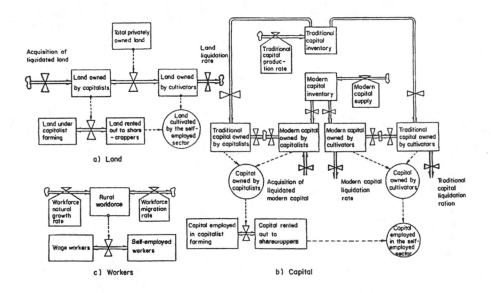

Figure 12.1   **Allocation of production factors in an agrarian economy**
Source: Saeed (1982); changes to the original model are shown in bold lines

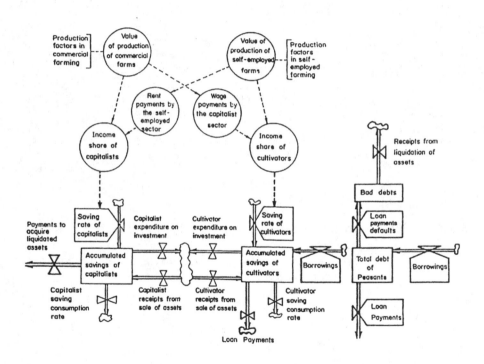

Figure 12.2   Disbursement of income
*Source: Saeed (1982); changes to the original model are
shown in bold lines*

The behavior of the model: understanding the role of the credit sector

The role of credit in the rural economy of Thailand is analyzed against the backdrop of the green revolution and the farm mechanization which has

300

been underway since the 1960s. The initial conditions of the model incorporate a concentration of land in the formal sector and the predominance of sharecropping practices.

The model covers a predominantly rice-growing area of 7000 hectares in the central region of Thailand in which 600 families live. The initial output elasticities of capital, land, and labor are 0.2, 0.5, and 0.4 respectively. A debt repayment time of four years and an interest rate of 20 percent are used in the simulation. Other parameters used in the model are obtained from the data compiled by Pongpaichit (1982).

The mechanization policy is simulated by exogenously introducing a constant supply of modern capital and the green revolution is simulated by doubling the constant term in the Cobb-Douglas-type production function used in the model. The pattern of changes occurring in the credit sector is shown in Figure 12.3. In the initial few years, the debt accumulated by the peasants increases slowly. This is followed by a phase of rapid increase in debt, and then by its eventual decline.

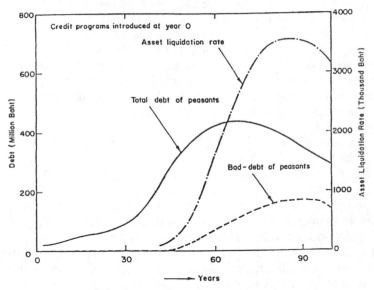

Figure 12.3   **Simulation showing behavior of debt, bad debt, and asset liquidation rate upon the introduction of credit program**

The accumulation of bad debt by the peasants and the loss of assets due to liquidation lag several years behind the introduction of credit facilities. Loan repayments by the peasants are relatively prompt over the initial few years. During this period, the borrowings of the peasants are more than their repayments and, thus, their financial position is improved because of the availability of loans. This increased financial capacity enables the

301

peasants to increase their farm investments which, in turn, increase the productivity of land and, therefore, enlarge their revenue. However, the land tenure pattern alters the impact of the above causal relationship. When most of the land tilled by the peasants belongs to the formal sector, as is the case in Thailand and many other developing countries, the improved productivity of the land causes the land rent to rise considerably. Through this increased rent, a portion of the revenue increase brought about by the use of credit is transferred to the formal sector. The increased land rent reduces the saving ability of the peasants, which has an adverse effect on their financial capacity.

On the other hand, because of the increased land rent the formal sector finds it profitable to rent out more land, which further increases the benefits siphoned away from the peasants. Thus, the income of the peasants does not increase proportionately with their increased farm investments which are made possible by the use of credit facilities.

The above causal relationships influencing the financial ability of the peasants are shown in Figure 12.4. The benign positive feedback loop, acting through capital investment, productivity, farm output and revenue, shows the relationship implicit in the general belief about the role of credit. If this were the only causal relationship, the financial ability of the peasants would increase monotonically and there would be no problem of loan repayment default. However, two additional interactions, one acting through the land rent and the other through the land under sharecropping, provide an explanation, in terms of the organizational arrangements, for the loan repayment defaults.

Since the negative feedback loops of Figure 12.4 appreciably influence the behavior of the system, the land tenure pattern, which is the underlying cause of this feedback relationship, becomes an important determinant of the performance of a rural credit program. In a rural economy where most of the land is owned by landlords and sharecropped by peasants, the renting of land acts as an economic device through which the benefits of credit facilities extended to peasants are siphoned away from them.

The increase in income of the peasants is not proportionate to their increased farm investments facilitated through the use of credit. Hence they default in their repayments with the consequent increase in their debt burden. Data from the central region of Thailand also indicate that debt is more pervasive among tenants and the debt burden of tenants is nearly double that of full owners (Onchan 1984).

Figure 12.5 shows the changes in land ownership and tenure patterns in two simulation runs, one with the credit sector in operation and the other without. At the beginning of the simulation run, most of the land owned by the formal sector is sharecropped by the peasants. The introduction of modern capital enables the formal sector to engage in commercial farming which reduces the amount of land available for renting. The use of machinery enables multiple cropping and increases the earning of the formal sector, a part of which is used for increasing the capitalists' land holdings. Commercial farming also increases the number of wage-workers, which decreases the peasants' utilization of savings to support their own farming operations.

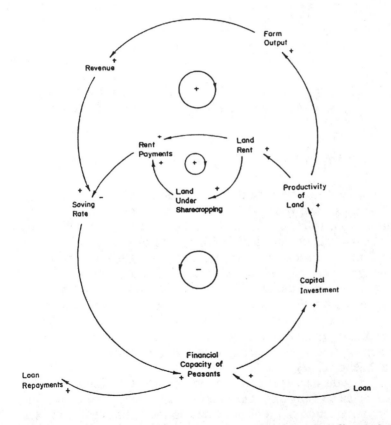

Figure 12.4   Causal diagram affecting the financial capacity of peasants

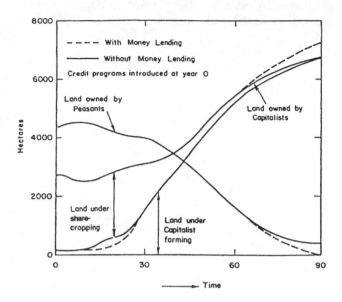

Figure 12.5   **Changes in the land ownership patterns, with and without explicit money lending structure**

The impact of credit on land ownership and tenure patterns

The wage rate does not rise because the compensation given to the wage-worker is not commensurate with the marginal revenue he generates, but is only the opportunity cost of not being self-employed. Thus, the saving rate of the peasants decreases and their land is bought out by the formal sector.

Land being a major factor of production and the basis of claim for income, the income share of the formal sector increases rapidly and the problem of income distribution worsens. This is shown in Figure 12.6. This phenomenon, under the impact of the green revolution and farm mechanization, has been reported in several developing countries (Griffin 1979). A detailed description of the causal interactions that operate to bring about this phenomenon and the policies to alleviate its undesirable effects can be found in Saeed (1982).

As Figure 12.5 indicates, the introduction of credit facilities for the peasants does not substantially alter the pattern of change in land ownership and tenure. The introduction of credit facilities, in the initial years, tends to slow down the rate of conversion of sharecropped land to commercial farms. This results from the increased land rent and the consequent decision by the formal sector to rent out more land.

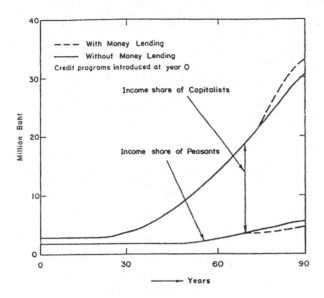

Figure 12.6   **Changes in income distribution, with and without money lending structure**

In the period of rapid transition, when the peasants lose most of their land, the existence of the credit sector has little impact. This is because, during this period, the amount to be repaid is much higher than the amount borrowed and there is no net improvement in the financial position of the peasants. In addition, this period is characterized by the high rate of loan repayment default and the consequent rise in bad debts (Figure 12.3). During this period the peasants lose most of their land because of their decreasing financial capacity, and the eventual limit to their borrowing is determined by the combined influence of the high debt-asset ratio and the worsening loan repayment records.

The accumulated bad debts of the peasants are recovered by liquidating their assets. In the initial years, the asset loss is minimal and reaches its peak several years after the introduction of the credit facilities (Figure 12.3). This is because of the initial low rate of accumulation of the bad debt and the long period required to effect the liquidation of assets.

Some researchers have tried to discount the problem of the worsening debt situation of Thai peasants by pointing out that the loss of assets due to liquidation is very low (Amyot 1976). The simulation shows that in the initial years, the loss of assets cannot be a reliable indicator of the mounting debts. These simulations show that the introduction of the credit

305

sector has not substantially altered the course of changes in the rural economy under the impact of the green revolution and farm mechanization.

Conclusion

This paper has presented an analysis of the role of credit in the rural economy of Thailand and provided a causal explanation for the high loan repayment default rate by the peasants. The increased investments by the peasants in farming operations made possible by the use of credit facilities improves the productivity of land. However, the increased productivity also increases the land rent. This increases the peasants' rent payment burden which, in turn, limits their rate of saving. Thus, the financial capacity of the peasants does not improve in proportion to the loans taken by them. Hence, they default in loan repayments. The eventual liquidation of their assets to recover the accumulated debts results in loss of land and consequent reduction in their income shares.

The analysis shows that the renting of land acts as an economic device through which the benefits of credit extended to the peasants are siphoned away from them. The model used for the analysis in this paper incorporates an explicit representation of the financial markets and their interactions with the other sectors of the rural economy, while in Saeed's model (Saeed 1983) these interactions were represented implicitly. It has been shown that credit policies on their own will not change the income distribution. However, the performance of credit schemes along with other policies that may influence the ownership pattern need to be further investigated.

References

Adams, D. W. (1984) 'Why Agricultural Credit Programs in Low Income Countries Perform Poorly' in *Credit Situation in Asia*, Tokyo: Asian Productivity Organization.

Ambali, J. (1983) *Role of Credit in the Rural Economy of Thailand: A Systems View*, unpublished Masters Thesis, Division of Industrial Engineering and Management, Bangkok: AIT.

Amyot, J. (1976) 'Village Ayuthaya: *Social and Economic Conditions of a Rural Population in Central Thailand* ', Social Science Research Institute, Bangkok: Chulalongkorn University.

Belshaw, H. (1959) *Agricultural Credit in Economically Under-developed Countries*, Rome: FAO.

306

Bhisalbutra, L. (1984) *National Policies for and Objectives of Farm Credit*, in *Credit Situation in Asia*, Tokyo: Asian Productivity Organization.

Demsetz, H. (1971) 'Information and Efficiency: Another View Point' in Lamberton (ed.), *Economics of Information and Knowledge*, New York: Penguin.

Griffin, K. (1979) 'Growth and Impoverishment in the Rural Areas of Asia', *World Development* (7): 300-340.

Ladejinsky, W. (1976) *Green Revolution in Bihar and Punjab*, New York: Agricultural Development Council.

Marcus, I. D. (1974) *Local Government and Rural Development in Thailand*, Special Series on Rural Local Governments, Ithaca, NY: Cornell University.

Ng, R. C. Y. (1979) 'Development and Change in Rural Thailand', *Asian Affairs* (10): 63-68.

Onchan, T. (1984) 'Credit Problems of Farmers in Thailand' in *Credit Situation in Asia*, Tokyo: Asian Productivity Organization.

Pongpaichit, P. (1982) *Employment, Income and Mobilization of Resources in Three Thai Villages*, Bangkok: ILO.

Rozental, A. A. (1970) 'Finance and Development in Thailand', New York: Praeger.

Saeed, K. (1980) *Rural Development and Income Distribution: The Case of Pakistan*, unpublished Ph.D. Dissertation, Cambridge, MA: MIT.

Saeed, K. (1982) 'Public Policy and Rural Poverty: A System Dynamics Analysis of a Social Change Effort in Pakistan', *Technological Forecasting and Social Change*, 21 (4): 325-349.

Saeed, K. (1983) 'Worker Compensation and Income Distribution in Agrarian Economies: Patterns and the Underlying Organizations', *Dynamica*, 9 (Part I): 20-32.

Senarak, B. (1976) *Land Alienation of the Farmers: A Case Study in Amphoe Bangmum Nak*, Masters Thesis, Faculty of Economics, Bangkok: Thammasat University.

The World Bank (1974) *Agricultural Credit*, Development Series Report No. 14, Washington, D.C.

13   Sustaining economic growth with a nonrenewable natural resource: the case of oil-dependent Indonesia[*]

M. Tasrif Arif and Khalid Saeed

Abstract

This study uses a system dynamics model based on an integration of micro- and macro-economic theories to understand economic growth with a nonrenewable natural resource. The case of oil-dependent Indonesia is used as an empirical reference for the study. Long-run growth patterns resulting from various intuitively appealing development policies are analyzed, and an attempt is made to identify the best policy set for attaining a sustainable growth pattern. The study shows that influencing factor prices to facilitate adoption of capital-intensive technologies accelerates development and is a key policy for sustaining growth in the long run.

Introduction

This article examines past oil-dependent economic growth in Indonesia and explores policy options to sustain growth over the next 50 years, during which oil reserves are expected to be depleted. A generic system dynamics model is constructed to analyze the problems of transition from an economy dependent on a nonrenewable natural resource to one independent

[*] Reprinted from *System Dynamics Review*, 5(1),   M. Tastif Arif and Khalid Saeed, Sustaining economic growth with a nonrenewable natural resource: the case of oil-dependent Indonesia, pp. 17-34, 1989, with kind permission from John Wiley and Sons, Ltd., Baffins Lane, Chichester, West Sussex PO19 1UD, UK.

308

of it. The model is based on an integration of macroeconomic growth theory and microeconomic market-clearing mechanisms. In addition, it incorporates relationships creating processes to consume the nonrenewable natural resource as the economy expands. Simulations with this model are used to examine alternative policies for sustaining economic growth after the nonrenewable natural resource is exhausted.

Development planning has traditionally required large-scale interventions by government (Morawetz 1977). Many of the well-known interventionist policies have been implemented in Indonesia. These include (1) increasing government spending, (2) encouraging investment, (3) controlling foreign trade, (4) subsidizing domestic consumption of oil, and (5) controlling factor prices. While implementation of such policies in Indonesia has created some short-run surges in the economy, it has not precipitated long-term economic improvement, and Indonesia remains dependent on oil revenues.

A study of the implications of these policies against the background of history helps to build confidence in the model and to explain the system under study. The emphasis of this study is also on influencing the day-to-day decisions of the participants in the system rather than intervening to fight internal trends. It is therefore necessary to elucidate the decision-making process itself instead of simply using the behavioral equations prescribed by the macroeconomic theory, as is often done in the case of econometrics (Tomkins 1981). Hence, the model used is somewhat large. Its general structure is discussed in this article; further technical details and a machine-readable listing of the model written in DYNAMO are available from the authors on request.

The study suggests that nonintervention by government might have created better economic performance than the interventionist policies listed above. The tendency of the economy to maintain a sustained growth pattern appears to be facilitated by the unencumbered working of the market-clearing mechanisms. Furthermore, when technological flexibility exists, influencing factor prices to efficiently increase capital intensity further helps, because it strengthens the accelerator mechanism and thus creates larger multiplier effects.

The Indonesian economy

An Overview under the so-called New Order (which signifies the assumption of political power by a new regime after a failed coup d'etat in 1965 by the Indonesian Communist Party) the rate of economic growth in Indonesia averaged nearly 8 percent per year over the period 1969-1981. This translated into a real per-capita growth rate of over 5 percent per year (McCawley 1983). As compared with a per-capita growth rate of -0.2

percent per year during the period 1960-1965 (the period of the so-called guided democracy) such a rate of economic growth is high, even by contemporary Asian standards, and much higher than that achieved in western Europe during the nineteenth century or in Japan between 1867 and 1914 (Arndt 1975).

This rapid growth rate has attracted many observers to study the mechanisms of growth of the Indonesian economy during the 1970s. It is widely believed that such rapid growth occurred largely because of revenues from the export of oil. Indeed, petroleum and gas currently account for 75 percent of total exports and for 60 percent of the government's budgetary outlays (Pitt 1985).

Although energy consumption in Indonesia is low, even by developing country standards, it has grown very rapidly over the past decade. Commercial energy consumption grew at an annual rate of 14.7 percent during 1972, which is among the fastest rates of growth in energy consumption in the world and is almost twice as fast as the GNP growth rate in Indonesia (Pitt 1985). In absolute terms, domestic oil consumption accounted for about 124 million barrels of oil equivalent in 1976, which was about 87 percent of Indonesia's total commercial energy consumption (Energy Planning 1981).

Apparently, a major factor behind the rapid growth in domestic oil consumption has been the Indonesian government's subsidization policy. Under the New Order, subsidies granted to producers for the domestic sale of refined oil products at low prices have become a sizable item in the state budget since the late 1970s. In the early 1970s, the price of domestic oil products was higher than production cost (Dick 1980). The increasing dependence of the Indonesian economy on oil export revenues must, however, be viewed with some alarm, since oil resources are finite and nonrenewable. The known reserves-production ratio is about 50 (Wijarso 1981). When oil runs out, the economy might experience a sudden and deep recession before it can make a transition into an oil-independent mode.

Past bases of development policy

It is widely recognized by the development planners that if population is growing, real income must also grow. Its failure to do so implies a reduction in living standards to the point where the population ceases to grow (Hamberg 1956). Thus, models of economic growth have become indispensable to designing strategies for the less developed countries. These models are further supplemented by humanitarian concerns and moral judgments as bases for development policy. Unfortunately, the policies issued on these bases often require large-scale government intervention that

310

counters the internal tendencies of a complex social system - a situation that can be economically wasteful and politically dysfunctional (Saeed 1986; 1987).

The relatively simple Harrod-Domar model, which is the best known of the various economic growth models, has been the main instrument of policy making in the past (Bhagwati 1984). According to this model, the basic remedy for the development problem is simply to increase resources to be invested. Two policy implications of this popular model have been to increase domestic savings and foreign aid. However, a particularly crucial assumption of the Harrod-Domar growth model is that production takes place under fixed factor proportions. This assumption denies the possibility of substitution through technical change and of market-induced changes in factor prices to eliminate slack (Solow 1969). Any excess of either capita or labor is therefore wasted.

The idea of market clearing is also closely related to the optimizing behavior of individuals, albeit within a bounded information set. People determine their individual choices of work, consumption, and so on, in order to make themselves as well off as possible. Market clearing implies that individuals who participate in and organize markets, and who are guided by self-interest, do not waste resources and thereby end up achieving efficient outcomes (Barro 1984). Last but not least, if policy intervention is to be indirect, it must aim at affecting the day-to-day decisions of individuals, not final policy outcomes. Thus, a policy model concerning economic growth must incorporate decision mechanisms affecting individual choices at the microeconomic level. There are, however, inefficiencies in the existing market because of legal norms, social class structure, fragmentation of the financial system, and technological differentiation between the various production sectors, which modify information bounds in which individuals operate (Saeed 1988). These inefficiencies have not been addressed in the model of this article. The integration of the market-clearing and growth processes attempted in the modeling effort, however, allows us to create an evolutionary development perspective targeted at individuals, which is different from an interventionist perspective obtained using only growth models.

A system dynamics model of economic growth with a nonrenewable natural resource

The model developed in this study consists of two parts: (1) a single-sector two-factor production system that incorporates national income accounting at an aggregate level, and mechanisms to determine price level, wage rate, interest rate, and technological mix; and (2) an oil production and consumption system representing the oil sector of the economy. Following are the key assumptions of the model:

1. There is only one commodity other than oil, whose rate of production depends on the potential production rate and the capacity utilization factor. Potential production rate is modeled as a function of capital and workers, whereas the capacity utilization factor depends on the short-run aggregate demand and the inventory condition.

2. Inventory decouples production and consumption and provides important information for determining general price level, imports, and exports. Inventory is introduced into the economic growth submodel as a level containing the physical accumulation of goods in the economy. It is increased through production and imports and depleted through capital investment, government purchases, consumer purchases, and exports.

3. Excesses in inventory can be exported, while shortages in inventory can be met by imports. Volumes of both exports and imports can be controlled through specified policy instruments. There is no limitation outside of the country for exports and imports.

4. Financial markets are cleared through changes in the real interest rate.

5. Fractional gross profits, tax rate, propensity to consume, population growth rate, export price of oil, electricity price, coal price, and subsidy on domestic oil consumption are specified as fixed model parameters that are exogenously determined depending on government policy. Government spending is also exogenously determined.

6. Desired oil exports are endogenously determined on the basis of oil reserves and the need for oil revenues, but they can be further modulated by the oil export policy.

7. Two main components of the oil submodel are the potential oil production and the desired oil production. Potential oil production is determined by capital stock in this sector and by its productivity, which declines as the remaining resources diminish. The model considers capital as the sole production factor input for producing oil, since the oil sector is highly capital-intensive. Oil production is used for domestic consumption and exports. Revenues from oil exports are assumed to be used for importing goods into the economy.

The following sections describe briefly the causal relationships incorporated into the model and the growth patterns generated by simulating it.

Growth mechanisms of the model

Income accounting in the model is based on the well- known identity

$$Y = C + I + G + (X - M),$$

where Y, C, I, G, X, and M are, respectively, income, consumption, investment, government spending, value of exports, and value of imports.

The growth mechanisms are embodied in the feedback loops representing the multiplier-accelerator principle first propounded by Samuelson (1939). However, instead of assuming the presence of a market equilibrium all along the growth path, the model incorporates the micro-level responses of producers and consumers to changes in market conditions, since market clearing, for both the goods and production factors, is the natural micro-complement to the macro-foundations that underlie the model (Barro 1984).

Income of the economy (in real terms) is obtained by multiplying sales by the equilibrium price. Sales constitute consumer purchases, capital investment, government purchases, and next exports in terms of goods. When the oil sector is also connected to this system, income is equal to sales times the equilibrium price plus the real value of domestic oil sales.

The multiplier mechanism is represented through a positive feedback loop, which is coupled with a negative feedback loop, as shown in Figure 13.1. The negative feedback loop represents the constraint imposed by inventory availability on consumption. The effect of wage rate on consumption, as a budget constraint, is not taken into account. The accelerator mechanism is represented through one main positive feedback loop, which is coupled with three supplementary positive feedback loops, as shown in Figure 13.2. These positive feedback loops are, however, coupled with several negative feedback loops, which are created by the market-clearing mechanisms.

Figure 13.3 shows the behavior of the model when it is disturbed from equilibrium by stepping up government purchases. In this experiment, the market-clearing forces are assumed to be absent and population is kept fixed. Also, the oil sector is kept out of the picture.

As seen in Figure 13.3, because of a step increase in government purchases, income rises to a new equilibrium through the growth forces embodied in the feedback loops of Figure 13.1 and 13.2. The new equilibrium occurs at a higher level of income than its initial value. Moreover, because of an increase in the desired production in the face of a fixed population, the unemployment rate decreases.

313

Market-clearing mechanisms of the model

Four market-clearing mechanisms are built into the model. These are real interest rate, general price level, wage rate, and technological mix indicated by the capital-labor ratio. Interest rate balances investment and saving rates, which are decoupled by a pool of uninvested savings. Uninvested savings, in excess of a level necessary to support desired investment at the current cost of capital, exert a downward pressure on the real interest rate, which encourages further investment. Interest rate is also influenced by price. An increase in price raises money demand to support existing exchanges of goods, which raises the interest rate.

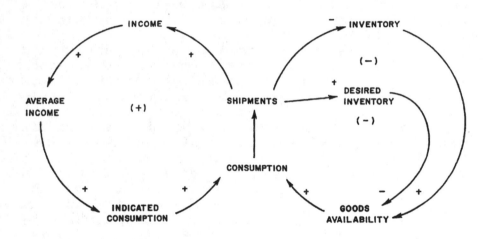

Figure 13.1   The multiplier mechanism and the controlling feedback loops coupled with it

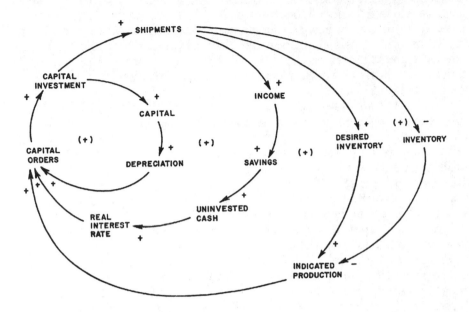

Figure 13.2   Positive feedback loops contributing to the acceleration process

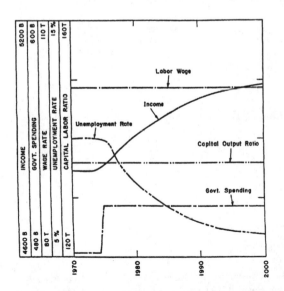

Figure 13.3   Behavior of the model incorporating only growth mechanisms, with a fixed economy assumption

315

General price level clears the goods market. It adjusts towards a desired level at which inventory is adequate to support shipments. General price level, in turn, also affects consumption and investment. Wage rate clears the labor market. An increase in the unemployment rate depresses wage rate. A depressed wage rate, in turn, will increase the demand for workers. Subsequent hiring of workers restores the balance between the workers and the unemployed.

Finally, it is also assumed that, in the long run, the optimal technology mix can be adjusted by using relatively flexible production methods, although this process may be quite slow. This assumption allows for substituting workers for capital in production without compromising on production efficiency. The study assumes that the optimal capital-labor mix will rise when the real wage rate is higher than the average value of the marginal productivity of workers. Presence of such technological flexibility, however, depends on how the government deals with the import of technology. Thus, the process of clearing the technology market should be considered a policy variable.[1]

Figure 13.4 shows the behavior of the model repeating the first experiment while the assumptions of fixity of price, interest rate, wage rate, and optimal capital-labor ratio are relaxed. As shown in Figure 13.4, income rises and levels off, as in the first experiment. Price (not shown) will first rise because of the inventory shortage and then decline, converging to its equilibrium value in its effort to balance supply and demand of goods. Wage rate increases and levels off at a higher level as

---

[1] A Cobb-Douglas production function incorporating constant returns to scales is used. The elasticities of production of capital and labor in this function are allowed to adjust towards those required by capital-labor ratio KLR and capital output ratio KOR, which are allowed to vary depending on market forces. The elasticities are computed as follows:

$$Q = A * K\mu * L1-\mu$$

where Q is production, K is capital stock, L is labor, μ is elasticity of production of capital, and A is a constant scaling factor.

$$(Q/K)\mu-1 = A*(K/L)\mu-1$$

Therefore,
$$KOR = A-1 * KLR1-\mu$$

$$\mu = 1- (\ln(KOR) + \ln(A))/\ln(KLR)$$
Also, at the time of initial equilibrium,

$$\mu = KOR * (IR + 1/LK)$$

where IR is interest rate and LK is life of capital stock. The initial values of the capital-labor ratio and other parameters provide an elasticity of capital of 0.17 and an elasticity of workers of 0.83. As compared with the U.S. economy, in which the elasticity of capital is 0.25 (Forrester 1982) this is plausible, since the Indonesian economy was more labor-intensive in 1970 than the U.S. economy.

compared with its initial value.

The increased wage rate raises the optimal capital- labor ratio. This means that the constant fraction of output accruing to capital is higher than its initial value. In other words, the economy becomes more capital-intensive compared with the first experiment. Consequently, at the new equilibrium, the interest rate is higher than its normal value. It should be noted that the unemployment rate is lower than in the first experiment, since increased capital intensity creates bigger acceleration and also raises subsequent multiplier effects.

Population growth

When population is allowed to grow exponentially and the increments are added to the pool of the unemployed, the wage rate is depressed, and this raises the demand for workers. When technological adjustments are possible, the reduced wage rate decreases the optimal capital-labor ratio, which further fuels worker hiring.

Figure 13.5 shows the model behavior repeating the second experiment, but without a step in government spending, while an exogenously determined fractional population growth rate is introduced. As described above, the rise in population raises the pool of the unemployed, which depresses wage rate, which in turn increases hiring. The consequent rise in production raises the level of inventory, which depresses price level (not shown).

The reduction in price is followed by a decline in interest rate (not shown) while the investment rate lags behind saving rate. The excess supply and the lower level of capital-labor ratio do not encourage further investment. Therefore, more and more capital is substituted by labor. This also limits acceleration and subsequently the multiplier effects as income declines. Thus, unemployment rate becomes high in spite of a low wage rate.[2]

---

[2] Since fractional population growth rate is exogenously determined and is not affected by the declining wage rate, while wage rate cannot go below a minimum needed for subsistence, the model simulations for very long periods will show rising unemployment with wage rate leveling off at the specified minimum value.

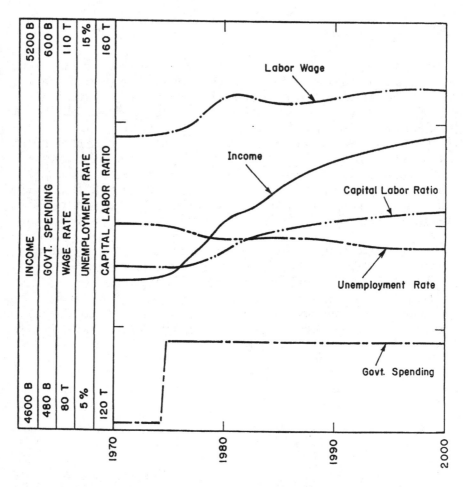

Figure 13.4   Behavior of the model incorporating both growth and market-clearing mechanisms, with a fixed economy assumption

318

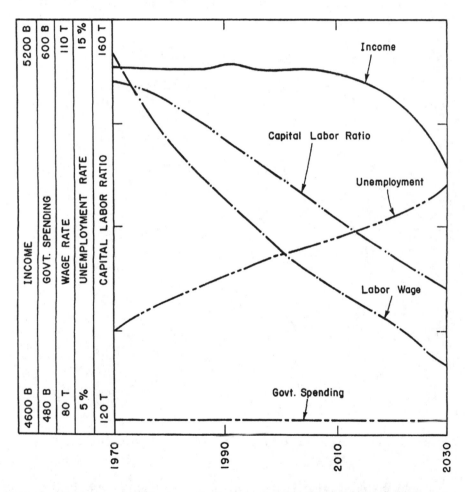

Figure 13.5   **Behavior of the model incorporating both growth and market-clearing mechanisms, with population growth**

319

The oil submodel

The oil submodel determines potential oil production and desired oil production. The potential oil production is given by multiplying capital in the oil sector by the productivity of this capital. The oil capital increases through capital investment in this sector, which is modeled as a function of the desired oil production and the forecast oil productivity of capital. A decline in oil productivity raises the capital investment needed to produce the same amount of oil. This productivity, in turn, depends on the level of the oil reserves remaining. Figure 13.6 illustrates the main causal loops of the oil submodel.

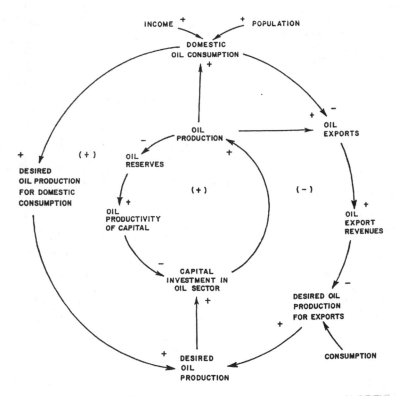

Figure 13.6   Feedback loops incorporated into the oil sub-model

Desired oil production is the sum of the desired oil production for domestic consumption and the desired oil production for exports. Desired oil production for domestic consumption is determined by forecasting domestic oil consumption. The desired oil production for exports is a function of the ratio of oil export revenues to income. When oil export revenues decline, there is a tendency to export more oil in order to offset the declining revenues, and vice versa.

The domestic demand for oil is modeled as a function of income, population, domestic oil price, and average energy price. The average energy price is an average of electricity, coal, and oil prices to the consumer. The electricity and coal prices are determined exogenously as policy parameters of the model.

Considering existing policy to make oil available for domestic use inexpensively, it is assumed that the price charged to the consumer will be linked with the cost of production as long as oil for local consumption is indigenously produced. This price will rise to that in the export market when oil for local consumption has to be imported.[3]

Figure 13.7 shows the behavior of the model when the oil submodel is coupled with the economic growth submodel. This experiment also assumes government spending to be a fixed fraction of the average income and allows population to grow, although at an exogenously determined rate. In this case, all market-clearing mechanisms are assumed to be working.

As shown in Figure 13.7, income grows. However, when income growth rate is less than the population growth rate, income per capita (not shown) declines and wage rate and optimal capital-labor ratio are also depressed.

Since different growth strategies may yield different growth patterns, the pattern of growth sought is the main basis in determining the alternative strategies of growth (Lewis 1984). The pattern being sought in our analysis is one of economic takeoff that might also overcome the problems of transition from an oil-dependent economy to an independent one. The appropriate strategy, in the long run, should maintain sustained growth and encourage the country to become self-reliant.

Unemployment rate rises, since the growth in income is unable to absorb the additional labor. Net exports are positive, indicating that there is excess inventory. Propelled by the need to support higher outlays as income rises, oil exports rise but are limited by the declining oil reserves towards the end of the simulation. The pattern generated in this experiment replicates the problems of increasing dependence on oil and the absence of an economic takeoff that were experienced in Indonesia.

---

[3] Because of the level of aggregation used in the model, the units of goods, capital, oil, and money cannot be defined in realistic physical terms. In qualitative terms, the export price of oil is assumed to be initially much higher than the cost of its production. The cost of production is computed as the cost of capital in the oil sector:

Cost of production = ((IR + 1/LKOS) * GPL)/AOPK

where IR, LKOS, GPL, and AOPK are, respectively, real interest rate, life of capital in oil sector, general price level, and average oil productivity of capital.

321

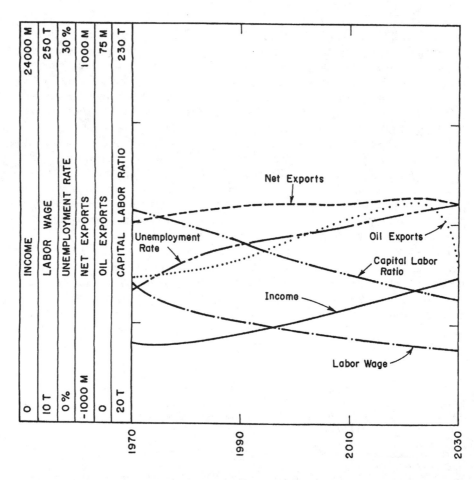

INCOME	24000 M	
LABOR WAGE	250 T	
UNEMPLOYMENT RATE	30 %	
NET EXPORTS	1000 M	
OIL EXPORTS	75 M	
CAPITAL LABOR RATIO	230 T	

Net Exports

Unemployment
Rate

Oil Exports

Capital Labor
Ratio

Income

Labor Wage

INCOME	0	
LABOR WAGE	10 T	
UNEMPLOYMENT RATE	0 %	
NET EXPORTS	-1000 M	
OIL EXPORTS	0	
CAPITAL LABOR RATIO	20 T	

1970   1990   2010   2030

Figure 13.7   **Base run showing behavior of the complete model**

A search for an appropriate growth strategy

It is also important that the instruments of change fall within the purview of normal intervention by government and that they not call for suppressing laissez-faire. Last but not least, these policies may not transfer costs of growth into the future. A good entry point for government intervention is the market. Some examples of policies to influence the market are the establishment of a minimum wage rate for workers or a ceiling on interest rates (Herrick and Kindleberger 1984).

We experimented with the following well-known development policies, using the model to understand how they propagate through the system: (1) increasing government purchases, (2) encouraging investment through cutting taxes, (3) encouraging investment through increasing saving propensity, (4) restricting imports and expanding exports (trade policies) (5) supporting wage and interest rates, and (6) subsidizing domestic oil consumption.

The policy of increasing government purchases is simulated by stepping up fractional government purchases to 20 percent of the average income as compared with 10 percent in the base run. The policy to encourage investment through tax cuts is implemented by stepping down the fractional gross profits tax by 50 percent. The policy to encourage investment through increasing saving propensity is implemented by reducing the propensity to consume by 10 percent.

Trade policies include making foreign trade respond faster to changes in excess inventory, introducing 10 percent positive non-oil exports, and doubling oil exports. Support of wage rate is implemented by holding the rate constant at its initial value. Oil subsidy is simulated by stepping down the oil price to domestic consumers by 50 percent. This policy has been seen as one in which the poor benefit from the oil bonanza. However, several studies have suggested that it helps the higher-income groups considerably more (Down 1983). The base run is made with fractional government purchases at 10 percent of average income, population growth rate at 2 percent per year, and absence of all development policies.

We also explored a set of policies that indirectly influence factor prices and technological mix. These include (1) stepping down interest rate normal (long-run interest rate) by 50 percent, which may be achieved by keeping discount rate low; (2) stepping up wage normal (long-run wage rate) by 50 percent, which can be achieved by fixing minimum wage at a high level; and (3) gradually increasing the goal of the capital-labor ratio to be almost twice its initial value by 2030, which can be achieved by giving fiscal advantages to capital-intensive industry.

The simulation results are compared in Tables 13.1, 13.2 and 13.3, giving the relative-order magnitudes compared to the base-run magnitudes, in each case taken as 1, respectively, of income per capita, unemployment rate, value of net exports, and capital-labor ratio in the year 2030. The initial conditions for all simulations are the same.

Table 13.1 shows the simulation results of the base run and the six development policies previously mentioned. When development policies are absent (base run) the introduction of flexibility in interest rate and technology, in addition to flexible prices and wages, not only decreases income per capita but also makes the system more labor-intensive while increasing unemployment rate. When the indicated development policies are implemented, the presence of such flexibility improves behavior mainly for the first, the second, and the fourth policy, while it worsens behavior for the rest.

Apparently, the presence of such a flexibility in the face of population growth makes the system move towards greater labor intensity, which is concomitant with a considerable weakening of the accelerator and multiplier effects. However, when demand is simulated, the same flexibility allows capital intensity to increase, which strengthens multiplier and accelerator effects.

It should be noted that stimulation of investment only at the cost of limiting demand greatly weakens the growth engine, while supporting wage rate also greatly discourages investment. Subsidization of domestic oil consumption produces results similar to the base runs while it also limits exports.

A comparison of the figures of Table 13.1 for the various computer runs shows that the capital intensity in the economy must rise to increase its growth potential through multiplier and accelerator effects, while at the same time, demand must remain high to stimulate investment.

Table 13.2 shows the simulation results of selected policy runs when capital intensity is increased autonomously to almost three times (283%) its initial value in 1970. The policy of encouraging investment through tax cuts while allowing complete flexibility of the market gives the best results, since it generates the higher multiplier and accelerator effects. Such a policy may also, in the long run, lead the country to self-reliance. On the other hand, the policy of increasing government purchases may create large deficits, and trade policies may increase dependence on the international markets, even if they are able to create some propulsion in the economy. These side effects seem significant enough to make a case for steering away from such policies.

An autonomous increase in capital intensity may, however, be hard to realize unless mechanisms of intervention are identified. The following policy runs attempt to identify means of such an intervention. One way to increase capital intensity might be to influence prices of the production factors. This can be done by keeping nominal interest rates at a low level and wage rate at a high level. Table 3 shows the results of such strategies.

324

Table 13.1
A comparison of the performance of well-known development policies

Nature of intervention	Economic indicator	Relative magnitudes of economic indicators			
		Fixed technology and interest rate	Fixed technology only	Fixed interest rate only	All market clearing mech. working
Base run: no intervention	Income per capita	1.00	0.95	0.53	0.66
	Unemployment	1.00	1.00	1.46	1.23
	Net exports	1.00	2.15	2.00	1.00
	Capital-labor ratio	1.00	1.00	0.57	0.66
1. Increasing government purchases	Income per capita	1.14	1.12	2.86	2.58
	Unemployment	0.69	0.69	0.23	0.31
	Net exports	-10.76	-10.25	-20.32	-16.73
	Capital-labor ratio	1.00	1.00	2.42	2.22
2. Encouraging investment through tax cuts	Income per capita	1.05	1.18	0.53	1.40
	Unemployment	0.92	0.69	1.46	0.61
	Net exports	-0.87	-4.52	1.97	-5.42
	Capital-labor ratio	1.00	1.00	0.58	1.16
3. Encouraging investment through increasing saving propensity	Income per capita	0.36	0.88	0.08	0.19
	Unemployment	1.85	1.15	4.60	2.15
	Net exports	5.24	5.44	1.19	2.69
	Capital-labor ratio	1.00	1.00	0.22	0.31
4. Restricting imports and expanding exports	Income per capita	1.13	1.11	3.03	2.71
	Unemployment	0.77	0.77	0.23	0.23
	Net exports	4.44	4.56	14.19	14.22
	Capital-labor ratio	1.00	1.00	2.56	2.33
5. Supporting wage rate	Income per capita	0.35	0.34	0.35	0.34
	Unemployment	5.69	5.77	5.69	5.77
	Net exports	-0.04	-0.01	-0.02	0.01
	Capital-labor ratio	1.00	1.00	1.00	1.00
6. Subsidizing domestic oil consumption	Income per capita	0.97	9.14	0.53	0.66
	Unemployment	0.92	1.00	1.46	1.23
	Net exports	-0.22	1.06	1.89	0.94
	Capital-labor ratio	1.00	1.00	0.58	0.66

325

Table 13.2
Performance of well-known development policies with autonomous increase in ambient capital-labor ratio

Nature of intervention	Income per capita	Relative magnitudes of economic indicators		
		Unemployment rate	Net exports	Capital labor ratio
Base run: no intervention	1.00	1.00	1.00	1.00a
1. Increasing government purchases	1.33	0.50	-2.27	1.00
2. Encouraging investment through tax cuts	1.42	0.50	-1.01	1.00
3. Encouraging investment through increasing saving propensity	0.83	1.37	1.69	1.00
4. Restricting imports and expanding exports	1.34	0.50	1.68	1.00
5. Supporting wage rate	0.95	0.37	1.19	1.00
6. Subsidizing domestic oil consumption	0.92	1.12	0.76	1.00

a. Base-run value of capital-labor ratio in this table incorporates an almost threefold increase (283%) from the base run in Table 13.1.

Table 13.3
Performance of well-known development policies with maintenance of long-term interest rate at a low level and long-term wage rate at a high level

Nature of intervention	Income per capita	Relative magnitudes of economic indicators		
		Unemployment rate	Net exports	Capital labor ratio
Base run: no intervention	1.00	1.00	1.00	1.00a
1. Increasing government purchases	3.98	3.03	-16.82	3.38
2. Encouraging investment through tax cuts	2.13	0.65	-5.32	1.79
3. Encouraging investment through increasing saving propensity	0.29	1.65	2.60	0.48
4. Restricting imports and expanding exports	4.20	0.25	14.37	3.54
5. Supporting wage rate	0.41	4.35	0.02	2.31
6. Subsidizing domestic oil consumption	0.99	1.00	0.94	1.00

a. Base-run value of capital-labor ratio in this table is the same as in Table 13.1.

Deficit spending, export promotion, and encouraging investment through tax cuts are indicated as best policies. The first two increase demand, while the third improve the ability to invest, although, as stated earlier, the first policy may create large national debt and the second may increase dependence on foreign markets in the long run. However, further helping to increase capital intensity through explicitly raising its ambient value, possibly by giving fiscal advantages to the capital-intensive industry, also sufficiently propels demand, even in the absence of deficit spending, export promotion, and tax cuts.

Figure 13.8 shows the growth behavior when tax cuts, low interest rate, and high wage policy are also linked with increasing ambient capital-labor ratio. Unemployment rate rises at first; however, it later declines below its initial value. Income and wage rate rise steadily. When oil exports start to decline because of the exhaustion of oil reserves in the face of robust demand, interest rate will rise to encourage savings in order to provide for the increased capital investment needed for supporting the existing level of consumption. This set of policies appears to be the best for realizing a self-reliant and sustainable growth.

Conclusion

This study has attempted to identify indirect instruments for attaining self-reliant and sustainable growth in an economy dependent on a nonrenewable natural resource, with specific reference to Indonesia. An important requirement of such an exercise is to incorporate into the model an appropriate "policy space". Thus, the market mechanisms to be influenced through indirect means must be included.

The best policy set identified in this analysis aims at increasing multiplier effects and acceleration in the economy. This is possible by making sure that demand is not limited, that there is sufficient financial ability to invest, and that a high degree of flexibility is maintained in the market. Also important is to increase capital intensity through influencing factor prices and having an explicit capital intensity goal, instead of the existing tradition, as a basis for determining appropriate factor proportions.

The study, however, relies on a theory-based model, although the attempt to integrate micro- and macroeconomic relationships leads to interesting policy choices. A large empirically-based model of an oil-dependent economy has been developed for Iran by Mashayekhi (1978) although he has not considered the policy issues we have addressed in this paper with a theoretical model.

328

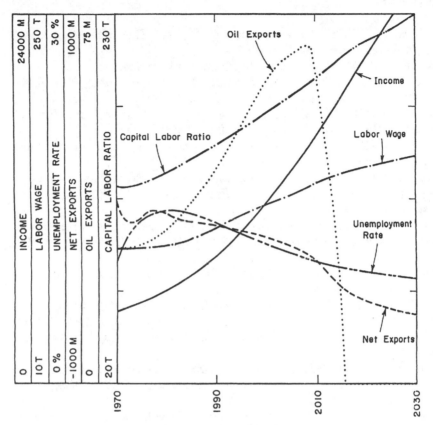

Figure 13.8   Simulation run showing best policy set, incorporating cutting down interest rate and taxes, increasing wage rate, and facilitating capital intensive production

The model of this study also does not address implications for income distribution. A dual-economy framework in which wages are determined through bargaining mechanisms has been suggested by Saeed (1988) for determining income distribution in agrarian economies. Such a framework appears quite appropriate also for studying income distribution in the industrial sector.

The results of this study may be generalized to some degree and may hold true also for non-oil economies. The analysis shows that the appropriate technology to be adopted by a developing nation should not depend on existing labor availability but should take into account the growth pattern desired.

References

Arndt, H. W. (1975) 'Development and Equity: The Indonesian Case', *World Development*, 3(283):77-90.

Barro, R. J. (1984) *Macroeconomics*, New York: Wiley.

Bhagwati, J. N. (1984) 'Development Economics: What Have We Learned?', *Asian Development Review*, 2(1):23-38.

Dick, H. (1980) 'The Oil-Price Subsidy, Deforestation, and Equity', *Bulletin of Indonesian Economic Studies*, 16(3):32-60.

Down, S. (1983) 'Household Energy Consumption in West Sumatra: Implications for Policy Makers', *Energy*, 8(11):821- 833.

Forrester, N.B. (1982) *A Dynamic Synthesis of Basic Macroeconomic Theory: Implications for Stabilization Policy Analysis*, Ph.D. Dissertation, Cambridge, MA: MIT.

Hamberg, D. (1956) *Economic Growth and Instability*, New York: Norton.

Herrick, B. and Kindleberger, C. P. (1984) *Economic Development*, New York: McGraw-Hill.

Lewis, W. A. (1984) 'The State of Development Theory', *American Economic Review*, 74(1):1-10.

Low, G. W. (1980) 'The Multiplier-Accelerator Model of Business Cycles Interpreted from a System Dynamics Perspective' in Jørgan Randers (ed.), *Elements of System Dynamics Method*, Cambridge, Mass: MIT Press.

Mashayekhi, A. N. (1978) *Strategy of Economic Development: A Case of Development Based on Exhaustible Resources*, Ph.D. Dissertation, Cambridge, MA: MIT.

McCawley, P. (1983) 'Survey of Recent Developments', *Bulletin of Indonesian Economic Studies*, 19(1):1-31.

Morawetz, D. (1977) *Twenty-Five Years of Economic Development, 1950-1975*, Washington, D. C.: World Bank.

Pitt, M. M. (1985) 'Equity, Externalities, and Energy Subsidies: The Case of Kerosene in Indonesia', *Journal of Development Economics*, 17:201-217.

Republic of Indonesia, (1981) *Energy Planning for Development in Indonesia*, Ministry of Mines and Energy, Directorate General power.

Saeed, K. (1986) 'The Dynamics of Economic Growth and Political Instability in Developing Countries', *System Dynamics Review*, 2(1):20-35.

Saeed, K. (1987) 'A Re-evaluation of the Effort to Alleviate Poverty and Hunger', Socioeconomic Planning Sciences, 21(5):291-304.

Saeed, K. (1988) 'Wage Determination, Income Distribution, and the Design of Change', *Behavioral Science*, 33(3): 161-186.

Samuelson, P.A. (1939) 'Interaction Between the Multiplier Analysis and the Principles of Acceleration', *Review of Economics and Statistics* (May):75-78.

Solow, R. M. (1969) 'A Contribution the Theory of Economic Growth' in *Readings in the Modern Theory of Economic Growth*, J. E. Stiglitz and H. Uzawa (eds.), Cambridge, Mass.: MIT Press.

Tomkins, R. (1981) 'Structural Features of a System Dynamics Model of the UK Economy', *Proceedings of the 6th International Conference on System Dynamics* (Paris).

Wijarso, (1981) 'National Energy Planning in Indonesia', *Energy*, 6(8):737-744.

14 The dynamics of indebtedness in the developing countries: the case of the Philippines*

Phares P. Parayno and Khalid Saeed

Abstract

The relationships between foreign capital inflows, the build-up of debt, and economic growth in a developing country are analyzed using a system dynamics model of the pertinent processes. The Philippines serves as an empirical case to apply the model. The model incorporates the macro-structure of economic growth, the micro-structure of market-clearing mechanisms, and an accounting of the money flows. The study shows that economic policies enhancing debt-servicing ability create better economic performance than those limiting acquisition of loans. Increasing capital-intensity is the most important part of such policies. They are further facilitated by encouraging investment through decreasing taxes and enhancing demand through increasing government spending and promoting exports. Thus, augmentation of domestic resources by foreign capital inflows appears to be a viable economic strategy.

Introduction

Guided by the economic models suggesting that growth rate can be stepped-up by increasing resources for investments, the developing country

* Reprinted from *Socio-Economic Planning Sciences*, 27(4), Khalid Saeed, The dynamics of indebtedness in the developing countries: the case of the Philippines, pp. 239-255, Copyright 1993, with kind permission from Elsevier Science Ltd., The Boulevard, Langford Lane, Kidlington OX5 1GB, UK.

governments have often resorted to foreign capital borrowing to supplement domestic resources in their efforts to fuel industrialization. The borrowed capital is also often used to finance capital imports necessary to expand the export industries and for capital outlays for upgrading the infrastructure. As further economic expansion is targeted, more capital imports are needed. As a consequence, foreign debt increases, which creates heavy debt service burden. When debt service payments begin to take a greater share of GNP, operating expenses and capital outlays for development purposes are reduced, which curtails growth. A remedy increasingly being suggested to decrease foreign debt is to reduce growth targets by decreasing the expenditure on industrial and infrastructure expansion [Feder 1978, Lamberte et. al. 1985]. However, many highly-indebted Latin American and Asian developing countries which adopted this policy, continue to endure high debt service payments while attaining either a minimal or no economic growth [Deitz 1986, Orlando and Tietal 1986]. It is, therefore, imperative to search for alternative policies which might be more effective.

This paper examines the relationships between economic growth and foreign capital inflows in an effort to understand the causes of the build-up of external debt coupled with stagnation in economic performance. The case of the Philippines is used as an illustrative example. An attempt is also made to search for appropriate policies for increasing growth without creating a heavy debt burden. The analysis is accomplished through a system dynamics model adapted from one developed by Arif and Saeed (1989) in a study on oil-dependent growth in Indonesia. Additional structure incorporating financial decisions to borrow and service debt have been added to the model of Arif and Saeed and the oil sector originally built into it has been deleted since it is irrelevant to the case of the Philippines. Technical details of this model are reported in Parayno [Parayno 1989]. The mathematical structure of the model is given in Appendix A. A complete listing of the model written in DYNAMO[1] can be obtained from the authors on request. Experimentation with this model suggests that economic policies enhancing debt-servicing ability create better economic performance than those limiting acquisition of loans. Such policies include increasing capital intensity and stimulating demand. The economic takeoff resulting from these policies may support high debt servicing which subsequently decreases debt levels and finally, also the dependence on foreign capital inflows.

---

[1] DYNAMO is a trademark of Pugh-Roberts Associates, Inc. DYNAMO is a powerful DOS-based modeling environment which is capable of 1) developing models of complex systems, 2) validating models, 3) examining dynamics, 4) testing alternate policies and assumptions and 5) reporting and evaluating results.

The Philippines' debt problem: an overview

As a part of her industrialization strategy, the Philippines from the late 1960s began to expand her light manufacturing industry which exported much of its production. Thus, in the late 1960s and early 1970s, over which the volume of world exports rose rapidly at an annual rate of 8.5%, the Philippines recorded favorable export earnings. Exports grew by an average of 20.7% per year as contrasted to 7.1% per year in the 1960s, with the share of non-traditional exports in the total increasing from 7.5% in 1970 to 38.0% in 1980 [Remolona, et. al. 1986].

This growth, however, incurred high investment cost. The government in its attempts to promote exports had to increase considerably its capital outlay for the export infrastructure. Many export processing zones were created in the 1970s. To maintain the momentum of growth, the government expanded its capital outlays by 25% per year from 1974 to 1982, which was a further increase from an already high expansion rate of 21% per year over the 1960s. Private investment rate increased by an average of 30% per year from 1974 to 1982 [Remolona, et. al. 1986, De Dios 1986].

The increase in government capital outlays for the export promotion infrastructure and the apparent import-dependent character of the manufacturing of the export products led to a heavy dependence on foreign capital inflows, which is seen in the increasing percentage of capital-goods imports: from 4.5% of potential output in 1973 to 7.1% in 1975. These heavy imports and the quadruple increase in prices of oil imports from 1973 to 1974 doubled import payments, causing current account deficit to GNP ratio to increase from 1.2% in 1974 to 5.7% and 5.9% respectively in 1975 and 1976 [Remolona, et. al. 1986, De Dios 1986].

The rapid increase of external debt made it difficult for the country to cover the concomitantly increasing debt service. The government resorted to foreign capital borrowing to meet the increasing amount of interest payments more so to short-term loans when the long-term and medium-term loans offering relatively easy terms became more difficult to obtain in the international financial market.

The increasing difficulty of interest payments is seen in the time series plot of Figure 14.1. The share of short-term borrowings in the external debt grew to about 43% of total outstanding loans over the period 1981-1983. With the political events of August 1983, the reduction in the confidence of foreign banks in the government caused them to refuse to renew short-term financing. Without replenishment from short-term borrowings, international reserves fell drastically from $2.54 billion at the start of 1983 to $1.43 billion at the end of September that year [Remolona, et. al. 1986, Hill and Jayasuriza 1985, Lamberte et. al. 1984, De Dios 1986].

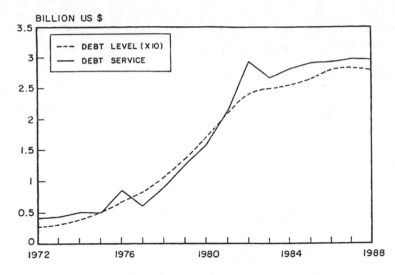

BILLION US $

- - - DEBT LEVEL (X10)
——— DEBT SERVICE

Figure 14.1   **Philippine external debt and external debt service burden, 1972-1988**
Source: Central Bank of the Philippines

As debt payment difficulty intensified, the government declared a 90-day moratorium on payments of principal on its foreign-exchange liabilities and also imposed foreign exchange restrictions. The government then began negotiations with its private creditor banks and the IMF for debt rescheduling and an additional financing of $3.6 billion for 1984. The government also agreed to cut expenses as a condition of the financing and increase taxes to augment the foreign capital inflows, so that additional expenses could be met. These conditions are reflected in the GNP figures shown in Figure 14.2.

The GNP actually declined after the balance of payments crisis in 1983. It should be noted that it was during this period that imports were restricted, government expenses cut, and taxes increased. The restricted imports cut down essential inputs to production, creating underutilized industrial capacity, which discouraged further investment. The cut in government expenses and increase in taxes further discouraged investment. This led to a decline in the GNP. With decreasing income, consumption was constrained and savings decreased, which further constrained investment. The decreasing income also meant that less taxes would be generated. Consequently, the country became even more dependent on foreign loans for its debt service payments.

In the first half of 1989, the government negotiated for another foreign financing from the IMF by agreeing to a further cut in government expenses and an increase in taxes in order to improve the country's balance

335

of payments situation. This may create in the future substantial negative multiplier effects especially when per capita income has already begun to decrease because of the population growth as shown in Figure 14.2.

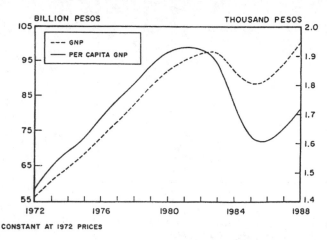

Figure 14.2   **GNP and GNP per capita, 1972-1988 at 1972 prices**
Source: National Economic Development Authority (NEDA) April 1989

A system dynamics model of economic growth and indebtedness

The model used in this study incorporates: 1) the debt accumulation processes; 2) the economic growth mechanisms; and 3) the market-clearing mechanisms, the latter two sets of mechanisms being adapted from the model of Arif and Saeed (1989). The coverage of market-clearing mechanisms is necessary to be able to identify pressure points through which day to day decisions of the actors in the system can be influenced.

The variables of interest in the debt accumulation processes include debt, the acquisition of foreign loans and debt repayments. Those in the economic growth processes include government expenditure, personal consumption, investment, taxes, exports and imports. Finally, the market-clearing mechanisms focus on the optimizing behavior of individuals confined in a bounded information set. The variables considered are general price level, interest rate, wage rate and the technological mix embodied in the capital-labor ratio. Capital-output ratio is modeled as a policy parameter representing the efficiency of capital investment.

Following are the key assumptions implicit in the model structure:

1. The need for loans is created when expenditure exceed revenue and the value of imports exceed the sum of the value of exports and the net factor income.[2]
2. The net factor income is considered exogenous to the system since it is often affected by government policy and actors outside of the system.
3. Loans can be obtained both from domestic and foreign sources.
4. Interest rate on foreign loans is exogenously determined.
5. There is only one commodity whose rate of production depends on the potential production rate and the capacity utilization factor. Potential production rate is formulated as a function of capital, workers and government infrastructure facilities [Eisner 1989]. Capacity utilization factor depends on the short-run aggregate demands and the inventory condition [Mass 1975].
6. Inventory is increased through production and imports but decreased through government and consumer purchases, capital investment and exports.
7. Excess inventory can be exported while shortages can be met by imports. Volume of exports and imports can be controlled through specified policy instruments one of which is related to debt. There is no limitation outside of the country for exports and imports.
8. Capital goods are assumed to be homogeneous.
9. Money creation is not considered in the model; hence, money-related inflationary effects are not included.
10. Population growth rate is exogenously determined.

Information relationships in the main sectors of the model are explained below:

Debt accumulation processes

The accumulation of debt is embodied in the positive feedback loops shown in Figure 14.3. Debt increases through acquisition of loans and accrual of interest. As debt increases, debt service consisting of principal payments and interest, rises. The consequent build-up of government expenditure draws down government money balance, which creates a need for taking more loans.

The insidious debt growth process explained above is, however, contained by several negative feedback loops striving to equate revenues

---

[2] This statement holds that $Sf = (G-T) + (M-X) + I - Sd - Af$ which is true for dynamic relationships. Our analysis here does not focus on equilibrium relationships. Sd and Sf are domestic and foreign savings, respectively; Af = income from foreign assets; G = government expenditure; T = taxes; M and X are imports and exports respectively; and I = investments.

and expenses. Increasing government spending decreases government money balance to a low level where it creates a pressure to limit government spending. An increase in revenues expands government money balance, which may call for cutting down taxes that would limit revenues. Also, payment of outstanding interest and capital amount decreases debt, which limits the amount of subsequent payments, while acquisition of more loans increases government money balance which decreases the need for more loans.

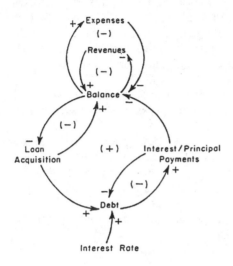

Figure 14.3   Positive feedback loop contributing to the accumulation of debt with appropriate controlling feedbacks

These debt accumulation processes are strongly coupled with other mechanisms in the model which can also prevent or facilitate escalation of debt. These are now explained.

The economic growth mechanisms

The economic growth mechanisms of the model are embodied in the feedback loops representing the multiplier-accelerator principle first proposed by Samuelson [Remolona et. al. 1986]. As in the original system dynamic model suggested by Arif and Saeed (1989) the multiplier is represented through a positive feedback loop coupled with a negative feedback loop as shown in Figure 14.4. The multiplication process is created by the mutual dependency of consumption and output. A disturbance in demand produces a change in output and a proportional

338

change in consumption which feeds back to further disturb aggregate demand. The consumption, however, is constrained by the availability of inventory as represented in the negative feedback loop.

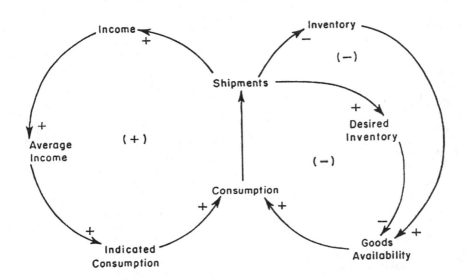

Figure 14.4 **The multiplier mechanism with appropriate controlling feedback loops**
Source: Adapted from Arif and Saeed (1989)

The accelerator mechanism is represented through four positive feedback loops as shown in Figure 14.5. The innermost positive feedback loop represents the classical accelerator implying that a rise in the demand of capital goods (capital orders) creates an increase in capital investment that further increases aggregate demand. The first adjoining feedback loop shows that a rise in shipments increases income of the economy that increases savings. A rise in savings depresses interest rates, which encourages investment, thus further enhancing aggregate demand. The second adjoining feedback loop establishes that production will rise as shipments are increased; the increase in production causing further increase in investment. The third adjoining feedback loop creates increase in production in response to the depletion of inventory resulting from an increased demand. These four feedback loops representing the accelerator reinforce one another.

The positive feedback loops representing multiplier and accelerator are, however, coupled with several negative feedback loops which are created by the market-clearing mechanisms.

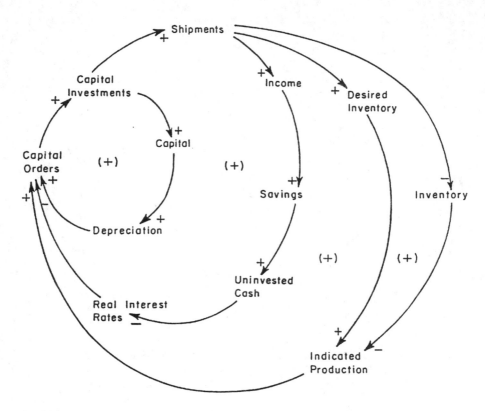

Figure 14.5   **Positive feedback loops contributing to the accelerator process**
Source: Adapted from Arif and Saeed (1989)

Market-clearing mechanisms

The market-clearing processes capture the basic structural mechanism representing the micro-level responses of producers and consumers to changes in the market conditions, since market-clearing for both goods and production factors is the natural micro-complement to the macro-foundations that underlie the model [Barro 1984]. The market-clearing mechanisms included in the model are interest rate, general price level, wage rate and technological mix indicated by the capital-labor ratio.

Interest rate is a mechanism that equates investment and saving rates which are integrated into a stock of uninvested savings. A downward pressure is exerted on the interest rate when the level of uninvested savings is in excess of the level necessary to support the desired investment. Interest rate is pushed up when the uninvested savings are less than the desired level needed to support investment. It is also pushed up by a rise in the general price level.

General price level adjusts towards the desired level necessary for equating supply and demand, but with a delay. Price tends to increase when inventory (representing supply) is less than the desired inventory (representing demand) and vice versa. General price level also affects consumption and investment.

Wage rate clears the labor market by maintaining unemployment rate at its frictional value. It is reduced when unemployment rises. This reduced wage rate, however, increases the demand for workers and the resulting increase in the hiring of workers finally restores the balance between the workers and the unemployed.

The technological mix allows the substitution of workers for capital in the production process without compromising on production efficiency. A sensibly high capital labor ratio is achieved when the system comes to equilibrium, the values of the capital labor ratio depending on the intensity of the policies implemented. This adjustment mechanism, however, involves relatively long adjustment times.

The presence of multiple growth and adjustment paths in the form of positive and negative feedback loops makes possible the existence of many economic patterns, including increasing growth at a high level of debt on the one hand and decreasing growth at a high level of debt on the other. It also appears from the causal relationships of the system that certain forces that allow economic growth to increase also allow debt to rise. Furthermore, the side by side existence of a variety of negative feedbacks shows that the system may resist some of the forces of change while the positive feedback loops may cause growth or decline depending on the gain over the course of an adjustment towards a dynamic equilibrium. Hence, it is possible that while debt continues to accumulate, economic growth is regressing or vice versa. Korea is an example of the former economic pattern while the Philippines and many other developing countries in South Asia and Latin America are examples of the latter pattern [Power 1983]. The increase in government spending which causes high deficits may not promote growth when interest rates are so high that investment is strongly discouraged or when capital intensity is at a low level. On the other hand, a high level of income may create a high saving rate and generate sufficient taxes to eliminate the need for loans which may decrease debt.

Many simulation experiments were performed to understand the economic pattern experienced in the Philippines and to prepare a policy framework for a change. These are discussed in the next section.

Understanding the Philippines' debt service problem

There exists a trade-off between representing a complex system as a complex model that tracks history precisely or simplifying its structure to communicate a clear understanding of the system, although the resulting model may capture only broad historical patterns. The simplified representation would limit the comparison of the generated behavior of a model with the real world behavior to qualitative aspects only, although it might still provide a sound basis for policy experimentation [Saeed 1992]. This study adopts the latter option. Hence, the behavior of the model may not exactly follow every aspect of the pattern shown by the time series data forming the reference mode.

Before simulation experiments are conducted, the model is initialized to represent the conditions of the Philippines in 1972. These include exports, imports, debt, net factor income, fractional government purchases and population growth, besides other economic variables. The initial values of parameters used are given in the Appendix B. The first simulation of the model with each starting conditions will be called the base run. The growth-debt pattern observed in the Philippines taken as the reference mode for further exploratory experimentation, is generated by progressively introducing the different policies adopted by the Philippines to the base run case.

The different policies incorporated into the model for generating the reference mode are the following: 1) increasing government spending in the early 1970s; 2) cutting taxes to encourage investments in export promotion in 1976; 3) keeping wage to a minimum to attract foreign investments; 4) promoting exports without, however, restricting imports; 5) rescheduling debt and limiting debt service to 20% of export earnings; 6) decreasing government spending and increasing tax in 1984 when heavy debt burden precipitated in 1983. The increase in world interest rates in 1978 decreasing the availability of the long-term loans is also introduced.

The policy of increasing government spending is implemented by stepping up the initial value of spending of 11% of average income to 22%. Tax reduction is implemented by decreasing the initial fractional gross profit tax by 25% in 1976. The policy of establishing a minimum wage rate to attract foreign investment is simulated by fixing in 1976 the value of wage rate instead of letting it float.

The rise in exports is introduced by increasing the share of exports in income by 30% of its initial value of 17.7% and making foreign trade respond faster to excess inventory. This would, however, also expand imports since exports selected by the government for promotion call for installing additional infrastructure and capital investment with high import content. This effect is simulated by increasing the fraction of income forming imports from 18.5% to 24%.

The policy of limiting debt service payments to 20% of the export earnings is simulated by formulating external debt service as the minimum of the outstanding interest and principal payments and 20% of the export value. Rescheduling is requested in the model when liquidity problems occur. The liquidity problem is assumed to take place when the level of external debt is 150% of the export value and government money balance is less than the desired government money balance [Schelzig 1989].

The government response in 1983 to the accumulation of a heavy debt burden in limiting spending and increasing taxes is simulated by reducing the share of income forming government spending by 20% and increasing the fractional gross profit taxes by 50%.

The reference mode simulation incorporating above policy agenda is shown in Figure 14.6. It is observed that investment decreases after the policies of reducing government spending and increasing taxes are introduced. Income also diminishes and then rises slowly. The low levels of income and investment can not support the increasing population, which creates rising unemployment. As population continues to increase, income per capita declines.

Though the debt service burden is reduced in the short run, the economy continues to be saddled with increasing debt in the long run. Since income does not grow as fast as the build up of the external debt, it becomes very difficult for the country to repay its debt. Thus, debt repayment is unable to reduce the level of external debt. To augment available domestic resources for repaying its debt, the country requires additional foreign capital inflows. But unless these capital inflows rebound the economy to a higher level of income, the country will sink to a crisis of high debt burden, low income and worsening unemployment rate.

The simulation of Figure 14.6 resembles in essence the historical pattern described in the earlier section of this paper. It must be recognized, however, that the model used in this study incorporates only the general economic relationships, excluding the mechanisms of political change. Thus, the political upheaval of August 1983 which partly explains the historical pattern depicted, is outside of the scope of the model. If socio-political explanation should be injected into the growth-debt problem of the Philippines, the model would have to be further extended to include the socio-political relationships. This might make the model much too complex to analyze easily.

The problem of socio-political change may, however, be dealt with separately from the problem of economic change by appropriately partitioning the system [Saeed 1990, 1992]. Our model deals only with economic change. Thus, it may not be expected to track history at every point although it should replicate the general economic pattern, which it does.

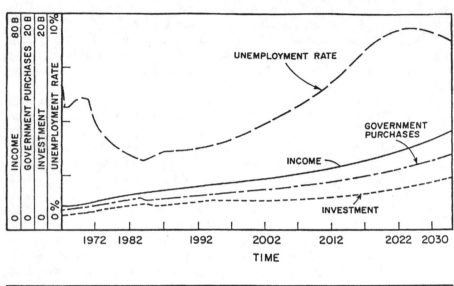

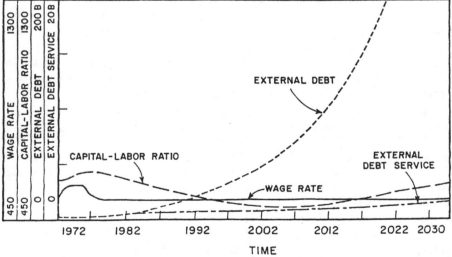

Figure 14.6   Reference mode

Sustaining economic growth without heavy debt service burden

The preceding simulation shows that the policies of decreasing government spending, increasing taxes and limiting debt service payments do not alleviate the debt problem which has beset many developing countries for many years. Such policies may appear to decrease the balance of payments, since expenses and debt service payments are reduced, they would also limit economic expansion because investments are discouraged. Thus, a reduction in the balance of payments may give only short-term benefits since the structural tendency to slow-growth is still present. To reduce a continually increasing external debt is almost impossible in a stagnant economy. In our search for an appropriate strategy, we keep in view the economic pattern in which the high level of debt of a country will finally be repaid by an economic takeoff that may be achieved through high investment.

In their simulation experiments searching for an appropriate growth strategy for Indonesia, Arif and Saeed (1989) suggested government intervention to increase capital intensity so that investment is encouraged. The specific policies accomplishing this are keeping interest rate at a low level and wage rate at a high level. These policies were seen to apply to our case equally well and are introduced in 1989 in all the simulation experiments that follow, searching for an appropriate growth strategy for the Philippines.

Additionally, we also experimented with several well-known alternative development and debt management policies. These policies are: 1) increasing government purchases; 2) encouraging investment through tax cuts; 3) encouraging investment through increasing savings propensity; 4) expanding exports and restricting imports; and 5) not limiting external debt servicing. Each of these policies is introduced in 1989 in the model producing the reference mode.

The policy of increasing government purchases is implemented by stepping up by 10% the fraction of income forming government purchases. The policy of encouragement of investment through tax cuts is achieved by making a 50% reduction in the fractional gross profit tax. The policy of encouragement of investment through increasing propensity to save is introduced by decreasing propensity to consume by 10%. Trade policies include making foreign trade respond faster to excess inventory and intensifying exports as debt increases but limiting imports. The policy of not limiting external debt servicing is implemented by removing the restriction of external debt servicing to 20% of the export earnings.

Each of the above strategies is tested for three intensities of government reactions to the changing balance deficit - moderate, prudent and radical. It is assumed that moderate government behavior does not normally resort to drastic tax increases when balance deficit develops as a result of the

345

increasing expenditure. Prudent behavior reduces government purchases as debt increases. It is represented by adding a negative causal link from the level of debt to fractional government purchases - as the level of debt increases, fractional government purchase decreases. Radical behavior increases taxes as government expenses increase. It is formulated by increasing the slope of the function representing government's response to money balance changes in changing the tax rate. Each of these policies is introduced in 1989 in the model producing the reference mode.

The simulation results are compared in Table 14.1 giving the relative-order magnitudes of the selected indicators compared to the magnitudes of Figure 14.6, in each case taken as 1. These indicators are income per capita, unemployment rate, external debt to income ratio, external debt service to income ratio, capital-labor ratio and net exports respectively in year 2030.

The comparative results of Table 14.1 show that the growth forces are weakened by the demand-limiting effects of decreasing government purchases as debt level increases. Income per capita for all policy runs has relatively lower magnitude in the prudent behavior assumption than in the other two assumptions while debt to income and debt service to income ratios are higher. Also unemployment rate is higher and capital-labor ratio lower. As demand is limited by reduction in government purchases, investment is decelerated causing a reduction in income.

The limited debt servicing capacity which is further abated by decreasing income in the prudent behavior produces greater debt levels than in the other two assumptions. When investment lags behind population growth, unemployment rises, which in turn makes the system move towards a higher labor intensity that further wanes investment. This leads to a worsening economic condition. On the other hand, though the radical behavior produces slightly better results than prudent behavior, there is no definite effect on investment. While investment is promoted by increase in government purchases it is, however, discouraged by a tax increase.

The simulation results using the policies of increasing government purchases, cutting taxes and promoting exports but restricting imports with the moderate behavior assumption show the most favorable performance of the system. The simulation incorporating a high propensity to save limits demand which weakens the growth engine and thus decreases income. The simulation which does not restrict debt service payments to a percentage of export earnings shows a large decrease in the level of debt. These simulation results point toward the premise that to achieve an economic takeoff without the increasing debt burden, the growth process should be strengthened by increasing demand while maintaining a high rate of debt repayment as income rises.

346

Table 14.1
Performance of alternative development and debt policies under different government behaviors

Nature of intervention	Economic indicators	Relative magnitude of economic indicators		
		Moderate behavior	Prudent behavior	Radical behavior
Base run	Income per capita	1.00	0.77	0.75
	Unemployment rate	1.00	3.52	3.50
	ED/income	1.00	1.21	1.36
	EDS/income	1.00	1.10	1.14
	KLR	1.00	1.08	1.04
	Net exports	1.00	2.92	2.91
1. Increasing government purchases	Income per capita	1.56	1.07	1.39
	Unemployment rate	0.81	1.17	0.93
	ED/income	0.60	0.82	0.70
	EDS/income	0.97	1.11	1.05
	KLR	1.54	1.20	1.49
	Net exports	-0.25	5.01	3.40
2. Encouraging investment through tax cuts	Income per capita	2.04	1.40	2.00
	Unemployment rate	0.58	0.91	0.59
	ED/income	0.53	0.75	0.57
	EDS/income	0.92	0.97	0.92
	KLR	1.65	1.50	1.64
	Net exports	-16.50	0.10	-14.67
3. Encouraging investment through increasing propensity to save	Income per capita	0.83	0.61	0.82
	Unemployment rate	1.40	1.64	1.40
	ED/income	0.90	1.20	0.93
	EDS/income	1.23	1.37	1.24
	KLR	0.90	0.78	0.91
	Net exports	7.68	8.12	7.83
4. Expanding exports and restricting imports	Income per capita	1.28	0.89	1.24
	Unemployment rate	1.00	1.32	1.04
	ED/income	0.69	0.94	0.74
	EDS/income	1.04	1.16	1.08
	KLR	1.35	1.08	1.34
	Net exports	3.20	5.86	4.51
5. Not limiting debt service to percent export earnings	Income per capita	1.02	0.87	0.80
	Unemployment rate	1.20	1.35	1.42
	ED/income	0.13	0.13	0.27
	EDS/income	2.23	2.15	3.43
	KLR	1.15	1.05	1.05
	Net exports	4.56	6.17	6.78

+ED = external debt; EDS = external debt service;
KLR = capital-labor ratio

Figure 14.7 shows the result of combining the policies of increasing government purchases, encouraging investment through tax cuts, increasing exports and restricting imports and not limiting debt servicing under the moderate behavior assumptions.

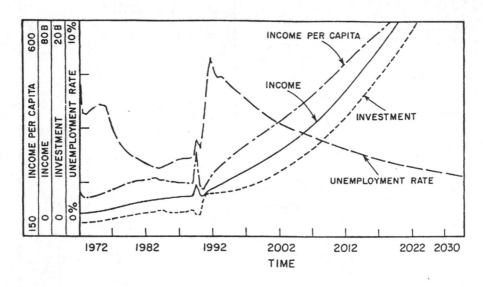

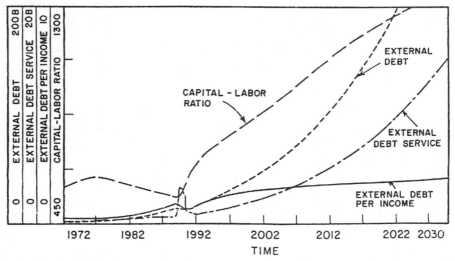

Figure 14.7   Simulation run showing the policies of increasing government purchases, encouraging investment through tax cuts, increasing exports and restricting imports - moderate case

Sensitivity of the proposed policy framework

An important instrument in the policy framework outlined in the preceding section is increasing capital intensity, which strengthens the growth process that, in turn makes debt financing a viable option by creating the ability to sustain a high level of debt service. This might appear contrary to the revisionist thought on economic development [Fie and Ranis 1964].

It has been argued in several studies on the Philippines and also those on other developing countries that the alternative labor-intensive strategies would not only raise the rate of economic growth, they would also yield lower unemployment rates. Thus, labor intensive development might yield higher social returns. Other studies have viewed that the quality of investment might also raise social returns by yielding a higher level of output for each unit of capital invested [ILO 1974].

A sustained increase of income and income per capita is seen but this is achieved by acquiring more loans. External debt, therefore, is much higher; yet, because of the faster rate of growth of income, external debt to income ratio remains low. Investment rate is high because of favorable low tax rate; unemployment rate, therefore, is maintained at a low value. External debt service to income ratio is also maintained at a low value.

We conducted additional simulation experiments to test the sensitivity of the debt management strategy issued by our analysis to changes in labor intensity and the efficiency of capital investment. Labor intensity was stimulated in these experiments by increasing interest rate and lowering wage rate. A policy of investing in socially efficient portfolios was simulated by reducing capital-output ratio. The simulations showing the outcome of the various combinations of these policies are plotted together in Figure 14.8 with the earlier plots of Figure 14.7.

It is noted that more efficient investments and labor intensive policies are helpful in bringing down unemployment rate and reducing the demand for domestic and foreign savings. However, income and income per capita growth are depressed by slow acceleration process of the growth mechanism as a result of low capital labor ratio. In effect, as income does not rise as fast as the increase of debt, the external debt to income ratio reaches higher values than that for capital intensive and more efficient investment policies. Hence, capital intensive strategies which speed up the acceleration mechanism including a more efficient investment portfolio and the set of policies incorporated in Figure 14.7 sustain growth and tolerable debt levels.

349

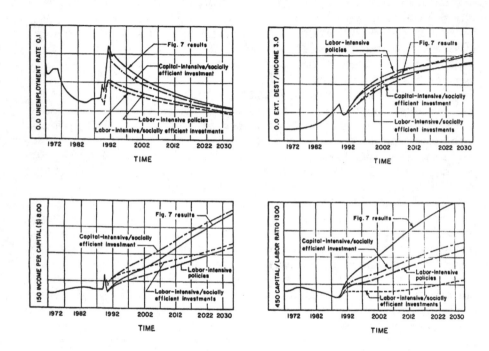

Figure 14.8   Comparative results of Figure 14.7: capital-intensive/socially efficient investment policies, labor-intensive policies, and labor-intensive/socially efficient investment policies

Conclusion

This study suggests that policies which are intuitively thought to reduce debt levels through a decrease in the need for foreign loans, do not eliminate the country's debt service burden. These policies, instead, limit demand through reducing target growth rates in general and reducing government spending in particular. While they may create a temporary relief through a decrease in government spending in that deficit is decreased, the subsequent negative multiplier effects adversely affect growth in income. In effect, the depressed income growth rate reduces the country's creditworthiness. Also the reduction in income generates a lower level of taxes which may further decrease the ability to pay the debts the country owes to the foreign banks and international financial institutions. Debt level may not increase fast but neither will it decrease fast. As growth rate is depressed, the country ends up still being burdened by a high debt service.

Limiting debt service to a proportion of the export earnings does not take the country out of its heavy debt burden. As debt repayment is reduced, debt level decreases very slowly. At the same time, with no apparent increase in investment, income remains depressed and the country continues to be in heavy debt.

Our analysis shows that the best set of policies propelling an economic takeoff not only requires the normal government influence on the market to intensify capital investment through keeping the interest rate low and wage rate high, it also should stimulate demand and investment. As income increases, debt servicing ability is also increased so that the level of debt decreases. The high level of income, therefore, eliminates the burden of debt servicing. Investment in socially efficient portfolios further facilitates this process, while labor intensive developments seem to weaken the growth machinery.

This study, however, does not consider the inflationary effects resulting from money creation and the changes in the foreign exchange rates. It also does not take into account the effects of income distribution on consumption and investment rates. These effects, if considered, would curtail growth, although, they may not change the proposed policy implications of our analysis.

References

Arif, M. T. and Saeed, K. (1989), 'Sustaining economic growth with a nonrenewable natural resource: the case of oil-dependent Indonesia', *System Dynamics Review* 5(1): 17-34.

Barro, R. J. (1984) *Macroeconomics*, John Wiley and Sons, New York.

De Dios, E. S. (ed.) (1984) *An Analysis of the Philippine Economic Crisis: A Workshop Report*, Quezon City: University of the Philippines Press.

Dietz, J. L. (1986) 'Debt and development: the future of Latin America', *Journal of Economic Issues*, 20(4): 1029-1051.

Eisner, R. (1989) 'Divergences of measurement and theory and some implications for economic policy', *The American Economic Review*, 79(1): 1-13.

Feder, G. (1978) 'Growth, Foreign Loans and Debt Servicing Capacity of Developing Countries', *World Bank Staff Working Paper No. 274*, Washington D.C.: World Bank.

Fei, John C. H. and Ranis, Gustav (1964) *Development of the labor surplus economy: theory and policy*, The Economic Growth Center, Yale University.

Hill, H. and Jayasuriza, S. (1985) 'The Philippines: growth, debt and crisis', *Australian National University Development Studies Center Working Paper No. 85/3*, Melbourne: Australian National University.

ILO (1974) *Sharing in development: a program of employment, equity and growth for the Philippines*, Geneva: International Labor Office.

Lal, D. and van Wijnbergen, S. (1985) 'Government deficits, the real interest rate and LDC debt', *European Economic Review*, 29(9): 157-191.

Lamberte, M. B. et. al. (1985) 'A review and appraisal of the government response to the 1983-1984 balance-of-payments crisis', *Manila: Philippine Institute of Development Studies Monograph Series No. 8*.

Mass, Nathaniel J. (1975) *Economic cycles: an analysis of underlying causes*, Cambridge, MA: Wright-Allen Press.

Orlando, F. and Teitel, S. (1986) 'Latin America's external debt problem: debt-servicing strategies compatible with long-term economic growth', *Economic Development and Cultural Change*, 34(3): 641-671.

Parayno, Phares (1989) *The Dynamics of Indebtedness: The Case of the Philippines*, Masters Thesis, Bangkok, Thailand: Asian Institute of Technology.

Power, John S. (1983) 'Response to the balance-of-payments crises in the 1970s: Korea and the Philippines', *PIDS Staff Paper Series No. 8305*, Manila.

Remolona, Eli M. et. al. (1986) 'Foreign debt, balance of payments, and the economic crisis of the Philippines in 1983-84', *World Development*, 14(8): 909-918.

Saeed, K. (1990) 'Government support for economic agendas in developing countries: a behavioral model', *World Development*, 18(6): 785-801.

Saeed, K. (1992) 'Slicing a Complex Problem for System Dynamics modeling', *System Dynamics Review*, 8(3): 251-261.

Samuelson, P. A. (1939) 'Interaction between the multiplier analysis and the principles of acceleration', *Review of Economics and Statistics* (May): 75-78.

Schelzig, W. M. (1989) 'The changing external debt situation in the Asian and Pacific region', *Asian Development Review*, 7(1): 70-97.

Appendix A
Model description

External debt ED increases through external loans acquisition rate ELAR and accrual of interests INT but decreases through debt servicing EDS.

$$\frac{d}{dt}[ED] \quad = \quad ELAR + INT - EDS \qquad (1)$$

ELAR is a fraction of the total desired loans DL, the remaining fraction being met by domestic loans. This fraction is decreased when the ratio ED/SALES reaches a value beyond which the country is perceived as possessing diminishing creditworthiness which moves the lending institutions to decrease the loans.

$$ELAR \quad = \quad FRNEX*DL*f1[ED/SALES] \qquad (2)$$

where $f'1 < 0$, FRNEX is fractional external loans and SALES are GNP in current terms.

DL is assumed to adjust balance towards the desired balance over a period DLAT. It is also assumed that the country does not become a creditor country when the level of balance exceeds the desired balance.

$$DL \quad = \quad Max[0,((DCABCAB)+(DGMBGMB))/DLAT] \quad (3)$$

where DCAB, CAB, DGMB and GMB are, respectively, desired current account balance, current account balance, desired government money balance and government money balance.

GMB increases through tax collection TAX and acquisition of loans LR - external and domestic, but decreases through government expenditures GE and debt repayment DREP.

$$\frac{d}{dt}[GMB] = \quad TAX + LR - GE - DREP \qquad (4)$$

DREP is the sum of external debt service EDS and domestic debt service DDS. EDS, consisting of interests and principal payments, is a fraction of external debt. This fraction increases to the given normal value when GMB/DGMB approaches one and decreases when ED/AEXV is greater than 1.5 at which point the country will start experiencing difficulty meeting the debt services which results in request for rescheduling of debt repayments. It is assumed that no rescheduling takes place for domestic debt servicing.

DREP	=	DDS + EDS	(5)
DDS	=	DD*FDDS	(6)
EDS	=	ED*FDS	(7)

353

$$FDS \quad = \quad FDSN*f2[GMB/DGMB]*f3[ED/AEXV] \quad (8)$$

where f '2 > 0, f '3 < 0. FDDS, FDS, FDSN and AEXV are, respectively, fractional domestic debt service, fractional external debt service, fractional external debt service normal and average export value.

GE, formulated as the product of government purchases GP and general price level GPL, increases when GMB/DGMB is greater than one, but decreases otherwise.

$$GE \quad = \quad GP*GPL*f4[GMB/DGMB] \quad (9)$$

where f '4 > 0.

TAX is formulated as a fraction of gross profit GPRO, the difference between INCOME and consumption C. It is assumed that tax rate decreases when GMB/DGMB is greater than one but increases otherwise.

$$TAX \quad = \quad GPRO*FGPT \quad (10)$$
$$FGPT \quad = \quad FGPTI*f5[GMB/DGMB] \quad (11)$$

where f '5 < 0. FGPT and FGPTI are, respectively, fractional gross profit tax and fractional gross profit tax initial.

Interests INT are the returns on the borrowed foreign loans.

$$INT \quad = \quad ED*IREL \quad (12)$$

where IREL is interest rate on external loans.

INCOME which is GNP in real terms, is taken as the measure of economic growth and is given by the following identity:

$$INCOME \quad = \quad C+I+GE+EXV-IMV \quad (13)$$

Consumption C depends on indicated consumption IC and inventory availability. Low level of inventory constrains consumption. Indicated consumption IC is a fraction of average income AINC where the fraction is the propensity to consume PC.

$$C \quad = \quad IC*f6[IN/DIN] \quad (14)$$
$$IC \quad = \quad PC*AINC \quad (15)$$

where f '6 > 0. IN and DIN are, respectively, inventory and desired inventory.

Inventory IN is increased by production PR and imports IMR and decreased by consumer purchases CP, capital investment CI, government purchases GP and exports EXR.

$$\frac{d}{dt}[IN] \quad = \quad (PR+IMR)-(CP+CI+GP+EXR) \qquad (16)$$

Capital investment indicated by capital formation rate KFR is a delayed process of capital orders KO through a pool of capital on orders KOO. It depends on product constraint given by the ratio IN/DIN and budget constraint given by the ratio UIS/DUIS.

$$KFR \quad = (KOO/TAQK)*f7[IN/DIN]*f8[UIS/DUIS] \quad (17)$$

where f '7 > 0, f '8 > 0. TAQK, UIS and DUIS are respectively, time to acquire capital, uninvested savings and desired uninvested savings.

KOO increases through capital orders but decreases through capital formation rate.

$$\frac{d}{dt}[KOO] \quad = \quad KO - KFR \qquad (18)$$

Capital orders KO are given to be the maximum of zero and the indicated capital orders IKO to prevent cancellation and negative orders for capital. IKO is equal to the average capital depreciation rate AKDR and a fraction of the difference between desired capital DK and capital K, and the difference between desired capital on orders DKOO and capital on orders KOO.

$$IKO \quad = \quad AKDR + (DK-K+DKOO-KOO)/TAK \quad (19)$$

where TAK is the time to adjust capital.

DK is a function of long-run average of indicated production rate for capital orders IPRKO and modulated with life of capital LK, interest rate IR and elasticity of capital EK. Indicated production rate for capital orders is the averaged value of desired production rate DPR.

$$DK \quad = \quad (EK*IPRKO)/(IR+1/LK) \qquad (20)$$

Production rate PR is a fraction of the potential production rate PPR. This fraction, called the capacity utilization factor CUF, is function of the ratio of the desired production rate DPR and the potential production rate PPR. PPR is a modified Cobb-Douglas production function of capital, workers and the significant contribution to private output from government infrastructure capital IS.

PR	=	PPR*CUF	(21)
CUF	=	f9[DPR/PPR]	(22)
PPR	=	A*(KEK)*(WEW)*f10[IS/DIS]	(23)

where f '9 > 0 and f '10 > 0. A, EK, W, EW, IS, DIS are, respectively,

355

technology constant, elasticity of capital, workers, elasticity of workers, government infrastructure and desired government infrastructure.

DPR is equal to average inventory usage AINUS plus a fraction of the difference between desired inventory and inventory.

$$\text{DPR} \quad = \quad \text{AINUS} + (\text{DIN-IN})/\text{IAT} \qquad (24)$$

where IAT is inventory adjustment time.

Interest rate IR is assumed to adjust over a period IRAT toward indicated interest rate IIR. Indicated interest rate IIR depends on the level of uninvested savings UIS and general price level GPL.

$$\text{d/dt[IR]} \quad = \quad (\text{IIR-IR})/\text{IRAT} \qquad (25)$$
$$\text{IIR} \quad = \quad \text{IRN*f11[UIS/DUIS]*f12[GPL/GPLN]} \quad (26)$$

where f '11 < 0, f '12 > 0 and IRN is interest rate normal.

General price level GPL adjusts over a period GPLAT toward indicated general price level IGPL. Indicated general price level IGPL depends on the level of inventory compared to desired inventory.

$$\text{d/dt[GPL]} \quad = \quad (\text{IGPL-GPL})/\text{GPLAT} \qquad (27)$$
$$\text{IGPL} \quad = \quad \text{GPLN*f13[IN/DIN]} \qquad (28)$$

where f '13 < 0 and GPLN is general price level normal.

Wage rate WAGE adjusts over a period WRAT toward indicated wage rate IWR. Indicated wage rate IWR depends on unemployment rate. An increase in unemployment rate decreases wage rate.

$$\text{d/dt[WAGE]} \quad = \quad (\text{IWR-WAGE})/\text{WRAT} \qquad (29)$$
$$\text{IWR} \quad = \quad \text{WAGEN*f14[UR/URN]} \qquad (30)$$

where f '14 < 0. WAGEN, UR and URN are respectively, wage rate normal, unemployment rate and unemployment rate normal.

Capital labor ratio KLR is assumed to adjust over a period KLRAT toward indicated capital labor ratio IKLR. Indicated capital labor ratio IKLR increases when wage rate is greater than the average marginal productivity of workers AMPW.

$$\text{d/dt[KLR]} \quad = \quad (\text{IKLR-KLR})/\text{KLRAT} \qquad (31)$$
$$\text{IKLR} \quad = \quad \text{KLRN*f15[WAGE/AMPW]} \qquad (32)$$

where f '15 > 0 and KLRN is capital labor ratio normal.

Appendix B

Values of key parameters in the base run case.

Fractional Gov't Purchases	=	11% of GNP
Exports	=	17.7% of GNP
Imports	=	18.5% of GNP
Net Factor Income	=	US $ -78.65 million
Foreign Debt	=	US $2.732 billion
Population Growth Rate	=	2.6% per year

15 Food self-sufficiency in Vietnam: a search for a viable solution[*]

Nguyen Luong Bach and Khalid Saeed

Abstract

This paper attempts to assess the effect on the agricultural resource system of the past and presently planned policies to maintain food self-sufficiency in a centrally-planned economy. Vietnam's case serves as an illustration. Experimentation with a system dynamics model of the food production system incorporating relationships concerning soil ecology and agricultural land management policy serves as a basis for this assessment. Short-run policies to increase production appear to be detrimental to maintaining food self-sufficiency in the long-run. It appears that a sustainable food production policy must incorporate soil conservation and improvement, and population controls. Although difficult to implement in a market system, such a policy agenda may be feasible to consider in a centrally-planned economy.

Introduction

Poor cultivation practices are known to depreciate soil quality. Soil degradation has occurred in many countries due to erosion, loss of nutrients, loss of texture, water logging and salinity (Bowonder 1981).

[*] Reprinted from *System Dynamics Review*, 8(2), Nguyen Luang Bach and Khalid Saeed, Food self-sufficiency in Vietnam: a search for a viable solution, pp. 129-148, 1992, with kind permission from John Wiley and Sons, Ltd., Baffins Lane, Chichester, West Sussex PO19 1UD, UK.

Centrally-planned as well as market-economy countries may encourage poor cultivation practices. The free market economies often tend to externalize private costs to the environmental commons since private decisions often view environment as a free resource (Hardin 1985). The centrally-planned economies, also, fail to internalize environmental costs because incentives are provided to managers to boost production, not preserve environment. Furthermore, since the resources placed in the hands of the managers reflect no scarcity value, no opportunity cost, and no real price, the cost of using resources is essentially irrelevant. Without incentives to conserve productivity of the soil, wide-spread inefficiencies of production and environmental abuse occur in many countries (Chandler 1987).

With only occasional exceptions, assessments of environmental degradation have had little effect on the considerations underlying national policy and decision making at the government level. First, a compartmentalized treatment of the complex systems that concern public policy tends to ignore the feedback between the various subsystems. Second, the planning decisions rarely consider the costs externalized to the environment, in terms of depleted resources and deteriorated soil conditions, for the preparation of development agendas. Thus, the effects of deforestation, soil degradation, and cropland abandonment are generally omitted from agricultural development strategy (Brown and Wolf 1986).

This paper attempts to assess the effect of the past and presently planned policies to maintain food self-sufficiency in Vietnam. The observations made can be generalized to some extent to cover all centrally-planned economies. The analysis uses a system dynamics model of the food production system that incorporates three subsystems: population, food production, and soil ecology (Bach 1988). It appears that short-run policies to increase food production to a level planned by the state are detrimental to maintaining food adequacy in the long-run. Designing a sustainable food production policy must consider population controls and soil conservation and improvement, and for Vietnam, also finding alternatives to grain in aquatic and synthetic nutritional sources.

The food production system of Vietnam: an overview

Vietnam covers an area of 329,600 square kilometers, three-fourths of which is arid mountains and plateaus. Only 17 per cent of the total area is arable land under cultivated crops. Food crops are mainly planted in the Red River delta in the North, and the Mekong River delta in the South. Although these plains are not very large, they are relatively fertile and especially suitable for food crops.

The country has a tropical climate with a humid monsoon season. There are two main seasons: winter, which is cool and dry, and summer, which is hot and rainy. In the rainy season, there is enough rainfall for crop planting over the whole year. However, without proper water conservation systems, the fields often suffer from drought during the dry part of the year. Abnormalities of season often create disastrous consequences, too much rainfall during the rainy season causing water logging and flooding while a prolonged winter delaying seed-sowing in the spring. During heavy rainfalls the soil erodes, and nutrients are leached.

The population of Vietnam is at present basically rural and is concentrated in the Red and Mekong river deltas. As a result, agriculture is basic to the Vietnamese economy providing direct employment for 70% of the country's labor force, and accounting for about 45% of the GDP. A population growth rate of approximately 2.4% per year doubles the population about every 30 years. Population has risen from 16.5 million in 1930 to 32 million in 1960 and to 64 million in 1987. A large population, coupled with limited cultivable land, maintains the arable land per capita at a low value.

Among the food crops, rice is the most important. All other crops are minor compared to rice. Nearly all areas suitable for rice are cultivated for this crop. Vietnam's strategy is to promote yield increases instead of expanding rice-growing areas. Except for short-term decreases in food output during adverse years, food production in Vietnam has experienced a long upward trend since 1930. Increased production was achieved mainly through increasing yield per hectare per crop and using multiple crops. However, population increased faster than food production. Population growth resulted in a downward trend in food per capita. Vietnam is no longer a grain exporting country as it was before the 1970s.

Furthermore, poor cultivation practices contributed to both physical and chemical degradation of soil. The losses of soil organic matter are particularly high. In many places, especially in the hilly areas, the soil has become barren. The most serious soil erosion has occurred on steep slopes in the highlands, such as in the Northwestern Region.

A system dynamics model of food production system

The food production system of Vietnam can be characterized by feedback loops shown in Figure 15.1. The organic relationships underlying the feedbacks loops span population, food production, and ecological subsystems as discussed below.

The population subsystem

Births and population form a positive feedback loop, which accounts for the observed exponential population growth. When calculating births per year, we can think in terms of birth fraction per year, but when considering a policy to decrease births, the fractional birth rate does not help in designing an implementation strategy. The birth rate is, therefore expressed in terms of tangible parameters such as fraction of population forming child bearing couples, their average fertility period, and children per couple born over this fertility period. A policy to reduce the number of children per couple is a concrete and implementable reality, especially in a centrally-planned economy. Population and deaths form a negative feedback loop which limits population growth. Deaths are assumed to be dependent on the self- sufficiency ratio which is food per capita normalized with respect to a defined value considered adequate. Sustained and increasing food availability leads to higher life expectancy, thus fewer deaths; and vice versa. The relative strength of these two feedback loops determines actual population growth path.

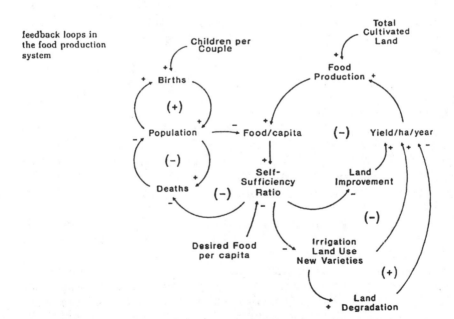

Figure 15.1   **Main feedback loops in the food production system**

361

The food production subsystem

Food supply and yield form several negative loops. As long as food per capita remains below a sustainable level, agricultural planners have no choice but to try to increase production by any possible method (normally the quickest and the least costly). For countries like Vietnam, where land fit for producing food is limited and most of the arable land has already been brought under cultivation, increasing the yield (output per unit cultivated area per unit of time) has become a major goal.

Well-known methods to increase yield are soil improvement, development of irrigation to permit multiple cropping, and adoption of high-yield varieties. So, a decline in food per capita leads to attempts to boost food production through the above methods which, in turn, causes food per capita to be increased, ceteris paribus. These self-correcting feedback loops explain why countries with large population but limited land can still experience a growth in food production to feed their population, as in Japan and South Korea.

The ecological subsystem

Soil chemicals needed for plant growth are classified into two main categories, macro-nutrients and micro-nutrients. Many types of micro- and macro- nutrients are necessary for the optimal growth of crops. However, the ingredient in lowest supply is the limiting factor in determining growth.

According to Allison (1973) nitrogen (N) is the most important macro-nutrient in soil organic matter when considered from the economic standpoint. Crop yields are often directly proportional to the N released from organic matter; N is required in very large quantities and is most likely to be the limiting ingredient. Hence, the model captures the nitrogen cycle as a proxy for all macro-nutrients. Nitrogen enters the system through fertilization, through leguminous plants and through crop biomass return. It leaves the system through the leaching process, which also depends on soil humus stock, and through the uptake by crops that are subsequently harvested.

Soil micro-nutrients, sometimes called trace minerals are represented in the model by the soil humus level. The humus level also represents many other factors important to plant growth such as soil structure and soil texture. Humus consists of soil organic matter which has undergone extensive decomposition. It is a dark, heterogeneous mass consisting of the residues of plants and animals together with the synthesized cell substances of soil organisms. Humus is not static but dynamic in soils; it is continually undergoing change (Forth et. al. 1978). Humus is created is created by the humification of organic residues as they decay. Humus is lost by oxidation of the carbon compounds in the humus. As cultivation intensity rises, more soil surface is exposed to air, which increases the oxidation rates for carbon in the organic matter and carbon in humus. Land degradation in the model is assumed to be caused primarily by the loss of soil nutrients (through erosion or multiple cropping) and by water-logging and salinization in poorly-managed irrigation of problem soils. Degraded land is conserved as "Adverse land".

Under population pressure and with limited arable land, high-yield technology which intensifies land-use and employs new high-yielding seed varieties tends to alter soil properties, unless the system is managed properly. Under poor cultivation practices, use of high-yield technology can lead to land degradation that will eventually cause crop-yield, total food produced, and thus the self-sufficiency ratio to decline in the long-run. Food production and poor land practices thus form a positive feedback loop that aggravates both land degradation and food production in the long-run.

A DYNAMO flow diagram of the model incorporating the feedback structure outlined above is shown in Figure 15.2. Values of parameters and initial conditions of the model are placed at Appendix 1 and model listing coded in DYNAMO in Appendix 2.

Following implicit policy assumptions are incorporated into model for the base run:

i)   A normal soil fertilization rate is defined so that the system is in equilibrium initially. The soil fertilization rate may be increased somewhat when the need for fertilizer is perceived. However, longer term mechanisms affecting soil dynamics, such as immobilization and mineralization, as suggested by Jones (1984) are ignored.

ii) Irrigation, new seed varieties, and soil productivity improvement (conversion of adverse land to good land) are assumed to develop at specified normal rates unless further modified by other processes. They remain unchanged as long as the average self-sufficiency ratio, which compares actual food per capita with a fixed target is greater than or equal to 1. When this ratio is less than 1, these activities will be stepped up.

iii) Intensity of land use for cultivation, which is referred to as "land use index" in the model, is formulated as a linear function of the percentage of the areas under irrigation - the "irrigation percentage".

iv) The population is aggregated into a single stock. It is assumed that the fraction of child bearing couples and children born per couple over the fertility period do not change over time, except through policy intervention. Average life span of population is a nonlinear asymptotic function of the average self-sufficiency ratio.

v)   Total land under food crops (consisting of good land and adverse land) is assumed to be constant, while the ratio of good to adverse

363

land will vary over time depending on the degradation rates experienced. The total land can be increased in the model for experimental purposes.

The normal rates in assumptions (i) and (ii) represent ambient conditions at the start of the simulation under traditional agriculture. The responses to the development of abnormal conditions represent centralized planning rather than laissez faire. The remaining assumptions represent simplifications that do not limit scope of the analysis with respect to the problem addressed.

Figures 15.3, a and b, show a simulation of the model giving the behavior of yield per hectare per year, land use index, self-sufficiency ratio, population, nitrogen and good land. Yield per hectare per year experiences an upward trend, slowly increasing during the early decades of the simulation time, then rapidly increasing due to the use of production-boosting instruments, especially the land-use intensity.

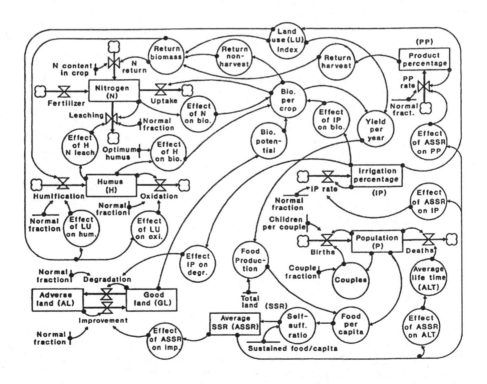

Figure 15.2   The flow diagram of the system

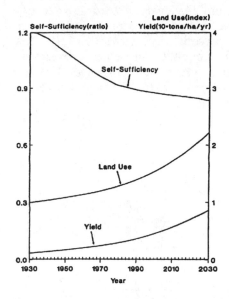

Figure 15.3a Simulation of the model giving the behavior of yield per hectare per year, land use index and self-sufficiency ratio

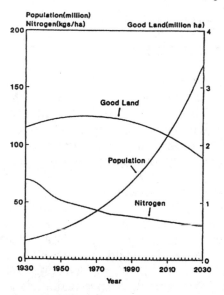

Figure 15.3b Simulation of the model giving the behavior of population, nitrogen, and good land

365

The model-generated outputs were compared with the available historical data for five key variables from the year 1930 to 1987 using a formal procedure suggested by Sterman (1984). This procedure requires examination of the root mean square percent error (RMSPE) the mean square error (MSE) and the Theil inequality statistics providing a decomposition of the error into its systematic (Um and Us) and unsystematic (Uc) components (Theil 1966). Table 15.1 summarizes the error analysis for the five key variables considered in the system.

Table 15.1
Error analysis of food production model for historical data from 1930 to 1987

Variables	Root mean square percent error (RMSPE)	Mean square error (MSE)	Inequality statistics (percent of MSE)		
			Mean (U^m)	Deviation (U^s)	Covariance (U^c)
Land use index	1.6201%	0.036	24.98	1.56	73.46
Yield/crop (kg/yr)	5.3283	13.69	0.655	1.542	97.793
Food production (kg/yr)	5.6488	$445 \cdot 10^{13}$	3.679	0.7563	95.564
Population (people/yr)	2.9449	$1,075 \cdot 10^{13}$	32.711	1.819	65.417
Self-sufficiency	5.4166	0.002	0.07786	9.534	89.694

RMSPE for all five variables is small (1.6% to 5.7%) indicating that the model adequately tracks all these variables. The inequality statistics in the table also show that most of the errors are due to unequal covariance, indicating that the simulated patterns track the underlying trends in the historical data, although they do not coincide with it point by point. Since point forecasting is not intended, the nature of the fit between data and model behavior is quite acceptable.

In the experiment assuming poor soil management practices, a downward trend appears in soil nitrogen stock, which is a proxy for land fertility. A high land use index changes the physical and chemical properties of soil, reducing the organic matter returned to soils and the quantity of good land in the long run. New high-yield varieties uptake large amounts of nutrients during the crop growth stage, depleting soil nutrient stock. Coupled with the continuing growth of population, land degradation gives rise to a decline in self-sufficiency ratio during the simulation, from 1.2 in 1930 to 1 in 1966-1967, then down to nearly 0.8 in 2030, as read from Figure 15.3a. It is noteworthy that these model-generated ratios fit historical records quite well. These results explain why the country, which used to be a net grain-exporter, became to experience grain-deficits.

A search for a sustainable food policy

An advantage of viewing the problem through a system dynamics computer simulation model is that the model can, when carefully developed, helps the modeler to identify the strengths and weaknesses of the model structure and modify it appropriately so it comes to represent the real system as precisely as possible. Furthermore, careful experimentation with a correctly built model helps to identify which policies are "good" or "bad". This second advantage can shed much light on the implications of the alternative policies to be adopted in the future for improving the system performances.

The experiments described below, carried out for testing the model, involved changes in the system parameters which affected almost all important parts of the system. The changes are not abstract but meaningful in the sense that they are related to concrete policies which can be implemented in actual practice.

Population controls

As can be seen in Figure 15.1, the positive feedback loop governing the birth rate is a powerful source of growth for the population which limits food per capita. So, it is reasonable to think that population-control measures to reduce the natural birth rate through family planning could maintain the food per capita and hence, the food self-sufficiency ratio at a reasonable level.

The simulation of Figure 15.4a incorporates a gradual reduction of the average number of children per couple from 3 to 2 (33%) over the period 1988-2030. This change appears to achieve self-sufficiency by the end of simulation in 2030. The simulation of Figure 15.4b incorporates a sudden reduction of children per couple after 1988 of only 22% (from 3 to 2.34). The self-sufficiency can still be achieved in the year 2015. Thus, when immediately enforced, even moderate population-control measures appear to yield considerable results. However, direct intervention to implement family planning might appear impractical, although there is evidence of its success in Japan and China. There is a need to develop appropriate policies to implement population controls.

367

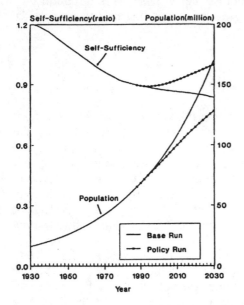

Figure 15.4a   **Gradual reduction of number of children per couple**

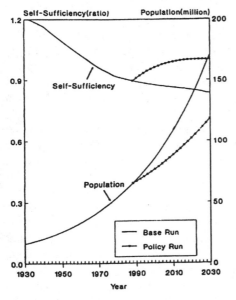

Figure 15.4b   **Sudden reduction of number of children per couple**

368

With the adoption of an intensive land-use policy and use of high-yield seed varieties, soil nutrients tend to be depleted as shown in the base run in Figure 15.3b. It is widely recognized that careful application of fertilizers, together with returning high residues to the soil, can sustain soil fertility. However, the model assumes the pressure to obtain quick returns on investment and the lack of incentives and financial resources for proper management will lead to large soil nutrient losses.

Figure 15.5a shows the behavior of soil nitrogen if fertilizer application is increased by 35% in 1988. The Nitrogen content of the soil rises quite fast but drops to almost the previous level after an initial overshoot. Such a behavior is created since Nitrogen in soil is constantly lost through crop uptake and leaching in proportion to its remaining stock.

Thus, a step increase in the fertilizer application rate may yield considerable increases in soil nitrogen, but temporarily. On the other hand, a highly annual increase in fertilizer application of 2.7% is to be sustained if nitrogen by the end of the simulation can be restored to its initial level as shown in Figure 15.5b. The fertilizer application policies alone, however, do not restore self-sufficiency ratio to its original level.

Crop residues returned into the soil after harvest, plus animal manure application, may improve the nitrogen stock in the short-term but not in the long-term, as seen in the simulation of Figure 15.6 incorporating a 50% increase in residues returned from 1988 and 2030, but this policy alone also does not improve self-sufficiency ratio.

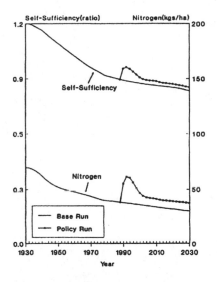

Figure 15.5a   35% increase in fertilizer application

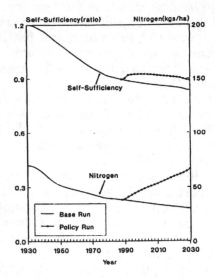

Figure 15.5b   **Fertilizer application increased at an annual rate of 2.7%**

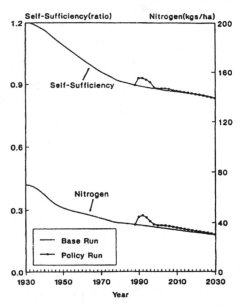

Figure 15.6   **Increasing residues**

370

Another policy choice is to increase investment to improve adverse land conditions. Figure 15.7 shows a simulation incorporating land improvement effected at the rate of 10%. It results in an upward trend of "good" land share, but since the resulting increase in food-production facilitates population growth, the self-sufficiency rises only for a brief period. In the long run, the rising population depresses self-sufficiency ratio, especially when the limit of total land places a limit on the conversion to good land.

It should be recognized that all policies aimed at improving land management experimented with above cannot maintain food self-sufficiency ratio above 1 in the long-run. This is mainly because population increases overtake food production increases while food production also suffers in the long run because of soil degradation.

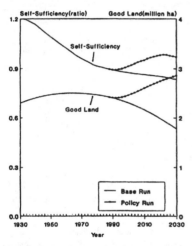

Figure 15.7   Improving land

Water management

A different strategy to boost food output is to increase quantity of land under irrigation. As shown in Figure 15.8, an 80% increase in irrigated land, which is only made possible at a high investment cost, steps up food self-sufficiency ratio in the short-run, but may also lead to water-logging and salinization in the long-run which, coupled with loss of soil nutrients, leads to a decline in productivity.

In all previous experiments, the total land under cultivation was assumed to be constant. Consequently, when population (and so the demand for food) continues to grow, the limited land comes under greater pressure. As an experiment, it was assumed that new land could be opened to raise the

371

total land planted to food crops. Land development, although a costly choice, would often tend to be seriously considered and adopted since its short-term impact is impressive.

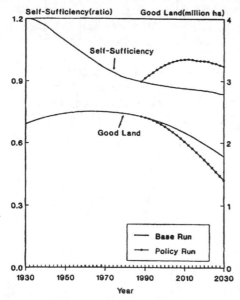

Figure 15.8   Stepping up irrigation

The simulation of Figure 15.9 assumes a 20% increase in new land development over the period 1988 to 2030. It is seen that the quantity of adverse land increases while self-sufficiency ratio only slightly increases first, then turns downward and continues to decrease. Because of the feedback between self-sufficiency ratio and population growth, an increase in land resources would only lead to creation of a larger population, without affecting the long-term trend of self-sufficiency ratio. Also, since the best land for food production has already been brought under cultivation, only marginal lands remain to be developed. The opening of new land, thus, largely increases adverse land, which limits even short-term impact of this policy.

A combination of moderate policies

Following policy package was considered for implementation after the year 1988:

i)   An annual 5% decrease in number of children per couple;

ii)   An annual 2% increase in fertilizer application to be made possibly

372

through all available sources (such as chemical fertilizer, animal manure, night soil, or silt) to replenish soil nutrients;

iii)   An annual 2% increase in residues returned into soil after harvest; and

iv)   An annual 5% increase in land improvement effort in terms of conversion of adverse to good land.

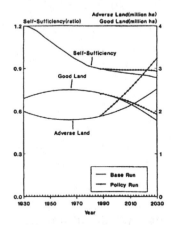

Figure 15.9   Commissioning new land

Such moderate changes in each system part may prove to be quite feasible in practice. The key is to introduce them together.

The long-term results generated by this policy combination are better than those achieved by any of the individual policies, as seen in the simulation of Figures 15.10, a and b, which incorporates this. Nitrogen stock is much higher than in the base run. Good land does not decline. Population, still increases, but at a rate lower than in the base run. These improvements account for the upward trend in the food self-sufficiency ratio, which reaches returns to the original level in 1930.

Conclusion

This paper has attempted to characterize at an aggregate level the interaction between the food production system and agricultural resources in a centrally-planned economy; using Vietnam's case as an illustration. A formal model representing this interaction was developed and experimented with using computer simulation to understand system relationships and implications of centrally controlled policies to maintain self-sufficiency.

373

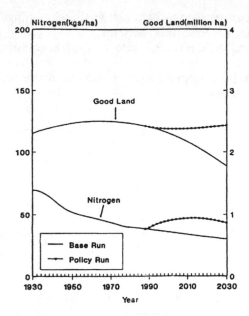

Figure 15.10a   Suggested moderate policy combination: good land and soil nitrogen

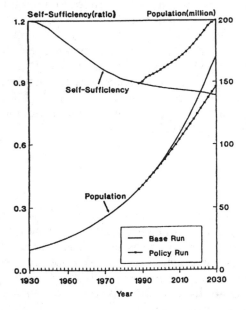

Figure 15.10b   Suggested moderate policy combination: population and self-sufficiency

Our analysis shows that policies attempting to keep food production apace with the population growth can create very harmful consequences over the long-term. Intensifying land utilization, expanding cultivation into marginal areas, using "miracle varieties" and extensive fertilizer application all might bring premature hope and lessen concerns over an exploding population and depleting agricultural resources. Such an optimism could lead to policies in which the trade-offs between present and future are not carefully considered.

The model of this study also demonstrates that food production beyond a threshold determined by the parameters of the ecosystem is basically an extractive activity, which is likely to lead to land degradation and decay of agricultural capacity. Population growth appears to be the fundamental driving force behind this process. Experimentation with the model also shows that proper population control measures (i) and good cultivation practices (ii, iii, and iv) can bring the system into a balance, which can be sustained for a long time. This calls for realistic and long-term planning, since degraded land takes a long time to recover and population also takes a long time to control.

The model developed in this study is, however, a simple and aggregate representation of the real food production system for a centrally-planned economy. It only provides broad guidelines rather than a detailed policy. In order to delineate a comprehensive food policy and its implementation strategy, the boundary of the system considered for analysis must be further expanded.

References

Allison, F. E. (1973) Soil Organic Matter and its Role in Crop Production, in *Developments in Soil Science*, 3, Amsterdam: Elsevier.

Bach, N. L. (1988) *Agricultural Land Management Policies and the Dynamics of Food Production in Vietnam*, Masters Thesis No. IE-88-29, Bangkok: Asian Institute of Technology.

Bowonder, B. (1981) The Myth and Reality of High Yield Varieties in Indian Agriculture, *Development and Change*, 12(2).

Brown, L. R. and Wolf, E. C. (1986) Assessing Ecological Decline, in Brown, L. R. et. al., *State of the World 1986*, Worldwatch Institute, W. W. Norton & Company.

Chandler, W. U. (1987) Designing Sustainable Economies, in *State of the World 1987*, Brown, L. R. et. al., Worldwatch Institute, W. W. Norton & Company.

Forth, H. D. (1978) *Fundamental of Soil Science*, 4th ed., New York: John Wiley and Sons.

Hardin, G. (1985) *Filters Against Folly*, New York: Viking Press.

Jones, D. K. (1984) *Soil Nitrogen Dynamics*, Master's Thesis, Hanover, NH, USA: Thayer School of Engineering, Dartmouth College.

Sterman, J. D. (1984) Appropriate Summary Statistics For Evaluating the Historical Fit of System Dynamics Model, *Dynamica*, 10(2).

Theil, H. (1966) *Applied Economic Forecasting*, Amsterdam: North Holland Publishing Company.

16 The dynamics of water policy in southwestern Saudi Arabia[*]

Anthony C. Picardi and Khalid Saeed

Abstract

The effects of water-supply policies on growth in southwestern Saudi Arabia are examined with the aid of a system dynamics model. The Southwest Zone is predominantly agricultural and relatively isolated by its difficult terrain. It is losing population to regions of the country in which industry, commerce, and the public sector are growing more rapidly.

The feedback loops which relate the demand for water, agricultural activity, groundwater extraction, aquifer recharge, and supply and demand policies are explained. Model runs which simulate the consequences of four alternative water-management policies are then presented. These policies are:

1. The replacement of groundwater supplies with desalinated water for domestic use.
2. The implementation of water-conservation and irrigation projects.
3. The recycling of domestic waste water for direct urban use.
4. The recycling of domestic waste water for recharging aquifers and for agricultural use.

The results of several simulations illustrate the effect of these policies on the competition for water supplies between the agricultural and the

* Reprinted with permission from *Simulation*, 33(4), Anthony C. Picardi and Khalid Saeed, *The Dynamics of Water Policy in Southwestern Saudi Arabia*, Copyright 1979, The Society for Computer Simulation, U.S.A.

domestic sectors within a population cluster and competition for groundwater supplies between adjacent clusters.

Three variations of a wastewater recycling policy were examined in Abha; of these, recycling water directly to agricultural use was the most successful in alleviating the competition for water resources while at the same time increasing potential supplies to neighboring users. Given the high costs of supplying desalinated water via pipeline to high-altitude areas in the Southwest Zone, water recycling emerges as the principal recommendation for these water-short areas.

Introduction

This paper analyzes the effects on population and agriculture of alternative water-supply policies in regions of Saudi Arabia in which water is scarce. The analyses are done with the aid of a computer model, the Regional Utility Simulation Model (RUSIM). Development Analysis Associates, Inc. (DAA) developed RUSIM to simulate patterns of water and power demand and use, physical growth, and demographic change in Saudi Arabia; it is described in more detail elsewhere.

This paper considers only the Southwest Zone of Saudi Arabia. This zone offers great potential for policy testing because of its diverse geography, groundwater and agricultural resources, importance in the Kingdom's agricultural development plans, and the occurrence of significant water shortages at certain locations.

RUSIM is a system dynamics model which was developed over the past three years by DAA for the Saline Water Conversion Corporation (SWCC) in Saudi Arabia to project demand for water and electric power. It is being used to examine how demand is affected by development policies, by projects undertaken by government agencies, and by the rapid demographic and socioeconomic changes now being experienced by the population.

DAA advises SWCC on water and electric power, a task that encompasses many activities besides simulation. These include the design and execution of field surveys, projection of future demands, policy analysis, the optimization of water and power supply networks, and the analysis of alternative desalination technologies and their future potential. The RUSIM model integrates information from the survey and statistical activities and provides demand projections for optimizing the water and power network.

For the purpose of estimating demand, the Kingdom was divided into five socio-geographic zones. A zone typically contains from three to fifteen watershed regions, each of which has one to five population clusters for which demands are calculated. The Southwest Zone consists of nine watershed regions and eighteen demand clusters as shown in Figure 16.1.

378

This paper examines four different water-related policies. These are: (1) the replacement of ground water with desalinated supplies, (2) the implementation of irrigation and water infiltration-promoting projects, (3) the implementation of water recycling projects for direct urban use, and (4) the recycling of domestic waste water for agricultural use. Different demand clusters will be used to illustrate each type of policy, according to the various clusters' socio-geography and the differing regional resources.

The numbers by the demand clusters are identifying numbers used in the simulation model. The double numbers refers to both the cluster and the watershed area. Thus (1,4) Abha means Abha is cluster 1 in watershed area 4 in the Southwest Zone 2.

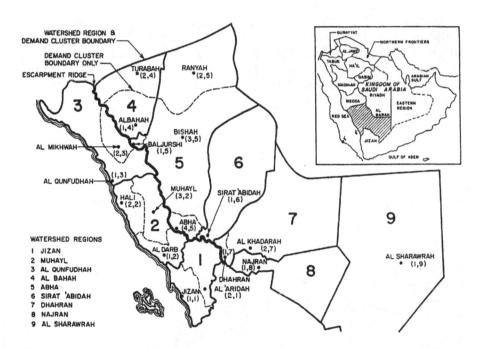

Figure 16.1   **Watershed regions and demand clusters in the Southwest Zone of Saudi Arabia**

Overview of the Southwest Zone

Growth and development in the Southwest Zone have been slow in comparison to other zones in Saudi Arabia. There are several reasons for this, one of which is the rugged terrain. A rift escarpment lying about 40

379

kilometers from the coast runs from the northeast to the southwest and sometimes rises from 100 meters to over 2000 meters over a distance of 50 kilometers. Travel to and from the clusters lying to the east of the escarpment is difficult because of the topography and lack of roads. Thus the principal population centers in this area are relatively isolated. The physical characteristics of the area have historically maintained the isolation of the population clusters in the zone.

Agriculture, the principal economic activity in the Southwest Zone, is for the most part entirely dependent upon rainfall and rainfall-induced flooding. Heavy monsoon rains during the summer (experienced nowhere else in Saudi Arabia) give the Southwest Zone a unique agricultural potential. The agriculture employs the greatest fraction of labor in the Southwest Zone, but farming is risky because of the unreliable rainfall. In comparison to the risky nature of farming, job opportunities in the Kingdom's rapidly growing cities are very attractive. This has caused a chronic out-migration from the Southwest Zone in recent years. Figure 16.2 shows that over the time horizon of the simulation, the projected population of the Southwest Zone declines as a percentage of the aggregate population of the Kingdom.

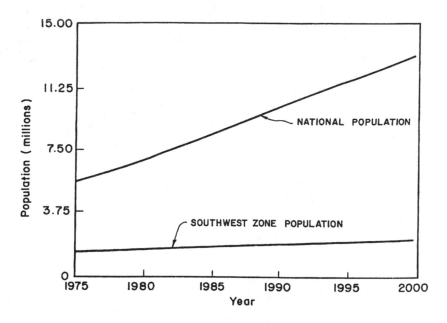

Figure 16.2   A comparison of the Southwest Zone's projected population level with the total projected population of Saudi Arabia

380

In the course of its household survey of the Kingdom, DAA found that the prevailing reason given for both emigration and immigration has been the search for better employment opportunities. Saudis from the Southwest Zone have moved both temporarily and permanently to the larger cities within this zone as well as to the larger cities in the rest of the country. At the time of the survey there were no observed cases in which Saudi citizens had migrated into the Southwest Zone from other zones in the Kingdom.

A significant portion of the recent immigrants in the survey came from North African countries. They are employed as skilled laborers in construction and in a variety of professional activities in the government sector. Immigrants from other Arab agricultural regions are settling in those parts of the Southwestern Zone where the more economically stable forms of cultivation such as groundwater irrigation are practiced.

Higher living standards are an incentive for people to migrate to the larger cities in the Southwest Zone. These higher standards result from the avail ability of electricity, reliable water distribution, schools, improved diet, and improved housing. In addition, government development projects have drawn population from the surrounding areas either by providing jobs or by improving living conditions. Examples of specific development projects are the Wadi Jizan Irrigation Project (which provides water for 8,250 hectares) and the Wadi Najran Flood Control Dam (which will also add 800 hectares of cultivated land) the Khamis Mushayt Military City (potential population 50,000) and the university in Abha. The reasons for the migration were noted during the household survey, especially in isolated rural villages. These villages, which were primarily dependent upon rain-fed agriculture, had no observed in-migration, a monotonous diet, no electricity, an often unreliable water supply, and a lack of roads and schools.

In spite of the ambitious development program now being implemented in the Southwest Zone, the attractiveness of the area will continue to lag behind that of the rest of the country, as is illustrated by the index of attractiveness generated by the model in Figure 16.3. Only for a brief period around 1985 will this zone be as attractive as the Kingdom as a whole. The Southwest Zone is expected to remain primarily an agricultural area, while Riyadh, Dammam, Jubayl, Yanbu, Jeddah, Mecca and Taif have been earmarked as the focal points of the national drive for industrial diversification and economic growth.

Basic mechanisms of water policies

The RUSIM model lends itself easily to the simulation of the consequences of alternative policies. Figure 16.4 is a diagram showing the types of sectors in a typical cluster and the general nature of the policies considered in the model. This paper, however, will only consider desalination, groundwater, and agricultural policies.

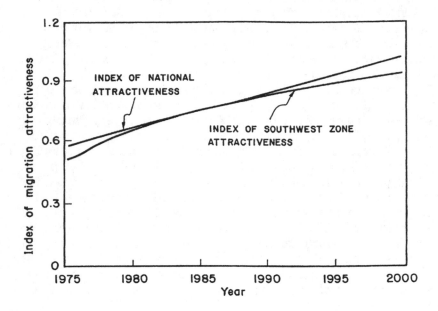

Figure 16.3   Relative indices of migration attraction used in the RUSIM model for the Southwest Zone and for the Kingdom as a whole

Figure 16.5 shows the basic mechanisms governing the use and distribution of water. This figure is a causal flow diagram. A change induced in the quantity at the tail of any one arrow causes a change in the quantity at the head of the same arrow. The reader should refer to Figure 16.5 to follow the balance of this discussion.

On the left of Figure 16.5, note that the availability of water is the sum of the groundwater apportioned to the specific cluster (on the basis of the cluster's share of the regional demand) and the available desalination capacity within the cluster. The demand for agricultural water depends primarily on the amount of land under cultivation. If abundant and reliable sources of water become available, the amount of cultivated land can be increased by government irrigation projects and by individual farmers.

Agricultural demand for groundwater can be reduced to the extent that domestic waste water is recycled directly to the fields.

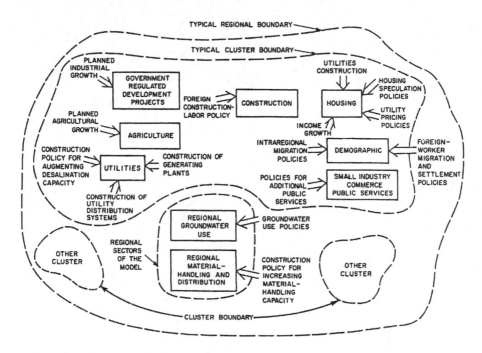

Figure 16.4   Types of sectors and policies incorporated in the RUSIM model

On the right of Figure 16.5, groundwater use is determined by the total water demand, less sea water desalinated and waste water recycled, and is limited by the extraction fraction. (The extraction fraction is the fraction of total groundwater demand that is actually pumped in a given year.) This fraction decreases below 100 percent of demand when water in the aquifer is drawn down below the level desired to prevent shortages during periods of low rainfall and when the yearly recharge from rainfall and recycling is insufficient to meet demands. Under these conditions it becomes uneconomic to pump water from an ever-shrinking reservoir. Actual groundwater (aquifer) reserves are the cumulative result of yearly recharge and yearly extractions. The recharge rate depends on the equilibrium between precipitation, surface runoff, evapotranspiration, infiltration, and the level of water in the aquifer from previous years. The groundwater recharge rate can be increased by spreading water over land and allowing it to percolate into the aquifer, or by well injection, or by the construction of dams that retain floodwaters and other surface water and increase the total infiltration. These groundwater extraction and recharge mechanisms are particularly valid for the shallow-water aquifers generally found in the southwest of Saudi Arabia.

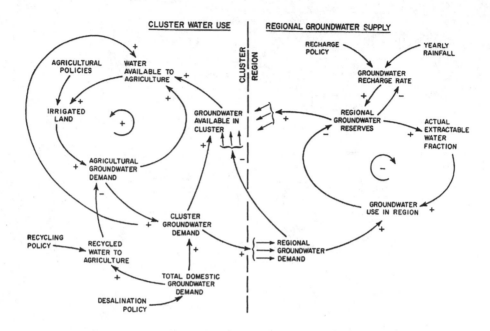

Figure 16.5   **Basic mechanisms linking the supply and demand for ground water, including the effects of local recycling and desalination policies**

The two main feedback loops of Figure 16.5 interact by means of the total regional water demand which, when modified by the extraction fraction, determines regional groundwater use. Net groundwater use, when added to desalination capacity in each cluster, represents the total regional water supply. Regional supply determines the water available to the specific clusters after it is apportioned according to cluster groundwater demands.

The individual causal relationships described in the above paragraphs combine to form a negative feedback loop structure (depicted by the negative sign within the circular arrow). This structure balances water demand and supply through internal adjustments made in the amount of irrigated land or the level of water in the groundwater reservoir, depending on which policies are implemented and the degree to which they are enforced. Note that the left-hand side of Figure 16.5 shows a positive feedback structure, indicating that the irrigated land would expand without limit if not influenced by another part of the system. In fact, the negative loop on the right serves to limit such an expansion through limitations on the groundwater available to the cluster.

The supply of desalinated water to Jizan

The Jizan cluster lies on the coastal plain in the southern-most part of the Southwest Zone. Although the principal city, Jizan, has a port, an airport, and a number of small industries, the majority of the population lives in small villages and is engaged in agriculture. Figure 16.6 shows that water use is dominated by agricultural demand with a small but steady increase in the domestic and commercial sectors. In spite of the slight increase in the availability of water (a number of dams have been built to increase infiltration) the total demand is now just above the availability, and any new supplies are quickly used.

The decline in agricultural demand for groundwater occurs because the total extraction rate is greater than the long-term average recharge rate. When this occurs, the extraction rate must decline simply because it is impossible to pump more water out of the aquifer for prolonged periods than is recharged into it.

While this behavior is qualitatively correct, it must be noted that the exact time at which the recharge and extraction rates come into equilibrium depends on the extraction policy. This policy incorporates elements of perceived variability as well as factors depending on the economics of extraction. The simulation shown in Figure 16.6 includes a policy which decreases the extraction rate significantly as the water levels in the aquifer reservoirs begin to be drawn down. This simulates a risk-avoidance policy in which a reservoir of water is maintained to use in years of below-average rainfall.

This policy makes sense in an arid region in which the rainfall varies greatly. Of course the actual rate of water extraction will depend on the future rainfall pattern and on how aggressive farmers are in drawing down the water table. The longer it takes people to reduce the extraction rate, the lower will be the level of water in the aquifer at equilibrium.

It must also be noted that the model deals only with average conditions and does not, for the sake of clarity, simulate stochastic weather conditions. This means that the real curves of water availability can be expected to vary above and below the curves shown in the figures in this paper.

The available evidence indicates that the current levels of extraction are higher than the sustainable yield. In a number of cases, wells have run dry, and it has become necessary to sink deeper wells. In the light of this evidence, the behavior shown in Figure 16.6 is qualitatively realistic. Since some of the information on agricultural extractions was gathered from reports published before 1975, the model cannot be quantitatively validated without more up-to-date information on the present extraction rates and levels of water in the aquifers.

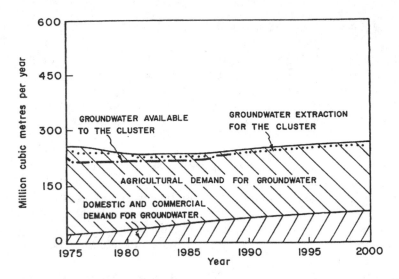

Figure 16.6   **Projected water supply and demand conditions in the Jizan cluster with no desalinated water supply**

Figure 16.7 shows the effect of gradually replacing the groundwater used for nonagricultural purposes with desalinated supplies. This replacement takes a long time because the population is dispersed in a large number of small villages and because building the required distribution network is time-consuming. Replacing groundwater used for domestic consumption by desalinated water slightly decreases the demand for groundwater in the desalinating cluster and slightly increases groundwater availability in other clusters using the same aquifer. Since the nonagricultural demand for groundwater is reduced within the desalinating cluster, more of this water can be apportioned for agriculture. The significant effect of desalinated water supplies in this zone is that a slightly higher level of agricultural activity can be supported, especially in areas contiguous to towns that compete with agriculture for scarce supplies.

Agricultural policy and inter-cluster competition for water

A rift escarpment runs parallel to the coast of the Southeast Zone, from northwest to southeast. The watershed to the north of the Jizan watershed drains the western slope of the escarpment (Figure 16.1); the population centers are almost totally agricultural villages. A small number of these villages have been identified by the Ministry of Agriculture as locations for land reclamation and irrigation projects, while other population clusters have no projects specified. The following simulation illustrates the dynamics of inter-cluster competition for water when clusters grow at different rates.

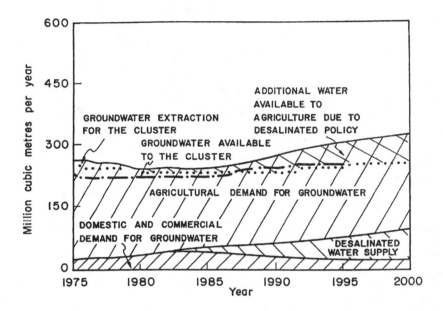

Figure 16.7   **Projected water supply and demand conditions with nonagricultural water demand gradually met with desalinated water**

Figure 16.8a shows the availability of water in Hali, a coastal cluster on the Tihama plain. In this base run (in which no agricultural policies are implemented) groundwater availability increases slightly in Hali as a result of a dam and irrigation-channel complex proposed for the late 1980s. Groundwater extraction also increases after a delay since, as shown by the feedback loops in Figure 16.5, the increased availability of groundwater eventually results in more use of groundwater for agriculture. Other clusters in the same watershed show the same behavior in response to the slight increase in the long-term availability of water.

Figure 16.8b shows the case in which agricultural development projects are initiated in the Hali cluster, but not in neighboring clusters, early in the simulation. Demand increases in advance of supply, and supply eventually

387

increases to a much higher level than in the base-run simulation.

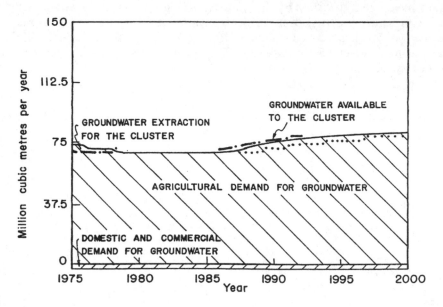

Figure 16.8a   Water supply and demand conditions in Hali cluster without implementation of irrigation policies

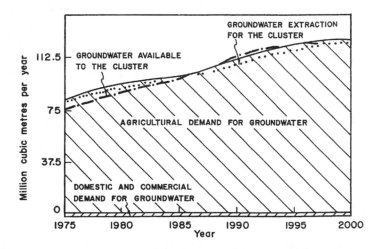

Figure 16.8b   Water supply and demand conditions in Hali cluster with implementation of irrigation policies

388

Where does the additional groundwater supply come from? Figure 16.5 shows that a policy of promoting agriculture increases total demand for water in the cluster. Government policy is to share groundwater in the region roughly in proportion to demand; consequently more water is available in those clusters which have increased irrigation needs, and less water is available in those clusters with no change in needs.

Figures 16.9a and 16.9b show that the history of the Muhayl cluster is the same as Hali's in the absence of an agricultural development program in Hali. However, as more water is apportioned to Hali under the agricultural land development policy, the availability of water decreases in Muhayl, resulting in decreased agricultural production there. Without new supplies in the watershed, new demands in Hali must be eventually balanced by decreased demands in Muhayl and other neighboring clusters that obtain water from the same aquifers.

The significant point is that groundwater is a common resource which is shared within a watershed among several clusters according to their demands. In a number of instances in Saudi Arabia, groundwater is piped or trucked from remote wells to demand centers, usually for domestic purposes. Although there is not presently a shortage of water in the Hali-Muhayl watershed, the implementation of significant irrigation projects in one cluster may decrease the availability of water in other neighboring clusters.

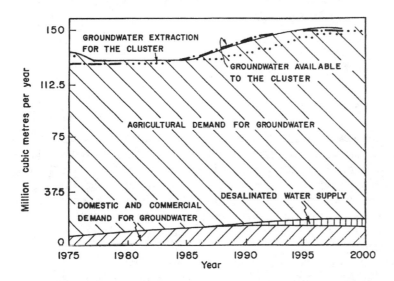

Figure 16.9a **The effects of competition for groundwater between clusters in a watershed: behavior of the Muhayl cluster with no irrigation projects in the adjoining Hali cluster**

389

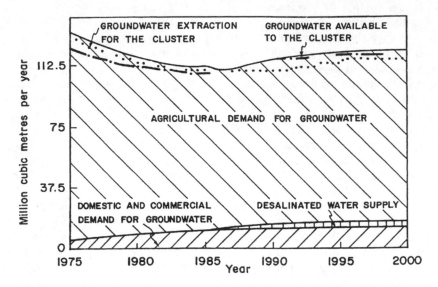

Figure 16.9b The effects of competition for groundwater between clusters in a watershed: behavior of the Muhayl cluster with irrigation projects in the adjoining Hali cluster

Waste-water management schemes

The need for water in Abha

One of the most severe water shortages in the Southwest Zone occurs in Abha, which is shown on the map in Figure 16.1 lying just east of the escarpment at the head of watershed 5. Abha is an urban cluster containing the town of Abha, which is a rapidly growing community of about 40,000 inhabitants. The total population of the Abha cluster is estimated at 139,000.[1] Besides the town of Abha, the Abha cluster also contains a new military town, a university extension, and several small flood-control and groundwater projects.

The Abha watershed contains four population clusters, but only the population of the Abha cluster is growing. Populations in the other clusters in the watershed are expected to decline. Such growth patterns can be attributed to the concentration in Abha of development in the public sector. This concentration draws population away from the other clusters in the region. Abha is located at the head of Wadi Bishah. This Wadi spreads until

390

it loses all identity as it flows from the eastern slope of the escarpment into the desert.

Abha is badly in need of water for domestic use. According to a recent geological survey of the region's groundwater, the alluvial deposits in the watershed are thin, and good-quality water is available only from some 20 wells located upstream of the Wadi. There is hardly any possibility of increased extraction. A dam to capture the surface runoff has been completed near Abha, but the total storage volume of its reservoir is only 1.7 million cubic meters, which is inadequate even for the needs of the city of Abha. There have been proposals for additional surface reservoirs, but the Wadis are small and separated in this highland area, making collection of significant amounts of water in any location difficult. The cluster's current domestic and commercial needs for water are estimated at 20 million cubic meters per year and are expected to increase rapidly.[1]

As an aside, we remark that DAA has investigated the feasibility of supplying desalinated water via a pipeline running from Jizan across the escarpment to Abha. The unit costs of water delivered through such a system are estimated to range between $2.50 and $7.00 per thousand gallons in addition to the desalination costs which vary between $5 and $7 per thousand gallons depending on the size of the plant, i.e., the total estimated cost is $7.50 to $14 per thousand gallons. This contrasts with a cost of $5 per thousand gallons for water presently delivered by tankers from wadi wells and about $1 per thousand gallons for water in suburban Boston. Since the Saudi Arabian government has a policy of supplying water at a price of $0.28 per thousand gallons through municipal distribution networks, most of the costs of delivering desalinated water will probably be subsidized. The huge size of this subsidy justifies the consideration of a range of water supply policies, including decreasing effective demand through recycling. The physical implications of meeting nonagricultural demand through desalination include increased availability of groundwater to the agricultural sector in Abha and a decrease in the water shortage in the adjoining clusters in the Abha watershed.

To return to the management of waste water, recycling may offer a viable solution to the water shortage in Abha and other watershed areas in the Kingdom, particularly in cases in which waste water from a primary application can be recycled for secondary uses with minimal treatment. Wastewater treatment generally depends upon the nature of the effluent and the final use. Commonly used treatments include sedimentation, oxidation, reverse osmosis, and microfiltration. These processes have been used in many parts of the world and, depending upon the degree of purity required, can recover from 20% to 50% of the waste water.

Currently, about 75% of the water used in Saudi Arabia is for agriculture, a use in which the consumptive losses, through

---

[1] DAA estimates.

391

evapotranspiration and evaporation, can be as high as 90%. The urban water use is largely nonconsumptive, with losses of 20% to 50%. Since urban water use is often concentrated over a small area, waste-water collection is usually feasible. Urban waste water can be recycled for direct urban use, for agricultural use, or for recharging the aquifers.

Several aggregate policies for waste-water management in the Abha region were simulated with RUSIM. The main aspects of these policies and their implications are discussed later. The simulations demonstrate the physical feasibility of recycling as a means of increasing the availability of water. The economic feasibility depends on a complete cost analysis of recycling as compared to desalination, which is beyond the scope of this paper.

Waste-water recycling policies for recharging aquifers

Waste water can be easily collected and recharged into the aquifers after primary or secondary treatment. Primary treatment consists of removing the solids and suspended solids from the effluent, while secondary treatment results in the additional removal of about 80% of the dissolved organic matter. While secondary treatment may be sufficient for some industrial uses, drinking water standards require removal of almost all the dissolved organics in addition to chemicals. With primary and secondary treatment, the recharged fraction can be as high as 50% of the water subjected to treatment. Figures 16.10a, 16.10b, 16.10c and 16.10d show simulation runs of the model with various recycling policies.

Figures 16.10a and 16.10b show that while agricultural and nonagricultural water demands in the simulation run with recycling through aquifer recharge do not differ appreciably from those in the base run, recycling the groundwater availability and the level of extraction are slightly greater toward the end of the simulation.

Since the water recharged into the aquifer spreads over a large area, no large-scale changes occur in the availability of water at specific locations in the watershed. However, the availability, and the levels of extraction, increase slightly over the entire watershed.

Waste-water recycling for agricultural use

The treatment necessary for recycling waste water for direct agricultural use is minimal since residual dissolved organic matter in the water may be beneficial to crops. Also, because such uses benefit specific locations, they do affect the intercluster competition for water. Figures 16.10a and 16.10c compare the effect of waste-water recycling for direct agricultural use with the base run. Note that, while the sum total of agricultural and nonagricultural water demands in this case remain practically unchanged, the agricultural demand for groundwater and total groundwater extraction in the cluster is considerably reduced as a result of meeting a portion of the agricultural demand by recycled water. Also, as the demand for groundwater in this cluster decreases, more of the water in the aquifer can be used by the other clusters. Consequently, they may increase their extraction and so enjoy a higher level of agricultural activity.

In general, recycling for local agricultural applications has two effects: First, the local agriculture becomes more and more dependent on the recycled water as its quantity increases. Second, water shortages in the adjoining clusters are eased as a result of the local cluster's reduced demand for groundwater, which leaves more groundwater for its neighbors.

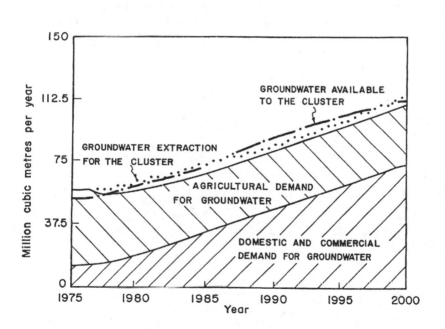

Figure 16.10a   Waste-water recycling in Abha cluster: base-run simulation incorporating no waste-water recycling schemes

393

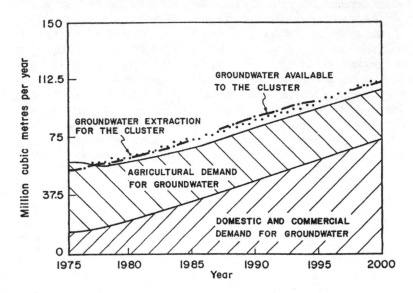

Figure 16.10b **Waste-water recycling in Abha cluster: simulation showing the effect of waste-water recycling for recharge into ground water aquifers**

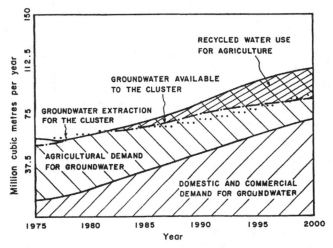

Figure 16.10c **Waste-water recycling in Abha cluster: simulation showing the effect of waste-water recycling for direct agricultural applications in the recycling cluster**

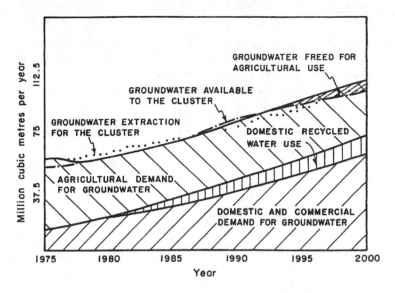

Figure 16.10d   Waste-water recycling in Abha cluster: simulation showing the effect of waste-water recycling for direct urban use in the recycling cluster

Waste-water recycling for direct urban use

Waste water subjected to primary, secondary, and tertiary treatment can be refined to a level of purity suitable for domestic consumption. The recovered quantities, however, are small (about 20% of the recycled water). Simulation of this policy results in a decreasing domestic and commercial demand for groundwater in the recycling cluster, thus allowing more of the cluster's share of groundwater to be used for agriculture (see Figures 16.10a and 16.10d). Because the amount of water recycled is small, only a little more water is available for agricultural use locally and in the adjoining clusters. The magnitude of this effect on adjoining clusters is much smaller than in the case of recycling for direct agricultural applications. The principal effect of this type of recycling is to alleviate serious domestic water shortages.

Depending on the pattern of growth desired, any of the recycling policies or combinations thereof can be implemented. These simulations indicate only the physical possibilities, limitations, and first-order intercluster feedback effects involved in a number of different policies.

395

Concluding remarks

This paper demonstrates the usefulness of the RUSIM regional simulation model in assessing the impact of a range of regional water policies. This model incorporates the principal modes of interaction among various population clusters and allows us to draw the following general conclusions about the Southwest Zone.

1. In the Southwest Zone of Saudi Arabia, a number of clusters are using water at or in excess of the average long-term sustainable yield. It is almost inevitable that continuation of this practice will lower the water table, increase the cost of extraction, and decrease the ability of the groundwater reservoir to supply needed quantities in years of rainfall deficit.
2. Nonagricultural water demand is expanding almost independently of the availability of water, while the level of agricultural activity is largely governed by the quantity of water available for it. Thus, unless special provisions are made for reserving water for agricultural use and for encouraging agricultural activity, agriculture can be expected to decline as a result of intersectoral competition.
3. Since groundwater resources are shared among various population clusters in a watershed region, changes in demand in one cluster affect the intercluster competition for water and consequently the levels of water-sensitive agricultural activity in other clusters in the region. Thus, provision of desalination facilities or the implementation of water-conservation projects is likely to have a ripple effect and to increase the water available to other clusters in the same watershed.
4. While several waste-water management schemes are viable, there are subtle differences in their effect on the demography and the economy of the recycling cluster as well as on adjoining areas sharing the same watershed. Waste-water management policies can now be undertaken after ascertaining whether the secondary impacts of these schemes on sectoral and spatial growth patterns in the region are in accord with the priorities and development goals of the government and the local populations.
5. Given the high costs of supplying desalinated water via pipeline to high-altitude areas in the Southwest Zone, water recycling emerges as the principal recommendation for these water-short areas. Since recycling to recharge aquifers and for agricultural use has a recovery rate of 50% (versus 20% for recycling for direct urban use) this type of recycling appears to be the most promising.

References

Anonymous (1978) 'Reverse Osmosis Moves Forward', *Chemical Week*, September 27: 67-682.

Linsley, B. K. and Franzin, J. B. (1969) *Water Resources Engineering*, New York: McGraw-Hill.

Ministry of Planning, Kingdom of Saudi Arabia (1975) 'Second five Year Plan', Riyadh, Saudi Arabia, pp. 63, 115.

Picardi, A. C. and Shorb, A. McK. (1978) 'A Regional Water and Electricity Simulation Model', *Proceedings*, International Conference on Systems Modeling in Developing Countries, Bangkok, Asian Institute of Technology, May 8-11, pp. 151-166.

Shorb, A. McK. and Picardi, A. C. (1978) 'Evolution of a Water and Power Demand', Projection Model for Saudi Arabia, *Proceedings*, Florida: Winter Simulation Conference, Miami, December 4-6: 454-459.

Conclusion

Sustainable development as an intellectual notion seems to have accommodated many adversarial positions rather than a shared common view of the physical reality on ground. Development policy, on the other hand, has been driven by simplistic aggregate models created either from situational evidence or from conjecture. The concepts of perfect information, infinitely wide distribution of wealth, equitable value claims for factor contributions, unlimited physical resources, homogeneous character of households, absence of considerations of political power, etc., which are the mainstay of the development models, are mostly figments of imagination rather than reality. The absence of perfect markets in reality for commodities, production factors and finance has often been attributed to defects in reality rather than a shortcoming of its models. Policies to correct such defects have often been irrelevant to the entry points potentially existing in the real system and have repeatedly called for indiscriminate intervention that invokes much resistance from the internal forces generated in the system.

An attempt to model reality carefully so it is able to track history, including the diverse situations lived in the past and the policy impacts that have actually been experienced, creates at the outset a model that resolves adversarial controversy by providing a shared common view of reality. Experimentation with this model provides additional learning experience that brings to fore feasible entry points for change. Development planning and policy design stand to gain hugely from the use of such an experimental process by creating robust policy designs that lead to sustainable solutions to social, economic, political, organizational and environmental problems.

This book has collected a number of attempts to model generic problems of sustainable development as well as to address specific agenda concerning selected country cases. These attempts have not only provided many insights into understanding developmental systems and identifying entry points for the design of public policy, they have also demonstrated the use of the experimental procedure of system dynamics for the design of policy for sustainable development. The Introduction to the book - the lecture delivered by the author when the earlier edition of this writing was honored by the award of Jay Wright Forrester prize - summarizes the key insights gained in the course of modeling and experimentation carried out for each attempt. It is only appropriate that the Conclusion attempts to summarize the learning process implicit in the implementation of the modeling regime used.

Prescribed procedure for system dynamics practice

The term *system* is used extensively both in the context of science and mathematics. In the context of science it implies natural and societal organisms which exist independently of how we view them. In mathematics, however, a system necessarily implies an abstraction visualized through perceptual and methodological filters. Although, it is impossible to see the natural and societal systems in their true natural forms, the various methodologies following the principles of science attempt to define criteria to create a consensus on how natural systems should be viewed, albeit only in terms of transcendental models.

The transcendental models of systems are also divided into two classes. The first - often termed concrete systems - concentrates on the common characteristics of natural and societal organisms, viewing them as living systems; the second focuses on specific functions or problems and is often referred to as abstract systems [Rappoport 1980]. The open system defined by Ludwig von Bertalanffy belongs to the former category [Bertalanffy 1968], whereas the closed system referred to by Jay Forrester belongs to the later [Forrester 1968]. Thus, a system dynamics model is an abstract system, conceptualized around a pattern of behavior and it may not represent any concrete system *per se.*

The classical system dynamics practice is aimed at arriving at a clear understanding of how information relationships in an abstract system create a problem behavior, so policies for system improvement may be conceived. The procedure followed in the classical system dynamics practice creates a cyclical learning process which calls for the development of a number of rather abstract concepts in a sequence requiring use of both cognitive and physical skills, which are not clearly defined. A widely recognized view of this process is illustrated in Figure C.1.

Empirical evidence is the driving force both for delineating micro-structure of the model and for verifying its macro-behavior, although the information concerning the macro-behavior may reside in the historical data and that concerning the micro-structure in the experience of the people. Thus, the modeling process draws on both historical and experiential data.

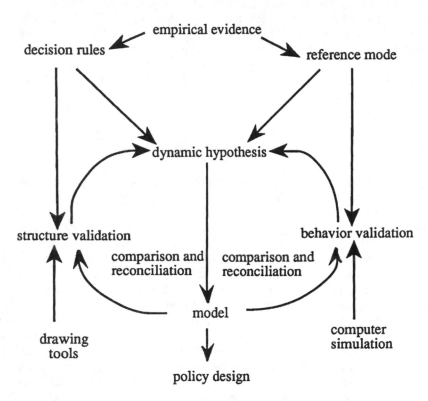

Figure C.1   A widely recognized interpretation of system dynamics practice

The first requirement of the method is to organize historical information into what is known in jargon as "reference mode". The reference mode, together with the experiential information about the decision process leads to the formulation of a "dynamic hypothesis" expressed in terms of the important feedback loops existing between the decision elements in the system that create the particular time variant patterns contained in the reference mode. The dynamic hypothesis must incorporate causal relations based on information about the decision rules used by the actors of the system, and not on correlations between pairs of variables observed in the

400

historical data.

A formal model is then constructed using the given rules of information structure and incorporating the dynamic hypothesis along with the other essential detail of the system relating to the problem being addressed. The boundary of the abstract system synthesized in the model must incorporate the dynamic hypothesis and also the policy space and the time horizon of the intervention considered. The model structure must be "robust" to extreme conditions and be "identifiable" in the "real world" for it to have credibility. A model might undergo several iterations in a cyclical process to arrive at an acceptable structure. This process creates a basic "understanding" of the information relationships in the system underlying the problem being addressed through an iterative learning mode it embodies.

Once a satisfactory correspondence between the model and the real world structure has been reached, the model is subjected to behavior tests. Computer simulation is used to deduce time paths of the variables of the model, which are reconciled with the reference mode. If a discrepancy is observed between the model behavior and the reference mode, the model structure is re-examined and modified if necessary, and this leads into to another cycle of behavior tests. This iterative process creates additional learning that further enhances "understanding" of the information relationships in the system and how they yield the problem behavior. In rare cases, such testing might also unearth missing detail concerning the reference mode, leading to a restatement of the reference mode, although for most cases, the reference mode delineated at the start of the modeling exercise must be held sacred.

When a close correspondence is simultaneously reached between the structure of the model and the theoretical and experiential information about the system, and also between the behavior of the model and the empirical evidence about the behavior of the system, the model is accepted as a valid representation of the system [Bell and Senge 1980, Forrester and Senge 1980, Richardson and Pugh 1981, Saeed 1992].

Since there exists large variability in the outcome of the modeling procedure described in Figure 1, in terms of the learning and new knowledge it creates, its accuracy in representing the actual process carried out by an experienced modeler is in question. It is instructive to look at a generic model of learning proposed by Kolb (1979, 1984) to identify the missing links in the prescribed procedure for system dynamics practice so it becomes possible to represent it more accurately.

A generic model of experiential learning

While there exist many views of the experiential learning process, a model developed by David Kolb appears most relevant to the system dynamics modeling practice [Kolb 1984, Hunsacker and Alessandra 1980, Kolb, et. al. 1979, Kolb 1974]. Kolb perceives experiential learning in his model as a four stage cycle illustrated in Figure C.2.

Kolb's learning cycle is driven by four basic faculties - watching, thinking, doing and feeling. For the learning process to be effective, watching must result in careful observation of facts, leading to discerning organized patterns. These patterns then must drive thinking, which should create a concrete experience of reality. The implications of the concrete experience must be tested through experimentation conducted mentally or with physical and mathematical apparatuses. Finally, this experimentation must be translated into abstract concepts and generalizations through a cognitive process driven at the outset by feeling, which would, in turn, create further organization for careful observation thus invoking another learning cycle.

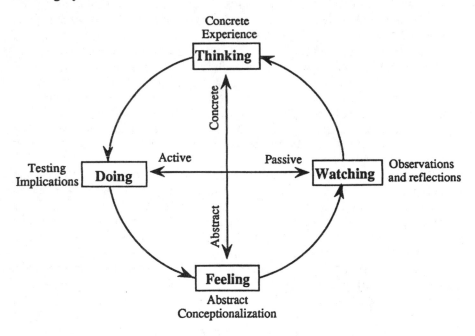

Figure C.2   Kolb's model of experiential learning

The learning faculties, according to Kolb's model, reside in two basic human functions, physical and cognitive, each integrated along two primary dimensions, which are also illustrated in Figure C.2. The first dimension, concerning the physical functions is passive – active. The second, concerning the cognitive functions is concrete – abstract. Thus, the faculty of watching is a passive physical function, thinking a concrete cognitive function, doing an active physical function and feeling an abstract cognitive function. Since the mental construction of reality and its interpretation must filter unwanted information, each faculty must be guided by certain organizing principles to affect learning. Additionally, the learner is required to shift constantly between dissimilar abilities to create opportunities for refuting the anomalies which would appear among the constructs of each ability.

Even though the practice of system dynamics on the simplistic lines illustrated in Figure C.1 may not appear to conform to Kolb's model of the learning cycle, it is known to have created learning and new knowledge, in cases when it has been carried out skillfully, by an experienced modeler. Clearly, Figure C.1 does not fully describe the process actually implemented when learning is created through system dynamics practice. Evidently, the skillful modeler implicitly goes through the steps of a learning process which are not explicitly known. I have attempted to draw on Kolb's model of experiential learning to help me describe those implicit steps.

A learning model for system dynamics practice

The oldest formal reference to the learning context of system dynamics I could find comes from Professor Jay Forrester, who underscored this context as far back as 1971 when he wrote a brief note to his Urban Dynamics modeling staff emphasizing the importance of the modeling process rather than the model it creates. This note concluded:

"In fact, for any particular real life implementation we can expect that there will be a series of models simultaneously existing and simultaneously in evolution. Different models will address themselves to different issues. The various issues will become evolved and clearer. New issues will arise which require new models, or combinations of models which previously had existed separately. Rather than stressing the single model concept, it appears that we should stress the process of modeling as a continuing companion to, and tool for, the improvement of judgment and human decision making." [Forrester 1985]

On the surface, two learning cycles appear in the modeling process described in Figure C.1, after a reference mode which in itself is an abstract concept, has been delineated. The first cycle corresponds to the structure validating processes and the second to the behavior validating processes. The first cycle walks the modeler through the construction of a dynamic hypothesis, model formulation and validation of model structure

403

through comparison and reconciliation with the evidence. The product of this cycle is a preliminary model which is further tested through simulation experiments. The second cycle requires going through the tasks of deduction of the model behavior and further comparison and reconciliation to achieve its behavioral validity. The conduct of the two cycles in theory must create enough learning about the abstract system represented in the model to issue a logical basis for a policy design for system improvement. In reality, this basis can be created only by a handful of artful modelers, who seem to possess a mysterious feel for the process. In my observation, the mysterious feel comes from carrying out implicitly a number of steps, which conform closely to Kolb's model of learning, but which are not reported in Figure C.1.

Carefully re-examining the system dynamics modeling practice in the backdrop of Kolb's model of experiential learning, I have attempted to represent in Figure C.3 the physical and cognitive tasks an experienced modeler actually performs in the pursuit of learning through system dynamics practice. These steps have seemingly gone unreported since they are learnt subconsciously through painstaking apprenticeship.

Evidentally, all components of the cyclical process described in Figure 1 indeed fall in the category of conceptualizations lying in the abstract cognitive domain and moving directly from one to another will be unproductive from the standpoint of learning. To create any learning, moving from one abstract conceptualization to another must involve a learning cycle calling on all learning abilities as described in Kolb's model.

Thus, reference mode must be viewed as an abstract concept created by first drawing upon the observation ability in the passive physical domain to examine historical evidence, which at the outset becomes a basis for delineating system boundary when processed through drawing on the thinking ability in the concrete cognitive domain. An effort is made then to graph patterns to represent the reference mode, which is an experimental process in the active physical domain. Finally, reference mode is conceptualized as a mental picture of a fabric representing a multi-dimensional pattern in the abstract cognitive domain. The graphed time profiles drawn in two dimensional space rather poorly describe the multidimensional mental image constituting reference mode - like the straight lines representing all two-dimensional objects in Abbot's flatland, whose real shape can only be imagined [Abbot 1987]. The graphs we create are nonetheless important for constructing a mental image of the multidimensional fabric the reference mode actually is.

The dynamic hypothesis represents an intuitive appreciation of the system at a highly aggregate level lying also clearly in the abstract cognitive domain. Its formulation originates, however, in the passive physical domain where role systems are carefully observed. This observation is followed by the delineation of the feedback structure in the concrete cognitive domain which creates the basis for drawing the feedback loops in the active physical domain. Conceptual images of how those feedback loops translate into an archetypal explanation of the reference mode constitutes the dynamic hypothesis.

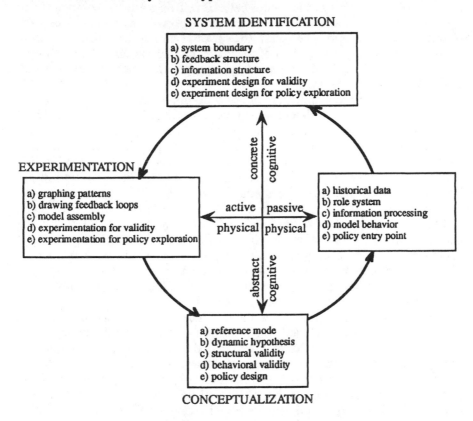

SYSTEM IDENTIFICATION

a) system boundary
b) feedback structure
c) information structure
d) experiment design for validity
e) experiment design for policy exploration

EXPERIMENTATION

a) graphing patterns
b) drawing feedback loops
c) model assembly
d) experimentation for validity
e) experimentation for policy exploration

concrete cognitive

active | passive
physical | physical

abstract cognitive

a) historical data
b) role system
c) information processing
d) model behavior
e) policy entry point

a) reference mode
b) dynamic hypothesis
c) structural validity
d) behavioral validity
e) policy design

CONCEPTUALIZATION

Figure C.3   A learning model for system dynamics practice

The structural validity of the model formulated is, likewise, an abstract concept creating the confidence that the model structure indeed represents equivalent information processing norms in the real world. Its appreciation originates in the passive physical domain through recognition of the information processing patterns discerned through experience and literature descriptions. The information processing patterns recognized lead to the formulation of the mental image of the information structure in the concrete cognitive domain. This image is translated through an experimental assembly process carried out in the active physical domain into an explicit model. The instrument so created forms the basis for comparison with real decision relationshps and arriving at the abstract concept of structural validity of the model.

The behavioral validity of the model is also an abstract concept bridging the gulf between the system decision relationships and its behavior through use of deductive logic. It originates in the passive physical domain through recognition of patterns in the model behavior. This leads to the creation of the experiment designs in the concrete cognitive domain to test the sensitivity of the model behavior to various assumptions and to refute anomalies observed. The results of this experimentation deliver an intuitive appreciation of the behavioral validity of the model, which resides again in the abstract cognitive domain.

Finally, the conceptualization of system improvement is an abstract cognitive process, which likewise the processes described earlier, originates in the passive physical domain through the observation of possible entry points into the system. Experimentation to investigate these entry points is conceived in the concrete cognitive domain. Experimental exploration occurs in the active physical domain and the results of this exploration are translated into system improvement concepts in the abstract cognitive domain.

The modeling practice represented in Figure C.3 involves five successive learning cycles described above. The shift from one cycle to the next occurs after the preceding cycle has yielded learning in its own context. The shift actually takes place when moving from the abstract cognitive domain to the passive physical domain. The five cycles, thus, lie on a spiral converging into system improvement concepts.

In performing above tasks over the conduct of the five learning cycles, the modelers draws upon both physical and cognitive functions as in the case of Kolb's generic model of learning. Also, the physical and cognitive tasks carried out in these cycles seem to appear alternately while they also lie at the opposite extremes of the continuums representing the physical and cognitive functions similar to Kolb's model of experiential learning. It is not surprising that system dynamics practice conducted in this way should create learning. Learning gets inhibited when above process is severely truncated from literally following the prescribed procedure for system dynamics modeling reported in the literature which seems to require moving between abstract concepts within the cognitive abstract domain of human functions.

Core competencies for system dynamics practice

The five tasks performed in each of the four domains of the learning system represented in Figure C.3 seem to display common characteristics translated into the labels placed on the boxes representing the various domains. The tasks performed in the passive physical domain have a common element of pattern recognition; all those in the concrete cognitive

406

domain seek system identification. The tasks in the active physical domain fall into the category of experimentation. Finally, the tasks in the abstract cognitive domain are all conceptual and are labeled conceptualization. The core competencies for practicing system dynamics are therefore defined as, *pattern recognition, system identification, experimentation* and *conceptualization.*

The core competencies discussed above seemingly arise from the learning faculties of *watching, thinking, doing* and *feeling* in Kolb's model. The acquisition of these competencies has also been difficult without the apprenticeship of a master modeler since what they entail is not clearly known. I recall a question from an undergraduate student while working as a teaching assistant in an introductory course on system dynamics at MIT. He asked me what makes a good model. I also recall my somewhat artless but perhaps not inaccurate reply that making a good model was like learning to swim or bike. The art of balance in those activities is acquired from carefully observing a biker or a swimmer and internalizing the process through practice. The same is needed in learning to build a good system dynamics model. The problem with this mode of learning, however, is that it is limited, whereas, the art learnt might also be highly stylized depending on the personal fixations transmitted through apprenticeship. It is not surprising that there has appeared a large variety in the practice of system dynamics while its growth is also greatly constrained by the apprenticeship opportunities available.

While the core competencies and how they should be called upon for the conduct of system dynamics practice has been illustrated in Figure C.3, the organizing principles that must be superimposed on the common learning faculties to yield system dynamics core competencies still remain largely unclear. The learning of these principles has to-date also remained implicit in the process of pursuing system dynamics through apprenticeship.

I have attempted to reflect carefully on my own experience as a modeler and a teacher to state explicitly the organizing principles guiding the four key competencies involved in system dynamics modeling – pattern recognition, system identification, experimentation and conceptualization. Each core competency is created by superimposing the indicated set of organizing principles on a related learning faculty. These principles, their relationship with the learning faculties commissioned, and the respective products delivered are listed in Table C.1.

The skill of pattern recognition stems from the fundamental learning ability of observation. It delivers organized perceptions of what is observed. The key organizing principle for delivering time patterns is the designation of an appropriate time horizon. Different patterns will often dominate different time horizons. Depending on what is the time horizon of interest, irrelevant patterns must be filtered out and relevant patterns highlighted.

Table C.1

Table C.1
System dynamics core competencies, relevant learning
faculties and their organizing principles

CORE COMPETENCY	KEY LEARNING FACULTY	ORGANIZING PRINCIPLE	OUTCOME
pattern recognition	watching	a) time horizon	a) time patterns
		b) decision space	b) decision patterns
		c) bounded rationality	c) information flow patterns
		d) time horizon	d) model behavior patterns
		e) parameter interpretation	e) policy sensitivity patterns
system identification	thinking	a) purpose	a) system boundary
		b) causation	b) feedback structure
		c) stocks/flows	c) information flow patterns
		d) validity criteria	d) model behavior patterns
		e) policy space	e) policy sensitivity patterns
experimentation	doing	a) multiple modes	a) graphs of time patterns
		b) diagramming tools	b) causal diagrams
		c) software structure	c) model assembly
		d) simulation	d) sensitivity scenarios
		e) simulation	e) policy scenarios
conceptualization	feeling	a) fabric	a) reference mode
		b) archetypes	b) dynamic hypothesis
		c) reality checks	c) structural validity
		d) deductive logic	d) behavioral validity
		e) feedback	e) system improvement

The key organizing principle for delivering decision patterns is the perception of the decision space in which the actors can be seen to play their roles. Structure outside of this space must be perceived as environment represented by a parameter set. Likewise the time horizon, the appreciation of decision space should help to filter out irrelevant decision processes and include the relevant ones in the system boundary. The organizing principle for delivering information flow patterns resides in the recognition of the bounded information sets in which we operate. All information in the system is not available at all decision points. Patterns of bounded information flow must be carefully discerned to accurately represent the information flow process. As in the case of discerning time patterns in the real world, the recognition of an appropriate time horizon is the key organizing principle also for discerning patterns in the model behavior. Finally, the ability to interpret parameters as policy levers will guide the observation of the policy sensitivity patterns in the system under study.

The skill of system identification is a manifestation of thinking in a concrete framework. It delivers the boundary of an abstract system, which does not have any physical existence, through the organization of a purpose for the modeling exercise. An appreciation of the cause and effect relationships helps to conceive feedback structure. The organization of stocks, flows and generic processes helps to conceive information structure. Validity criteria deliver a design for validity experimentation and a recognition of the policy space from the point of view of the model user leads to the creation of a productive design for policy experimentation.

Experimentation is a function of the faculty of doing, which resides in the active physical domain. An appreciation of multiple modes helps to separate different modes of behavior while graphing patterns. The organization of the diagramming tools delivers causal diagrams. The software icons and specification rules create a model assembly process, while the knowledge of the simulation process helps to create accurate and error-free behavioral deductions from the model structure.

Finally, abstract conceptualization stems from the faculty of feeling. A focus on a multi-dimensional fabric rather than isolated graphs helps to conceive a reference mode; the recognition of archetypal structures delivers dynamic hypothesis; reality checks deliver structural validity; deductive logic delivers behavioral validity; and the perception of feedback helps to conceive designs for system improvement.

For achieving sustainable solutions to developmental problems, we need to move away from the adversarial views of reality and come to a shared world view. System dynamics modeling as illustrated in the essays of this volume allows to achieve a shared world view thus resolving controversy and creating a basis for identifying positive policy endeavors.

System dynamics modeling has, however, often been likened to an art, learnt through apprenticeship rather than from books and this has created considerable heterogeneity in system dynamics practice as well as a large variety in the expectations from its use. The core set of skills needed for the practice of system dynamics is not clearly defined, hence acquiring them is difficult. Using a widely recognized model of experiential learning, I have attempted in this chapter to outline the steps in the practice of system dynamics that should facilitate its use for learning about the problems of sustainable development and developing solutions to those problems. Also

409

outlined are the core competencies needed for system dynamics practice and the organizing principles of each of these competencies, which should facilitate carrying out the practice on the lines illustrated in this book.

References

Abbott, E. A. (1987) *Flatland*, London: Penguin.

Bell, J. A. and Senge, P. M. (1980) 'Methods for Enhancing Refutability in System Dynamics Modeling', A. Legasto, Jr., J. Forrester, J. Lyneis (eds.), *System Dynamics*, Amsterdam: North-Holland.

Bertalanffy, L. von (1968) *General System Theory*, New York: George Braziller.

Forrester, J. W. (1968) *Principles of Systems*, Cambridge, MA: MIT Press, Wright-Allen Series.

Forrester, J. W. (1985) "The" model versus a modeling "process", *System Dynamics Review*, 1(1).

Forrester, J. W. and Senge, P. (1980) 'Tests for Building Confidence in System Dynamics Models', in *System Dynamics*, A. Legasto, Jr., J. Forrester, J. Lyneis (eds.), Amsterdam: North-Holland.

Hunsacker, P. L. and Alessandra, A. J. (1980) 'Learning How to Learn', in *The Art of Managing People*, Englewood Cliffs, NJ: Prentice Hall, pp. 19-49.

Kolb, D. A. (1974) 'On Management and Learning Process', in *Organizational Psychology: A book of Readings, 2nd ed.*, Englewood Cliffs, NJ: Prentice Hall, pp. 27-42.

Kolb, D. A. (1984) *Experiential Learning*, Englewood Cliffs, NJ: Prentice Hall.

Kolb, D. A., Rubin, I. M. and McIntyre, J. M. (1979) 'Learning Problem Solving', in *Organization Psychology: An Experiential Approach, 3rd ed.*, Englewood Cliffs, NJ: Prentice Hall, pp. 27-54.

Rapoport, A. (1980) 'Philosophical Perspectives on Living Systems', *Behavioral Science*, 25(1): 56-64.

Richardson, G. P. (1986) 'Problems with Causal loop diagrams', *System Dynamics Review*, 2(2).

Richardson, G. P. and Pugh, A. L. (1981) *Introduction to System Dynamics Modeling with Dynamo*, Cambridge, MA: MIT Press.

Richmond, B. M. (1994) 'Systems Thinking/System Dynamics, Let's just get on with it', *System Dynamics Review*, 10(2-3).

Saeed, K. (1992) 'Slicing a Complex Problem for System Dynamics Modeling', *System Dynamics Review*, 8(3).

Index

413

global sharing of resources, 205
governance, 4, 132
government control, 27, 31, 35, 41, 220, 222, 223
government spending, 82, 309, 313, 317, 321, 332, 338, 341, 342, 343, 345, 350
green revolution, 208, 214, 265, 297, 300, 301, 304, 306
green revolution inputs, 265
green revolution technologies, 208
groundwater extraction, 377, 383, 393
growth of knowledge, 159

H

heroic assumptions, 122, 138
higher education, 183
horizontal integration of firms, 243, 245, 254
hunger prone condition, 202
hungry population, 202

I

ideological and social dogmatisms, 38
income distribution problem, 265
income distribution system, 264, 265, 266, 267, 270, 273, 279, 289, 290
indirect intervention, 127, 138, 139, 143, 147
Indonesia, xxiv, 5, 308, 309, 310, 321, 328, 330, 331, 333, 345, 351, 358
industrial revolution, 56, 57, 242, 243, 245, 246, 249
information technology, 128

infrastructure development, 89, 171, 236
innovation, xxiii, 4, 15, 157, 158, 163, 169, 171, 184, 235, 236, 237, 238, 239, 240, 241, 242, 245, 246, 247, 248, 253, 254, 255
innovativeness, 182, 186, 188, 190, 192
institutional charter, 182, 193, 195
institutional finance, 240, 254
institutional structure, 132
institutionalized financial assistance, 99
instrumentalism, 184, 188, 192
insurgence, 27, 28, 32, 33, 34, 37, 40, 42, 223
intangible products, 184
interest groups, 27, 117
internal deficiencies, 203
international global order, 205
international trade, 20, 204
international transfers, 204, 205
interventions by government, 309
investment in technology, 163, 169
irrigation projects, 377, 382, 387, 389, 390
iTHINK, 186

L

labor productivity, 14, 52, 96, 160, 175
laissez faire, 364
land management, 141, 266, 273, 280, 281, 282, 358, 371
land management practices, 141
land ownership patterns, 280, 304
land reforms, 265, 283
land rehabilitation, 141
large capitalist firms, 159

latent information structure, 73
Limits to Growth, 23, 116, 129,
131, 132, 150, 151
living standard, 89, 99, 101, 103,
210, 310, 381
loan repayment default, 293, 294,
302, 305, 306
low income countries, 4, 10, 14,
18

M

machiavellian attitudes, 184
management training, 254
managing material resources, 114
manifest and latent roles, 184
manifest power, 184
marginal factor costs, 55, 80, 111
marginal productivity of labor, 93
marginal revenue product of
capital, 162, 165
marginal revenue product of
labor, 52
marginal revenue product of
workers, 55, 56, 58, 67, 78, 79,
110, 163, 165, 169, 271, 276,
277
market clearing, 124, 139, 161,
311, 313
Marxist theories, 68, 73, 251
material resources, 113, 114, 117,
124, 125, 127, 128, 221
migration, 284, 285, 298, 380,
381, 382
military hardware, 21
modal change, 9, 134
modal variety, 134, 135, 150
modern technology, 69, 96, 160,
164, 167, 169, 170, 282, 287
monopolistic formal firms, 14,
157, 161, 177
multiple cropping, 280, 302, 362,
363

multiple modes, 8, 9, 10, 11, 134,
408, 409
multiple patterns, 10, 13, 73

N

nonrenewable natural resource,
308, 309, 311, 328, 351
normative policies, 133
nutritional energy, 202
nutritional needs, 204

O

occurrence of feudalism, 164
opportunity cost of capital
investment, 277
organizational charter, 188, 193
organizational citizenship, 186
organizational performance, 133,
184
organizational slack, 113, 114,
125
organized economic development
effort, 160
ownership of resources, 14, 60,
62, 64, 65, 67, 68, 88, 93, 96,
106, 225, 230, 270, 276, 290

P

Pakistan, xxi, xxii, xxiv, 46, 47,
48, 74, 76, 106, 107, 159, 160,
178, 180, 212, 231, 243, 256,
259, 263, 264, 265, 266, 272,
273, 279, 280, 282, 284, 290,
291, 292, 307
peasant economies, 60
penalizing unearned income, 173,
175, 176

technology embodied in capital, 162, 169

technology embodied in workers, 162

technology policy, xxiii, 14, 137, 146, 158, 164, 176, 177, 218, 219, 221, 224, 229, 230

Thailand, xxi, xxiv, 180, 181, 231, 259, 293, 294, 295, 296, 300, 301, 302, 306, 307, 352

theories of value, 22, 52

trade flows, 18, 20, 149, 204

traditional capital, 56, 65, 82, 268, 298

traditional development effort, 106

triage strategy, 205

U

unadjudicated collegial system, 182, 189, 190, 195

uniform returns to scale, 66

V

value creation, 183, 186, 188, 189

value patterns, 12

value processes, 185

Vensim, 164

venture capital, 173, 245, 248

Vietnam, xxiv, 5, 40, 358, 359, 360, 362, 373, 375

vulnerability to food shortage, 86, 103

vulnerability to hunger, 208

W

wage and income distribution patterns, 51, 53, 73, 251

wage bargaining position, 101, 279, 282, 287

wage determination, 51, 52, 53, 55, 67, 73, 99, 161

wage employment, 160, 163, 273, 277

water conservation, 360

water management, 390, 392, 396

water resources, xxiv, 378

water supply policies, 391

watershed regions, 378

weapons trade, 21

welfare of human society, 124

women entrepreneurs, 238

worker households, 54, 78, 93, 102

world hunger, 201, 206

Y

youth entrepreneurs, 237, 240